MANOR HOUSES
IN NORMANDY

Photographs by Régis Faucon

Text by Yves Lescroart

Manor Houses in Normandy

KÖNEMANN

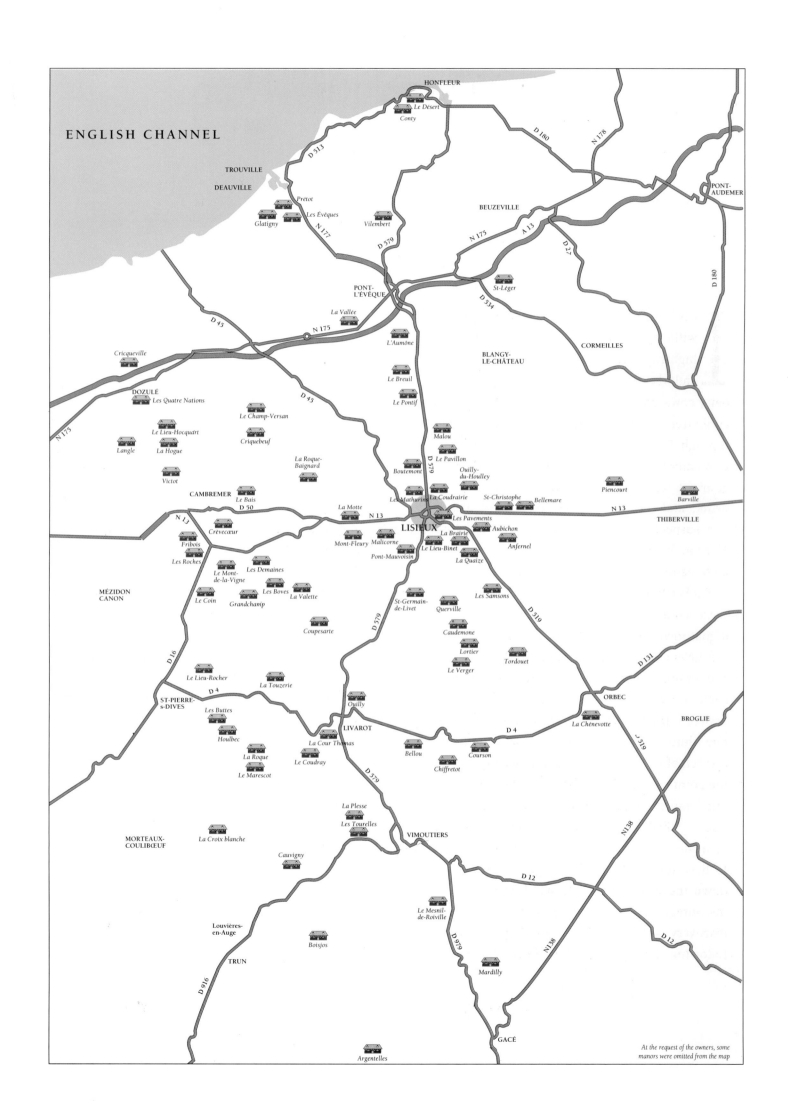

Foreword

It is possible to pass through the Pays d'Auge without actually realizing it. Driving along the highway which leads from Paris to Deauville and the Côte Fleuri, you see the beautiful dairy cows grazing against a background of twisted apple-trees and half-timbered cottages. Passing through Pont-l'Évêque, not far from Livarot and Camembert, you will be reminded that this is a gourmet region, appreciative of good food, good drink, and, essentially, the good life. Little does one suspect that behind this picture postcard of Normandy "at its most Norman" lies a wealth of architectural treasures: the manor houses.

Timber-framed or constructed in brick and stone, these country houses and residences erected by dignatories to mark their successes in bygone centuries range from small and modest to very large and impressive buildings. There are hundreds of such houses in the Pays d'Auge, an area which lies between the Eure and the Orne and occupies only one third of the *département*, or administrative district, of Calvados. Discreet and secretive, often to the point of distrust, neither the Pays d'Auge nor its inhabitants willingly present themselves to outside scrutiny. Sheltering behind the whims of a delicately tormented landscape, the inhabitants of Auge seem to have retreated behind the groves and hills and down the valleys and long winding lanes, as if to discourage attention from prying eyes. Thus, the discovery of this region is not simply a matter of following the signposts, but those who persevere will be richly rewarded. However, very few of the manor houses are actually open to the public. This is, of course, regrettable but it is also an important part of their charm: these are first and foremost living houses. Norman families such as Lecoeur, Courtmanche, Graindorge live in manors with names like Montfleury, Saint-Hippolyte-du-bout-des-Près, la Planche, l'Aumône, Coquainvilliers, Fiquefleur, Ouville-la-Bien-Tournée, Pennedepie. These houses breathe to the rhythm of grazing herds and harvest cycles, or the will of an "outsider" who has fallen under the spell of the forces of nature which sustain this fertile ground.

This book is the fruit of a twofold passion for Normandy and photography. I grew up with the former and remain deeply attached to its pastures, ploughlands and hedges. Having discovered the thrill of capturing and preserving beauty, truth, and the unusual at a young age with the help of the latter, I have continued to practice it throughout my life.

This labor of love, which started out seven years ago, was primarily intended as a photographic work. However, the erudition of a rigorous and passionate specialist was deemed necessary to do true justice to the subject matter. And there is no man more equal to this task than Yves Lescroart.

We hope to succeed in sharing with you, the reader, the joy we both experienced in producing this book.

Régis Faucon
Paris, October 1995

© 1995 Éditions Mengès, Paris

Concept and implementation
Éditions Eric Koehler, Paris

© 1997 for the English-language edition
Könemann Verlagsgesellschaft mbH
Bonner Str. 126, D-50968 Köln

Translation from French: Paul Aston,
Eithne McCarthy, Jackie Smith
for Hart McLeod, Cambridge
Copy-editing: Susan Cox
Typesetting: Goodfellow & Egan, Cambridge
Production Manager: Detlev Schaper
Printing and Binding: Partenaires Fabrication, France
Printed in France
ISBN 3-89508-703- 3

Contents

Contents

An inventory of the manors of the Pays d'Auge

Contents

Richness and diversity of seigneurial architecture

Four centuries of architecture

Discovering the Pays d'Auge

The Pays d'Auge, the heart of Normandy

Normandy is composed of a mosaic of highly distinctive *pays*, or localities, each with its own legacy stretching further back than the duchy which was once an integral part of its history. Prior to relinquishing its political autonomy in 1200 AD, the region enjoyed a short period of dominance and conquest spanning almost two centuries.

The Pays d'Auge is one of the elements in this historically-based mosaic. However, its real identity is that of a natural region which covers the basin of two coastal rivers, the Dives and the Touques, and opens onto the English channel and the Seine estuary. Deposits from the sedimentary bed of the Paris basin form modest hills giving the area its unique landscape. The presence of permeable layers of limestone and sandstone, alternating with clays capable of sealing these aquifers, has resulted in the formation of an undulating landscape of streams and springs. The former score the plateau breaking up into noisy meandering *douets*, or brooks, as they weave their way through valleys of alder and willow trees to the nearby coast.

Compared with the plateaus of Ouche and Lieuvin and the plains of Caen and Argentan, the Pays d'Auge has a most distinctive landscape. Sometimes the sun can be seen rising over a valley scored by a web of streams with a gentle, subtle beauty which does not rely on grandiose and spectacular effects. Sometimes it can be seen setting behind small groups of hills which roll gently down to the valleys and the hillsides where the tightly criss-crossed hedges and trees of holly, hawthorn, hazel and oak alternate with the young apple trees. A handful of timber and stone houses, a slated church spire, and some graveyard yews set the scene for the village which is composed for the

Le Bais, a traditional image of the Pays d'Auge with its manor house and its apple trees in blossom.

most part of scattered manors and houses situated at the end of shady lanes. The survivors of the ancient forest, *saltus Algiae*, the tall trees which once populated the entire Pays d'Auge, still grow in clusters on limestone outcrops made fertile by the presence of silt. The Pays d'Auge is a region of gentle hills and modest green valleys, lofty apple and occasional pear trees in orchards surrounding the houses. It is also a region of rich valley pasture lands, lush meadows, and marshlands known as *les prés baignants* which are skillfully irrigated by the river Orbec. It is said of the meadows in the Dives valley that " if you leave out a stick overnight, you will find it almost over-grown with grass the following day" (Etienne Pasquier 1611).

Whereas the Pays d'Auge is well defined in terms of its natural and geographical features, the origins of its name and administrative boundaries, which were only fixed by official decree in 1942, are less clear. Straddled between the two regions of Upper and Lower Normandy and the three *départements*, or administrative districts, of Calvados, l'Eure, and l'Orne, the administrative status of latter-day Pays d'Auge is for the most part a legacy of the Ancien Régime when it was torn between the three *Généralités* (financial constituencies in existence prior to 1789) of Caen, Rouen, and Alençon. Thus, though the Pays d'Auge is a clearly definable region, the actual term "auge" has been used throughout history to refer to highly diverse sections of this district and never to the area as a whole. In a charter signed between 1050 and 1060, William the Bastard (later known as the Conqueror) assigned every "church in Auge" falling under his jurisdiction to the Abbey of Bec. From this we can deduce that he was referring to several parishes surrounding Orbec. Between 1080 and 1082, William also assigned the parish of Saint-Pierre-Azif, again a parish belonging to Auge, to the Abbey of Saint-Étienne in Caen.

Prior to this, in 1077, Roger de Montgomery had bequeathed "the village of Trun and the forest of Auge" to the Abbey. Robert de Montbray had also bequeathed all his possessions "in the region of Villier, which is in Auge" to the same Abbey. These references from the ducal period refer to a series of places bordering the latter-day Pays d'Auge and largely reflect the current administrative organization of the region. Similar references are echoed in a much older text dating around 887. This text alludes to a certain monastery of Montreuil (Montreuil-la-Cambe?), itself situated in "the forest of Auge".

The financial and administrative district of the viscounty of Auge as it stood in the 17th century only accounts for the north-western quarter of the Pays d'Auge as we know it today. Although slightly smaller, the boundaries of the viscounty were similar to those of the religious district of the "archdeaconry of Auge".

As illustrated by the map drawn up by Danville in 1727, the boundaries of the Pays d'Auge tally quite neatly with the boundaries of the old bishopric of Lisieux. As a rule, the oldest bishoprics have preserved the administrative organization of the ancient Gallo-roman cities. After the fall of the

The logis of Le Marescot, manor house set amidst sloping pastures and plateau forest. The seigneur could survey his entire estate, which was under his direct control, from his logis.

The manor of Le Bais. Until recently, the wealth of the estate stemmed from its lush meadows and orchards, whose yields were sufficient to enable the tenant farmer to pay his dues.

The seigneurial manor

Empire due to the torrent of barbarian invasions, the bishoprics and first centers of Christianity took over the territorial unit of the ancient "pagus" of the Gallic people known as the Lexovii: Caesar referred to this phenomenon on several occasions (*De bello gallico*, IX, XI, XVII, XXIX). Generally, and certainly in this instance, the old territories were left intact.

In Normandy, this administrative continuity from ancient "pagus" to bishopric and then to "pays" is repeated in the Bessin, which can be traced back to the ancient "pagus" of Bajocasses and its chief town of Bayeux. Similarly, Cotentin can be traced back to the ancient bishopric of Coutances and so forth. There can be no doubt that the Gallic Lexovii founded their identity on the natural environment in which they lived, that is, the Pays d'Auge as we know it today. Thus, despite two thousand years of administrative division and reorganization, distant historical facts can be seen to coincide with natural surroundings which survive to this day.

Ambiguous in contemporary parlance, the term "seigneurial manor" is randomly applied to an infinite variety of constructions which tend to be characterized by a modest but painstaking quality of workmanship, their rustic settings, their size, and a number of mostly visible features indicating a *raison d'être* above that of a farm and simple abode.

Incorrectly considered a cross between a farm and a castle, the manor is often associated with a wide range of terms, all of which focus solely on the physical aspect of the building, or group of buildings, which typify the manor. This ignores the fundamental political significance of the manor. Based on the feudal legal system, the manor is an expression of a type of social and territorial organization and society which lasted for most of the last thousand years. Having adapted itself to the political and economic structures of the different provinces, the feudal system reached its apex during the 15th and 16th centuries.

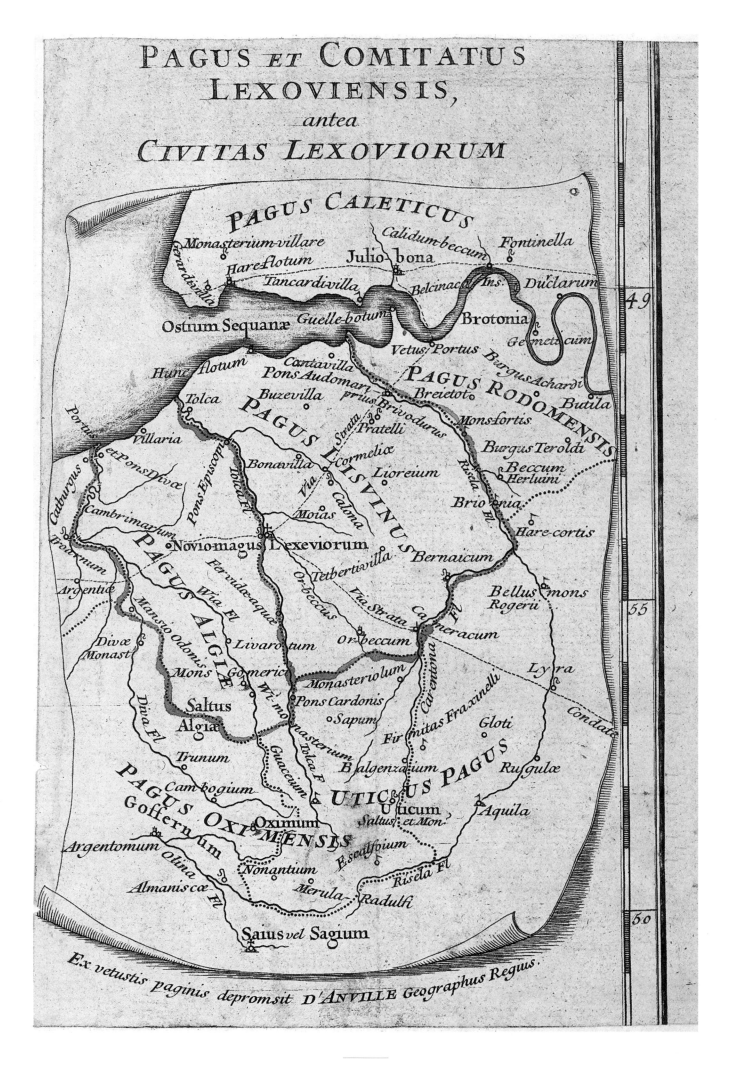

Drawn up by Danville and engraved in 1727, the map of the diocese of Lisieux includes a small vignette showing the position of the Gallo-Roman pagi *before* the civitas (Roman administrative district) of the Lexovii was established, predecessor of the diocese of Lisieux. The borders of the archdeaconries correspond approximately to each ancient "pagus". The present Pays d'Auge is composed essentially of the ancient Pagus Algiae and part of the ancient Pagus Lisvina (Lieuvin).

The manor house or *logis* was the focal point of the estate which the seigneur received in fief from his feudal lord. The notion of property ownership as we know it today did not exist within the pyramidal hierarchy of feudal society.

The bond of trust, or loyalty, which existed between the suzerain and the different ranks of vassal was based on control over the land, whose basic element was the seigneury. Various rights and duties operated at each level of the feudal hierarchy. These related to the exercise of justice both great and small: military affairs, such as military service and guard duty; taxation; other economic matters, such as taxes in kind and various duties; and religion, notably rights of parochial patronage and church appointments.

The manorial estate is therefore the physical expression of a complex state of affairs. Part of it is the 'seigneurial reserve': the demesne or home farm, i.e. the lord's ordinary residence, center of the farming activities which he directs through his servants, mainly in order to satisfy his everyday needs. Other parts may be leased to tenants who may, in turn, be considered his vassals. As Élizabeth Gautier-Desvaux has pertinently commented, "The material aspect of the bond between suzerain and vassal is late in appearing. The corner-stone of feudal society, laid during the creation of the principalities, is the bond of trust which the weak placed in the strong, the former pledging help and advice in exchange for his protection. The fief was entrusted to the vassal initially at his master's pleasure and later could be inherited." ("L'habitat seigneurial reflet de la vie rurale au XVI siècle", in Le Château en France, edited by J-P Babelon, Paris, 1986).

The manor house is also a tangible expression of the social rank of the seigneur and the obligatory rights attached to his fief. Although the seigneury lies at the lowest echelon of the feudal system, it still possesses a number of distinct prerogatives.

That of fortifying the manor house against attack, albeit in a symbolic way, is limited by the seigneur's obligation to pay due respect to the Consuetudines et Iusticiæ drawn up by William Rufus in 1091, which remained in force until the 17th century: for example, 'No-one in Normandy has the right to excavate a defensive ditch on flat land unless it is possible to throw out the earth from the bottom without the aid of a ladder, nor to erect a palisade, unless it be of a single row of fencing without enfilades or salients.' (quoted by Michel Bur, "Le Château et le Droit" in *Le Château en France*.)

His vassal is obliged to pay homage to the new seigneur when a fief changes hands: "The vassal is obliged to pay homage in person to the seigneur, in the seigneurial manor, by placing his hands between those of the seigneur and delivering the following words: 'I am your servant and I will show you respect and loyalty over all people except the King' (Custumal of Normandy)". Thus, the seigneurial manor is not simply a residence, it is the setting in which concrete expression is given to the feudal bond of each generation.

The seigneur is also entitled to exercise a variety of judicial rights. In this respect, Norman legal custom distinguishes itself from practices in other provinces in the kingdom: "Despite the general maxim that fief and judiciary should remain distinct entities …, this does not hold in Normandy where fief and judiciary are not usually separated".

The seigneur also had the prerogative of exercising his 'ordinary useful rights' in the dependent buildings forming part of the 'seigneurial reserve'. For example, the Customs of Normandy state that "The rights attached to the dovecote, (which are) purely feudal rights … are not relinquished if the building goes out of use or is demolished; to conserve these rights, it suffices if the remains of the dovecote may be made out." This demonstrates the importance attached to this highly symbolic building.

Against this background the more prominent features of the manor or, more precisely, the seigneurial enclosure, emerge. Constructed with or without outbuildings, the *logis* originally consisted of a simple square wooden tower standing on an earth *motte* encircled by ditches and light defenses. The generally less well defended outer bailey enclosed outhouses, garrets, cow sheds, stables and a cider-press, all of which were usually centered on the dovecote.

This arrangement developed fully during the 15th century; however, as considerations of layout outweighed the diminishing need for security, it gradually evolved to more traditional forms.

The art of building in the Pays d'Auge

Although only a few traces stand today, descriptions of this arrangement have fortunately been preserved in a number of documents. For example, a legal statement dated June 1st 1688, which is quoted by Arcisse de Caumont in his *Statistique Monumentale de Calvados*, describes the *logis* he owned in Méry-Corbon. Seat of the old quarter fief of Montfreule and under the jurisdiction of the King, the manor house was composed of "an inner and outer bailey, an adequate *logis* consisting of a hall and kitchen, four bedrooms over two stories, a cellar, and two structures on which the attic stands. The entire building has a tiled roof and is surrounded by stone and half-timbered walls with four small galleries, at the end of which stand four small rooms clad with shingles, all of which is attached to the principal *logis*."

There are two other buildings attached to "the gate of the aforementioned outer bailey, on top of which there was a chamber with a tiled roof". There was "a chapel for saying mass", and everything was surrounded by ditches.

Any mention of the "Normandy house" invariably conjures up images of half-timbered thatched cottages surrounded by orchards and cattle grazing in peaceful herds. It would appear that the universal presence of wood in the architecture of the Pays d'Auge has given the entire Norman province one of its most distinctive features. However, it would be too much to classify every residence or structure, in which wood features as either a component or simply as part of the decorative façade, as being in the "Normandy style".

Nonetheless, the Pays d'Auge has certainly exploited its timber resources to the full. Until the 17th century, almost all urban *logis* were entirely constructed from wood. Most survived until 1944 when the majority of towns were destroyed by bombardment.

In the space of a few days, the finest group of medieval houses in the Pays d'Auge at Lisieux were reduced to ashes by fire; these houses had been rightly acclaimed for the quality and abundance of their carvings. Although a comprehensive pictorial record of these houses remains, an in-depth study

Houses situated on the corner of Rue de la Paix and Grand'rue in Lisieux, destroyed by fire in 1944. The Gothic structure and details date from the second half of the 15th century.

aimed at capturing the wealth of this chapter of civilization, similar to that undertaken by Raymond Quenedey on housing in Rouen in the late 1920s, was, alas, never compiled. The destruction of similar buildings in towns such as Pont-l'Évêque and Vimoutiers, meant the loss of the basic fabric of urban architecture in the region.

It is, today, difficult to fathom the devastating effect of World War II on the province of Normandy. Notwithstanding the influence of urban classicism, this medieval heritage had survived five centuries of relative peace and prosperity. Were it not for the tenacity of scholars such as François Cottin in Lisieux and Jean Bureau in Pont-l'Évêque, all trace of these buildings would have been lost for posterity. Happily, however, the towns of Orbec and Honfleur survived unscathed to bear witness to the role played by timber in the towns in the Pays d'Auge.

Timber also played an important role in the religious architecture of the Pays d'Auge. One such building, the church of St. Catherine in Honfleur, which was built towards the end of the 15th cen-

The house known as that of the "monks of Jumièges", which stood in Vimoutiers, was destroyed by shelling in 1944. Its destruction marked the loss of one of the most remarkable examples of secular urban Renaissance architecture.

tury, still stands today. The original structure closely resembled a barn or market hall, featuring a central nave flanked by two aisles. Covered by a vast roof, the church was dimly lit by windows inserted in the side walls. The meticulously molded decorations and numerous carvings show that the church was not a temporary edifice intended for use until the resources required to build a stone church became available. The addition of a second nave at the beginning of the 16th century and the insertion of high windows in the roof above the aisles clearly demonstrate that this church was intended to last a long time. Several timber churches or chapels which were built in the 15th and 16th centuries are also extant. Examples include modest castle chapels such as Fort-Fresnay in Saint-Hymer and Saint-Martin parish church in Mesnil-Oury, which is concealed behind 18th century rendering. Timber porches, which can be found in churches in numer-

ous regions, often reached the dimensions of veritable narthexes in the Pays d'Auge, for example the porch which is grafted onto the stone nave of the church of Saint-Aubin-de-Bonneval. Built towards the end of the 15th century, the porch of this romanesque church consists of two timber stories and supports the church spire. Numerous structures demonstrating the absolute faith of the builders in timber still stand in Normandy, and particularly in the Pays d'Auge, to this day. The timber-framed roof and paneled vault rest on a series of wooden posts and the masonry walls were built to enclose rather than support the building. There can be no doubt that timber was the favorite construction material of builders in the Pays d'Auge and its continued use in manor houses up to the 18th century is a feature which is specific to this part of the province.

The availability of quality timber and the relative shortage of stone is not sufficient, however, to

The château of Saint-Germain-de-Livet is mainly built in stone. The actual logis is the only building constructed in timber, which illustrates the importance attached to this material.

which followed its own course and followed its own very distinct logic to the highest level of technical sophistication during the 16th century? Moreover, contrary to the perceived time-lag of about fifty years between town and country, the Pays d'Auge kept effortlessly abreast of new decorative repertoires and the evolution of plans, while also developing its own system of ornamentation and an array of original designs.

A number of recent studies have shown clearly that timber construction does not necessarily cost less than its more prestigious stone counterpart. It is interesting to note that in Norman towns where high quality Caen stone is readily available, the side walls and the rear elevations of buildings are often constructed in Caen stone, whereas the street façade is built in timber. And whereas wood easily lends itself to the most sumptuous decoration (52–54 rue Saint-Pierre in Caen), it is equally capable of bringing out strength, sobriety and rigor in a structure with the help of nothing more than the substantial section of the exposed timbers. (Maison des Quatrans, rue de Geôle in Caen).

Normandy is not an isolated case in this context and numerous similar examples can be found in both Brittany and the Loire Valley. However, the

This small logis in the late-15th-century manor of La Valette is a beautiful structure built with long bay posts. The mullioned and transomed windows on the second floor have been preserved and the continuous rail provides additional support. The large dormer window was added during the 16th century.

explain this unshakable attachment to wood. The 12th and 13th century secular and religious buildings, many of which still stand, prove that masons were quite capable of building in masonry. It is highly significant that although stone is much in evidence in the majority of important castles and medieval fortifications, the actual *logis*. while supported by defensive stone walls, was usually constructed in timber. Examples of such structures can be seen at Crèvecoeur and Saint-Germain-de-Livet.

Should the Pays d'Auge be classed as one of those conservative timber-frame regions on the periphery of a substantial West European movement which was intent on guiding architecture away from the primitive log cabin towards the more dignified stone castle? Should it not be said rather that a veritable "culture" of timber evolved in the Pays d'Auge

Stone gives way to timber in this curious dormer bretèche *above the entrance to the manor of Aumône.*

The manor of Pontif provides an excellent example of the use of marl, lime rendering, and brick. Contrary to normal practice, the brick forms the decorative element.

Here we see architectural terra-cotta put to a variety of uses. The roof tiling (logis of the manor of Langle, left) produces a sumptuous effect. Fragments of broken tile — often recycled roofing debris — are mixed with other materials such as limestone and flint (Vieux-Manoir at Orbec, right).

An example of wattle and daub nogging, bare or lightly plastered with lime, on outbuildings (La Cour Thomas above, left). Fragments of tile nogging in the roof of the dormer window in the logis at the manor of Ouilly (above, right).

Brick was mostly used in larger structures. For example, the outhouses of the château of Manerbe (left) have brick walls interrupted by vertical bands of toothed ashlar (left). Rows of stone separate brick walls decorated with a lozenge of glazed headers in the logis at the manor of Saint-Léger (right).

originality of the Pays d'Auge lies in the prominent role played by timber in the construction of its manors, the talent and craft employed in the construction of these manors, and the fact that many of these buildings still stand today. The only other comparable location in Western Europe is possibly South East England. This may well be the result of a shared tradition dating back to when ducal Normandy extended across the English Channel.

Although wood is certainly the predominant construction material used in the Pays d'Auge, the originality of its manors also lies in the variety of materials used in their construction. Drawn directly from the

land or indirectly from other substances, these materials were used to insulate, embellish, and protect against inclement weather. Local geology provided builders with the widest variety of stone.

From the point of view of texture, appearance, and color, these include – to mention but a few examples – white and green flaky limestone, resistant gold 'pierre de marne', tufa extracted from the rocks of petrified springs and impermeable to several centuries of inclement weather, a mixture of fertile silt and straw known as "wattle and daub", ochre-toned cob, black flint extracted from the cliffs of the Pays de Caux where it is used to ballast ship holds, roughly hewn or carefully napped gray, yellow, and brown colored flint.

Terra-cotta appears to have quickly replaced thatch and was used not only as a roof covering in the form of small flat tiles but was also used extensively in the nogging, the material used to fill the spaces between the members of a timber frame. Recycled from roofing debris, fragments of broken tile were the main material used to create decorative nogging with geometric and figurative motifs. The use of brick in fillets, nogging, and checkerwork walls did not become widespread until the early 17th century.

What characterizes the use of these vastly diverse materials in the Pays d'Auge is the way in which they are juxtaposed in mosaics of varying colors and forms. In some late-16th-century nogging, it is possible to find pink tiling alternating with brown and gray flint, and limestone *cabochons* cemented together with pale colored mortar. Similar diversity can to be found in string-courses – even in those manors which are constructed completely in stone.

The range of colors, which were derived either directly from the soil or following a preliminary treatment, proved inadequate to the needs of the builders who eventually turned to glazed terracotta, a material which reached the height of its popularity in the workshops of Manerbe and Le Pré-d'Auge in the 16th century. In addition to using this technique to glaze clay tiles and slates, they also glazed bricks green and yellow, accentuated the roof ridges in similar style and punctuated them with the finials which are so typical of the region. Meticulously ornamented plinths, vases, bouquets, arches, human, animal, and plant-like figures were mounted on these fragile structures which often reached a height of two meters. Although little evidence remains today, the effect was a feast of greens, browns, yellows, violets, and marble against a background setting of blue skies. All of this can only hint at the depth of this passion, this mania, for color. A collector's item since the 19th century, these finials are now mostly found in museum showcases or in the homes of enthusiasts. This style of roof decoration, which was particularly popular during the Renaissance, in fact represented the fruition of a trend which originated in medieval times. The roof of the cathedral in Lisieux was covered

with large yellow, green, and brown tiles from the 12th century onwards and some of the tiles can still be seen hooked over the roofing laths under the north tower.

Timber – the material with which houses were built

Necessity and fate were not the only factors which determined the choice of material for the construction of houses in the Pays d'Auge. There is a symbolic link which constantly pervades the intimate relationship between the builder and his work. As opposed to stone, which is inert and dead, wood is a living organic substance – a clear case of warm versus cold.

With the help of its veins and sap, wood grows and matures before being felled and prepared for

Built over four centuries ago, the timber in the logis *of the manor of Querville has not lost any of its original qualities. The detail on this astonishing front is beautifully rendered by the lifelike qualities of the wood.*

the great "work". It is chosen for the quality of its texture, its fiber, and its silver grain. It will lose its sap only to breathe again in tune with the cycle of the seasons whilst protecting the seigneur's *logis* from the winter chill and summer heat. The exact use to which the timber will be put is determined by the curve of the grain, a slight bow which makes it suitable for load-bearing beams or for the construction of the braces used to support jetties.

Wood is often depicted as a precarious material, eminently perishable, vulnerable to the effects of water, fungus and wood-eating insects, and easily destroyed by fire. These reasons would appear to justify the absolute superiority of "the masonry buildings", were it not for the evidence to the contrary provided by the use of oak in the manor houses of the Pays d'Auge. When used in accordance with the rules of the trade, oak proves remarkably resistant to all but the latter of the aforementioned sources of attack – fire. Although fire certainly poses the most ominous threat to wood, this is tempered by the extraordinary stability of timber frames in this context. While retaining most of its mechanical resistance, the surface of the wood burns slowly leaving a charred layer which insulates and protects the wood within. Paradoxically, metal and reinforced concrete structures are actually much more vulnerable to the effects of fire. Providing it is adequately protected from rain and water running off the roof, wood is almost indestructible. Unlike stone with its inherent rigidity, wood retains its strength and other technical characteristics almost indefinitely. Proof of this can be found in any building erected several centuries ago. The freshness of the facing, the detail on the moldings, and meticulously crafted carvings often still bearing the trace of the chisel, are all clearly discernible today. Once a living organism, wood wrinkles and splits slightly, its features become more etched with time. When initially shaped, timber is usually yellowish in color; it turns gray after a few years and, providing it is not painted, will eventually turn a silvery white color. Unlike stone façades with their inherent risks of efflorescence and chemical decomposition, timber façades do not require regular restoration.

Astonishingly, it is precisely because of this that the authentic structure of most manor houses has been preserved to astonish the viewer. Restorations are usually the result of misguided alterations and the failure to implement basic maintenance.

Timber framing: an insufficiently known building technique

The study of timber architecture, which was hitherto viewed as a minor specialization, has only recently begun to attract attention in France. Timber was rarely used in the construction of important French buildings and seldom warranted mention in books such as Jacques Androuet Du Cerceau's *plus excellents bâstiments de France* (outstanding French buildings).

Moreover, regional idiosyncrasies did little to salvage the crude and somewhat defunct image associated with timber architecture. By developing original designs, with little regard for the principles of classical architecture, timber architecture was seen as little more than the popular expression of a more prestigious type of architecture. Ironically, it was precisely this "rustic" character which became the focus of the new-found enthusiasm for timber dwellings – typified by the chalets of the first "Romantics". This developed into an interest in the holiday home which was subsequently replaced by the farmhouse-style country residence, viewed as an indispensable complement to the "town house" by a strata of society largely ignorant of the true art of timber construction.

This chain of events did little to diminish the mostly condescending view of timber architecture. The interest expressed in these buildings by the first local associations seemed to reduce them to the level of simple rural curiosities. However, the Pays d'Auge did prove something of an exception to this vision. Deeply affected by the bombardments in 1944 which virtually wiped out the region's entire urban architectural heritage in a matter of days, several prominent personalities joined Henri Pellerin in 1951 to found the association known as *Le pays d'Auge*. The association, which launched a campaign aimed at preserving what remained of the architectural heritage, soon enjoyed the support of several thousand members, and their combined efforts led to the recognition of these manor houses as a precious reminder of the region's identity.

Nonetheless, the study of these buildings, and of timber-architecture in general, suffered from the failure of two very disparate professions – the historians and technical analysts – to join forces. The art historians worked on dating techniques, decorative detail, design, and the distribution of mass, and concentrated their efforts almost exclusively on stone architecture. Meanwhile, the technical analysts tended to focus exclusively on the development of construction techniques, the establishment of typologies of multiple joints specific to individual parts of the structure, and the functions of these joints. The lack of convergence in these parallel approaches often resulted in erroneous conclusions which ultimately restricted progress in the study of timber architecture.

Architectural treatises are also conspicuously silent on matters relating to timber architecture. The first book to refer to timber architecture, entitled *Théâtre de l'art de charpentier*, was published in 1627 by Mathurin Jousse. Most of this book is devoted to the timber roofs of public buildings and urban residences. Only a handful of pages and a mere four illustrations relate to timber-framed façades. The same observation applies to all subsequent editions of the book published prior to the 18th century. The only other reference to timber architecture to be found in the other treatises of this period consists of a single drawing taken from the *Manière de bien bastir pour toutes sortes de personnes* by Pierre Le Muet (1623), and features a clearly archaic illustration of a timber-framed building.

The fifth tome of *La Statistique monumentale du Calvados*, which was published by Arcisse de Caumont in 1867, was the first document to give a detailed analysis of the manor houses of the Pays d'Auge. It included a section of the jettied façade of the *logis* of La Pipardière manor house illustrated by Bouet. Unfortunately, the engraving was so incomprehensible to the printer that it was inserted upside down, which, needless to say, did little to enlighten the reader. Despite De Caumont's groundbreaking work (he was also the founder of the Normandy Society of Antiquaries and later of the French Archeological Society), he all but ignored the manor houses of the Pays d'Auge although he did produce the first perfunctory inventory of these buildings as part of his *Statistique*.

In the same work, he recounts with utter indifference how he himself "had a large 16th-century timber and stone building demolished" in his manor at Montfreule. He did, however, show an interest in Belleau manor house, mostly due to the richness of its exceptional decorations which he featured in several illustrations, and arising no doubt from a premonition of its imminent demolition.

Information about the manor houses finally became available in the form of the superb watercolors of the manor houses of La Pipardière, Le Coin, and Fribois and Grandchamp château which were painted between 1886 and 1888 by Gabriel-Ruprich-Robert, an *architecte-en-chef* in the French Historic Monuments Service. The scrupulously meticulous preparatory sketches he made of these

Mozin Chalet, Trouville, built in 1844 by the painter Charles Mozin examplifying the interest of the first Romantics, who were responsible for the "discovery" of the Norman coast, in this type of architecture.

Lithograph based on a drawing by Felix Benoist from around 1860. The logis *of the manor of Belleau was perhaps the only building to attract the attention of 19th-century engravers. The fine carved details of the* logis *featured in an illustration by G. Bouet and described by A. de Caumont in the final volume of his* Statistique monumentale du Calvados. *Despite this, however, the house was demolished in 1870.*

buildings reveal something of a discrepancy between his idealized vision and the houses as they stood in reality, which only goes to demonstrate the profound admiration he felt for these houses. The few documents published subsequently were mostly limited to heliographic plates accompanied by a few brief lines of commentary. The first in-depth analysis of the manor houses appeared after 1951 in a review written by Henri Pellerin and Jean Bureau and published by the association *Le Pays d'Auge*. The review was largely based on historical fact, the authenticity of which was established in a rigorously scientific manner by Michel Cottin. Monographs included in studies published by Philippe Deterville in 1982 and 1985 have also featured pieces on a number of hitherto unpublished manor houses.

As is the case with most timber constructions, the analysis of these houses is often hindered by two principal factors. Firstly, the carpenter is free to alter existing structures with relative ease, providing the basic structure of the house is not affected, and secondly, although each alteration leaves a multitude of visible traces, the sheer abundance

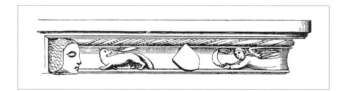

of this evidence often renders accurate analysis extremely difficult.

The task of updating a medieval façade to accommodate contemporary taste and fashion could hardly have been more simple. Because there was no need for shoring, basic chisels and saws were all that was needed to re-model any moldings and decorative details which were considered outmoded. This is why when examined today some buildings prove older than their details would indicate. A little basic shoring made easy work of the renovation of an entire story. The astonishing results which could be achieved here are demonstrated by a townhouse on Place Victor-Hugo, Lisieux, which was destroyed in 1944. Comprising three stories, the first two floors could be dated from the 17th century, whereas the details of the third floor definitely dated it in the 15th century. In the absence of

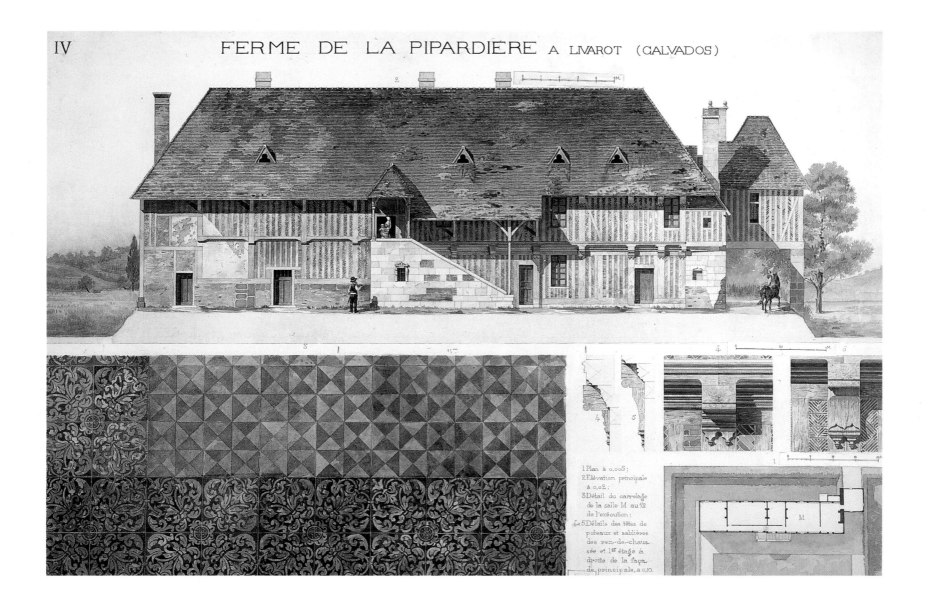

IV   FERME DE LA PIPARDIERE A LIVAROT (CALVADOS)

1 Plan à 0,005 ;
2 Élévation principale
à 0,02 ;
3 Détail du carrelage
de la salle M au 72
de l'exécution ;
4 5 Détails des têtes de
poteaux et sablières
des rez-de-chaus-
sée et 1er étage à
droite de la façade
principale, à 0,10

thorough investigation, such occurrences often caused consternation and certainly contributed to rash conclusions about so-called archaic styles.

Carpenters took advantage of this possibility, and where they intervened, a large body of evidence remains. As opposed to stone architecture where any individual feature can be replaced relatively discreetly, a timber structure can rarely be altered without leaving a discernible trace. For example, when a piece of timber has been removed, it will leave the trace of the mortise and peg-hole. A window which has been sealed will retain the outline of the chamfer which once surrounded its frame. The initial location of an ornamental decoration can be determined by the slightly less worn appearance of the original timber surface, and the latter often bears traces of the tool used in the operation. The use of basic shoring can be ascertained by the presence of characteristic notches on the vertical posts, etc.

Such analysis requires a perfect understanding of the technical procedures used in these alterations. Without this knowledge, the sheer volume of information is likely to overwhelm the observer, leading him to draw false conclusions concerning, for example, the possible reuse of existing timbers.

Materials were certainly recycled in timber construction, although this rarely occurred during the 15th and 16th century. Nonetheless, timbers were frequently moved around during this period to enlarge or alter existing openings; the distinctive markings on the timbers enabled them to be easily restored to their initial location. Where timbers have clearly been reused, it is often possible to ascertain their original function by characteristic markings which remain in the wood. Carpenters have also occasionally been known to take individual features of exceptional quality, for example entire sets of mullioned windows, and to insert

A water color depicting the logis of the manor of La Pipardière, painted by Gabriel Ruprich-Robert in March 1888.

able evidence of such practices in Normandy. These include a report drawn up in 1457 by the executors of Agnes Sorel's will concerning the Cour du Mont manor house in Duclair: "I acquired (…) a completely new timber house in Duclair. I had it transferred to the Court du Mont where it was then plastered and roofed".

In the other instance, whereby a building is modified before being transferred, it is possible to piece together a complete account of the operation. I observed such a case in the *Pays d'Ouche*, in the *logis* of Le Buquetière manor house near Jonquerets-de-Livet. The building has two bare eaves walls with few openings. The walls are constructed from long rough timber posts with a single jutting gable, in which despite the abundant moldings and decorations the openings have been sealed. The building is actually a 16th-century town house with its gable facing the street which was removed in the 17th century to a clearing in the forest of Broglie. The shop front on the ground floor and the set of windows on the first floor survive intact. Windows have been hastily inserted in the blind eaves walls to create a main and rear elevation. Another example worthy of note concerns La Pipardière manor house. Here the 16th-century *logis* was extended during the 17th century to include several bays, all of which originated from a timber structure built two centuries previously and were subsequently enlarged to accommodate the building in which they now stand.

The conversion of old, obsolete *logis* to a new use was also very common. Many observers have been surprised to note the care with which presses and other farm buildings appear to have been built – that is until they realize that these buildings have actually been converted from former *logis*. The latter generally had its chimneys removed in order to free up valuable space, and a new more fashionable *logis* was usually built nearby.

Finally, in cases where certain structures are not considered worthy of reuse, their materials are often recycled on the spot. A perfect example of this is to be found in the 17th-century *logis* of Querville where the molded and carved jetty bressumer was sawed into short timber rafters prior to being moved to an adjacent building. This phenomenon

Number 22, Place Victor-Hugo in Lisieux, destroyed in 1944. This building constitutes a perfect example of the disturbing extent to which timber architecture can be remodeled. The structure of this 15th century façade allowed the complete restoration of the second story in Renaissance style, without damaging the upper medieval stories.

them in the façade of a farm building constructed almost two centuries later: this can prove yet another source of misleading information when it comes to dating such structures.

More extreme cases of such "recycling" practices involve the complete reutilization of homogenous structures by transferring them to other locations. Such structures would have been completely dismantled, relocated, and possibly modified. If the structure is not modified, the building will rarely retain traces of the operation. In such cases, difficulties could arise when it comes to classifying the legal status of the structure as a moveable or fixed asset! A number of documents provide irrefut-

can often be found in the roofs of several very large buildings. For example, the purlins from the buildings of the Abbey of Bec-Hellouin recycled as rafters conserve sufficient elements from the previous structure to enable the reconstruction of the medieval trussed-rafter roof.

Anonymous works of art?

Les Normands have a reputation for being reticent and discreet when it comes to disclosing their age. The same can also be said of the builders of the Pays d'Auge who have left us little information by way of dates and names. In other areas, it was common practice to clearly display the names of both the client and carpenter, and to include a short verse from the Bible. In the Pays d'Auge, only one 15th-century building bears the carpenter's name and a precise date of construction. The *logis* of the manor house of La Grue in Capelle-les-Grands, which was subsequently converted into a cider-press, features a moving inscription in Gothic characters and Roman numerals. It has been etched with a marking awl, a tool normally used for marking the position of assembled timber frames on a full-scale floor plan, and reads as follows:

"A carpenter by the name of Thomas le Coutelier built this fine house in MCCCCLXXVI." It is rare to see a carpenter express himself so clearly, but he certainly had reason to be proud of his fine house which was built with commendable skill.

Scarcely a dozen dates, all of which should be treated with caution, remain to document the history of the 16th-century *logis*. In several cases, the dates merely refer to important modifications which the master builder or client wished to signal. More frequently, these dates were inscribed to mark the addition of Renaissance details to a medieval structure. Examples of this can be found in the *logis* of Langle, where an entire set of mullioned windows was completely modified, or at the *logis* of Foyer where a new dormer window was inserted in 1583. In each instance, the date is deliberately affixed in such a way that the nature and importance of the modification is quite clear but only to someone who has worked out the methods used by the carpenter. The construction date for several

The old medieval logis of the manor of La Bruyère. Outmoded and uncomfortable, the original logis was converted to a farm building in the late 16th-century when a new logis was built nearby.

manor houses has been miscalculated by more than a full century by not understanding such methods.

In the absence of detailed notarial registers, which would, no doubt, throw some light on the contracts concluded between clients and master builders, we still know very little about the carpenters other than in the case of Thomas Le Coutelier and also "Michelle Noelle and J(o) ha (nus) Moley" who have left an inscription dated 1521 on the church porch of Saint-Martin-du-Mesnil-Oury. It is unclear whether this date refers to the porch or to the entire church.

Carpenters working on the Courtonne-la-Meudrac church also signed their work with simple initials engraved in beautiful Gothic letters, below which they have carved an axe, a symbol of their trade. The carpenter who worked on Belleau manor, which was destroyed around 1870, thought so highly of himself that he fashioned a coat of arms from his initials and his tools, and mounted it alongside the Breton coat of arms and that of families allied to the tenant of the fief, René de Lyée. The similarity of the carpentry in religious architecture (which is better documented) has been instrumental in the elucidation of the history of timber architecture.

Dendrochronology has been used for several decades to determine the date on which a tree was

A coat of arms taken from the manor house of Belleau which was illustrated by G. Bouet and described by A. de Caumont in the final volume of the Statistique monumentale du Calvados. *Unlike other regions, it is extremely rare to find dates and signatures on the manor houses of the Pays d'Auge. The oldest inscription was discovered in the former logis of La Grue, where, quite exceptionally, the carpenter's name was also included. Occasionally, carpenters signed with their initials and their tools which they displayed in an irregular-shaped coat of arms. The inscription of dates occurred more frequently during the second half of the 16th-century. (The Old Manor, Orbec, 1568).*

felled by examining the relative widths of annual rings on a piece of timber. Providing the sample has retained some of its sapwood and a sufficient number of rings exist, the date of construction can be estimated to within a year of the exact date. In the Pays d'Auge, a systematic campaign will be able to complement meticulous observations made during the course of recent restoration projects. Dendrochronology may eventually provide completely accurate construction dates for the manor houses. It will certainly have an important contribution to make, providing the procedure is implemented with maximum scientific rigor. Full responsibility for the construction of a building was usually entrusted by the client to the carpenter. Compared to a stone mason of similar standing, a good carpenter will have had a dis-

tinct aptitude for proportionality and abstract thinking. A master of the "art of line", the carpenter sketched a full-scale drawing on the ground on which he then laid his timbers before cutting them to size. He then marked out the joints in the timber frame, elevation by elevation, followed by the gables and trusses. These full-scale obey a simple logic and use a specific module, on the basis of which harmonic relations are established, which can sometimes be demonstrated by reconstructing the *épure*. Until the late 16th century, floor plans were almost always very accurate and the module often revolved around the longest piece of timber available which was pivotal to the overall cohesion of the structure, i.e. the top plate which was always constructed from a single piece of timber.

Inside the manorial enclosure

The alignment of the buildings along the perimeter of Les Tourelles' manorial enclosure have as important a role to play in its symbolic defense as the slim entrance turrets. The principal structures, the logis *and the dovecote, stand in the middle of the enclosure.*

A survivor from early feudal times, the manor house of Piencourt on its motte *surrounded by ditches, which are now filled in, stands next to a church which was probably the old manorial chapel.*

The manorial enclosure and its defenses

The manor is a symbol of power and, thus, by definition destined to bring out the covetous rivalry between fiefs. Its defense system, for the most part symbolic and actually incapable of holding at bay a large resolute army, is mainly concerned with the expression of this power, of which it is a symbol.

Almost all medieval manors have defense systems of varying levels of sophistication. Having relinquished their *raison d'être* in the late Middle Ages, most of these systems disappeared and in some cases all that remains is an outline in the form of a quadrilateral surrounding the manor. In its basic form, the layout perpetuates the formula of a *logis* on a *motte*, a steep mound of earth excavated from a circular ditch which was generally filled with water. The *motte* was surrounded by a simple wooden fence, or *plesse*, or sometimes a modest hedge of impenetrable thorns. A perfect example of this can be found in Piencourt manor with its 15th-century

logis which probably replaced an earlier structure. The manor house consists of a timber-framed second story resting on a stone first story and stands on a circular motte which is still clearly discernible. The other buildings, barns, sheds, and outhouses of the seigneurial reserve (home farm) are located in a second, more extensive enclosure – the outer bailey – and are surrounded by ditches which are now barely recognizable. The adjacent church may well have been the original manor chapel.

This layout is closely based on the motte-and-bailey, with the ensemble of buildings divided between an inner and outer bailey as can be found at the château of Crèvecoeur. At Crèvecoeur, the inner bailey consists of a square stone keep and a timber-framed *logis* surrounded by moats and walls and defended by a drawbridge. The outer bailey, which is significantly bigger and less well defended, included the dovecote, the chapel, and various other farm buildings. This arrangement is reproduced in the château of Saint-Germain-de-Livet which, however, has no keep but includes a timber *logis* in the inner bailey, which is defended by a chatelet and ditches with flowing water. The outer bailey is accessed from a portal in the enclosure wall, of which only fragments remain.

This preoccupation with defense, which is more pronounced in actual châteaux than in the manors, partly explains why the manors tend to be positioned at strategic locations. Such locations include valley floors, which, as in the château of Grandchamp, provided convenient *isolation* with the help of usually artificial ditches; blocked-off mountain spurs as in the case of Quilly-du-Houlley; and high isolated sites such as Le Mont-de-la-Vigne.

There were other constraints to be taken into account, particularly that of the supervision of the seigneurial reserve, which was located, where possible, on a direct line of sight from the manor house,

as recommended in 16th century treatises. Most of the manor houses in the Pays d'Auge were actually built on hillsides. Theoretically, this location was considered less favorable, as it made the excavation of ditches more difficult and the manor was more exposed to attack from above. The manor also had to be situated in close proximity to a water source to ensure the essential supply of water. These obstacles were successfully overcome in many instances and numerous hillside manors survive today: the water in the ditches of the manor of Le Pontif, which is built on a hillside, are supplied by a single stream; a minuscule tributary of the river Touques,

blocked by a mound of clay some thirty meters from its source, forms a large reservoir whose waters supply the diminutive *motte* on which Le Verger manor was built; and the hillside manor house of Malou in the Touques valley retreats behind the steep drained ditches of the *motte* on which it stands. The latter still retains a modest postern flanked by a pair of towers, similar to the postern found in the chatelet of Saint-Germain-de-Livet, near the château of Crèvecoeur, to which it was transferred from the chatelet of Beuvillers in 1970. The manor house and dovecote of Le Bais, both of which are situated on a rectangular platform, are

At the manor of Malou, the defense system of the modest hillside fort is barely distinguishable from the actual building. The pair of towers flanking the postern are attached to the roof and walls of the adjacent buildings.

defended by a moat and a postern with a drawbridge. Curiously, however, the imposing two-story barn, which was constructed in the 15th century, was left in a fold in the valley completely undefended.

However, real defensive walls are rarely found on manor sites. The manor of Le Coudray is one of the few significant exceptions to this rule, but in this instance the inclusion of defensive walls was primarily due to the importance of this full fief which had that various feudal prerogatives, including significant judicial rights.

The defenses in a small number of manors were limited to the actual *logis*, or included, at most, a minuscule enclosure; the pepperpot-shaped towers of the manor of Coupesarte are set at an angle to the main *logis*, and a recent clean-up of the moat has revealed the foundations of a round tower on the opposite side.

The outbuildings

Occasionally situated within the inner bailey, but more frequently relegated to the outer bailey, the farm buildings associated with the home farm – barns, stables, stalls, sheds, cider-presses, and ovens – include highly varied structures, a detailed study of which is unfortunately beyond the scope of this

book. These simple structures, whose size reflects the lesser significance of the seigneurial reserve, are rarely attached to the dwelling. Meticulously built, with few windows, and comprising one, or more rarely, two stories, these farm buildings were an integral part of an organized arrangement centering on the privileged position of the *logis*.

As a rule, the barn was the largest structure. For obvious safety reasons, the bakehouse was generally detached and the sheds were situated at the far end of the stables and stalls. In more recent buildings, the presence of a cider-press is marked by a square-shaped return wing which housed the actual press. The structure of these cider-presses is often quite astonishing. A profusion of moldings, carvings, galleries, and jetties would indicate that they were built in an exceptionally meticulous manner. However, closer analysis usually reveals that they have simply been converted from the former *logis*, as is the case with the presses at the manors of La Bruyère and La Grue.

The dovecote, a seigneurial prerogative

As the most visible symbol of seigneurial prerogative, the dovecote was treated with the utmost importance. It usually stood alone in the center of the inner or outer bailey. The importance of the fief is expressed by the number of niches or pigeonholes in the dovecote. A source of delicate meat for the seigneurial table, it was also a source of valuable high quality manure. Equal in importance to the *logis*, in some instances, e.g. La Valette, the *logis* was built in timber and the actual dovecote in stone.

As a rule, the structure of the Normandy dovecote is largely determined by its functions. The

The stables and sheds of the manor of Coupesarte are aligned along the outer bailey. The first two dormer windows probably originated from the main logis, prior to its conversion in the 17th century.

The outhouses in the manor of Cauvigny are aligned in two long rows enclosing the bailey behind the logis. The sheds form a third row at the center of the bailey.

ABOVE:
The well, above, was generally housed in a small free-standing structure, as seen here in the manor of La Cour Thomas. The winch is sheltered by a pyramid-shaped roof.

RIGHT:
The main elements of the press at the manor of Les Évêques are still intact. The horse-driven grindstone was used to crush apples which fell directly from the loft into a circular trough; the large press.

pigeonholes are usually fitted to the full height of the inner walls or occasionally along the upper half of the structure, which is then accessed from an oblique rotating ladder. The vast majority of dovecotes are therefore circular or hexagonal in plan, although a number of square ones exist. Access is through a single narrow door at ground level and the pigeons enter via dormers at the base of the roof or, more rarely, through a louver at the top. As a rule, the roof of the dovecote is pyramid-shaped, although rare examples of square dovecotes with pitched roofs do exist, such as that at Crèvecoeur. For the most part, circular dovecotes, which are generally constructed from brick, stone, or wattle and daub, have cone-shaped roofs. Although commonplace, the construction of a cone-shaped roof on a hexagonal dovecote was certainly a test of

the carpenter's skill in making the transition from a polygonal to a circular plan and crowning it all with the famous glazed terra-cotta finial, which was often topped by a pigeon or pelican.

Chapels and oratories

The effort expended in asserting the importance of one's fief, i.e. erecting a suitable *logis* with adequate defenses, building the necessary farm buildings, and constructing an opulent dovecote, did not exonerate the seigneur from attending to matters of the soul. Several manors had their own chapels which, like the château chapels, e.g. at Crèvecoeur, often outlived them. In most cases the chapels were free-standing randomly positioned structures, e.g. at Belleau-Belleau, Anfernel, and Mont-de-la-Vigne. However, the position of the chapel at Cuvinière manor shows how it could also be integrated into a rigorous traditional plan.

As testified by the archives of the manor of Courson, the chapel was sometimes limited to a modest oratory attached to the main *logis*, the external wall of which was decorated with tiles bearing religious motifs. The chapel at the manor of Saint Léger certainly represents the most original solution in this context. Here, the builders daringly attached the chapel – a completely oversailing structure with a three-sided apse supported by a series of curved brackets – to the side of a straight staircase turret.

A coupled rafter roof in the chapel at the manor of Le Mont-de-la-Vigne.

The conical roof of the defensive turret at the manor of Les Tourelles, from which the manor takes its name (i.e., tourelle translates as turret), is echoed in the adjacent timber-framed dovecote.

ABOVE:
The dovecote at the manor of Crèvecoeur is a simple structure based on the old principle of resting the corner posts on the angle of the sole plates.

ABOVE, RIGHT:
The timber-framed chapel at the manor of Saint-Léger is an oversailing structure attached to the staircase tower.

The manor of Cauvinière is built on a traditional plan. The pavilions situated at the angles of the platform, which is encircled by ditches, are the chapel and the chaplain's house.

A chronological outline

From random medieval enclosure
to the structured manorial plan

Oriel, spiral staircase and gallery, the key major elements in the evolution of the manor house. Left: the manor house of Conty. Above: The manor house of Le Désert.

Randomly composed of buildings and spaces, the layout of the medieval manor house was developed in response to a variety of requirements and betrays a general lack of concern for a structured plan. Although a degree of hierarchy existed between the various buildings, security was clearly the main concern.

The *logis*, which usually comprises two stories and a steeply pitched roof, stands at the top of the courtyard and dominates the inner bailey. A tower, which occasionally includes an oriel, was directly attached to the *logis*. The tower was functional in terms of the access it provided to each floor, and also symbolic in that it figured in the symbolism of the feudal hierarchy: Charles V's tower at the Louvre, symbolic of royal power, and the tower in the seigneurial manor house reflected the hierarchical tiers of the feudal system descending from the suzerain-lord to the humble vassal. Dovecotes, chapels, and barns were arranged as was best possible within the limited space available in the courtyards, and the outbuildings leaned on the enclosure defenses.

This scheme, which was used for impressive châteaux and humble manors alike, was eventually abandoned with the emergence of the new Renaissance ideas at the beginning of the 16th century. This new influence initiated a complete revision of the style of ornamentation and, subsequently, architectural composition in Normandy.

Gothic decoration, ogee lintels, flamboyant niches, and tapered pinnacles gave way to molded architraves, arabesque and grotesque pilasters, projecting half-balusters, and medallions. These changes to the architectural repertoire initially resulted in the crass juxtaposition of the medieval heritage, in which a harmonious balance had been struck between structure and ornament, and the new style: the results were often of a particular taste with, for example, timber-framed houses being decorated with motifs specifically developed for stone architecture. Capitals returned with a vengeance; they had been discarded at the end of the Gothic period, which had done much to unify the decorative repertoire of timber and stone respectively by encouraging the art of the molding. Perplexed sculptors were frequently faced with the daunting task of updating the decoration of timber-framed structures with Corinthian capitals, fluted pilasters, and arches with volute key-stores. For the most part, they succeeded in their task, and often with great subtlety and taste. They incorporated wide gadroons into jetties, carved Classical dentils onto cornices and wall plates, and transformed the grotesque beasts, which once decorated the timber beams in the late Middle Ages, into delicate foliated bands, dolphins or foliate masks.

This renewal in ornamental style was soon followed by a similar development in architectural composition. The simple Gothic *logis* with its elongated rectangular plan and pitched roof, which had previously shown little concern for symmetry, even if the façade was marked by a staircase turret, gradually evolved into a more systematic structure. Inspired by François I, who in 1528 decided to

Most of the medieval details on the logis *of the manor of Caudemone has been borrowed from stone architecture. Here, the pinnacles, ogees, and small columns are protected by the overhang of the jetty.*

The decorative details on the logis *of the manor house of Querville, such as the grotesque animals extending from the bressumer, are specific to timber architecture. The large Renaissance window, which was imposed on the Gothic structure, is ornamented with pilasters and scrolled capitals, features normally associated with stone architecture.*

The proportions and profiles of timber moldings underwent substantial change in the second quarter of the 16th century. Whereas the grotesque figures were mostly left intact, torus, cavetto, and ovolo mouldings soon gave way to ogee and cyma reversa moldings. The jetty at the Old Manor at Orbec served little purpose other than providing a pretext for the gadroon molding, which is liberated from the strict rhythm formerly created by the end-stops of the transverse beams.

The latter part of the 16th century is marked by a dramatic break with Gothic traditions. The manor house of Le Mesnil-de-Roiville is a perfect example of the new architectural styles which brought about a profusion of projecting pavilions, varied roofing structures and the absolute dominance of symmetrical lines.

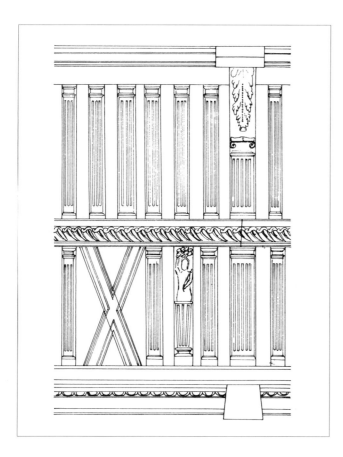

"reorganize and restore the aforementioned castle (the Louvre)", the plans and layout of castles and manor houses throughout the entire country were radically overhauled. This work was also inspired and guided by a series of models, which gradually became more widely available thanks to the development of printing.

Slightly projecting pavilions began to appear at the corners of the main façades of some *logis*, often with the intention of balancing a square staircase turret on the rear elevation. The pavilion roofs on these structures clearly distinguished them from the main hip-roofed *logis*. The enormous chimney stacks, which were previously positioned centrally making it impossible to locate the main entrance on the central axis, gradually evolved into two structures on the side elevations. Thus, the increasingly symmetrical *logis* become the central focus of the ensemble.

Renaissance ornamental styles were used, for example, on the timber gallery of the château of Mesnil-Guillaume where the upright timbers take the form of fluted antique-style pilasters.

A rigorous Classical style dominates at the manor house of Prétot. Built from traditional long timber posts, the imposing bulk of the logis is enhanced by the decorative slanted timbers at either side of the main façade, which also visibly reduce the distinction between the two stories.

The late 17th century saw the advent of a key architectural trend which, while imparting an air of sober grandeur, enforced a rigorous form of symmetry that left room for only small exceptions. An example of this can be found in the main façade of the logis of the manor of Saint-Léger.

The elegant *logis* of the Classical period

This emphasis on rigorous composition and abundant ornament gradually forced the builders to simplify the lines and volumes. Although it retained its central position, the external staircase, still common until the early 18th century, was gradually integrated into the quadrilateral of the *logis*. The winding staircase was abandoned in favor of straight dog-leg stairs, and its natural corollary, the open gallery, which had been progressively eliminated in the interests of comfort, also disappeared completely.

Logis constructed in stone and brick became more commonplace and decorative detail was mostly confined to the polychrome features of these materials, the rhythm of their toothing stones, cantilevered rustication, and flush or slightly projecting string courses. Very occasionally, a pediment was fitted over the entrance or above the dormer windows.

Carpenters were gradually replaced by stone masons. Until now, the carpenter's technical expertise had played an important role in the development of specific forms and features. The logical use of short timbers in timber-framed architecture had popularized the jetty until it was gradually outlawed in the towns by the royal edict of 1498 in Orléans and the municipal edict of 1525 in Rouen.

The gradual application of these edicts gave rise to the disappearance of oversailing structures in timber-framed *logis* and the emergence of a new trend in carpentry which favored uniform paneled façades. The stories no longer climbed irregularly, tier upon tier, supported by the oblique breast-summers. The successive bays of windows and window breasts accentuated by the jetties separating each floor were replaced by the uniform façade in which the ceiling joists were joined to the inner side of the timber posts.

Decorative detail was mostly confined to the timber framework, with timbers arranged in the shape of a saltire under window breasts or simply positioned at oblique angles extending across the height of the story. Horizontal members were occasionally accentuated by moldings, and in the more prestigious buildings, the vertical elements were still embellished with foliation and fluted pilasters.

From this time onwards, the focus shifted to refining the layout and internal decor of the *logis*. The timber frame was virtually relegated to the status of an anonymous construction material which, like stone, merely served in the realization of the architect's vision.

These trends continued uninterrupted throughout the 18th century. The steeply pitched roofs,

Logis *built in the 18th century, such as at Lieu-Hocquart, were more unassuming, relying on clear and simple volumes for their effect. Symmetry is still imperative. Here the roof is less steeply pitched and the only ornament consists of the cross braces on the window breasts.*

Timber architecture is extremely versatile. An upper floor of radically different design was added to an originally single story logis *which had been built as the presbytery of Saint-Michel-de-Livet at the beginning of the early 17th century. Between the windows of the new story, were alternating panels of intersecting cross-bracing and herring-bone patterns.*

The manor house of Les Quatres Nations is an excellent example of the art of timber architecture in the 18th century. The wide and narrow bays are differentiated by the width of the fern motifs. The carpenter clearly preferred this kind of motif to the more traditional arrangement with vertical members and also applied it on the side elevations.

Timber architecture gradually fell from favor in the late 18th century, and the timber frames of numerous logis, such as that of the manor house of Le Bais, were often covered up with a mixture of lime and crushed brick.

which were beginning to lose favor in the preceding century, were replaced by more gently sloping roofs.

This trend was accompanied by the emergence of more complex plans developed in response to new concerns surrounding physical comfort and the demands of social life. The floor plans, which more than doubled in depth, now included alcoves, corridors, anterooms, and chambers which were often decorated with wood paneling. Upstairs, a corridor spanning the entire width of the building afforded individual access to each room.

External decoration was, therefore, reduced to curvilinear lintels and carefully orchestrated, rigorously symmetrical openings, and, occasionally, a projecting frontispiece. The timbers of the façades were arranged in a profusion of motifs, including saltires, herring-bone and fern patterns.

In the late 18th century, wood was no longer fashionable and even the gleaming nogging with

its fragments of broken pink tiles had fallen from favor.

The façades of numerous prestigious dwellings were reworked by applying chestnut lathing which could then be covered with lime plaster in order to simulate rusticated corner masonry and terra-cotta panels imitating brickwork.

The country house

The medieval seigneurial property had indeed moved a long way from its origins by the early 19th century. If not simply abandoned, or at best, converted into farm buildings, the manor houses were eventually converted into farms, residences, or country houses.

The results were often quite astonishing. What should be done with the now defunct dovecote, if the owner is not partial to pigeon flesh? Several dovecotes were converted into small workshops in the gardens which replaced the original bailey. In the case of Le Bais manor, the dovecote was fitted with an external staircase, lozenge-shaped windows were inserted in the roof, and the walls were fitted with roundels to create a peaceful place for meditation, not unlike the dovecote at Les Tourelles, which, although it has fewer windows, is also ideal for peaceful contemplation.

As a rule, *logis* were converted into simple country houses. Inspired by their medieval past and great beauty, when the first "Romantics" discovered the Normandy coast, they borrowed much from the

Neglected for almost a century, timber-framed logis were rediscovered by the first enthusiasts of the Norman "summer house". As the land is often suitable for raising horses, many logis were converted into reputable stud farms like this one which is situated on the former estate of La Rivière.

By the late 18th century, the new trend for converting old buildings into workshops and summer cottages brought about astonishing transformations, as seen here in the conversion of the former dovecote of the manor of Le Bais.

Built facing the Seine estuary, "Chalet Guttinger" played host to the literary circles of the first "Romantics". Built in 1829 at the edge of Saint-Gatien forest, the building now stands in pitiful ruin.

manor houses of the Pays d'Auge in the construction of their new homes. A native of Rouen and of Swiss extraction, the poet Ulric Guttinger constructed his chalet in 1829 at the edge of Saint-Gatien forest opposite the changing skies of the Seine estuary. In this, the first country house of its type which was inspired by both the Swiss chalet and the Norman manor house, Guttinger entertained a literary set, including his friends Nodier, Musset, and Saint-Beuve.

Timber-framed architecture

Materials and structures

The material at the disposal of the master builder is the key to the way he builds. Timber, the most widely available building material in the Pays d'Auge. inspired its master carpenters to develop the framing techniques and variety of structures which play a major role in determining the originality of this architecture.

The characteristics of this material must first be summarized. Due to its fibrous texture and variable density, unlike most other materials, building timber can work both in tension and flexion, depending on the type of timber, its thickness or 'scantling', and the way it has been converted from the original tree. It is the grain of timber which,

The manor of Les Buttes. Each element in the timber-framed wall expresses its function: supporting the roof, enclosing the building, maintaining the balance of the structure.

The different functions require joints of varying complexity, from the basic juxtaposition of elements to the very elaborate joints required for the jetty where at least six pieces of timber converge on one point.

above all, allows three criteria to be met: straight-grained timbers are best for constructional members in tension; beams subject to flexion require timber of sizeable scantling; and timbers in compression, used 'end on', need to be of even greater cross-section. The carpenter's choice of joints depends largely on which of these features is dominant.

Hardwood-yielding broad-leafed trees have always outnumbered conifers in Normandy. Conifers are generally used to provide straight timbers of uniform scantling, which are ideal for use in simple structures and for building walls log-cabin style. In contrast, broad-leafed, hardwood trees produce timber of widely varying cross-section. The relatively scarce timbers of large scantling and the more numerous pieces of smaller section allow a main frame to be built into which the smaller timbers can be inserted with a secondary function. This is the basic concept of timber framing.

The very nature of wood, its texture and lightness, prevents the builder from using it in the form of simple juxtaposed or stacked elements. It is used instead in the form of "articulated" elements rendered stable by joints which vary according to the function of the member in question, be it in tension, flexion, or compression. The basic model for such joints was inspired by the natural fork of the branch and the first joints were constructed using ties consisting of fibrous material from plants or bark. The carving of a longitudinal or transverse notch into the material eventually led to the development of the art of joinery.

The location of a joint at the center of superimposed timber members gives them a stability which is based on their own weight, and if a lap dovetail joint is used, the members can work in tension. However, it was the appearance of the mortise

The outbuildings of the manor of Le Lieu Rocher include one of the finest repertoires of simple types of joints used in the Pays d'Auge. Here, the projecting tenoned post, which is keyed using two pegs, is reinforced by a strong juxtaposed bresummer fitted as a tenon and slot scarf joint and keyed using a single peg.

and tenon joint which brought about the most significant progress in this field. Straight or chase-mortises, through-tenons, key wedges – their alignment exploits the alternating grains of the pieces of timber and the pegging only serves to lock an inherently stable joint.

The elements of the timber frame

Irrespective of what it is made of, a wall has two main functions: to provide support for the roof and floors and enclose the building. The timber framework is a complex structure which evolved with the aim of fulfilling these requirements. In the traditional masonry wall, these two functions are largely undifferentiated; in most cases the wall is a homogeneous mass with successive courses which combine to form a self-supporting unit. The concept of the timber framework differs completely from that of the

Once the frame and infill-frame are in place, the nogging is used to seal the wall.

masonry wall in that it consists of different elements which correspond to the varying functions of the wall. Each piece of wood has a clearly defined role and it is the arrangement of these individual elements which makes the timber framework into a

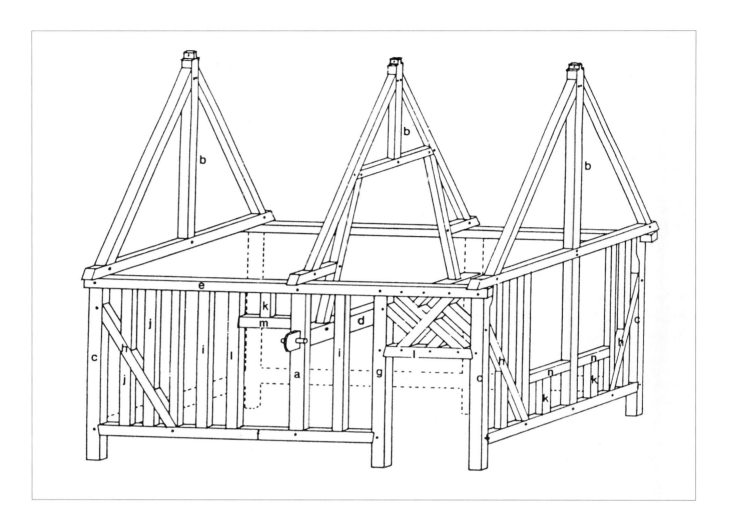

Elements used in the main frame and the infill framing.

structure, in which a perfect balance exists between the forces of tension, flexion, and compression exerted on each individual member and the role of each element.

The timber frame is far more dependent on the other elements of the building than its masonry counterpart. Because it is not self-supporting, its stability depends on its relationship to the adjacent walls, with which it often shares common elements.

The ceiling joists have an important role to play in ensuring the structural cohesion of these timber frameworks. Whereas in masonry structures they are simply inserted into the walls, in the case of timber-framed structures, they are meticulously joined to the timber framework and act with it in stabilizing the two supporting walls. The roof carpentry, which usually simply sits on the last leveling course of masonry walls, is securely anchored on the top horizontal piece of the timber framework and, thus, lends rigidity to the top story of the building.

Thus, while in theory the technology behind the timber framework is solely concerned with the interior and exterior walls, it also encompasses an overall concept which differs radically from that of masonry construction.

The timber-framed structures found in Normandy consist of two distinct sets of timbers: the main frame infill which constitutes the actual load-bearing structure and the frame which reinforces the wall and encloses the building by supporting the infill or nogging. This differentiation between the frame and the infill framing is clearly expressed by the scantling of the timbers used in each.

Oak was used almost exclusively until the 18th century. After this, elm was a partial substitute particularly in the construction of less prestigious rural buildings, though generally restricted to the infill framing.

The frame provides reinforcement for the timber-framed wall and encloses each of the panels in the infill framing. It is divided into a series of bays corresponding to the trusses in the roof frame.

The bay posts (a) provide the support for each of the roof trusses (b). The posts at the corners of the building are known as corner or angle posts (c).

The transverse beams (d) are joined to the posts or rest on the top plate (e). The ensemble rests on horizontal ground sills or sole plates (f) which are anchored to the corner posts or door jambs (g).

The vertical stability of the frame is provided by the gable walls which are composed of the same elements and share corner posts. This structure still lacks lateral stability, however, as rectangular frames or squares formed in this manner tend to distort into parallelograms. Different systems are used to brace this timber frame. These systems tend to differ from one region to the next and often provide the pretext for decorative details which tend to vary in the extent of their elaboration. They are all based, however, on oblique elements, the most simple of which is the brace (h) which is joined to both the sill beam and post, or the sill beam and a wall plate.

The joints used in the frame are simple: mortise and tenon joints with minimal pegging. Bridle joints and jowling are found in more sophisticated structures to overcome the weakness of simple tenons, which are prone to instability under excessive vertical load. A far wider variety of joints occurs, however, between anchor beams and bay posts: the beams could simply have rested on a slight jowl, formed on the post then tenoned and secured with two pegs; this solution did not, however, provide adequate resistance to withdrawal. Carpenters frequently responded to this problem by developing a range of more effective solutions: through-tenons keyed externally by one or two substantial square pegs; bridle joints, whereby the beam narrows at a notch formed about six inches from the end and is then dropped into a long slot formed in the top of the post before the wall-plate is installed; and, finally, by the use of certain clasping joints used in the formation of jetties.

Thus, the primary function of the wall – the support of the roof and the floors – is adequately fulfilled by the timber frame. It now remains for the building to be given a shell or skin. This is the main task of the infill framing which consists of the group of timbers – mainly vertical and narrower than those used in the frame – whose purpose is to hold the infill or nogging. These members are referred to in various medieval Norman texts as studs (vertical members, i.e. posts and studs) (i), a term which has aptly been related to the Latin term *columna* (column). Studs interrupted by braces are called interrupted studs (j) and short studs (k) when they are reduced to short pieces parallel to the openings.

Doors and windows are fitted into the timber frame and accommodated on the basis of the openings in the frame. To avoid any threat to the stability of the structure, the openings are located in the framework adjacent to the frame timbers, or isolated in the center of a panel. The vertical members surrounding the doors and windows are the door/window jambs (l) and the horizontal members are known as the lintels (m) and sills (n).

All that remains now is to fill in the spaces between the timbers to provide a continuous shell for the building. The nature of the filling material used determines the spacing of the posts and studs. In Normandy, despite the wide variety of materials used, this space is usually equal to or greater than the width of the timber members, in accordance with the distribution principle "equally full and empty" which was prescribed in several surviving building estimates.

The simple long-post framework

The use of long timbers, or more precisely "long posts", is considered to the present day as the oldest technique in timber-framing. All too often used as a criterion for dating such structures, the decline in the use of long timbers is usually identified around the 14th century and seen as a parallel development to the progressive shortage of long lengths of timber. Normandy had its fair share of these famous timber châteaux just like the quadrangular timber towers perched on their *mottes* which feature in several of the scenes depicted in the Bayeux tapestry.

The great timber "donjon" (actually the chamber block) of the château of Grandchamp, whose storey posts span the three stories of the building to a height exceeding ten meters, is a late example of these structures and is unique of its kind. Most of the medieval Norman manor houses consist of only two stories crowned by a roof.

The material is in such generous supply in these buildings that the carpenters clearly did not hesitate to lose a considerable quantity of it in forming the jowls needed to the support the rails which span the

Long-post frame at the château of Grandchamp

This type of frame, which uses a large quantity of long timbers of large scantling bay posts, disappeared around the end of the 15th century. Here in the outbuildings of the manor of Courson, the posts rise through two stories behind an intermediate rail. The braces and center stud are on the interior side of the timber frame.

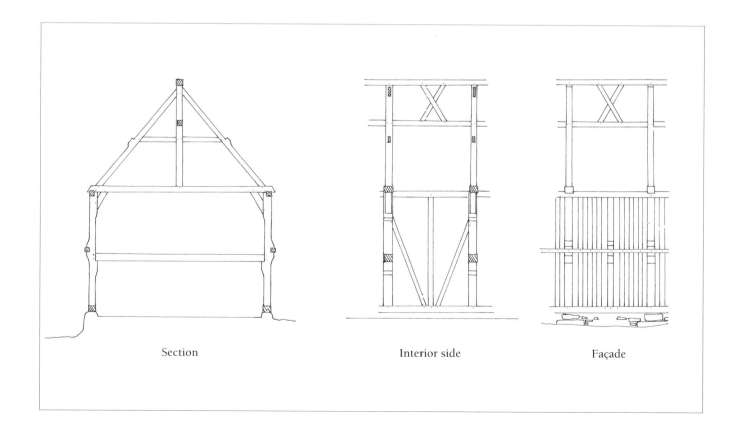

Section   Interior side   Façade

entire width of the façade and are notched to each post or stud. Timbers of this dimension disappeared at the end of the Middle Ages. The facts have to be faced: wood became increasingly scarce in the Pays d'Auge in the course of the 15th century just as it did all over Western Europe. This scarcity mainly affected the availability of large-scantling timber.

The classical model for long-post structures consists of short intermediary mid-rails which connect the posts, mark the position of each story, allow studs to be used which are only one story high. Other types seem to have also existed, like that observed in an outbuilding of the manor of Montgommery and a late medieval house near the church at Manneville-la-Pipard. Despite having two stories, these structures do not have intermediary plates: the bay posts and the studs, both of which are very wide, rise uninterrupted from the ground sill to the wall plate which supports the roof.

The short-post frame

The principle behind this type of frame is deceptively simple: if timbers which are long enough to be used for the entire height of the structure are no longer available, all you have to do is to insert a top plate on top of the posts on each story, which then doubles as a base plate for the posts in the next story. However, the organization of these pieces of timber converging on one point necessitated the use of joints which could undermine the stability of the extremities of these timbers. A complex joint linking the upper part of the frame to the roof frame can be found in the original long-post system: the top of the post is jowled to accommodate two tenons making it possible to join to it both the wall plate and the tie beam, both of which are located on different planes. This system was subsequently adopted to ensure a perfect connection between the timber posts, plates, and beams in the short-posted frames. This system was in fact the precursor of the jetty, one of the justifications for the way in which it enables the carpenter to distribute the multiple joints at this crucial part of the frame.

Although the long-posted frame applied to the entire building, it is rare to find multi-story structures based entirely on short-posted frames in the

manors of the Pays d'Auge. This could perhaps be explained by the fact that timber was in more abundant supply there than in other regions. However, it is more likely that the jetty, which was developed for the most part through the use of short timbers, won favor with the master carpenters by virtue of the technical – not to mention aesthetic – possibilities it offered. In economic terms, there is nothing to be gained from its use; the cube of timber required to construct the jetty in its most sophisticate form necessitates three horizontal timbers where one sufficed in the long-posted frame.

The aesthetic preference is obvious: short timbers and jetties dominated façades of buildings up to the

Houses on Rue au Char, Lisieux, which were destroyed in 1944. This group of three three-story short-posted structures has a wide variety of jetties, corner jetties on dragon beams and simple jetties on bresummers.

second half of the 16th century whilst long posts were often used to reinforce the rear elevation and support the oversailing or projecting galleries.

Jetties

The jetty on the bresummer was widely practiced until the mid-16th century. Above: the jetty on the dragon beam requires exceptional skill in coordinating the nine pieces of timber which converge on a single point (the manor of Courson). Right: corner jetty on the logis of the manor of La Brairie.

The generic term "jetty" covers a wide variety of structures within a short-post system which make it possible to accommodate cantilevered floors which vary in the extent to which they oversail or project. The innumerable variants which exist on this theme have already been described in great detail and they all bear the marks of their technical evolution and the practices common in the different regions in which they were adopted. The design of the jetty is dependent on the design of the floors in conjunction with the façades which support them. In the Pays d'Auge, the jetty is usually supported by the projecting ends of the transverse beams.

The jetty forms part of the logical structure of the building by introducing an equilibrium between the oversailing elements. It also contributes to the stability and robustness of the short-timbered frame by augmenting both the size and number of joints, each of which has a precise function: the two dovetails of the transverse beams work in tension preventing the walls from bowing, and the open mortise joints between the jetty plates and the posts prevent lateral displacement. The joints are, moreover, carefully distributed to avoid undermining the strength of any of the individual members converging on the same point.

Jetties are usually only found on the main façade as their structure is based on the principle of the projection of the transverse beams and is basically not suited to being built on a side elevation. In other regions, the jetty is mainly supported by floor joists; however this version is virtually nonexistent in the Pays d'Auge.

In urban structures, for example buildings which stand at the corner of two streets, the carpenters were concerned to carry the jetty motif round both façades and thus continued it on a facia board which they grafted on to the ceiling joists of the

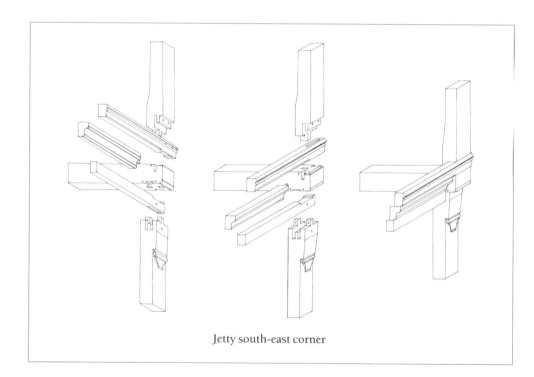

Jetty south-east corner

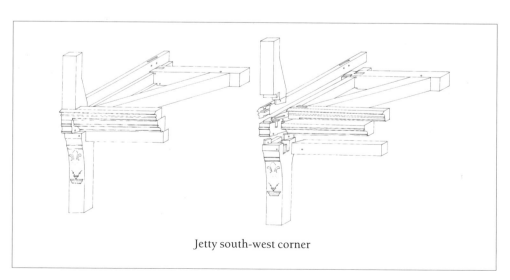

Jetty south-west corner

same bay. The main difficulty here consisted in the treatment of the angle, the junction at which the various timbers converged. The jetty was supported by a dragon beam assembly, the joints of which are conceived with an ingenuity which is unequaled by the methods used in other regions, such as Brittany or the Loire Valley. It is worth remembering that the carpenter had to find a way of connecting at least nine pieces of wood converging on one single point! To achieve this they used posts with triple tenons and main beams with double dovetails, the complexity of which remains fully hidden from the eye of the observer.

Jetties can be found on some of the side elevations of our manor houses. One of them, Les Pavements, even has a jetty which continues along three sides of the building.

The use of the jetty is sometimes justified in terms of the added interior space it created in restricted urban contexts. This argument falls flat, however, when jetties are found on rural structures where optimizing the use of space cannot have been a key priority. Thus, the optimization of space cannot be interpreted as a prime motivation in any context.

It is undeniable, however, that the jetties and oversailing structures constructed in this way provided a solution to one of the most pressing conservation issues, namely the problem of the run-off of rainwater on multi-story façades. The jetty made it possible to drain the water at each level with the help of the moldings on the wall plate which almost always has an integral moulded drip-course.

One last observation on the justification of the jetty: it goes without saying that it contributes to the aesthetic beauty of the timber-frame building. The overhang catches the light and stands out against its own shadow, it introduces a strong horizontal emphasis and provides the carpenter with ample space on three superimposed timbers for decorative carving and gives the sculptor a space well protected from run-off for the introduction of a wide variety of delicate motifs. Thus, the justification on the grounds of decoration alone, which could even be described as showing off, is self-evident.

The construction of buildings using long and very heavy posts continued in the Pays d'Auge when alternative short-timbered solutions already dominated elsewhere.

With considerable prodigality in the use of timber, carpenters in the Pays d'Auge even went as far as constructing jetties on some of the long-post buildings. A post with a 'normal' scantling on the ground floor thickened at the next story to receive, on each side, the tenons of the false bressumers which supported the studs of the story above. These bressumers, equal in depth to the thickened part of the post, had the same decorative moldings as those found on the bressumer(s) of a jetty of traditional Pays d'Auge design. One of the most remarkable examples of this system can be found in a timber building at the manor of La Pipardière, dated by dendrochronology to the late 15th century. It had obviously been recycled following the extension of an existing *logis* and introduced to its new location at the end of the 16th century.

The discovery of this kind of jettying, hitherto unpublished, demonstrates to us that the jetty had become an aesthetic form peculiar to timber-frame structures, and that it was deemed acceptable to use it even if there was no structural justification for its use. Every respectable timber building of this period had to have a jetty – at least on its main façade – even if it was constructed using long posts.

Thus, the evolution from long to short posts and jetties did not follow a straightforward and linear

Some long-post structures have false jetties which are formed by thickening out the posts. This demonstrates the sheer delight in the aesthetic qualities of the short-post system (the manor of Fribois).

The false jetty often only consists of a modest molding, or even a simple chamfer (Manor of Ouilly).

course which was solely dictated by the decline in supplies of timber. Exceptionally sophisticated forms and techniques in timber architecture were characteristic of this extremely creative period of the late Middle Ages in Western Europe generally, and the Pays d'Auge in particular. The jetty which was, in effect, invented to overcome structural constraints also marked the extension of restricted urban spaces, provided a particularly suitable opportunity for decoration and embellishment, and became in itself a characteristic form to the point of an exercise in pure virtuosity, in which the carpenter could demonstrate the sophistication of his talent behind this concealed element.

Banned in urban buildings by royal and municipal edict, the jetty gradually disappeared from the frames of the manor houses of the Pays d'Auge during the last decades of the 16th century and with it the technical virtuosity of its master carpenters.

The frames of the timber-frame structures in other French regions were almost exclusively constructed using short posts. The Pays d'Auge is the exception to this rule due, no doubt, to the availability of more abundant supplies of suitable timber, and also due to a tradition of excellence which prompted the carpenters to be rather skeptical of the possibility of attaining perfect stability using superposed short timbers. For the most part, the timber *logis* retained their two stories during the 17th and 18th centuries: thus, the carpenters adapted their version of the long-post frame to the new situation by reducing the sections of the timbers they used and splitting the two levels of the "paneled façades" into sub-groups. This made it possible to use shorter lengths of wood and reserve the use of the available long timbers for the actual posts.

Infill framing

Once the main frame has ensured the stability of the building, it is the job of the infill framing to enclose it by providing a matrix for the nogging. The infill framing is divided into bays, demarcated by the vertical posts and horizontal members, and often includes stiffening elements; the latter can either be concealed or may form a visible part of the actual infill framing.

Timber was abundant, and the carpenters of the Pays d'Auge seldom observed the "equally full and empty" rule, whereby the studs and nogging are supposed to be of equal width.

In its most basic version, the infill framing consists of a strictly vertical arrangement of studs and posts known as 'close studding'. Master carpenters often exploited the purity of this arrangement to aesthetic ends by concealing the angle braces on the inner face of the wall, for they would otherwise have undermined the sobriety of the external face with its strict vertical rhythm established by the wide posts.

Braces can, however, be integrated into the composition of the façade: they may tie a post and a horizontal member, or link any adjacent pair of

horizontal timbers. Arranged with extremely precise symmetry on both sides of the posts or at each extremity of the building, they can be found aligned parallel in groups of two, three, or four.

The temptation eventually arose to join several braces, initially in the form of simple saltires and subsequently in cross-braces of increasing complexity: this also made it possible to use timbers which varied significantly in length. In the late 18th and, primarily, during the 19th century, increasing skill with short timbers resulted in the frequent use of horizontal and vertical arrangements of fern and spike motifs, the angular elements of which provided the stiffening required for the wall.

The Pays d'Auge may have been responsible for the development of some original forms; however its repertoire did not include any of the well known

The jetty provides an ideal surface for decoration. This example has statuettes at the top of the bay posts, grotesque masks and urns with volutes on the lower bressumer, and cable and other mouldings on the upper bressumer.

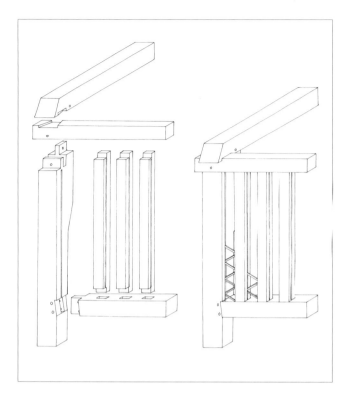

System of joints used in the infill framing: the vertical studs are mortised into the nail and wall-plate.

forms from other regions such as the Loire Valley and central France, where the carcass consisted exclusively of saltires the full length of the façade, or lozenge formations.

Up to the second half of the 16th century infill framing existed only as a vertical structure extending along the entire height of each story, and was not interrupted by an intermediary girding-beam. When this horizontal member extends across the entire width of a bay (as a rail at mid-height, intended to maintain the distance between the studs and posts) it is simply face-peged to the infill framing, without cutting into any of the vertical members: studs, door posts, window jambs, or mullions. With the demise of the "jetty", the "paneled façade" blurred the basic unity inherent to each [62] story, which, however, was subdivided into

Close studding at the logis of the manor of La Brairie.

ABOVE:
Timber frame with three rows of braces (outbuildings of La Roque, left) and window breast with cross braces (Coupesart)

BELOW:
The two angle braces at first floor level complement the stability already provided by the window breasts with St. Andrew's crosses (logis of La Brairie, left). A lean-to with three rows of braces on an outbuilding at Boissey.

adorned by saltires or cross-braces, which were sometimes separated and sometimes joined in a continuous frieze along the entire width of the façade.

The plinth

The timber frame, which had been marked out then assembled on the *épure* – a full-scale working drawing marked out on the framing floor – was erected like a fence with closely-spaced bars; its posts resting on blocks of timber. It was then the turn of the mason to make his contribution by providing the plinth, chimneys, and nogging.

two levels separated by a rail: the actual windows, and the window breast below them. The simple vertical infill at the level of the openings (i.e. between the windows) tended to deflect the emphasis to the area of the window breast, a focal point

Plinths come in a wide variety of forms – from a narrow low rubble wall (outbuildings of the manor of La Roque, left) to limestone and black flint checkerwork covering an entire story (logis of the manor of Le Désert, right).

With its dressed stone at the corners and points where the load of the frame is concentrated - the bay posts and door jambs – the plinth also expresses the structural logic of the building. Such plinths, in which the corner posts and some of the bay posts are inserted, represented an improvement on the old system, of which few examples have survived.

Initially composed of simple earth-fast posts, the timber frame had a horizontal ground sill or sole plate from Roman times onwards. This sole plate initially rested on the bare ground and was subsequently damp-proofed with the aid of a masonry ground-course or a more or less rudimentary plinth. The base of the structure thus consisted of a grid of horizontal sole plates, crossing over at their extremities and slightly projecting to ensure the solidity of the halved joints which connected them. The posts and studs were then assembled and erected on the base framework. The disadvan-

tage of this system was that the load was concentrated on the sole plate at certain points, directly below the posts. Already undermined by direct contact with the plinth, which is exposed to rising damp, they constituted the weak point of the frame.

The idea of separating most of the posts, particularly the corner posts, from the sole plate, and transmitting the weight of the frame directly onto the dressed stone of the plinth represented a major step forward and became common practice from the 15th century.

Plinths of dressed stone, or checkerwork in limestone and brick or knapped flints were found only in more prestigious buildings. Mass walling of flint from the plateaus, in a mortar matrix, tended to be used for more modest dwellings, whereas limestone rubble was was more common in those built around the Caen and Argentan plains.

Nogging

Nogging of several kinds occurs in the Pays d'Auge, depending on the geographical location and the quality of the building. Some *logis* have retained their nogging of cob – a mixture of clay and vegetable fibers – usually reserved for farm and other outbuildings and more often than not covered with a thin coat of limewash. Its support is provided by oak slats slotted into grooves on the sides of the timber posts, or, in later versions, by split oak laths nailed to the inside of the timber frame.

In rare cases, nogging consisting of flat beach pebbles is found slotted into the grooves of the timber posts, beneath the lime plaster of buildings near the coast. This rendering and the constituent elements of the nogging, including the building debris, can be recycled several times using a variety of methods developed in different regions.

Colored nogging is an outstanding feature of the timber-frame buildings in the Pays d'Auge and this art is unparalleled by work in any other region. It involved the recycling of terra-cotta products, the quarrying and cutting of stone intended specifically for this purpose, and, in some rare instances, the manufacture of specific products. Craftsmen in this area showed a particular talent for combining materials of varying appearance, size, and color. The only rule strictly adhered to was that the nogging be directly applied to the plane surface of the external side of the timber frame without even the slightest offset which would inevitably result in the collection of water, leading to accelerated rotting of the timber in the frame. It would also cause aesthetically unpleasing shadows on the walls.

Early evidence has been found of the use of broken tile fragments. In the 15th century, broken tile was put to a wide variety of uses in the more delicate masonry elements of buildings – hearths, firebacks, and chimney stacks. Its use in nogging was initially cautious and limited to small horizontally coursed elements with a single set of colors consisting of orange-pink colored tile and light mortar. One of the oldest extant examples of this work can be found on the south gable of the *logis* of the manor of Courson which is protected by an extension built in the late 17th century.

The temptation to expand this range of colors by introducing layers of knapped flint and then play on these tones varying from pitch black to gray-white, passing through all the nuances of yellow and brown, eventually proved too strong to resist.

However, the resulting horizontal emphasis then proved too monotonous and by the second half of the 16th century, compositions composed of triangles of limestone, introducing a shimmer of bright color and mesmerizing patterns, began to appear. The introduction of this motif may correspond to the construction of the Old Manor at Orbec in 1568 which inspired similar structures throughout the region, particularly the manor of La Chapelle at Bellou and the manor of Piencourt. Orbec is situated on the edge of the Ouche region, a factor which no doubt played a part in the

Cob in beautiful ochre tones is a very durable material, generally reserved for use in outbuildings (the manor of Le Lieu-Rocher, above). Complex compositions in tile, flint, and limestone arranged in regular triangles were used for the most prestigious buildings (Old Manor at Orbec, below).

perfection there of this type of polychrome nogging and is, above all, responsible for its prolonged application until the end of the 18th century.

This profusion of color had been in decline since the 17th century in the Pays d'Auge and was replaced by the development of the exclusive use of broken tile fragments in an exceptionally wide variety of forms. The most simple motif, for which tile debris of all sizes can be used to suit the variable width of the nogging, consists of series of alternating triangles. More complex forms appeared quickly, including chevrons, or a mosaic of criss-crossing stripes former out of numerous tile fragments.

LEFT:
Some compositions go as far as breaking free from the rigorous grid of vertical studding and depict large lozenges against a tile background (La Chénevotte).

LEFT:

Some compositions go as far as breaking free from the rigorous grid of vertical studding and depict large lozenges against a tile background (La Chénevotte).

RIGHT:

Painted brick, which is generally reserved for checkerwork effects, is also found in the nogging, as seen here in the logis *at the manor of La Quaize.*

The masons' imagination overflowed in the creation of purely ornamental patterns, such as rosettes, or motifs copied from religious symbols, e.g. crosses, suns, and monstrances. These sometimes indicated the function either of a whole building or part of it, such as the extension to the logis at the manor of Courson which houses the oratory. In some cases the broken tile nogging bears the coat of arms of the builder: François de Mailloc, the master of Les Éteux at Meulles, inserted three mallets, the coat of arms punningly referred to in his blazon, between the studs of the façade of his logis. More rarely, the nogging reveals a date: 1671 on the *logis* at the manor of Courson, and 1737 on one of the two *logis* at La Cour Thomas, here also including the name of the owner.

Brick nogging laid horizontally or obliquely did not enjoy the same popularity and is found only in a few 17th century buildings. The few remarkable and exceptional examples of its use include either green or multicolored glazed elements, as can be seen in the *logis* of the manor of La Quaize.

Elements specially produced in order to decorate nogging were also used in other regions; for example, the terra-cotta motifs on the elevations of the house at 54, rue Saint-Pierre in Caen, or the Renaissance molded plaster details at 85, rue des Carmes, in Rouen. Known examples in the Pays d'Auge seem to be limited to bricks laid in diamond shapes.

Door and window openings

Access to the outside world from the close-set, enclosed framework had to be provided somehow. Doorways and window openings were constructed in accordance with very rigid but ingenious rules, the evolution of which is relatively easy to trace. For windows, the most basic opening involved interrupting the nogging to create a simple gap. The basic principle involved in creating openings of sufficient size, for example, for a doorway, is to omit several studs in order to accommodate a horizontal lintel joined to two vertical members. In a few very ancient examples which still exist, the doorway sill is the actual sole plate extending along the width of the façade. Exterior doorways, always substantial in size, required a good sized lintel; it was almost always notched in and secured with two pegs.

Far greater variety can be observed when it comes to window openings. Up to the early 17th century, the maximum width of the window was limited to the opening created by omitting a single stud; thus windows had to be arranged in twos and threes to provide adequate light. They were either isolated in the center of the bay or arranged in pairs, with one or two on each side of a bay post. Timber-frame construction lends itself particularly well to windows with mullions and transoms. The window jambs are simply chamfered or molded above sill level, and the same chamfer returns along the tran-

A stud interrupted to accommodate a lintel and a sill: the construction of a window could not be more simple (logis of the manor of Lisores, left). Based on the same principle but involving the studs on both sides of a post, one of the forms of mullioned and transomed window found in the Pays d'Auge (logis of the manor of Aubichon, right)

som, which is mortised into the central mullion, the latter being no more than a stud exactly aligned to the bay post.

The technique of timber-framing gave rise to a specific type of window opening which continued in use until the late Middle Ages. This consisted of a juxtaposed series of windows along the entire length of the façade; the bay posts and window jambs acted as mullions, and horizontal articulation was provided by rows of saltires along the window breast and by rails continuing the line of the transoms of the oopenings. An extended sill is then face-pegged along the entire length of the wall. This arrangement is often fund in urban buildings, where it gives maximum light to the gable stories facing the street. It also occurs on several *logis* in the manors of the Pays d'Auge, mostly on the façade and very occasionally on the gable.

A few very rare examples of the fittings found in these windows survive. The most simple of these consists of wooden shutters, are hinged on iron hooks and are closed by a latch or a flat bolt. The inhabitants of these houses had two options to choose from: being warm in the darkness or enjoying the light while suffering from draughts. Another common feature was that of sliding timber shutters, the only traces of which generally remaining are the

The doors of the oldest dwellings were inserted above the ground sill. This can still be seen in the barn at Le Coudray where a fragment of the ground sill still exists under the left door post.

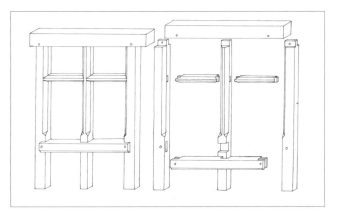

System of joints used in a mullioned and transomed window in the center of a bay (the manor of Courson).

LEFT:
Juxtaposition of a series of windows at the logis of the manor of La Brairie.

RIGHT:
The former logis of the manor of La Bruyère still has some of its sliding shutters in the side grooves of the window jambs.

grooves on the window jambs: when open, th shutter was lowered to the entire depth of the window breast. Thus, it was possible to pull it up partially, or completely to cover the opening entirely, and to lock it in this position by means of a wooden peg, the mark of which can often be found on the window sill. This explains the frequent correspondence between the height of the window breast and that of windows of this type. The windows on the upper story were generally covered with oiled paper or parchment which allowed a little light to filter through.

During the 16th century, windows mostly had casements fitting into a simple rebate in the timber frame. There was no actual window frame. The casements were generally divided into two sections, each of which had its own interior shutters. The upper section had stained glass and the lower section had wooden panels pierced with minute decorations either of Gothic tracery or Renaissance motifs. Some rare extant examples bear witness to the level of sophistication of these elements, which are also found in relatively modest buildings. They are often fitted with high-quality metalwork, with the openings of the filigree plates highlighted by red or blue velvet behind them.

Windows with mullions and sills integrated into the timber frame disappeared in the 17th century in favor of actual framed windows, which involved the skills of joinery rather than carpentry. The carpenter provided an opening in the timber frame which the joiner then fitted with a complete unit consisting of a frame, often containing a mullion and a single (or double) transom, and four (or six) opening lights, to which internal shutters were attached.

The timber frame was losing its special place, and 17th century joinery became identical to that of other stone buildings. Stained glass cut into diamonds or shapes resembling milestones was used for the entire surface of the window, with one or two panels per casement. This trend continued during the 18th century. Mullions and transoms gradually disappeared, and advances in the manufacture of glass made it possible to replace series of small framed lights with large individual panes. The straight lintel gave way to the segmental arch, and sometimes doubled the mid-rail, which had previously served as a lintel.

Roof construction

The roof was fully integrated into the structural logic of the timber frame, to which it is closely linked in terms of function.

In the left opening of the logis of the manor of Saint-Léger, the 17th century window frame consists of a timber mullion and transome set into the masonry. The upper casements with very small square panes have survived. The window frame on the right has a simple transom.

An important question must be addressed in this context: did the manorial *logis* represent the continuation of the long-lived medieval tradition of the open hall, i.e. the common living room, open to the roof? The open hall is well known in England up to the 16th century and is a familiar feature of the buildings of Normandy from the 11th to the 13th centuries, as the recent work of Edward Impey had highlighted. It is also known in Brittany.

A single example seems to have survived from the Middle Ages in the Pays d'Auge, and can be found in a *logis* at Orville, although it no longer stands in its original state, which consisted of a coupled-rafter roof lines with oak panelling.

Nevertheless, the complete or partial survival of several roofs with purlins and arch-braces in the plane of the roof – a more decorative than functional arrangement – seems to indicate their possible origin in halls with exposed roof frames.

Another vestige appear to hark back to the tradition of buildings with coupled-rafter roofs: those gables with overhanging flying rafter couples, common in medieval urban dwellings, which include all the significant features of buildings of this type. There are two sole-pieces at the base, which are supported by the projecting ends of the wall plates and by two brackets, the inner of which corresponds to the inner wall plate normally found in a buiding with stone walls. These structures support arch-braces rising to a short collar. This overhanging flying rafter is the end rafter of a series which covers the interior of the building, here found on the outside.

However, all that remains today are roofs with purlin structures whose tie beams merge with the ceiling beams of the top floor, a system which, by the way, adapts perfectly to the rhythm of a building divided into regular bays. The bay posts support in turn the ceiling beams and the rafter trusses with an

Roofing materials

The manor houses have plain tile roofs, the laborer's house has its thatch, and more modern structures their slate roofs? The answers are not quite so evident.

Plain tile has always dominated in the roofs of the Pays d'Auge. Small in dimension, it is attached to the split oak tile lath using a simple lug. In the 12th and 13th centuries, the tiles became much bigger and thicker and were fitted with oak pegs and thus were additionally secure. This practice appears to have endured until the late Middle Ages. The spread of the hip roof in the late 16th century would appear to have led to the development of a number of previously unknown accessories.

The roofer was only familiar with the plain tile and the ridge tile and "lapped" the tiles to cover the large curved valleys at the meeting of two slopes. The increase in the number of arrises on both the main slopes and on the dormers, and the principle of strict alignment of the rows of tiles on each side of the roof, led to the creation of the hip tile, which was more or less curved to match the pitch of the roof, and a corresponding inverse valley tile so that valleys could be tiled without metal flashings and thus ensured the continuity of the tile courses.

As a material which had to be imported and was thus rather costly, slate was reserved for larger, such as Fervaques and Cricqueville, where it was chosen for the way in which it complemented the polychrome appearance of brick and stone. It was mainly used in Renaissance structures, and is particularly common in the Loire valley.

Slate roofing was accompanied by the obligatory, equally costly, lead work used to produce the finial, ridges and vents.

The use of shingles, those fine tiles of riven oak, was limited to structures with circular plans and the tapered ridges found on turrets. They were also used to protect the timber frame, most often at the gable or the façade most exposed to the effects of the weather, and an even more rudimentary use was to form the link between a timber second story and stone first story. These shingles covered the steep roofs and chimney stacks of the modest bell towers of the Pays d'Auge for a long time right up to their eventual replacement by thin slates in the 19th

"The Manor of Formville", Rue aux Fèvres, Lisieux, destroyed in 1944.
A rare example of a jetty combining the bressumer and joist systems. The flying rafter which supports the edge of the roof is without doubt the last vestige of the coupled-rafter roof, which was probably practiced during the 13th and 14th centuries.

ideal distribution of loads which are then transmitted to the ground.

These structures do not generally have any individual features particularly worthy of mention. The trusses are simple with a false tie beam at mid height. The only sign of particular attention to detail can be found in the diagonal bracing, which in the 16th and 17th centuries was generally provided by sassor-bracing and multiple angle braces. The attic story, a common feature found in urban dwellings as a way of providing increased living space, it is almost completely unknown in the manor *logis*.

A beautiful group of tiled roofs at the manor of Le Lieu-Rocher.

Slate roofs on the towers of the château of Cricqueville.

century. Their relative fragility, however, restricted their use to very steep structures and they were never used forthe main roof. Thatch, which undoubtedly provided an important roofing solution for modest dwellings, was quickly replaced by tiles from the late Middle Ages. Unbroken stalks of rye or wheat straw were tied to the laths using split twigs. The ridges were produced using clumps of mud, the density of which was maintained with the help of the slight moisture produced by vegetation, such as irises and other plants, whose flowers also added an extra note of color. Thatch was sometimes used as a replacement during various periods of poverty, particularly when the *logis* and manorial ensemble were converted into simple agricultural buildings and stripped of their function as seigneurial abode.

The oldest of the extant *logis* all have a rectangular – almost square – plan and are covered by a

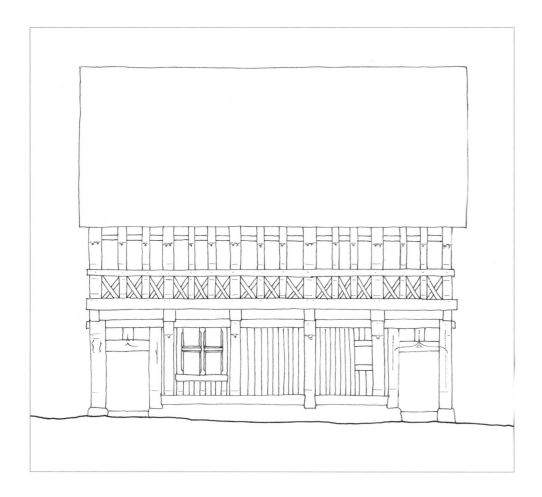

Simple pitched roof for the logis at the late 15th century logis of the manor of Saint-Gilles de Livet.

As seen here at the manor of Bouttemont (above right) , the exposed gables and sometimes the entire façade was clad in oak shingles.

The gables could also be protected by tiled awnings which were supported by the projecting wall plates (logis of Crèvecour, right).

The most common roof design involves the alignment of the dormer windows with the bays of the lower story(s). This example is from the logis of the manor of Courson during its partial reconstruction at the end of the 15th century. The left dormer was removed at the beginning of the 20th century.

simple steeply pitched roof with no openings at attic level, except a minute opening in the gable. The spiral staircase which was located in the corner of the single room on each floor was not reflected in a specific volume on the roof. An unusual feature found in some such structures consists of a straight awning on the west or south-west gable which provided perfect protection against inclement weather.

The roof was eventually made habitable through the installation of dormers, which were mainly developed during the late 15th and early 16th centuries. The most original type of dormer found in the Pays d'Auge is located on the central bay, creating a transverse gable, which often has the same system of windows as the lower floor – a series of three or four small windows side by side, sometimes limited to two twin openings.

The alignment of the dormers with the windows of the lower stories is more common, however. These dormers tend to be narrower or equal in width to the bay of the timber frame and are always constructed as gables with a slope equal to that of the main roof. The appearance of the projecting staircase turret, which was initially square and then polygonal in plan, led to the multiplication of the roof slopes and, less commonly, to the development of conical roofs. The creation of upper chambers, or oriels, on top of these staircases made these structures with independent roofs even more animated. The fashion for hipped roofs in the late 16th century frequently involved the restructuring of large medieval gables and their transformation into hipped gables whilst conserving the steep pitch. At the same time, plans were also becoming more complex which meant the multiplication of

the angle elements which projected to varying degrees and the increased detachment of the staircase turrets, all of which were crowned with pavilion roofs, pierced with sharp dormers.

The chimneys, which were originally built as a single unit with four flues arranged back to back in pairs and rose from the roof in a single stack from one or other side of the ridge-piece, gradually shifted to the ends of the mass and accentuated the symmetry of the composition with two high stacks at the base of the side slopes.

The gambrel roof, which is often incorrectly referred to as a "mansard", is very rare but when it appears it is very successfully executed as can be seen in the *logis* of the manors of La Coudrairie and Le Bois-Simon, with lines softened by the addition of sprockets which raise the slope of the roof at the lower edge.

The roof finally relinquished its prominence in the 18th century, becoming a sober, unified mass which crowned the now more substantial *logis*, sometimes doubled in depth, strewn with small timber dormers, and occasionally centered on a pediment which conveyed an air of solidity as opposed to the former impression of elegant nobility.

Fireplaces

Normandy was early to adopt this feature of architecture – and physical comfort – while England, for example, remained true to the concept of the open fire in the middle of the hall with the smoke escaping through an opening in the roof.

The oldest chimney-pieces from the 13th century were incorporated into masonry walls and the fireplace opening was covered by a very tight segmental arch or a lintel with voussoirs. They were later grouped two-by-two back to back in a block at the center of the *logis*: their timber lintels joined by flanking beams, formed a robust timber frame supported by aligned columns.

The transfer of the load onto the columns, which were more sturdy than the thin wall separating the flues was a particular concern: a relieving arch transferred the thrusts laterally and demarcated the double chimneyback which was built in tile, a more suitable material to withstand the heat of the fire. The mantel had to provide a sufficient overhang to support the columns of the upstairs fireplace.

The fireplaces on the upper stories were built on the same structure, the only difference being that the mantel gradually tapered to adapt to the section of the flue while clearing the ceiling trimming beam.

The medieval model was adapted to the architectural trends in later centuries. The Classical fireplace did away with the antique timber lintel and replaced it with a molded frame in stone, stucco, or timber around the fireplace opening and transformed the mantel into a straight molded hood crowned by a cornice which concealed the ceiling trimmer. Integrated in the majority of cases into wood paneling, the 18th century fireplace, which was made of timber or parts of it in Caen stone projecting on a hearth with rounded angles, was clearly adapted to the models common to secular architecture.

LEFT PAGE:
ABOVE: *Classical fireplaces, on the second floor of the logis of the manor of La Hogue, have very prominent moldings or large* trompe l'œil *paintings.*

BELOW: *Two fireplaces typical of the large Gothic logis from the manor of La Brairie. On the ground floor, a robust stone structure with a relieving arch on the mantel which supports the lighter first-floor fireplace; the mantel gradually tapers to match the section of the fireplace.*

RIGHT PAGE:
ABOVE: *One of the very beautiful fireplaces in Caen stone at the manor of Le Lieu-Hocquart demonstrates the elegance of 18th century decoration.*
BELOW: *In the staircase turret at Le Désert, a first flight of stairs in stone is followed by a second flight with timber treads and risers around a central mast.*

despite being a timber structure, it looked more like a piece of furniture which could be placed at will in any convenient corner of the room.

The division of the large primitive room to form two separate volumes separated by the back-to-back chimneys resulted in the shifting of the staircase to a central position. It now took the form of a stack in the middle of the rear elevation, or remained part of the main body of the building in a very original arrangement which could be fully integrated into a piece of furniture. Few examples of the latter have survived: they consisted of fragile timber structures consisting of a closed octagonal frame, made of long panels, which was inserted between the wall of the façade and the chimneys and contained a spiral staircase with treads and risers. Was the intention to provide easy access to the attic? The top of the frame extended to this level in a kind of large gable dormer which was easily recognizable through the absence of windows in the axis. All that generally remains of

Stairs and galleries

A staircase was required to provide access to the two stories and the attic floor of the standard *logis*. Staircases varied considerably in form from one period to the next and, in some cases, were based on very diverse concepts during a single period, dictating a highly differentiated treatment of interior space and exterior volumes. The simplicity and the very basic development of the *logis* would appear at a first glance to have dictated a very rudimentary horizontal layout. This was not at all the case, and the motif of the gallery, which varied in function, represented a particularly successful solution to the approach to the staircases.

In the oldest *logis*, which had one room on each story, the impact of the staircase in terms of the structural composition of the building was minimal. Positioned in one of the corners of the room, its frame was inserted into the openings in the ceiling between two beams. The steps of the spiral, formed of single pieces of timber, were fitted around a newel post which rose from the ground to the middle of the roof. Nothing on the outside of the building betrays the presence of the staircase. thus

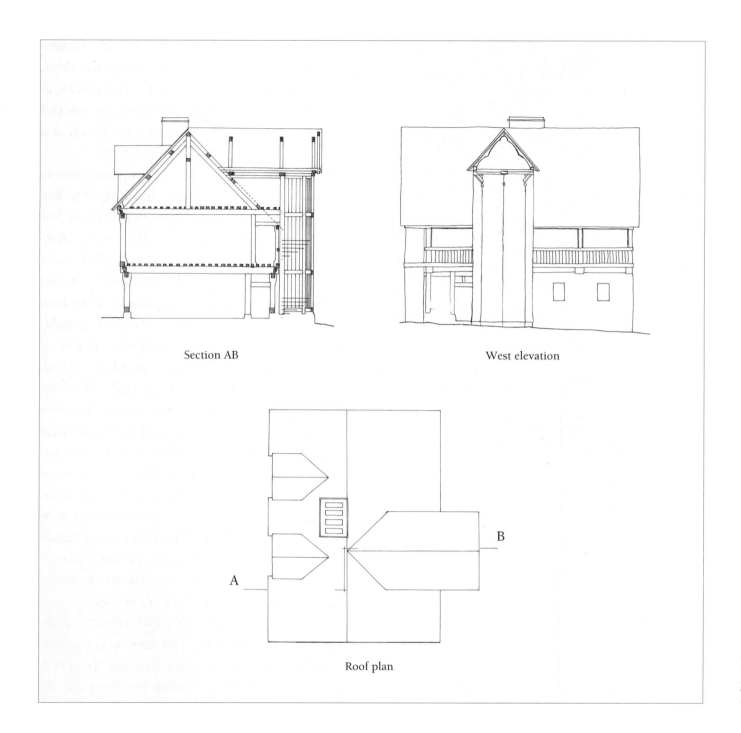

Section AB

West elevation

Roof plan

The open gallery and staircase in the logis *of the manor of Courson during its partial reconstruction at the end of the 15th century.*

these ephemeral structures, condemned by their fragility to inevitable disintegration, is a few characteristic panels which have been recycled for other uses, the octagonal opening, and the chimneystack shifted to the back slope of the roof to avoid blocking the staircase on the other slope.

The location of the staircase in a projecting structure, i.e. in a tower forming a generally large pentagonal or hexagonal projection on the rear elevation, thus became the standard model. Each of the two rooms on the upper floor could be reached directly from the staircase. The staircase normally opened on the first floor onto a gallery, which provided access to the two rooms, and was termi-

nated at roof level by a sloping or conical roof. In a few cases, the staircase turret was able to support an upper chamber – the oriel – which was reached from a small secondary spiral staircase mounted onto the main staircase. This feature is very familiar and described in detail by Queneday in the houses of Rouen and can be found in some urban and rural residences in Normandy.

This upper gallery is a motif frequently found in *logis* built in the Pays d'Auge between the late 15th and mid 16th centuries. Accessed from the staircase turret, mostly open, and covered by a roof supported by a row of narrow posts, the gallery could either project fully or rest on projecting beams over

Stairs and open gallery at the logis *of the manor of Conty.*

The logis *of the manor of Le Désert has the unusual feature of a gallery which is completely dissociated from the staircase turret.*

the timber portico situated on the ground floor. The extension of the roof to cover the projecting gallery gave rise to an imbalance in the volume of the *logis* on the rear elevation. The upper floor gallery was complex in function. An area for access, service, socializing, transition from the exterior to the interior, it was also very popular during the short period of the Renaissance when the Italian gallery was very fashionable in France. Its fragility and relative inconvenience in a temperate climate quickly condemned it to become a simple corridor with a few windows – the wide bays gradually shrank – which provided the inhabitants with access from the ground floor to the upper chambers without being exposed to uncomfortable draughts.

The same features can be found in urban *logis* of the same period. Due to the relative scarcity of space,

the staircase turret of buildings with street façades was located at one of the extremities of the rear elevation; the gallery extended across the entire width of the building and a second gallery, sometimes repeated on several stories, extended to join the stories of a second building at the back of the courtyard.

Vertical access resumed its development following this brief intermission featuring the gallery. The staircase turret was seen as increasingly archaic and considered as a distraction from the pure architectural lines. The spiral staircases gradually became integrated into the main body of the house, the last vestiges of their frames being disguised as false dormers, before finally being replaced by straight-run staircases which, however, took the central space previously allocated to the chimney block which was split in two and moved to the gable. The main entrance was finally centered; the entrance door now provided direct access to the ground floor rooms from the hall and those on the upper floor from the staircase.

This evolution did not take place over night: the old features enjoyed a long life. For example, despite being familiar with the straight-run staircase, the master builder of the 17th century manor house of Prétot could not resist the temptation of inserting a square turret right in the middle of the rear elevation to accommodate two privies.

From this point to the late 18th century, all the different forms of timber architecture in vogue were applied to the central staircase – straight-flight half-turn stairs, the winding stair on four newels at the château of Grandchamp, and even suspended winding stairs, sometimes installed in the old medieval frame, as in the manor of La Morsanglière.

The art of line

It is impossible to speak of architecture in wood without referring to the "art of line", an art in which the old master carpenters excelled. The "art of line" is the practice of marking out or tracing, a process which made it possible to transcribe a project from a reduced scale to a full-scale working plan, or *épure*. This provided the carpenter with a basis on which to cut each of the pieces of timber required for the structure.

The *épure* is marked out onto a perfectly even surface with the help of very basic instruments – a com-

pass, a rule, and a line. In the case of more complex structures, this activity assumed a perfect knowledge of the rules of line using simple modules, which when combined – depending on the skill of the master craftsman – could create harmonic proportions of varying degrees of perfection which dictate the underlying architectural quality of the structure.

There are significant differences between the practices of the master masons and master carpenters in their use of the *épure*. The former do not need to avail themselves of the *épure* when working on simple elements and reserve its use for more complex tasks, such as the tracery for a rose window or other openings. In this instance, the *épure* allows the mason to produce timber templates which are used as a basis for the cutting of each individual stone element. The *épure* can, therefore, be marked out on the ground or on a vertical wall in the case of smaller elements.

The master carpenter, however, had to use the *épure* for all elements, no matter how basic. When faced with the task of constructing a roof truss or a timber-framed façade, the *épure* provides the carpenter with a full-scale plan, on which he can position each of the pieces of wood to be cut and trace the various joints onto them without the intermediary aid of a template. It is,

therefore, essential that the *épure* be marked out on the ground of the building site.

In the case of more basic structures, the *épure* can be positioned directly on the area to be marked out without the need for preliminary drawings. However, the master carpenter was always strongly advised to mark the *épure* with lines representing harmonic proportions, which were generally based on a single module.

The making of detailed drawings of existing structures mean that it is possible to reconstruct, without difficulty the tracing of the *épure*, on which the timber structure was cut. An analysis of the façade of the mid-16th century *logis* of the manor of Les Pavements provides without doubt the finest example of this kind of research.

An initial observation was made on the basis of an extremely accurate drawing of the main elevation of this building: the equal widths of the two extreme bays and the height of the roof are exactly the same as the combined heights of the first two stories. The function of the *épure* as a regulating pattern became obvious in the grid obtained when the elevation was divided into a series of four identical compartments.

Inside the rectangle formed by the line of the roof ridge A, the vertical lines from the north and south

LEFT:
The two-flight stair at the logis of Prétot.

RIGHT:
This new position of the staircase in the interior, the disappearance of the tower, and the shifting of the chimneys to the extremities of the roof finally allowed the entrance to take central position on the façade. However, the master builder of the logis of Champ-Versan still had some difficulty with this new concept.

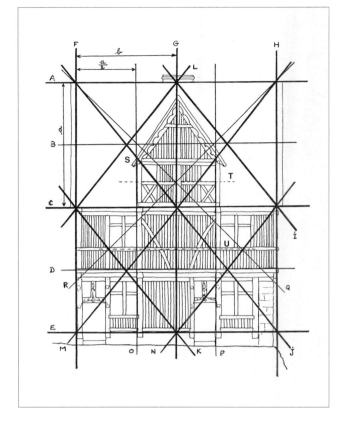

The west elevation of the logis of the manor of Les Pavements. Attempt at reconstruction of the regulating pattern.

gables, F and H, and the ground floor sills E, the symmetrical vertical axis G corresponds to that of the large dormer, and the horizontal center axis C to the width of the eaves. The top plate along the upper edge of the jetty D, i.e. at the exact level of the floor upstairs, can be traced at the intersection of the diagonal lines K, M, N, and J. The two side bays are, therefore, composed of four superimposed squares, the vertical lines of which – F, O, P, and H – are intersected by the horizontal lines A, B, C, D, and E. This marks the delineation of the central bay which includes the large dormer. The outline of this dormer obeys the same rigorous rules: the base of the gable corresponds to the line S which is defined by the intersection of the diagonal lines J and M with the vertical lines O and P. Finally, if the diagonal lines Q and R of the two squares ABFO and ABPH are extended, their intersection and meeting with the diagonal lines K and N of the two rectangles CEFG and CEGH, provide in T the level of the window sills of the dormer and in U that of the rail which runs along the entire width of the façade under the upper floor windows. The entire composition is based, therefore, on the combination of two modules, the rectangle a x b, and the square $a/2 \times a/2$.

The ingenuity of this plan comes as no great surprise: a concern for clarity and harmony of expression in every creative act, be it graphic or architectural, was very often the motivation behind the application of this exercise, as demonstrated by the illustrations in Villard de Honnecourt's album.

Interior decoration

Due to the change of taste, regular renovation as a result of constant use, and frequent developments and innovations with regard to the comfort and physical well-being of inhabitants, relatively little is known about the original decor of the manors of the Pays d'Auge, particularly in the earlier periods.

The floors have generally survived better than the walls and ceilings which were subject to the application of successive layers of paint, soot from the chimneys, vandalism, and inexpert renovation involving intensive, careless stripping.

Flagstones, flint cut in geometrical patterns, terracotta tiles: the oldest of the floor coverings found on the ground floor of these manor houses show an astounding variety, the careful study of which in many cases will reveal a detailed stratigraphy. Up to the early 18th century when bare tiles, stone paving, and parquet flooring became definitively

established, glazed terra-cotta was the preferred floor covering for all floors in the dwellings. Heraldic motifs, *fleur-de-lis*, rosettes consisting of four elements, scrolled borders with mixed glazings of yellow, green and brown were popular until the late 16th century. Running foliage decorations and palmettes – still in the same colors – were popular combined as checkers up to the late 17th century until an original product, Lisieux paving, introduced a new type of decoration. This flooring consisted of earthenware enameled in blue and white in addition to the usual colors and combined in simple geometrical forms. The vivacity of the colors and the precision of the design, which was astonishing in its modernity, attracted builders until the end of the 18th century. This type of flooring was widely used; this is documented by invoices at the palace of Versailles.

Wear and tear from clogs and steel-tipped shoes caused the disappearance of most of these beautiful floors, traces of which can still be found hidden under some well-placed cupboards.

Why then were the walls and ceilings excluded from this taste for vivid color?

The most common error made in the restoration of these timber-frame *logis* is in treating the interior walls as though they were external façades and pursuing this obsession with "exposed timber" at all costs by juxtaposing the dark-colored wood with light-colored infill. This treatment does not even have much in common with the original exteriors as demonstrated by recent research on the polychrome nature of timber-frame façades. White interior walls with black zebra stripes, an all too common sight today, were almost non-existent in former times. The contrasting of materials was in fact replaced by decorations based on the fully paneled

wall, going from the simple whitewash clad with delicate wall coverings and wood paneling to all possible varieties of decor, depending on the means at the disposal of the builder: painted walls, plain colored walls, geometrical or foliated patterns, a wide range of stenciled motifs, and *trompe-l'œil*. The disappearance of the whitewash due to a failure to reapply regularly too often led to the belief that walls were left untreated. The whitewash brightened the interiors and was an effective insecticide. Occasionally, certain elements in the timber frame – posts, studs, and beams – were painted in different, and possibly alternating colors – ochre, red or yellow ochre.

If the master of the house in the late Middle Ages could not afford one of the expensive floral or rustic tapestries, he had the motifs painted directly onto the timber frame and even went as far as decorating it with a *trompe-l'œil* border to complete the illusion. This kind of decoration was extremely difficult to conserve. The fragility of the nogging meant it required far more frequent repair than the timber frame. Moreover, the different behavior of this heterogeneous support – mineral and organic – and its often hasty preparation were the cause of early decay, which was even more prevalent in the case of the interior side of outer walls. In effect, the very varied thermal conductivity of the two materials, i.e. the timber and the nogging, made the conservation of the part of the decoration completed on the nogging very unpredictable as it was far more sensitive to variations of temperature, and all the more so because the walls were rarely more than four inches thick. No decoration of this type would appear to have survived to the present day. Other fitted decorations appear to have been applied in trompe-l'œil, including embossed leather, remains of which from the 16th century discovered on the third story of the château of Grandchamp have undergone interesting restoration processes.

In the case of cob nogging, the support could be provided by a new layer of the mixture of straw, clay, and gravel applied on a lattice of oak and covered with a thin film of lime. If the thermal conductivity and hygrometry of the support was subsequently gradually eroded, its fragility often resulted in its disappearance.

The untimely stripping of the wallpaper at the manor of Tonnencourt allowed the – rather belated – discovery of a battle scene, complete with inscriptions, representing the battle of Marignan, in which the seigneur of the manor, Guillaume de Lyée, had participated. The theme of the *trompe-l'œil* decoration on the well preserved blind arches on the stone of the gable wall on the second floor originates without doubt from Italy: the eave wall has, however, lost all trace of such decoration for the reasons explained above. Circular arches, punctuated by oval fielded panels are surrounded with floral motifs at the corners and rest on a socle which is an imitation of the wide chamfered Classical rusticated masonry. The awkwardness of the bases and capitals of the columns and pilasters fades into insignificance in the presence of this rich decoration in yellow and red ochre with wide black and brown lines feigning relief under a dentil cornice indicated by white lights on a black background. To judge by numerous vestiges found in various manors, this type of decoration, which appeared in the Pays d'Auge in the first half of the 16th century, was very popular.

Indeed, the art of *trompe-l'œil* was also used to transform simple timber posts which supported the ceiling joists into Corinthian columns, conceal chimney mantels, and disguise doors.

During the following century, new motifs appeared whereby the Classical linearity was replaced with large panels decorated with foliated motifs. The most beautiful example of this can be found in the manor of La Chapelle at Brocottes where all of the wall and ceiling decorations in the upstairs room have been preserved. Running foliage decorations centered on large circular cartouches embellished with flowers and fruits are found above a plinth inherited from the preceding century and hastily covered with flecking and wide stripes. The line is incisive, the colors of the plinth and "pilasters" vividly juxtaposed. The decoration of the posts and beams undertaken in the same spirit alternates baskets of flowers and bouquets with a rather inauthentic false timber reserved for the underside of the floor above. The only modification to have been made to this exceptionally well preserved decoration consisted in the painting of naive landscapes

on the false marble of the panels which is believed to have been carried out some years later.

While on the subject of – for the most part unpublished – decoration, it is also important to mention the exceptional ensemble preserved at the manor of Coupesarte. Indeed, an almost complete repertoire of 15th and 16th decoration can be found in these modest buildings. Several enormous beams on the ground floor alternating in red and yellow ochre are no doubt part of the 15th century structure. Important vestiges of decoration consisting of extensive rustications and *trompe-l'œil* panels remain on the south wall of the first-floor 16th century wing. The joisted ceiling with stenciled beams and multi-colored flowers and "incrustations" of false timber is also intact. The *chambre d'amour*, or "Cupid's chamber", in the *logis*, which was renovated at a later stage, was

decorated with painted timbers: vases and crowns intersected with foliate swags alternate on the decoration of the socle; above this a series of mythological figures surround Cupid and Juno in cameo beneath a molded ceiling which is dominated by garlands and braided leaves encircling a sky in *trompe-l'œil*.

The final touch consists of a skillfully constructed window opening on a garden – also a *trompe-l'œil* – with its box hedges, shapely trees, and gushing fountains. Similarities confirmed in the treatment of ornamental elements between this ensemble and the decoration of the seignneurial chapel at Louvagny near Coupesarte, the date of which is firmly established, would date the decoration of the *chambre d'amour* at around 1650.

After this period, all sophisticated *logis* were decorated with simple wood paneling. Stucco was sometimes imitated and used to render old French ceilings uniform, disguising their archaic joists up to their robust oak beams. In its final incarnation, wood paneling was limited to the surface beneath the wallpaper, the most interesting remnants of which should still be collected today. The old rustic timber frame was, however, in decline and the star of "petrophile" architecture in the ascendant.

In the "chambre d'amour" at Coupesarte, Juno and the peacock stand next to Cupid who is forging his arms.

Detail on one of the beams at the manor of La Chapelle.

The chimney mantel and "sky" in trompe-l'œil in the "chambre d'amour".

An inventory of the manors of the Pays d' Auge

Argentelles

Situated at the foot of the last hills on the southern fringes of the Pays d'Auge, the manor of Argentelles bears some of the distinct characteristics of the work of builders from the neighboring regions of Perche and the Argentan plain. It borrows from them the warm colors of rubble stone and ochre mortar and a more marked concern for the defensive provisions, even within the walls of the *logis*. However, the carpenter's skill is superbly expressed in the building's dominant feature, lending the *logis* a grace and lightness typical of the manors of the Pays d'Auge itself.

The manor house, which stands on a vast, slightly raised platform, had substantial defenses, being surrounded by ditches which, even today, are partially water-filled. Within this outer enclosure, a narrow moat surrounds the circular *motte* which was probably the site of the original fortified *logis*, relegating the service buildings and chapel to the outer bailey. In keeping with a phenomenon observed in several manors and châteaux, it is the dovecote – a distinctive symbol of seigneurial prerogative – which later came to occupy the summit of the *motte*.

The *motte* was actually too small to accommodate a *logis* of a size suitable for a powerful lord in the early part of the 15th century. It was Guillot d'Ouilly, a loyal vassal of the king of France, who was responsible for the construction of the existing *logis*, in about 1410. He was driven out by the English occupying forces in 1418, and his estate was assigned to Roland Leyntall, Lord of Hereford and governor of the nearby fortress of Exmes. Richard d'Escalles, a descendant of Guillot d'Ouilly, reclaimed his family rights at the end of the Hundred Years' War and found the noble residence virtually intact.

A rectangular coursed-rubble structure, the *logis* still stands firm on the northern side of the outer bailey. It is primarily a domestic *logis*, whose two floors boast an adjoining hexagonal tower on the courtyard side. Both floors of this elegant building are amply lit by large mullioned and transomed windows. The high window openings are framed by torus moldings intersecting at the corners, the door is crowned by an ogee under an equilateral arch, and the sills and cornices are also decorated with moldings. The plain gable walls are coped and a dripstone marks the transition from the ground to the upper floor.

This is also a well-defended building. It has four round corner towers constructed in dressed stone with loopholes looking out on each side of the building. The ground floor windows are protected by sturdy bars. The defensive structures over the doors, which open on the north and south sides of the building, are a most unusual feature. These consist of jettied bartizans decorated with elaborate moldings and linked by elegant ogees.

But the most significant feature of this manor is, without a doubt, the upper chamber in the central tower, an effective look-out post topped by a six-sided roof and reached from a small staircase located to one side in a tiny adjacent turret. The thinness of the timber framework and its design as an oversailing structure meant it could be made into a good-sized room with a fireplace. Here, the carpenter gave free expression to his art, using a double cornice which was as useful for stopping water from running down the walls as it was essential as a suitably impressive feature with which to crown such a work.

There are clear similarities between the manor of Argentelles and other buildings in neighboring regions, for example the manor house of Pommereux at Montgaroult near Argentan.

The interior of the *logis* fulfills the combined requirements of comfort and security. The quality of

The logis at Argentelles is distinguished by the rather unusual position of a hexagonal staircase turret on the main façade. The turret is topped by an upper chamber which is accessed from a secondary staircase.

The manor of Argentelles has kept part of its moat. The original fortified logis was doubtless built on a circular motte surrounded by water. The dovecote was erected on the motte during the 15th century, at the time of the construction of the current logis.

The frame of the dovecote does not date back any further than the 17th century. It initially included two horizontal frame structures, the lower of which has disappeared. In the upper one, the principal rafters are supplemented with diagonals for added stability.

A small sundial engraved with Gothic numerals is inlaid in the south face of the stair turret.

the fireplaces, which have straight hoods and a relieving arch on the ground floor, and on the first floor slope slightly inwards to meet the chimney stack, is paralleled only by the attention paid to the convenience of the loop-holes or the staircase exits where ample space is provided for the drawing of swords! No effort was spared either on the splendor and the dignity of the great hall, home of the famous "bed of justice", a magnificent Gothic canopy under which the lord of Argentelles exercised his rights, and which is now kept in the Philadelphia Museum of Art.

An old description mentions a motto inscribed on the tympanum of the main door: "Ayme aux trois coeurs" ("Love with three hearts"), no longer visible today. Was this the motto of Guillot d'Ouilly? The first word appears again on the pediment of the imposing dormer window above the windows aligned to the left

The sturdiness of the masonry work, in which the color of the plasters merges with that of the stone with the sharp arrises, contrasts with the delicate timberwork of the upper chamber.

of the door. This was built in 1632 by the descendants of Jean Lefranc, to whom Argentelles had passed in 1571. This feature had a matching counterpart aligned with the windows on the right-hand side, which disappeared following a long period of neglect.

Indeed, it is difficult to imagine the appalling state the manor had fallen into at the start of this century: although the stone walls, which were admirably well founded and constructed, had resisted the ravages of time and man, the roofs, timbers, and floors of the *logis* had collapsed, with the

exception of the upper chamber whose delicate timber framework had remained intact on the staircase turret. The dovecote on the turret was in a critical state and the chapel was falling into terminal ruin beneath the sprawling ivy. The manor house was slowly succumbing to neglect and indifference. The project undertaken in 1957 by Count Robert du Mesnil du Buisson, initially aided by young volunteers and later with the support of the historic monuments service, restored Argentelles to its former splendor within a few years.

Aubichon

The manor house of Aubichon with its discreetly colored timber façades stands at the edge of the plateau at the source of the stream which flows into the valley of Orbiquet. Time has barely left a mark on this seemingly fragile structure: were it a stone building, it could easily have succumbed to a slight weakness in the foundations. However, the timber was able to maintain its cohesion, and today the west part of the façade still gently echoes the slopes on the edge of the valley.

The old fief of la Folletière probably came under the barony of Glos, which was owned by the bishops of Lisieux until it was handed over to the Aubichon family, who gave its name to this small estate from then on.

The present-day *logis* consists of a long building with a two-story nine-bay timber framework, the lower floor supporting a prominently oversailing jetty. The six west bays form a perfectly homogene-

ous frame which, however, is lighter than the frames usually found in buildings of this size at the end of the Middle Ages. The last two east bays are clearly part of a second construction phase, which is not as neat as the first, and has no decoration other than cross braces under the upstairs window breasts. A mediocre and purely utilitarian diagonal brace spoils the pleasant equilibrium of the vertical members, but the new section respects the proportions of the original building, and the carpenter even went as far as maintaining the appearance of a jetty, a practice which was actually obsolete by the time this extension was being built.

The window arrangement on the upper floor is preserved intact in the oldest part of the building and the windows on the ground floor are still discernible. Despite the many modifications they have undergone, it is still possible to reconstruct accurately the original plan and elevation.

The Aubichon *logis* differs slightly from the usual models, which consist of two rooms per story with a central block of four chimneys positioned back to back in pairs. The model is closely adhered to on the four bays centered on the chimney stack where the layout is perfectly symmetrical. The upper floor, which is accessed by a staircase fitted between the chimney block and the façade, has two more rooms with a view to the south through two windows with mullions formed by the bay posts. To meet the client's requirements, however, the builder added two additional bays to the west of these four bays. This made it possible to add a room with a door to the ground floor, which mirrors that in the adjacent bay, and a chamber on the upper floor. However, neither of these additional rooms had a fireplace.

The decoration of the frame is particularly fine. The horizontal members, i.e. the jetty plate and upper jetty bressumer, and the continuous rail on the upper floor, have a set of drip moldings, and the

The bay posts, to which the horizontal cross pieces are fixed, act as the center mullions in the windows on the first floor. The mullioned and transomed window in the first bay of the ground floor is now filled in and its transom has been removed. There were originally double doors to the right of this window, the posts of which are still in place.

The shields carved on the first floor posts, and, particularly, that of cardinal Jean Le Veneur, bishop of Lisieux, in the second photograph from the left, accurately date the construction of this logis between 1505 and 1535.

The manor house of Aubichon has been extended by two bays on the east side, these are particularly identifiable from the presence there of the only diagonal lines on the façade.

The coat of arms of the parish of Saint-Jacques of Lisieux at the west extremity of the building.

lower jetty bressumer has a quadrant profile carved with slightly raised snarling beast-heads linked by a series of three cavettos.

The vertical members, i.e. the bay posts and door jambs, each have a base bracket supporting the projecting molded window-sill on the first floor, and a bracket on the ground floor with two small trefoiled bases under an ogee, which stands out against a background of red ochre and marks the thickening of the post to accommodate the jetty bressumers or the door lintel.

The finest of both the vertical and horizontal moldings terminate in downward spikes in the form of a kind of spearhead and are emphasized by their contrasting color. They are found both at the base of the jambs of the mullioned and transomed windows on the first floor and at the junctions of the upper jetty bressumer and continuous rail.

The successful restoration work revived the vestiges of the original polychromy, highlighting the slightly raised elements, the fangs and the eyes of the ferocious beast-heads and the single or double based brackets. The restoration also restored the legibility of the shields which adorn the six posts of the upper floor.

The most valuable of these shields, which is carefully distinguished by its jig-saw outline, bears the coat of arms of cardinal Jean IV Le Veneur, "argent a bend azure charger three soltires or". It was he who held this fief in his capacity as bishop of Lisieux from 1505 to 1535. The other shields include the coat of arms of the chapter of the cathedral of Saint-Pierre in Lisieux, "azure two crossed keys argent", and that of the parish of Saint-Jacques of Lisieux, "gules a bourdon or in pale charged a besare or and two cockles in chief or", in which the manor is located.

It would be impossible to over-emphasize the two apparently contradictory aspects of the Aubichon *logis*: could this fragile infill framing have been preserved in its original state almost six centuries after its construction? An objective analysis leads us to confirm this opinion without the slightest reservation.

On the upper floor of the logis, *the walls and ceilings once again convey the impression of an abundance of light achieved in the past by whitewashing, a practice too often forgotten today.*

The two easternmost bays, added in the 17th century, were more roughly executed. The beams seen on the ground floor here were barely even squared.

Identical fireplaces stand in pairs, back to back on both stories. The projecting piers support a frame consisting of four molded beams supporting the stone mantel.

The molding has been removed from the west fireplace on the ground floor. The spiral staircase was situated on the right between the fireplace pier and the front wall.

Le Bais

The buildings of the manor of Le Bais stand out like a patchwork of shimmering colors at the bottom of the small valley of the Grandouet. The tiled roofs with scattered glazed elements, the dark slate, the checkered pattern of bricks and stones turned gray with lichen, the pink and white plasterwork, and the timber framework combine to form a harmonious collection of exceptionally diverse structures.

The stream feeds the running water moats which encircle the small enclosure containing the widely contrasting buildings which make up this manor. They were built or rebuilt over the centuries of the eventful history of this fief, which is well documented in the pages of its chartulary.

The first reference to a lord of Le Bais dates back to the 12th century when Robert du Bais contributed to the foundation of the Cistercian abbey in nearby Val-Richer. In 1149, the same Robert du Bais and his sons Jean and Guillaume are mentioned as having made donations to the priory of Montargis, a daughter-priory of the abbey of Tiron built on a promontory overlooking the nearby alluvial plain of the Dives. Robert du Bais is also known for his generous gifts to the parish of Saint-Denis de Cambremer mentioned in a charter of 1165 in connection with the consecration of the new church. There does not seem to be any significant feature at the manor of Le Bais dating back to this period, except for the bases of a few walls beside the ditches. The entire manor must have been constructed from timber with a single stockade reinforcing the defenses of the moats.

The earliest material contained in the archives dates from after the end of the Hundred Years' War, when Le Bais was occupied by a gentleman of no significant wealth, Jean Le Gouez, who went to a great deal of trouble to get himself recognized as a nobleman, several years after being rejected in 1463 and forced to pay tallage. Fortunately, this was rectified by the greater benevolence shown towards his son Robert in 1540 by the Examination of the Elect of Lisieux. However, the Le Gouez lineage ended with the marriage of Jeanne Le Gouez to François de Malfillastre in 1560. Jean Le Gouez probably built the extant *logis* at the end of the Hundred Years' War in the form of a sturdy long-post structure along the south side of the enclosure. Evidence of this has been revealed by the recent restoration of the east gable which bears the traces of an open gallery on the second floor, which was fitted with a row of small rectangular windows and originally supported by beams with a series of diagonal ties. A similar arrangement can still be found in the former *logis* of the manor of La Bruyère.

This long-post structure must date from the same time as the huge farm building located a few dozen meters away outside the moat enclosure. This building was constructed with remarkable care and includes both a storage loft and a press. There were doubtless other buildings next to it which have now disappeared and been replaced with more recent stone buildings, which nevertheless maintain the presence of a service courtyard unusually situated without even the slightest defenses alongside the actual manorial enclosure.

In the early years of the 16th century, the family of Le Gouez also constructed an octagonal timber-framed dovecote opposite the gatehouse. The dovecote plan is traditional, as is the simple close studding frame which is reinforced by several slanting braces. The rather unusual lantern at the top of the conical roof could, however, date from the extensive alterations which were carried out on this building at the end of the 18th century.

The Malfillastre family's affluence allowed them to undertake the reconstruction of the essential defensive feature, the gatehouse, shortly after they settled at Le Bais.

The gatehouse was built in the second half of the 16th century, its walls decorated in a perfectly regular checker pattern, which lends the building its delightful elegance. A slight outward curve is a feature of the ridges of the roof, itself covered in scallop-tiles. The defensive provisions are still very much in evidence, for example, the very discreet loop-holes inserted amongst the checker squares and between the timbers of the bretèche.

The gatehouse, which is built on a rectangular plan, projects slightly over the east moat and has a small square staircase turret on the manor side of the structure. The builders chose the very finest materials for this building: the stone and red-brick checkerwork is perfectly executed and finished and bears no decoration except for the flat fillet separating the two stories and the gateway arch. The deep grooves which used to hold the rails of the drawbridge in the raised position actually contribute overtly to the overall harmony of the structure, as the master builder went to great lengths to hide the small loop-holes and firing holes which are discreetly cut into the squares of stone.

Great attention was paid to the profiles of the roofs, which show the same richness of color. The gatehouse itself is crowned with a short hipped roof which reflects the rectangular plan. The square staircase turret has a pavilion roof, a shape which is repeated in the pyramidal covering of the timber-framed dormer on the main body of the building. Despite its delicately ornate appearance, this dormer also plays a role in the defense of the gate: it rests on two stone brackets which interrupt the lovely ogee cornice to accommodate a *bretèche* which would pose a real threat to any intruder daring to cross the lowered drawbridge.

The gatehouse, the logis *and the dovecote: three buildings, three periods, three very different styles in a single manor.*

The enemy who happened to succeed in lowering the drawbridge would then come up against a sturdy iron-studded gate.

moats were cleaned out. The base of the turret finial has a female head with a broad forehead and curly hair on a huge starched collar, on top of which stands a square vase with plant-like volutes on the sides, which terminate in bearded heads surmounted by a palmette holding a bouquet of four flowers attached to a stem supporting a dove. Even more rare are the two ridge tiles at the top of the main body of the building which are decorated with the same female head resting on a green-glazed base. These are the only surviving trace of a fine roof crest which probably comprised two finials and four ridge tiles of this type.

On 25 July 1706, Marguerite, daughter of Jean-François de Malfillastre, squire and lord of Montreuil and Le Bais, married Jacques du Bois, squire and lord of Berville, a descendant of an illustrious family, some of whose members were companions of William the Conqueror. Thus, the du Bois family became the owners of the manor of Le Bais. They were not content, however, with merely placing their coat of arms windward of the weathervane which still crowns the finial on the pepper-pot turret of the gatehouse, but embarked on a subtle transformation of the *logis* and the dovecote, leaving the gatehouse intact.

It was Louis-Thibault du Bois du Bais who was responsible for most of the subsequent modifications to the manor. A former bodyguard of the king, but with some sympathy for the new ways of thinking and strongly influenced by Jean-Jacques Rousseau, he undertook the adaptation of the antiquated medieval manor to the taste of his time. The timber skeleton was preserved, but high wide windows were added between the posts. All of the façades were rendered in pink plasterwork, originally made from crushed brick, and edged with whitewash framing. The interior decor was also completely renovated and the dovecote, in particular, benefited from the builder's skill and expertise.

This disciple of Rousseau became known for his advanced opinions when, in 1789, he published a tract entitled "My well-founded opinion, or the wishes of a Norman gentleman", in which he appeals for the nobility to rally together to face the profound changes about to take place.

Thus, he probably attached little importance to

The defensive provisions of the gatehouse, probably judged inadequate, were later supplemented with a pepper-pot watch turret on the north-west corner of the tower, with firing holes in the walls.

These defensive devices are, however, easily outshone by the elegance of the roofs with their scalloped tiles, some of which still show traces of green, red or brown glazing at the edges, the vestiges of a geometrical decoration which is no longer distinguishable but would have been as precise as the checkerwork on the façades. The two pavilion roofs on the dormer and the staircase turret still have their varnished finials. The finial on the turret with its four square-sectioned elements is an original, while that on the dormer is a meticulous reproduction, reconstructed from the elements which were still in place and the remnants recovered when the

Three pyramids of glazed scalloped tiles with harmonious, rigorously parallel outlines above the meticulous checkered masonry.

The moat is not merely a ditch, but a wide expanse of running water. The two arches leading to the drawbridge project over the moat.

The postern dormer has regained the finial on its roof ridge, reconstructed from fragments collected in the moat. A true bretèche resting on two brackets, the dormer was also an effective defense element.

the prerogatives associated with the possession of the dovecote: he got rid of the birds and decided to transform this feudal symbol into a pretty country pavilion. For Louis-Thibault du Bois du Bais, the fortress enclosure surrounded by moats had the charms of an island bathed in clear water. The tower at the end of the "island" would make a marvelous place for meditation and meant that there was no need to build one of those structures which adorned fashionable new gardens at that time. He created an external staircase which followed the contours of the octagon, fitted a circle of eight slate-roofed dormers in the original conical roof, and inserted four lozenge-shaped openings into the lantern.

Le Bais' feudal past was, thus, erased, and Louis-Thibault was the first to make his mark on the manor in its new role as a country residence.

Bellou

The roofs of the manor of Bellou are surrounded by the loveliest apple orchards to be found on this plateau and its *logis* is the most imposing timber-framed structure in the Pays d'Auge. It is now difficult to trace the original layout of this manor, such is the extent of the successive changes it has undergone from a fortified building to the country residence and the farming center it still comprises today.

The *logis* with its large roof covering a very varied collection of volumes dominates the cluster of buildings. The main timber-framed body of the building is adjoined on the east side by a large wing of the same height. A smaller wing, consisting of an upper timber-framed floor resting on a stone plinth, is attached at the south-west corner; this design is repeated in the north façade which has turrets at the corner, and a monumental central stone doorway. A timber-framed dovecote stands at a short distance to the south-east of the *logis*, together with a bakehouse and a small, two-story timber *logis* with a gallery supported on individual posts. A building which originally served as the stables, shed, and tack room stands to the north, at right angles to the main *logis*.

The fief of Bellou, occupied by the family of the same name, seems to have belonged to the Moutiers-Hubert family in the 12th century. In 1213, the knight Guillaume de Bellou possessed the right of patronage of the nearby church of Sainte-Marie. The estate, which had passed into the hands of Guillaume de Friardel, was then divided into several smaller fiefs. At the end of the Hundred Years' War, it belonged to the Michel or Le Michel family, who remained the owners until the end of the 17th century. Guillaume Le Michel had his proofs of nobility rejected in 1519; however, he or his son Denis succeeded in obtaining this status by 1540. Ownership was passed down to Mathurin Le Michel,

squire and lord of Bellou in 1562, then to Philippe Le Michel in 1666, and lastly to Adrien Le Michel in 1696. We do not know the circumstances under which the fief of Bellou came into the hands of the La Pallu family: in 1765, it was occupied by the noblewoman Marie-Jeanne Baudouin, widow of Charles Robert de La Pallu. Several descriptions and statements bear witness to the existence of ditches around the *logis*: the only remaining evidence of these today is a large pond to the south-west of the site.

Construction of the present *logis* started in the second half of the 15th century. Preserved in its entirety, it occupies the central part of the six-bay two-story building, centered on the two diagonal braces on the first floor. It extended from the inside corner of the large wing to the second last bay before the small west wing, as demonstrated by the corbelling out of the jetty members, which show perfect continuity. Examination of the structure of the original roof reveals a gap in the series of purlins on the south side. This is the only proof we have of the original position of the chimney stack, which was presumably situated in the center of the *logis*, leaving enough space for the staircase between this block and the former north façade.

Thus, the original *logis* consisted of two rooms on each story with each room extending across three bays. The two central bays are particularly narrow and, furthermore, do not have any corresponding trusses in the roof frame: their main beams were originally embedded in the chimney stack – a practice which was very common at the time. The infill frame of the south façade has also undergone extensive modification to allow the determination of the exact position of the openings; however it is likely that there was a single window for each room in the middle of the center bay. The outer bays had wall braces similar to those indi-

cated on the center bay on the upper floor giving the building a very symmetrical appearance.

The frame has an interesting feature on the upper floor consisting of a molded rail, the central part of which is preserved. The remainder is now poorly reproduced across the entire façade and acts as a sill for the windows on this level.

It is joined to each post by a vertical tenon on the central thickened part of the post. The position of the door on the ground floor remains uncertain: traditionally, in cases where the chimney stack occupies the center of the building, the door or doors are located at the extremes of the façade, and this was most probably also the case here. The mortises, which could have held the lintel of two axial double doors, one on either side of the center post, probably correspond to two diagonal braces identical to those on the upper floor. The jetty which extends across the front façade was continued along the east

gable, as indicated by the bressumer placed diagonally at the end of the building. The living space was restricted and, in the decades that followed, the *logis* was extended by one bay towards the west. The moldings of the jetty were roughly copied and the elegant terminal motif simplified.

By the second half of the 16th century, people wanted more living space. Mathurin Le Michel, or his son, decided to add a much larger wing to the original *logis*, extending it to the north and south. The analysis of this extension has proven extremely complex because of the numerous reworkings which have since been undertaken. The first phase of the extension was limited to the section centered on the dormer directly above two mullioned and transformed windows.

This dormer is abundantly decorated and literally covered with carvings in slight relief: stylized foliation adorns the small posts of the window breast, the sill is

The small residence of the south outbuilding, erected in the 15th century, comprises an exterior gallery on the first floor. It is supported by posts which are now incorporated into a timber framework from a later date.

incised with cable moldings and foliate swags identical to those at the Old Manor at Orbec, which dates from 1568, and the plates and braces are covered with palmettes, roses and, interlaced scrolls.

This wing was twice extended further to the east: very little time elapsed between the modifications to this part, as is evident from the dormer on the east façade. It is decorated in a very similar manner to the south dormer: a few new motifs are used such as lozenges and medallions, but it is still the work of the same sculptor. The owner took the opportunity to have part, if not all, of the decoration on the medieval windows of the old *logis* modernized. Indeed, the window breast of the last but one west window on the upper floor contains a number of small posts with stylized foliate decorations and the remains of carvings are still attached to the wall plate above the other window openings. Michel Cottin judiciously indicated the importance

of the recycled timbers used in this large wing, which included complete wall frames. This would explain the various discrepancies between the probable date assigned to the remains of the painted decoration preserved on the timber structure of the upper floor of the large wing and the carving on the dormers, which clearly dates from a later period: the running foliage decoration, the little hunting scene, the curved garlands, and the figure of Saint Cecilia are several decades older and are comparable to the decorations found at the manor of Tonnencourt.

While on the subject of the importance of the recycled timbers at Bellou, we must consider the date of the creation of the dormers with Renaissance-style decoration described above: were they cut on site, or do they also derive from another building? Why do the successive extensions of the wing culminate in the positioning of a dormer on

the east side which is clearly the work of the same craftsman as that on the south façade?

Two other dormers of the same type were reused at the time of the construction of the stables, which date back to 1720, and whose structural elements include numerous other recycled timbers: a jetty plate with cable moldings, a post with palmettes, etc., all of which appear to originate from the same Renaissance building.

Is it possible that a consignment of timber from the demolition of some magnificent building was brought to Bellou and incorporated into the buildings on this new site over the years? Were the two dormers reused in the construction of the stables in 1720 originally located on the south slope of the roof of the *logis*? These questions remain unanswered today, but the theory that there was considerable recycling of timbers is again confirmed by the structure of the octagonal dovecote built in the same period between 1560 and 1570. This uses only new, untouched timber and has decorative carving which is radically different from that of the dormers of the *logis*, despite the fact that it dates from the same period. The thick gadroons and the strong cable molding on its cornice are quite different from the carvings on the dormers. Is it possible

View of the complete south façade. The original logis *comprising six bays is centered on the two diagonal braces on the upper floor and was originally extended by one similar bay towards the west. The large wing was constructed in three successive phases towards the end of the 16th century: the small west wing was added in the 17th century at the same time as the new north façade.*

Detail on the dormer on the east wing which is covered with ornamental carvings, stylized foliation, cable moldings, scrolls, and palmettes.

On the south-west wing: a loop-hole with a wooden hinge inserted between two broad stones and present since the original construction.

possibility of creating a rigidly symmetrical structure on the south side was rejected and it was decided to build a more modest counterpart to the large east wing. This wing is attached to the south-west corner and has an upper story constructed in timber which rests on a ground floor constructed in high quality medium-sized ashlar. It is topped with a hipped roof which is separated from the roof of the central block. As on the large east wing, the timber framework is still strictly vertical and is barely intersected on the east face by a rail which continues that found on the central block. The timber-framed upper floor is slightly oversailing, supported by a three-step jetty treated as a sort of quadrant-shaped cornice which conceals the protruding ends of the transverse beams. Defensive provisions are also present: each side of the small wing is equipped with hinged loop-holes which made it possible to guard the façade of the *logis*.

that there were two sculptors with such contrasting styles working on the buildings of the same manor at the same period?

The most important modification to the manor was made at the beginning of the 17th century and gave the *logis* of Bellou its definitive silhouette. The

Hunting scene painted on a red ochre background on the wall plate of the upper floor of the east wing. The lack of connection between this scene and the plant patterns on the timber frame would indicate the use of recycled timbers whose original decoration was preserved.

However, it was the north façade which underwent the most extreme alterations. The various outbuildings on the south side of the *logis*, which included the dovecote and the bakehouse adjoining the main façade, made it impossible to achieve an attractive layout, an important aim to which builders aspired from the early 17th century.

It was therefore decided to relocate the main façade on the north side of the dwelling and take advantage of this opportunity to increase the depth of the building, which had not changed since the end of the Middle Ages and probably did not allow very convenient access to the upper floor.

The new façade was built several meters in front of the old one, incorporated a wide closed gallery on the ground floor, and was cornered by two projecting round turrets with conical roofs. The medieval roof frame was preserved but enlarged with a fairly rough extension which took the ridge of the roof to a

Stag hunting scene on a background of yellow ochre painted on a wall plate in the same room.

considerable height, its sheer size being further emphasized by the absence of any opening in the roof. This new façade is marked by an overwhelming and majestic air of sobriety: the ground floor made of stone originally incorporated a few narrow

The holy figures painted on the posts alternate with running foliage and curved garlands.

openings. It supports a timber upper floor with two levels whose small rectangular windows punctuate the bays along the purely vertical timber frames. The only ornamentation to which the builder consented consists of a quadrant-shaped jetty, the bressumer of which bears a discreet scalloped frieze, and the small drip molding on the jetty sill.

This façade needed a strong axis, which was provided by the central portal integrated into the timber frame: its molded pediment has two projections immediately above the Tuscan pilasters with which it is framed and between which lies the round-headed doorway. The juxtaposition of stone and timber, as practiced on this portal, may seem surprising. However, it did not worry the builders at the start of the 17th century, who gave priority to the architectural lines and applied them to all materials, no matter how diverse.

Nevertheless, the tradition of the Pays d'Auge is well represented in the treatment of the nogging, which at that time was harmonized into a rich tile arrangement with alternating herringbone, chevron, and triangle patterns. The same decoration was also used in the dovecote and all the roofs were fitted with ridge finials, the bases of which still exist in some cases. However, the austerity of this last part does not seem to have lasted long, and no later than the end of the 17th century, major modifications were made to the window openings, which were considered too parsimonious: the narrow rectangular openings, the mullions and cross pieces of the medieval parts had to make way for large mullioned windows with double transoms inserted in the half-timbering of the south façade. Each window was then fitted with six lead-set glass lights and the same number of internal shutters. During the course of the 18th century, the north façade was fitted with large sash windows with small panes, whose pattern was copied when filling the windows of the south façade, leaving out the lead-set glass lights and fitting small wooden panels in the existing frames. Bellou can thus be regarded as something of an anthology of the arts of carpentry, masonry, and joinery.

Boisjos

The terrible days experienced by the manory Boisjos in August 1944 serve to illustrate the permanence of this strategic site on the southern fringes of the Pays d'Auge. Boisjos manor is indeed a fortress built on a blocked-off spur: its moat is now less sharply defined, but some of its circumvallations are still in place and the buildings are still grouped in an irregular ovoid pattern. The well-dimensioned *motte* is situated a hundred yards to the south on the plateau. The *motte* preceded the construction of the existing manor of Boisjos, which was probably built for the most part by Richard Le Cloutier during the second half of the 15th century. The Le Prévost family succeeded the Le Cloutiers: at the time of the survey of 1666, de Marle found the manor inhabited by François Le Prévost, lord of Boisjos.

The *logis* consists of a main stone section which is extended to the east by a shorter building of the same width. An outward-projecting polygonal turret, which houses the staircase, stands on the north façade facing the slope opposite the courtyard. The *logis* features a particularly interesting arrangement on the west gable in the form of two turrets built on the skew: the first consists of a very narrow structure similar to a thick buttress on the north-west corner, which is topped with a small tile roof and acts as both a defensive flanking structure and a latrine, and the second is a small square tower surmounted by a tall slate pyramid on the south-west corner. The latter is executed with particular care in comparison to the *logis* as a whole and houses a tiny chapel on the first floor, whose diagonal ribs rest on *cul-de-lampes* .

The façades of the main block are almost intact with the exception of the façade looking onto the courtyard, which has been extensively reworked and has had windows added. The two drip moldings which mark the transitions from one floor to the next are fashioned in attractive stone from the valley of Dives. This building was clearly the work of a master builder of quite exceptional competence, which makes it all the more regrettable that the main decorative feature of the façade overlooking the courtyard has disappeared: raking lighting reveals the complete outline of a large door with a slender ogee arch. Unfortunately, all of its moldings were ruthlessly destroyed at the same time as the drip molding which intersected it. This door gave access to a large hall which occupied the entire ground floor of the dwelling and opened to the chapel, the turret for the latrines, and the staircase to the upper floor. The three shields on the large beams of this hall had fortunately been described by Xavier Rousseau before being replaced after the building was damaged in the last war and are awaiting identification. The first is a lozenge horizontally with three crescents, two above and one below, the second showed three hands, and the last bore a lion or leopard rampant, its tail curled back, above a damaged lower register.

One detail gives us further evidence of the care taken in the construction of this *logis*: a small, double-faced sundial engraved with Roman numerals in beautiful Gothic script can be found on the south corner of the chapel where it is still protected from the weather by a delicate drip molding which returns around the angle.

The main block was very soon extended towards the east. However, the previous concern for perfection did not figure in the latter part of the 15th century: three bays of timber framework were considered adequate. The molded cornice and the upper part of the posts are all that remains of this timber frame, which today is merged into the rubble masonry applied to harmonize the appearance of the *logis* at the end of the 16th century.

A narrow rectangular turret and a small square wing which houses the chapel are joined diagonally to the gable of the logis. *The outbuildings, which were part of the extension of the dwelling and open onto the courtyard, contribute to the defense of the manorial enclosure.*

The staircase tarret projects from the rear elevation. Drip-stones cut from excellent quality limestone separate the different floors and continue across each elevation. The walls are mostly built in very hard rubble cemented with mortar of the same color.

The perfection of the stone cutting is particularly evident in the dressing of the window openings.

Boutemont

It would be impossible to present the manors of the Pays d'Auge without mentioning some of the châteaux in this area, which sometimes share very similar architectural features, or are the work of the same master builder. This will enable a better assessment of the differences and similarities between the manors and the châteaux .

A fortress at the bottom of the valley, Boutemont was one of a series of fortified sites along the banks of the Touques river guarding the route leading to its estuary. It was a full fief with its own coat of arms which belonged to the barony of Fauguernon and had been owned since the ducal period by a family of the same name.

The Boutemont family initially built a *motte* at the base of the hill which is still visible today about a hundred yards from the present-day château. The *motte* was abandoned before the end of the Middle Ages in favor of a site which was better able to fulfill the defensive requirements and meet the needs of everyday life in a demesne of some importance.

They therefore settled on the current site which was made into a huge quadrangular enclosure surrounded by moats fed from the Touques river. During the course of the Hundred Years' War, Boutemont changed hands and passed to the Servain family, who had lived in the Pays d'Auge for a considerable time and had been in possession of the lordship of Manerbe since the 12th century. On 10 January 1405, Jehan Servain applied to the king for recognition of the fief of Boutemont, mentioning the dovecote and the seigneurial manor, the foundations of which may have been incorporated into the present dwelling. By 1434, the Servains had been succeeded by the Borels, since in that year, Jehan Borel, lord of Boutemont, presented the priest assigned to the chapel of Notre-Dame-de-Boutemont to the bishop of Lisieux.

In 1525, a different Jehan Borel handed over Boutemont to Philippe Paisant, recently ennobled in 1522, in return for a payment of five hundred *livres*. Having obtained recognition from the king on 26 March 1538, Paisant devoted large amounts of money to the construction of the large stone *logis*, which was erected in the south-east corner and substantially oversails the moat. The two floors of the south wall, which are separated by a drip molding and featuring a window with moldings in the Gothic style, still survive, as does the east wall to which a latrine is attached, supported by three brackets. Philippe Paisant was also responsible for the construction of the four small towers at the corners of the walled enclosure.

Paisant's successors turned their attention to the château entrance at the start of the 17th century. It had previously consisted of a doorway inserted in the wall. A proper gatehouse was constructed immediately above the doorway in the original wall in a mixture of brick and rusticated quoins. This neat masonry is intersected by the double slots which hold the rails of the drawbridge for the carriage gate and the slot for the single rail of the footbridge. At that time, i.e. the early 17th century, machicolation was no longer required at the top of the walls. However, this motif was used to build impressive brackets above the band of stone to support the overhang of the roof which terminates in sprocketed eaves. The hipped roof displayed a multicolored pattern of scalloped tiles, which today is, alas. reduced to a few horizontal stripes.

Whilst the north face of the gatehouse overlooking the moat remained austere, the south face above the porch was positively majestic. Here, a timber framework consisting of a spandrel with two small cross braces per bay, a large cross brace on each side of the axial window, and a multitude of small straight upright wall members extends across three levels and bays.

All the vertical members in the upper level and the dormer have carvings representing long stylized leaves and fluted pilasters. The side cheeks on the upper story are merely extensions added at a later date.

The building work commissioned by the Paisant family probably also incorporated the other buildings in the courtyard, which have since been substantially altered. Boutemont then passed into the hands of the Le Bas family. The considerable wealth of this *noblesse de robe* was used to transform the former fortress into a delightful château: the walls which blocked the views from the *logis* towards the valley of the Touques were demolished, the old *logis* was enhanced with stone and brick facing in the form of large pilasters and window dressings, and arched galleries were added to the north and east walls of the courtyard.

On 12 June 1745, the daughter of Gabriel-Pierre Lebas, a counsellor at the Parliament of Rouen, married David Guéroult, who had also been accepted as a counsellor at the Parliament of Rouen in 1733. Guéroult thus took possession of the land and the château of Boutemont which their son retained until he emigrated in 1791. The Guéroults were responsible for raising the height of the east outbuildings in the courtyard.

The history of the manor of Boutemont demonstrates particularly clearly one of the very common courses taken by property ownership in Normandy after the Middle Ages. The fortress inherited from the ducal period often remained under the same ownership until the Hundred Years' War but had passed into different hands by the end of that turbulent century. In the 16th century, the estate was generally taken on by a recently ennobled, often extremely rich, family before becoming the property of a *noblesse de robe* and remaining thus until the end of the Ancien Régime.

RIGHT:
The four corner towers and the moat were left intact when the surrounding walls on the west and south sides were destroyed in the 18th century. The gatehouse and its roof of glazed tiles faces the logis, *the two being linked by a gallery of arches, now filled in.*

LEFT:
Detail of the timber framework on the upper floor of the gatehouse, which dates from the early 17th century. The double windows and their fluted pilasters are framed by large cross braces. The nogging between the vertical and horizontal timbers consists of diagonal tile patterns while the nogging between the diagonal timbers consists of vertical and horizontal tile patterns.

Le Breuil

The attractive appearance of the château of Le Breuil could almost make one forget that it was originally an important fortress situated in the middle of the valley of the Touques river, which once fed its now dried-up moats. It was owned in 1300 by the knight Jean de Bouquetot and remained in the family until 1611.

The genealogy of the Bouquetot family is fairly well known from the writings of Yves Nédélec, who mentions Robert de Bouquetot in 1340, Martin de Bouquetot, and his son Girard. Then at the end of the Hundred Years' War came Jean II de Bouquetot, a lieutenant under Guillaume Oldhalle in the viscounty of Orbec and a chamberlain of the Duke of York in 1447. They were succeeded by Guillaume de Bouquetot, his son, and in 1540 by his grandson, also called Guillaume, lord of Le Breuil. Subsequently linked by marriage to the Hautemer family, amongst others, the Bouquetot dynasty died out with Suzanne, daughter of Jean III of Bouquetot, who passed away in 1611. In 1593, Suzanne de Bouquetot had married Gabriel II de Montgommery, lord of Ducey, the son of Gabriel, the man responsible for the death of King Henry II at a fatal tournament.

There is probably nothing left of the work undertaken by the Bouquetot family in the present-day château, which shows great concern for an orderly appearance and owes its rigorous organization to the Classical age and the personalities of Gabriel and – subsequently – Louis de Montgommery.

The château is built on an unusual plan: a stone portal built on a curved projection of the enclosure opens onto a courtyard with the dwelling on the east side facing the outbuildings on the west side. The portal at Le Breuil is extremely elegant: the carriage gate, which is covered by a semicircular arch of rusticated masonry, is positioned between two pedestrian gates with a straight lintel.

The *logis* comprises a central brick and stone section which is flanked by two slightly wider and higher timber-framed wings. The entire building rests on a plinth of cut stone with rusticated masonry at the corners. Were the funds insufficient to finish the work entirely in stone, or did the Montgommerys more or less lose interest in their Le Breuil estate? We have reason to believe that this is the case judging by the extent to which – at least until 1658 – the land was rented out to farmers "with the exception of such rooms and buildings as designated by the said lord, these being within the enclosure of the seigneurial manor". However, there is no denying that the château of Le Breuil bears witness to the great skill and spirit of invention of the architects, who succeeded in creating a superb edifice based on the most varied of materials.

The central part of the *logis* has retained its Classical characteristics on the main façade overlooking the moats. This façade features rusticated ashlar, platbands, and stone modillions which stand out against the brickwork. The courtyard façade was reworked during the course of the 18th century using the same materials but a much simpler form.

The two two-story symmetrical wings at the extremities of the main body of the dwelling are each topped by a sizable hipped roof; an imposing chimney stack and a large dormer, adjoined by two smaller dormers on the north side of the north wing, project from the top of the roof. These wings have an unusual structure consisting of two separate superimposed frames. The bay posts are expanded at the top to enable them to support a small awning above the first floor and the overhang of the sprocketed roof over the second floor.

A similar intermediate awning also existed until recently on the long-post structure of the château of Grandchamp, and other examples can still be found on a range of more modest buildings. At Le Breuil,

The château was completely surrounded by water-filled moats. The logis and outbuildings stand facing each other on either side of the entrance gate. They were built a century apart, but based on the same principle: a main block flanked by two square wings. The timber wing includes a two-story short-post structure with no jetty. The posts, thickened at the top, support a small awning and above that a high cornice.

this feature perfectly fulfills its function of protecting the most fragile part of the frame, namely the point at which two superimposed structures are joined. The bottom two-thirds of each corner post are decorated with rustication echoing that of the stone plinth, thus creating an element of continuity between the different materials. The timber carcass conforms to a strict structural pattern and shows a concern for economy, placing cross braces side by side, thereby making it possible to use very short timbers and provide bracing, while avoiding the need to position the diagonal and cross braces per-

fectly symmetrically. The highly original treatment of the timber framework on the south wing is also worthy of note; here the timber partition, which has no nogging, is constructed from wall members which are laid side by side and alternately recessed and projecting to produce a checkered effect.

The fief of Le Breuil changed hands at an unknown date between 1658, date of the last known record, and 1696, the year of the death at his château in the Pays d'Auge of Adrien Bence, lord of Le Breuil, advisor and secretary to the king. The Bence family remained in possession of this estate

The logis was no doubt to be constructed entirely in stone but funds proved insufficient to complete the project in the intended manner. The disparity in the styles of the timber frameworks of the two wings was certainly attenuated – or even effaced – by the application of a uniform color to the entire building.

The outbuilding, today opened out from top to bottom, reveals the structure of its gambrel roof. It now houses maturing casks on the former site of the coach-houses.

The frame posts of the wings were clearly designed to blend in with the central masonry structure: they were decorated with slab rustication which resembles stone pilasters.

until 1734. They were responsible for the construction of the beautiful outbuilding facing the *logis* in the early years of the 18th century. This building was constructed in a combination of brick and stone and was hardly less imposing than the actual *logis*. The lower floor of the main body of the building takes the form of a series of open semicircular arches. The structure has a gambrel roof and is flanked by two wings with three bays of rectangular window openings surmounted by dormers with pediments. Work was started on the renovation of the roof of the central part of the *logis*, doubtless in order to copy the roofing of the outbuildings, but this did not progress beyond the initial stage.

La Bruyère

The juxtaposition of these two very well-finished buildings puzzled researchers for a long time. They are now known to have been two successive manorial logis and display very different characteristics: one of them faces the valley while the other is turned in towards the manor courtyard.

Besides the unusual gable gallery, the medieval residence displays a curious lack of symmetry caused by the presence of an aisle which does not seem to be a later addition.

To our knowledge, there is no record of a fief of La Bruyère in the district of Auvillars: a text from 1602 merely mentions a place called "La Brière", which was very clearly linked to the lordship of Auvillars. The ruins of the château of Auvillars can be found close to the church and barely betray its military importance during the Hundred Years' War.

La Bruyère dominates this site on the edge of the plateau and includes, alongside various farm buildings, two remarkable buildings, built at right angles to each other, which served as two successive *logis*.

The more imposing of the two buildings is rather long and consists of two very different juxtaposed structures. At the north end, two timber-framed floors rest on a masonry plinth. The scant lings of the timbers are all very substantial, perhaps even excessively so. This building is largely asymmetrical along the longitudinal plane: the north gable has a timber frame of three bays on two floors, perfectly aligned with the roof ridge, and a sort of aisle covered by the roof extension over this single level. A broad transverse open gallery stands on the top floor projecting over the three bays of the gable. It is supported by the projecting ends of the beams and braces with the same section, which take the weight of the gallery and are protected by the overhang of the roof slope. The two stories of this gable and the east façade are punctuated with rows of small rectangular windows, which share a common sill treated as a continuous molded rail above a window breast incorporating small straight upright members. A similar rail runs half way up the outer wall of the aisle and is interrupted level with the three doors, which are all fitted with strong timber lintels borne by small corner-pieces.

This is one of the oldest timber-framed *logis* still extant in the Pays d'Auge. Dendrochronology should allow us to pinpoint the date of construction, which could be earlier than the 15th century. There are few stylistic clues: the ornamentation has been reduced to a few drip moldings and a highly archaic profile on the jetty, on the sill which runs along at the base of the windows, and on the window lintels. Some of the windows are fully preserved and still have their shutters which slide in the grooves in the jambs. There is no fireplace or staircase whose design might provide a clue to the construction date. However, it is tempting to draw comparisons between the general layout of this dwelling and that studied by Edward Impey in Rumesnil, which dates back to the 13th century and comprises a huge room – the "hall" – with a passage backing on to it.

Could the older *logis* at La Bruyère be a surviving example of this type of *logis*? The southern part is

very different, despite being contained within the same exterior volume. It too now has two floors, but its long-post structure does not include an intermediate plate. The studs extend almost four meters from the base of the bottom plate to the wall plate. The structure is reinforced with a few braces and with a rail incorporated half way up, along the entire width of this section. Finally, it is also worth mentioning that the roof framework, which does not include any beams running below the ridge, is meticulously executed: the large arch braces which connect the common rafters to the king post would indicate a desire to liberate the large space of the upper floor, which possibly served as a vast hall with an exposed roof framework and no ceiling, similar to those found in medieval *logis* in Brittany and England.

This *logis* was inhabited up until the end of the Middle Ages but the proximity of the château of Auvillars and the fact that La Bruyère was not a true manor resulted in its exclusion from the modifications which most such dwellings underwent during the major rebuilding period that followed the troubled times of the Hundred Years' War.

It was not until the latter part of the 16th century that it was decided to build a new *logis* at the "place called la Brière", which Charlotte du Quesnel, dowager of Auvillars, certainly considered to be an integral part of her estate in 1602.

The former *logis* was carefully preserved. It was transformed into a farm building, barn, grain loft, cellar, and cider-press, and a new dwelling was constructed which was more in keeping with contemporary taste. A two-story structure built on a rectangular plan, its two chimney stacks rise from the sloping extremities of a steep tiled hipped roof. The masonry on the side walls is still in an archaic checkered pattern but stacks above these walls are executed in neatly toothed brick and stone. The south-facing main façade still features a slight overhang between the two stories, which is provided by the slight thickening of the long corner posts but reduced to the projection of a single plate and not a jetty consisting of three elements. The spiral staircase is also given a prominent place at the center of the rear elevation but the exterior tower, which should have housed it, is reduced to no more than a

simple projection from the roof in the form of a dormer.

Many things had changed, and this new *logis* at La Bruyère truly heralded the advent of the age of Classicism. The master builder still adhered to the tradition of double doors in the middle of the façade but abandoned mullioned and transomed windows in favor of a single thin mullion. The exterior decoration is extremely sober and limited to fine ogee moldings forming long hollow grooves on the sills, mullions, and lintels; the only carved elements are three scrolls and a half-rose, in very slight relief, on the door posts. This is the same pattern as found in the interior on one of the upstairs fireplaces where the entire chimney breast is decorated with scrolls with palmettes and roses.

The restoration work revealed the remains of some very fine decorations which covered the walls of one

The "new residence" still bears some archaic features on the rear elevation, such as the projection of the staircase turret on the roof and the overhanging latrine.

Apart from the use of the central double doors, medieval tradition is well and truly abandoned on the main façade with its separate chimneys, each with its own stack, on the ends of the roof.

of the upstairs rooms. These include trompe l'oeil panels in yellow and red ochre and, in a corner now covered over, the fading vestiges of a Corinthian capital, thus giving the modest timbers of the new *logis* an antique slant.

Separated into two properties which even shared the new *logis*, the manor of La Bruyère gradually fell into ruin. Traces of a fire were visible on the façade of the old *logis*, although the core fabric of the building had not been damaged. The manorial ensemble retained the fading charm of slow decay and some stately old trees lent it a distinct air of nobility.

It would have been easy to maintain the rural setting in conjunction with the exemplary restoration of the buildings. However, the person responsible for the restoration, a knowledgeable enthusiast, wanted to apply a measure of creativity and commissioned Russel Page to create a formal garden, making use of the very pronounced slopes, the few surviving trees, and the marvelous landscape in which the manor is situated. As a result, La Bruyère can now boast one of the most beautiful gardens in the Pays d'Auge.

Caudemone

The manor of Caudemone is situated half-way up the west slope of the Touques valley on a projecting terrace which provided an ideal site, both for keeping watch over the estate and for the construction of the dwelling and its outbuildings. These outbuildings are, for the most part, intact and still include an octagonal dovecote and a 17th century timber-framed farming and residential building of excellent proportions, which stands at right angles to the valley.

The history of this fief is remarkably well documented from the end of the Hundred Years' War onwards. Raoul Anfrey, or Auffray, promoted to the nobility by Charles VII in July 1454 in recognition of his skill as a warrior, lived at Caudemone. He also bore the title "Lord of Le Verger", an estate on the other side of the valley. He appeared at the "General demonstration of nobility for the bailiwick of Évreux" held at Beaumont-le-Roger on 17 and 18 March 1469 "dressed as a man of arms, with three horses", which suggests the extent of his wealth. In 1540, Caudemone was inhabited by Pierre Anfrey, who presented his patent of nobility before the Elect of Lisieux. Several years later his daughter, Marguerite, married Jean III de Bonnechose, whose family remained in possession of Caudemone for no more than three generations. He was succeeded by their son Jean IV, and it was Richard de Bonnechose who did homage to the barony of Auquainville for his fief of Caudemone in 1596. Madeleine de Bonnechose, who had married the squire David de Bernières in 1573, thus, brought the fief into this family. It remained theirs until the end of the 17th century, when it was passed on to the Lebas family. The *logis* is a complex structure consisting of three very different timber volumes side by side, which are perfectly aligned on the east façade but are staggered on the west façade. The two stories are in fact adjoined by various lean-tos which are dominated by a large square staircase turret.

The first three south bays form a coherent initial structure whose rich Gothic decoration contrasts with the next three bays, which are shorter and limited in terms of ornamentation to a jetty with fine moldings on quite a slender structure. Finally, prior to a quite radical restoration project, the last two north bays showed the traces of a long-post structure on two floors, with the upright wall members themselves extending from the sole plates to the wall plate.

Contrary to previously-held views, it would appear that the rare vestiges of the long-post structure were once part of the original *logis* at Caudemone, even if the results of the recent restoration now give it the appearance of a 17th century structure. This original *logis*, probably attributable to Raoul Anfrey, could not have been adequate to the needs of the master of such an estate in the long term and his immediate successors embarked on the construction of a new *logis* on the same axis before the end of the 15th century. This new *logis* consists of the three south bays on the building as it stands today.

The manor house is built on a very simple plan and consists of a vast room on each floor with a large fireplace on the north wall of each room; the staircase was possibly located in the north-west corner. This arrangement is identical to that still found in the dwellings at Tordouet and Querville manors. The master builder devoted his full attention to the decoration of the east façade, which is exceptionally rich. The short timbers of the frame on this side have an impressively large cross-section as compared with the timbers used in the carcass, which, despite having normal dimensions, seem almost fragile next to the oversized bay posts and sturdy jetty. There are two braces on the upper floor,

The Gothic decoration on this logis demonstrates the vitality of the work of the craftsmen towards the end of the 15th century. The robustness of the small columns and pinnacles contrasts sharply with the fluidity of the leaves, rolled up or stretched out along the ogee arch, and the finial.

The manor house was constructed in three successive stages: on the right it retains the vestiges of a long-post structure and on the left is the new logis *dating from the end of the 15th century. These two structures are linked by the lighter central portion dating from the 16th century.*

linking the rail and the wall plate rather than a post and the wall plate, and a single brace on the first floor; this was necessitated by the insertion of a door at the left extremity of the building.

Traditionally, three-bay *logis* with a single room per floor constructed at this time got by with one window per floor. However, due to the large dimensions of this dwelling, a different arrangement was deemed necessary, which is still clearly visible today despite the numerous additional windows. The upper floor had two pairs of twin window openings, one on each side of the second and third bay posts. The first on the left is the only one which is still in place and has retained its molded sill with rounded-off corners and its window breast bearing Gothic decoration with small blunt columns overlapping this sill. The adjacent window can only be identified from the traces of the window breast decoration, which is also visible to the left of the third

post. The last window on the right was simply filled in at a later date; the sill with rounded-off corners was not, however, removed and is still in place. The first floor had the same type of windows arranged in the same pattern, traces of which can be discerned in the third bay.

By far the most interesting feature of this *logis* is, of course, the quality of its carvings, which accentuate the lines of the frame and frame the openings. The carpenter left sufficient timber protruding from each bay post for the sculptor to carve a small column with cable moldings in high relief covered with scales and imbrication, encircled with a band halfway up, and crowned with a short pinnacle with carved crockets. The concepts are clearly borrowed from stone architecture but treated very imaginatively. The sculptor did not mind that the posts were thicker at the top to support the projecting ends of the transverse beams: he shaped the tops of

the pinnacles so that they followed the curve and was clearly unconcerned about creating a balanced appearance. The highlighted features are carefully positioned; the double pinnacles framing a shield in exaggerated relief are reserved for the first floor posts of the central bay and the size of the small columns is in proportion to the height of the timbers, as can be seen on the window breasts and the impost.

The entrance door is, of course, the most elaborate element. A pointed ogee arch with curled foliation starting at the bands on the small columns surges upwards to culminate in a superb finial. Each of these decorative elements is very similar to those found on many houses in Lisieux dating from the 1500s and, in particular, the manor of La Salamandre in rue au Fèvres. A shield projects at the center of the lintel and there are others on the adjacent posts. This may once have borne the coats

of arms of the Anfrey family, "gules eight bezants or in orle; sable three crescents or, bordure or."

Less than a century later, the house was extended by three bays to the north, on a much smaller scale and probably designed to match the height of the remaining original structure on this side. The many modifications undertaken on this section of the building make it impossible to identify the positions of the original windows. The structure, proportions, and profile of the jetty, however, allow us to date the construction of the building in the second half of the 16th century. The owner probably took this opportunity to install the staircase tower on the north side in order to provide better access to both the old and the new *logis*. Modifications were also made to the window openings: there is clear evidence of a very large window on both levels of the second bay and a central axial window opening in the south gable where the timber carcass is divided into four horizontal bands.

A large painted decoration was created at the time, which coincided with the marriage of Madeleine de Bonnechose to David de Bernières in 1573. This was rediscovered in 1926 and, no doubt, enthusiastically restored at the time.

Unfortunately it was removed when it was classed as a mediocre decoration from the last century during a new, somewhat excessive restoration project. It is, however, interesting to recall the description from 1927: "Some superb illuminated joists and summers appeared beneath the plaster ceiling. The walls were painted with imitation marble: white rectangles with black and red flecks, and, conversely, black rectangles with white and red flecks, separated by white joints and beds … . On the hood of the fireplace were caryatids, or rather sirens … . The ceiling joists are decorated by hand, with variations in the pattern (in the middle is a cartouche between two palmettes, and at each end there is half a cartouche with a single palmette; light green lines and palmettes; blue and red cartouches; brown background)."

Subsequent additions and modifications to this *logis*, especially on the rear façade, are of lesser interest, with the exception of the tiny red brick extension built in the 18th century on an east-west axis aligned with the gable. This structure served as the manor chapel and has also disappeared recently. The dovecote, which was built at the end of the 16th or beginning of the 17th century, deserves particular attention due to the harmony of its proportions and originality of its lines. The main body has eight sides each divided into two square sections with strictly vertical studs and posts and not a single diagonal member. The conical roof has two dormers, the hipped ends of which are curiously divided into two slopes and very precisely aligned with the arris of a tapered hexagonal lantern which is clad with shingles. Normally, when an architect decides on a square, hexagonal, or octagonal plan, he uses the same form for each element of the structure. This bold breaking of the rules gives the dovecote at Caudemone an interesting profile, enlivened by the double-sloped dormers which were probably then copied on the *logis*.

Although the decorative carving is the most attractive feature of this manor, the other buildings are also distinguished by their remarkable forms and styles. This is true of the outbuildings which stand at right angles to the logis, *and especially the octagonal dovecote with its brick nogging.*

La Chénevotte

It is true that, at first glance, the former inn of La Chénevotte gives the impression of a manorial residence. However, there is no dovecote and no specific decoration, nothing but a beautiful and well constructed house, whose exceptional quality lies in its timber framework which is filled in with a most attractive arrangement of tile fragments and flint.

There was never any fief of La Chénevotte, and therefore no manor. However, this does not detract in any way from the interest surrounding the building which bears this name today. The site falls within the fief of La Minière and place name derived directly from an agricultural activity which had always been practiced there: this is where hempseed was sown which, after retting, produced the "*chénevotte*", the woody substance from which the tow was extracted which was used in the manufacture of canvas.

Situated by the side of the ancient main route between Orbec and Vimoutiers, the site was ideal for the establishment of an inn, which is known to have existed from the 16th century when it was owned by the Mailloc family. Their innate flair for business and a series of settlements allowed them to take possession in the mid-17th century of the entire estate of La Minière, from which La

Chénevotte had been dissociated after the Hundred Years' War.

La Chénevotte is, therefore, a former inn, which displays all the characteristics of a very simple timber-framed *logis* dating from the late 16th or early 17th century.

Its long-post structure, recently restored to its original form, comprises above all some remarkable nogging which presents a skilled combination of graphic and polychrome patterns, very typical of the methods then in use in this southern part of the Pays d'Auge.

It incorporates patterns of tile fragments used both on their own in imbricated triangular patterns and in combination with the brown and gray flint found on the plateaux, which inspired some very attractive imaginative decorative uses. On the west end of the rear elevation there is little divergence from the standard models in which the triangular tile arrangements are interrupted at irregular intervals along the horizontal bed by large square flintstones. The west part of the main façade was meticulously finished using only these two materials. The mason used the vertical arrangement of the timber wall members as his basis and superimposed the diagonal pattern of a flint lattice forming lozenge-shaped tile patterns intersected by the upright wall members.

The marquetry and polychrome effects are particularly successful in the way in which they exploit the contrasting materials, combine the ashen shades of the timber with the dark shine of the stones alongside the warm shades of the terra cotta, and enhance the graphic effects of the finish.

The building was restored with meticulous attention to detail, which was even extended to the roofs, the outlines of which were softened by the perfect continuity of the valleys of the dormers and the curved hip rafters.

The tiling and timberwork of the façades have been faithfully restored at the "manor" of La Chénevotte, preserving some astonishing features like the post with its forked end resting on the ground sill.

Very free interpretations have, however, been applied in the treatment of the interior and exterior spaces, particularly in the creation of a small open gallery on the upper floor, or, stranger still, the omission of a ceiling, exposing the unsightly roof frame.

Chiffretot

The manor of Chiffretot occupies a site very similar to that of Caudemone slightly further up the Touques valley on a projecting terrace on the slope of the left bank, not far from the *motte* of the château of the Paynel family, barons of Moutiers-Hubert.

There are several surviving buildings on this site, including the timber-framed *logis*, which was constructed for the most part in the latter part of the 16th century and consists of a two-story main section on a rectangular plan, which is crowned with a hipped roof supported by large chimney stacks on the gable. This rather compact building would be rather devoid of originality were it not for the presence of an octagonal three-story turret half projecting from the south-east corner. This asymmetrical arrangement is not unique: a good example can be found on a much larger scale in another manor, Caudemone, situated in the district of La Chapelle-Haute-Grue.

The hillside location of the manor of Chiffretot gives no hint of the presence of this vast pond so similar to that at Caudemone. The unusual depth of the logis *and the addition of the single corner turret are characteristic of the experimental spirit of 16th-century architects following their liberation from the strict medieval traditions.*

The main body of this *logis* was constructed in a single phase and owes its solid proportions to the combination of a fairly low roof and a plan of double depth.

The timber structure consists of a long-post frame divided into five wide bays, reinforced on each level by diagonal braces which support the extremities of the façade and the central bay. The architect clearly wanted to introduce an element of symmetry, which is still perceptible despite the various alterations carried out to the layout of the rooms and the windows during different periods. The door is in the center of the east façade and the original windows were divided into twin openings on either side of the second and fifth bay post. It is easy to identify their positions and sill height by examining the fragments and pegging which can still be found inserted in these same posts.

The decoration on the timber framework, although very discreet, is nonetheless extremely detailed. It is limited to the girding beam separating the two stories and the door lintel where the cartouches can still be discerned. The same motif, certainly the work of the same craftsman, appears on the lintel of the door of the *logis* at the manor of Courson. Judging by the recycled timber on one of the upstairs window openings, a simpler version seems to have been used for the ornamentation of the window sills.

The presence of a half-projecting turret gives rise to questions as to the date of and circumstances surrounding its construction. It differs quite noticeably from the main body of the building in that it incorporates a lower floor made of stone containing narrow openings centered on each side – probably loop-holes which have since been enlarged – and has a timber framework which differs quite significantly from that of the main part of the building.

Indeed, the only point of similarity between the two structures is the position of the turret plinth and the intermediate plate with its cartouche decorations at the same level. The two bands of vertical wall members are reinforced by an intermediate band bearing saltires, a motif which is completely absent from the main part of the building. Also, the timbers used in the turret are much smaller in section than those used in the rest of the dwelling.

The turret must, therefore, have been added at a later date, probably in the very early years of the 17th century, as indicated again by the lack of similarity with the main section and its decoration of painted wainscoting.

Although the turret was constructed partly for esthetic reasons combined with the perception of the tower as a powerful symbol and the desire to provide access to those small rooms which added to the space and comfort of *logis* at that time, there does not seem to have been any plan to create a symmetrical turret on the opposite corner. A photograph taken soon after the last war confirms the importance placed on the defensive provisions which, although modest, were real enough: apart from the loop-holes on the first floor, the first band of timberwork contained a series of small lozenge-shaped openings in the tile nogging, which made it possible to scan the surroundings of the *logis* beyond an angle of 180°. These, however, have since been filled in.

Thus, numerous manors like Chiffretot continued to retain defensive provisions of this sort behind their pleasant exterior.

The manor buildings are spread over a very large area: the square dovecote built of ashlar and crowned with a pavilion roof occupies the south-east corner of the former enclosure overlooking the bottom of the valley.

The turret encircles the corner of the logis and slightly overlaps the wall supporting the fireplaces. The gallery was traditionally located on the first bay of the second floor

Here we see a monument to time, which breaks its own measuring instruments, whilst the look-out behind the loop-hole in the turret ensures the seigneur's peace of mind.

Coupesarte

Coupesarte is one of the most striking of the manors of the Pays d'Auge. Despite appearances, it is also one of the most complex. The original timber frame has remained intact throughout the subtle restoration work.

With its two *bretèches* projecting above a wide running-water moat, its magnificent framework of timbers turned gray with lichen, and nogging of red tile fragments, whose subtle harmonies are reflected in the water, Coupesarte is one of the places which best embodies the true essence of the Pays d'Auge. This is achieved in the quality of the site on the broad valley floor and, of course, the quality of its architecture, but more especially in its authenticity which has been carefully guarded by its occupants over the years. The carefree ducks noisily break up the reflections in the water, the barns are crammed full of hay and straw, and the masters return from the fields to their *logis*, just as their ancestors have done for the last five centuries.

The Anisy family is known to have occupied Coupesarte at the end of the Middle Ages: Montfaut's survey mentions "Guyon d'Anesy" in 1463. These

This trefoil dormer, now incorporated in the outbuildings, probably originated from the 15th century logis, from where it could have been moved during the major alterations carried out two centuries later.

records show that Jacques d'Anisy held two fiefs in 1552, but we do not know the circumstances under which it was acquired by the Le Prévost family before the end of the 16th century. Was it Thomas, master of Le Coin at Mesnil-Mauger and ennobled in 1544, his sons, or grandsons, Guillaume or Nicolas, reputed to have considerably enlarged the family inheritance, who acquired the manor? The available documents do not throw any light on this. François Le Prévost, master of Coupesarte, is certainly mentioned in 1653. His descendants remained in possession of Coupesarte until 1767, the date when the last daughter bearing that name inherited the estate from her brother, thereby bringing it into the Le Viconte family. With properties in other parts of Normandy, the Le Prévosts probably did not reside at their manor of Coupesarte for very long at the end of the 17th century. preferring their house in Caen, or their fief of Amblie, despite the elegance of their property in the Pays d'Auge.

The square *logis* is aligned along two sides of a quadrangular platform surrounded by water. When the moat was cleaned out, the foundations of a tower were discovered on the opposite corner – whether it was a small stone dungeon or dovecote, we will never know. A single timber stockade no doubt completed the defensive provisions.

Although there are numerous descriptions of it, the manor of Coupesarte did not particularly hold the attention of Arcisse de Caumont when he wrote the entries for the last volume of his *Statistique monumentale*: "... a lovely manor consisting of two buildings forming a square. These buildings, constructed in timber with bricks between the timbers, are surrounded by moats filled with water...". And nothing more. The buildings in fact occupy two sides of the square platform enclosed by the waters of the Douet de la Cour Fromage.

The complete long-post frame and a large trefoil dormer are all that remains on the moat side of the original logis. Among the features which verify its great age is the open-mortise attachment of the main tie beams on the upper floor. Most of the infill framing was replaced in the 17th century making way for a breast band bearing cross braces on this elevation to match that on the north wing.

These two wings are of the same height on both the courtyard and the moat side: the ground floor with its framework of strictly vertical timbers supports an upper floor comprising a window breast with cross braces which contains several diagonal braces and timber members interrupted at the window sills. In contrast, the four hipped dormers, each containing a small window opening perfectly centered above a window breast with cross braces, differ noticeably from the dormer on the east façade facing the moat, which is wide with a trefoil pediment crowning two twin window openings.

None of the elevations has a regular window arrangement. The current arrangement on both the courtyard sides and overlooking the moat gives no indication of a strictly defined layout.

However, some elements do lend a sense of the unity intended for this ensemble, which remains coherent despite the transformations the manor has undergone over the centuries. This is firstly conveyed by the symmetry of the two turrets on the north-east and south-east corners; these slim pepper-pot turrets are attached to the upper floor, and supported by three long timber braces and topped with a chestnut shingle roof. This overall unity is also suggested by the window breast of the upper floor which bears a pattern of cross braces running as a continuous band across all four façades and is adapted to the often very different widths of the bays and half-bays. And finally, it is demonstrated by the pink coloring of the tile and brick nogging which is executed in very neat and varied geometric patterns. Numerous other details, however, clearly demonstrate that these two wings originate from two different periods, an observation which is further substantiated by the awkward join between their respective roofs at the point where the west wing is at its shortest and narrowest.

The outbuildings facing the logis originate from different periods: the 17th century in the case of the barns, stables, and cow sheds with their vertical wall members, and in the following century in the case of the building in the foreground, which has triple braces and summers with a through tenon fixed with two pegs.

The original *logis* was in the south wing and extended as far as the right-hand side of the staircase which opens onto the courtyard via a wide door in the corner of the building. It has a powerful frame consisting of four main bays, each of which is subdivided into two half-bays. A very prominent jetty supports the overhang of the upper floor on the ends of the transverse beams and the weight is taken by thick brackets. It would actually be more correct to describe them as alternating transverse beams and false transverse beams. The latter, which mark the division into half-bays, are merely short timbers intended solely to support the middle of the jetty plate between the bay posts.

The division of the bays is actually much more evident on the façade overlooking the moat, where it appears flat and bare due to the absence of a jetty. The four bays, which are separated by vertical long posts, are not intersected by the many stop ends of

the transverse beams, as is the case on the façade facing the courtyard, and the upper story only appears to have half-bays due to the presence of two cross braces per bay.

Closer examination of this rather complex frame in its entirety reveals that the timber infill framing has been almost entirely renovated and that its appearance was noticeably different on the two façades. The south part of the ground floor, which has served as a storeroom for a very long time if not always, has remained intact on three sides: its timber framework comprises close studding, reinforced on the interior face with large braces designed to stiffen the frame. This system, which leaves only the vertical timbers visible on the façades, was probably used on the whole of the original building before the upper floor was subdivided into two horizontal bands, divided by the molded sill which runs along the base of the windows and delimits the window breast with its cross brace structure. The only trace of the original windows appears in the form of the mortises which are still clearly visible on the brackets on both levels, and which held the tenons of the horizontal timbers acting as the window lintels.

The technique and decoration used on the jetty are helpful for pinpointing the date of this first structure. The jetty has been preserved intact – as has the whole of the frame, of which it is an essential element – and is the only part to have been subtly decorated with moldings. This jetty is of a type described by Quenedey as archaic: the forked transverse beam is anchored to the post by a large open mortise at the top of the post, and its end is supported by a thick pegged bracket, supported by a small molded jowl on the post. The jetty plate is reinforced by a cross-bar with its ends simply fixed into hollows on the sides of the anchor beam and resting on the upper face of the anchor beam with a dovetail to counteract any movement and prevent it from slipping outwards. The post of the upper floor, which is mortised both to the anchor beam and the jetty plate, contributes to the overall cohesion of the structure. This type of jetty is very rare in the Pays d'Auge, and the example found at Coupesarte

On the courtyard side, the façade of the old residence has retained all of its original frame, sole plates, bay posts, and jetty dating from before the major alterations carried out at the start of the 17th century, when the cross bracing on the chimney breast was extended to all of the façades.

The extraordinary economy in the treatment of the materials used in the construction of the two corner turrets contrasts sharply with the effect achieved: a few slender timbers supported in a fashion by three oblique shores, some tile nogging, and a shingle roof all combined in the exceptionally well-balanced proportions.

by the subtle arrangement of timbers. All of the horizontal timbers are identical in width: the impressive jetty is replaced with a thin girding beam of the same cross-section as the window sill. This bare façade is made up of three unevenly sized horizontal bands: a large first floor with vertical timbers only, followed by a narrow window breast with cross braces, and an upper section with vertical timbers intersected by diagonal braces arranged in pairs on either side of the posts framing the windows. This part of the building is very homogeneous. At most, it is possible to distinguish a hesitation or interruption to the building work in the last three west bays which is indicated by the changeover from a window breast with two cross braces per bay, to a single longer cross brace between the posts. The same hesitation is perceptible with regard to the windows, which go from two windows, arranged one on each side of a post, to a single large window between two posts crowned by a dormer.

The construction of this return wing in the early part of the 17th century was accompanied by a complete overhaul of the *logis*: only the frame was preserved, and the very simple medieval infill framing was replaced by timbers arranged so as to match the appearance of the new wing. The old *logis* had to be completely stripped and reduced to the skeleton of its frame before the carpenter could add the elegant window breast with cross braces similar to that on the new wing but adapted to the larger width of the original bays and half-bays.

After this major transformation, the only remaining parts of the original construction were the frame, the large trefoil roof light, and the upright wall members of the first bay on the courtyard side, which can be identified from their large cross-section and by their cob and lime nogging. The majority of the floors seem to have been preserved, recognizable by the exceptional width of the joists, which are laid broad side down. Two hipped dormers with fully centered window openings and a window breast bearing cross braces were created on the roof of the original *logis*, again with the aim of creating a uniform appearance on the façades on the courtyard side. In those places where it proved impossible to create a new molding profile on the original frame, the carpenter was content to nail on

is almost unique. In fact, the archaic nature of the system by which the anchor beam is joined to the post corresponds to that of the decoration on the cross-bar, which consists of a single very hollow chamfer bordered by two blunt torus moldings at each end.

All of this part of the *logis* – or at the very least its frame and the few remaining vestiges of the original carcass on the first floor – dates from before the end of the 15th century.

The return wing, which is separated from the original *logis* by the bay housing the staircase, looks very different: its elevations have no oversailing elements. The jetty has completely disappeared and the timbers are much thinner. The powerful interplay of shapes, shadow, and light provided by the oversailing upper story described above is replaced

simple molded panels, and an example of this can be seen on the middle rail on the south wall. The splendid tile nogging which extends across all the walls clearly also originates from this second phase.

The two turrets, which served as latrines, must have been added shortly afterwards. It is difficult to imagine their being built for any other purpose, except perhaps as a way of emphasizing the uniformity of the rear elevation.

The remains of the interior decoration of the return wing confirm the suggested date of this major reconstruction phase: although the window openings right in the center of the dormers bear some similarity to those – copied from stone architecture – found on other timber buildings from the Renaissance period, the upstairs fireplaces, the ceilings painted with floral motifs, and the walls decorated with *trompe l'œil* panels would situate it more towards the beginning of the following century.

The lines, cartouches, and stenciling enhanced with trompe l'œil studs are exceptionally vivacious. These ceilings also provide an amazing record of the flora of that time: each joist bears a carnation, a rose, a lily, or some other flowering plant.

The upper chamber at the south end of the logis is adorned with remarkable painted wood paneling, portraying a series of mythological figures including Cupid and Juno on a wood-effect background.

Apart from some modifications to the windows, the manor of Coupesarte has not undergone any major renovation work since then.

In the course of the 17th century, emphasis shifted to the interior decor which was extremely elaborate, particularly on the upper floor of the original *logis* which is decorated with wood paneling and glazed tiles from Le Pré-d'Auge. Particular care and attention was given to the south chamber, which was quite unusual in a modest-sized manor house like this. A series of mythological figures, including Cupid and Juno, is portrayed in grisaille, under a molded ceiling featuring garlands and foliate circles surrounding a *trompe l'œil* sky above a painted section of wood paneling decorated alternately with vases and crowns, intersected with palms or leafy swags.

The lower panels depict alternating vases and crowns, monochrome urns, and palms beneath a frieze of lightly sketched garlands. The cartouches have trompe l'œil studs at their corners and Juno, wearing a helmet with an owl on top, looks towards a depiction of a shepherd.

It is all an illusion, even the trompe-l'œil garden with a perfectly crafted false window opening onto it. The eye focuses on the view of an embroidery garden with the dolphin of the fountain spewing forth water in front of a country house, which could easily be a design by Androuet Du Cerceau.

The glazed terra-cotta floor tiles from the kilns of Manerbe or Le Pré-d'Auge form a carpet of shimmering colors. Each motif, often composed of four tiles combined, covers a section bordered with bands bearing a strictly linear design.

Evening sunlight on the monochrome figures of the painted wood paneling: Cupid sits astride a lion between Juno with the peacock and Juno the warrior.

Evening sunlight on the floor patterns, which have faded over the years. Some of the tiles have been restored, giving a hint of the original intensity of color of these interiors.

The east moat at nightfall reflects this exceptional building which was badly damaged in the last war but was preserved with the help of careful restoration.

Courson

Behind the exterior of a modest manor house, Courson reveals itself as one of the most appealing seigneurial dwellings in the Pays d'Auge. It boasts a long history stretching back over nine centuries and skillful architecture which bears witness to the development of the art of carpentry – enhanced here by the superb red tile nogging – between the end of the Middle Ages and the Classical period.

The compact timber-framed *logis* stands on the edge of a plateau and is extended at right angles to the main section by a wing which serves as the outbuildings and was probably once part of an irregular enclosure punctuated by a circular dovecote and possibly by a second tower indicated by aerial photographs. A line of timber-framed farm buildings was later built opposite the *logis*.

Could this be the original home of the illustrious Curzon family from across the Channel, known, amongst other things, for providing Britain with a

viceroy of India. The theory is a plausible one, since the name Robert de Courson appears in the Domesday Book in the list of those who accompanied William the Conqueror in 1066. The first known lord of this estate, holding a full knight's fee, he was probably responsible for the construction of the small timber keep which used to stand on top of the *motte* encircled by ditches and which is still recognizable at some distance from the existing manor. The name of Hubert, one of the last Coursons, is mentioned in 1225 before the fief passed by marriage to the Courtonne family, mentioned in 1320, and then to the Belleau family. They owned it for little over a century until the marriage of Marie de Belleau to Jean de Neufville in about 1437. Their son Ancelot, who appeared in 1469 at the "General demonstration of nobility for the bailiwick of Evreux" "dressed as a vouge-bearing soldier, mounted and armed accordingly", was granted the title lord of Courson. This was when the new manor house was constructed – or reconstructed – on the current site, at the end of the Hundred Years' War.

The estate was first sold in 1662 to Nicolas du Houlley, counsellor at the Parliament of Normandy. Two generations later, in 1714, the fief of Courson was transferred by marriage to the Rioult de Neuville family, which disposed of it in 1797.

The text of an itinerary written by Charlotte des Ursins, Baroness of Ferrière, gives us an interesting picture of the estate in 1604: "Item, Gabriel de Neufville holds, within my said barony, a whole knight's fee, called the fief of Courson... , which fief has independent powers of justice and jurisdiction, its own men, allegiances, hills, thirteenths, income in deniers, grain, birds, provostship services, and other rights and privileges belonging to a full fief, there is the land in fee and not in fee, the manor, houses, dovecote, workable and unworkable land, woods, heaths, and extensive pastures... ." The

The reconstruction dating from the end of the 15th century centers on the staircase turret on the rear elevation. The open gallery has been closed in on the right and concealed on the left by the pentice of the oratory.

construction of the manor had been commissioned by Ancelot de Neufville about a century and a half earlier. The *logis*, which faced east, must have extended over quite a considerable length corresponding to the first nine bays of the present-day building, resting at the north end against a stone gable and terminated to the south by a timber gable, now incorporated within the building since the extension.

A timber *logis* of smaller dimensions with its two floors leaning against the stone gable was built adjacent to this original structure in the latter part of the 15th century. The four regular bays are centered on a double chimney stack of four flues, back to back in pairs. There is a hexagonal staircase tower on the rear elevation and an open gallery on the upper floor. These two elements of spatial distribution have several unusual features. Firstly, the gallery is not built in the usual way as an overhanging structure but is integrated into the body of the building. As a result, the ground floor rooms, and the hall in particular, are of a large site and offer space which the two chambers on the upper floor, limited by the presence of the gallery, did not really need. Secondly, the polygonal staircase turret is curiously topped with a pitched roof with scalloped edge rafters. There was no doubt a plan, which was never implemented, to create an upper chamber similar to the oriels which are familiar features in Norman architecture.

The attractive appearance of this four-bay *logis* was formerly enhanced on the west end of the main façade by two dormers aligned with the two large windows on the upper floor and positioned symmetrically on either side of the chimney stack: that closest to the stone gable has survived. The single door was originally positioned at the far right-hand end of the structure in the position now occupied by a window.

The polygonal staircase turret seems to have been designed to carry a quadrangular oriel and not a simple pitched roof.

and bearing the three round coronets of the Neufville coat of arms. Its position on the outer wall of what was no doubt the main hall of the *logis* is significant; this was distinguished on the interior by the presence of a sizable stone fireplace with two double doors to the side of it and lintels finely carved with oak and vine branches on either side of a second shield with three coronets.

Several decades later, the *logis* was extended to the south in two consecutive phases. The first phase involved the construction of the two adjacent bays and was very respectful of the design of the existing structure. This extension can probably be attributed to Thomas de Neufville, mentioned in 1540, who no doubt wanted to provide his *logis* with a grander entrance. To this end, he had a new finely ornamented door fitted: the protruding lintel is carved with cartouches with alternately square and rectangular knotwork and bordered with fine cable moldings, a motif already encountered at the manor of Chiffretot. The coat of arms appears again on a shield with a waved outline placed on an oval cartouche edged with stylized foliation.

A final extension was built in the second half of the 16th century and extends right up to the last bay, the surviving part of the original *logis*. It is indicated by a large dormer with a pitched roof, and geminated windows on the upper floors, which were built much less meticulously using numerous recycled timbers or timbers of small scantling. The coat of arms of the Neufville family appears here one last time in full: "gules in chief ermine and three coronets or".

Nicolas du Houlley took possession of the ancient *logis* in 1663, although it was probably hardly in keeping with his status as counsellor at the Parliament of Normandy. He was careful with his money, no doubt pious, and apparently limited his ambitions to the creation of a chapel, or rather a tiny oratory, on the ground floor of the north-east corner between the staircase turret and the stone gable. However, by commissioning the admirable tile nogging, which is decorated with lattice work, rosettes, herringbone and chevron patterns, he gave this venerable *logis* its loveliest feature. The date 1671 is inscribed in the middle of these motifs beneath the sill of the last bay to be built.

The decoration is extremely austere and sparse being limited to the chamfer of the mullions and transoms of the windows, the sturdy moldings on the jetty and cornice, and the small trefoil ends of the posts supporting the projecting ends of the bridging beams.

The building's status as a seigneurial *logis* is, however, affirmed by the presence of a raised shield on the fourth post bearing a coat of arms showing a man's head, which has become very worn over time,

Crèvecœur

The fortified site of Crèvecœur is situated in the valley of the Vie river not far from where it joins the Dives. It is an important fortress, and in his *Roman de Rou*, Robert Wace mentions a lord of Crèvecœur who fought alongside Duke William in 1066 at the time of the English conquest, a service for which the vassal would have been rewarded with several properties across the Channel. Later, we find the manor inhabited by Jehan de Crèvecœur, mentioned in the "Rôles de l'Échiquier" (Exchequer List) for Normandy in 1195. His descendant, who bore the same Christian name, was conscripted into the king's army in 1236, after the conquest of Normandy by Philippe Auguste.

This fortress at the bottom of the valley comprises two enclosures surrounded by deep moats. The outer bailey, which was defended by a gatehouse with a footbridge and drawbridge, shows no trace of outer walls and was probably enclosed by timber stockades. It contains the chapel, built at the end of the 12th century, the dovecote, and various outbuildings. These include an extant large timber *logis* known as the "gatekeeper's house" which was built at the end of the 17th century. This first enclosure gave access, via a second drawbridge, to a second enclosure containing a large *motte* surrounded by high walls without flanking, on which one can identify the traces of a large, square tower, a timber *logis* on the west side, and a well, which was originally covered with a roof on four wooden posts.

This *logis* is very typical of the houses built up to the end of the 15th century: it was, no doubt, constructed to replace an earlier *logis* destroyed during the English occupation before the fortress was taken by Dunois and the Counts of Clermont and Nevers in 1448. It consists of five timber-framed bays on two floors, now supported by a lower floor built in stone which has undergone numerous modifications. The robust long-post structure, which is not decorated in any way, is strengthened by diagonal braces. The original window arrangement has recently been restored. The large rooms of the *logis* have two mullioned and transomed windows on the ground floor and two windows with just a mullion on the first floor. The originality of this *logis* lies in the structure of the south gable wall, the side of the house which is most exposed to the elements, where the carpenter created an almost vertical awning which rests on the projection of the plate and is supported by an arch brace. A similar arrangement exists at the manor of Le Logis at Beuvron-en-Auge and is known to have existed at the manor of Tordouet before it was extended in the 17th century.

The dovecote in the outer bailey was probably built during the same period. It has a square plan

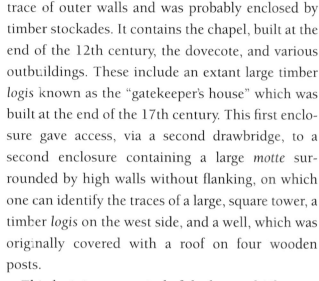

The outer bailey, which is circled by moats, contained all the buildings connected with the running of the estate as well as the chapel and the dovecote.

The defensive walls of the timber logis *on the* motte *support the long-post structure, which is protected on the south side by a large tiled awning supported by the projection of the wall plate.*

and shows a more marked concern for the perfection of the lines than the actual *logis*. Its long very thick posts rest on plates with beveled joints which enclose the two horizontal bands of a strictly vertical infill framing. The dormer, which provided an exit for the birds, occupies the central bay of the south roof slope and contains two openings above a window breast patterned with saltires.

The *logis* on the *motte* and the dovecote were probably built by the same carpenter: this is evident from the concern shown for the protection of the structure. The roof overhangs are particularly well defined using edge rafters to form a perfect full arch on the dovecote dormer and projecting trusses with

a collar beam, ties, and arch braces on the two gables. However, the carpenter was not happy to leave it at that: he formed a discreet drip molding on the ground sill and created a series of sills cut into semi-trefoils around the four sides of the building, making it possible to produce the elegant projection of the weather tiling which covers the upper section.

Judging by the position of the chimneys on the west wall, the molding on the sill of the first floor windows, and the rail running half way up the upper floor, the large *logis* in the outer bailey was built at the end of the 16th century.

A timber stockade probably stood alongside the moats around the outer bailey and linked all the buildings together. The dovecote, unusual in that it is square in plan, has reverted to its original function and still has its pigeonholes in oak planks and its revolving ladder. The large building which contains the entrance gate to the outer bailey was known as the "gatekeeper's house" in the 17th century.

View of the motte showing the water-filled moat, the defensive walls, and the manor house. The chapel, gatekeeper's house, and dovecote can be seen in the background.

OPPOSITE:
The dovecote has had a tiled roof since it was first built. The eaves are supported by a series of brackets pegged to the upright wall members, similar to those which support the awning over the exit window on the gable.

FAR RIGHT:
The motte, its moat, and the defensive wall, which the logis backs onto.

Criquebeuf

Architectural experiments abounded in the late Renaissance and early Classical periods. The master builders who designed the manors of the Pays d'Auge were no exception when it came to experimenting with new forms, varied volumes, and skillful compositions. They tried, with varying degrees of success, to interpret the great models familiar from engravings, or sought inspiration from employers whose wealth enabled them to engage the most skilled and talented craftsmen.

The *logis* of the manor of Criquebeuf was built as part of this movement and represents one of the interesting expressions of these experiments from the latter part of the 16th century. It consists of a central structure with two half-projecting towers at the corners of the main façade.

The du Mont family owned the Criquebeuf site in 1378 before it was sold by Jeanne du Mont to Étienne Labbey on 21 May 1433. He kept it for only a few years, selling it on 6 November 1454 to Jehan Rioult, lord of Le Vaudorey at Bonnebosq and of La Pierre at Auvillars. We know that this estate belonged to Étienne Michel from 1523 to 1540 and it is likely that he used the name "Étienne de Criquebeuf" when he was admitted to the nobility.

In 1600, Louis Le Gouez was lord of Criquebeuf. He sold it to Guy Hue and in 1633 it passed into the hands of Nicolas Patry, squire and master of Mutrécy, whose descendants retained possession of Criquebeuf until 1726.

The client who commissioned the construction of the manor house was not short of money: he decided to use beautiful green-tinged ashlar taken from the limestone beds on the edge of the plateaus overlooking the valley of the Dorette. He was, however, prevented from realizing his dream of a large residence constructed solely in this material.

The timber-framing of the south façade of the central section contrasts with the homogeneous ashlar facing of the corner towers and the rear elevation.

The client wanted to banish any reminders of medieval times by abolishing the archaic staircase turret from the rear elevation. Thus, the staircase turret had to be integrated into the main body of the residence with the result that the space available on the interior was reduced. By deciding to keep the line of the roof ridge of this part level with that of the corner towers, he was forced to give it a much gentler slope, thus contributing to the compact appearance of the building.

The two towers are built on the same, roughly square, plan and have the same platband marking the separation of the two floors; nevertheless they display some distinct differences. On its upper floor, the east tower has a tiny, perfectly centered window, which is bordered with a small flat molding and has a loophole on each side. The roof of this tower rests on a timber cornice supported by strong ogee brackets. The window on the same level of the west tower has a wider and off-center window and a series of small square window openings beneath the cornice.

In view of the numerous discrepancies between the original plan and the building as its stands, it is possible that the person originally responsible for the design issued the instructions, led the first construction phase, and then handed over responsibility for the completion of the residence to another master builder. The first phase appears to include the east tower, the rear elevation of the central section, and the first floor of the west tower. The second phase would, thus, have included the upper part of the west tower, the timber façade of the central section, the additional band running around the four elevations, and finally, the roof of the central section.

The logis of Criquebeuf is almost completely hidden behind its flourishing garden, although the corner wing and the slightly projecting turret on the rear façade are still visible.

Criquebeuf

The timber-framing of the main façade is treated very simply and contrasts with the care bestowed on the elements constructed in large cut stone. This no doubt indicates that the work was carried out by two successive master builders with different budgets at their disposal.

The first phase included one of the towers and most of the masonry on the rear elevation.

The irregularities of the building, which appears to have been completed with some difficulty, can be completely ignored thanks to the design of the gardens which now give the manor of Criquebeuf a totally new architectural perspective.

Cricqueville

The lofty roofs of the château of Cricqueville rise at the foot of the hill overlooking the valley of the Ancre. These three amazing slate peaks, which one might expect to find on a far more prestigious building, contrast with a surrounding landscape of hedges and trees, rather than blending with a formal expanse of gardens laid out in a continuation of the bold lines of the residence, which would normally surround such a building. All this only adds to the astonishment at finding such architecture here, and the perfection of the proportions indicate that it is the work of an excellent master builder well versed in the very best techniques. The former fortress of Cricqueville probably stood on the site of the present-day *château*. The outer bailey, still surrounded by walls and adjoined by the buildings connected with the running of the estate, is certainly still as it was in medieval times, the only difference being that most of the moats have disappeared: the cider-press, cow sheds, barns, lofts, stables, coach-houses, garden, pond, and orchards, all described in great detail in a valuation report dated 20 February 1793, are still virtually intact, their timber-frames originating from many different periods having been repaired, reinforced, and adapted over time.

The master builder reserved his most distinctive work for the rear of the château, both in plan and in elevation, setting the bold checkering of the walls against the soaring slate roofs.

All that is missing today is the octagonal dovecote, which was extant at that time.

In the 13th century, the fief of Cricqueville was owned by the de Silly family before coming into the possession of the Launay family; it is not known why this change of ownership came about. Guillaume de Launay was lord of Cricqueville at the end of the 15th century, and his eldest son, Benoît de Launay, a priest, was recognized as a nobleman in 1540. His heir was his nephew Guillaume de Launay, who married the daughter of Marguerite Le Veneur, whose high lineage and aristocratic status no doubt played a part in the projects carried out at Cricqueville by their son Robert. In 1576, the latter was in the service of Tanneguy Le Veneur, count of Tillières, the king's lieutenant in Normandy. By way of recognition for his renowned war exploits, the king appointed Robert de Launay as a gentleman of his Court and knight of his Order. His first marriage was to the widow of Guillaume d'Annebaut, but he later married Marguerite Richard, daughter and heir of a counsellor at the Presidial of Caen. Robert de Launay then embarked on the reconstruction of the *château*, whose residence was completed in 1584; this date appears on one of the ground-floor fireplaces.

The house is built on an extended quadrangular plan. It has two floors and two small octagonal turrets on the corners of the south façade. The north side, which stands opposite the rather solid central section of the *logis*, has two quadrangular towers on the north-east and north-west corners and a three-floor center tower, all three of which are crowned with outstanding hipped roofs. Their impressive height is part of the tradition of enormous roofs erected in such large numbers by the Normans from the start of the 16th century. The walls are constructed in extremely regular brick and stone checkerwork with a single band separating the floors.

The highly elaborate ogee cornice is supported by double brackets separated by simple square rustication and follows the forms which were well developed in France in the 16th century. A portal frame, located on the ground floor between the central tower containing the staircase and the north-east corner tower and consisting of three perfectly finished arches, represents the motif of the gallery which became fashionable at that time and was the sign of a quality building.

All of the apertures are still in their original positions, with the exception of one window on the upper floor of the central section near the north-west tower. Apart from the three full arches of the portal frame, the openings are all relatively tall with a single casement and are evenly arranged in vertical bays, with the exception of the openings in the north-east tower which differ on account of the presence of a door on the ground floor. The staircase windows are grouped in pairs and offset towards the east to allow for the installation of latrines in the return wall.

The tiled roof of the main body of the building does not have any roof openings. These are reserved for the slate roofs of the towers: there are two openings on each of the corner towers and one on the east return of the central tower. These stone dormers are one of the features commonly employed on the Caen plain in the 16th century and are found in several residences in the Pays d'Auge. They consist of small arched window openings cut into thick shaped blocks and faced with a curvilinear pediment whose carvings have almost completely disappeared. There are several small roof vents in finely worked lead bearing the initials of the builder, "R de L", on the upper parts of the roof. These provide ventilation for the roof and add a note of variety to the slate surface.

The elegant appearance of this manor house easily detracts attention from the defensive provisions still in use at that time of its construction. The north façade merges with the continuous wall defending the outer bailey, and although the gallery appears as a prestige feature largely open to the exterior, the two end towers are constructed on a bastioned plan. The three openings in the lower part of the central tower, which were intended for holding weapons, can still be seen.

Since its construction, the north façade seems to have been designed to look out onto a garden, the size and layout of which are completely discernible: it had a rectangular plan aligned with that of the façade and bordered on the other three sides by gently sloping levees, which, in keeping with the traditions of lawn design, no doubt overlooked a lawn on a slightly lower level.

The south façade has been greatly modified; the large windows featuring segmental arch lintels on both floors of the central section and the plasterwork which conceals the original surface of the walls were added in the 18th century.

However, the overall shape has barely changed, or at most through the addition of an unsightly pointed pediment in the center, no doubt designed to rival the high roof of the central tower of the

There are no long uninterrupted views from the château of Cricqueville. Instead, the approach routes were lined with hedgerows or passed through small orchards, and led to what was once the enclosed, formal garden at the foot of the three towers.

The many buildings of the outer bailey stand against the walls of the former enclosure and are centered on the large pond.

Although the buildings were modified many times in response to changing requirements, the covered staircase leading to the apple loft above the cider-press still survives.

north façade which rises above the roof ridge. The main gate in the south wall of the outer bailey on the axis of the house also dates from that period.

Observation of the evidence preserved in the walls of this façade enables us to reconstruct its original state with certainty: the checkered pattern of brick and stone continued on the side façades and over the whole of the ground floor, including the octagonal towers. Above that there was a slightly jettied timber-framed structure, probably including one level for the window breast bearing saltires beneath the window openings, a mid-rail serving as a continuous sill, and an upper level containing the windows.

This arrangement involving a first floor entirely constructed in masonry became increasingly popular in the 17th century. The novel feature at Cricqueville, however, is the octagonal turrets at the corners of the house. This is a rare example of a symmetrical

composition and the development of this motif can be noted in other buildings of that time, such as the *logis* at the manors of Caudemone, La Chapelle-Haute-Grue, and Chiffretot, which, however, only have a single tower of this type.

The interior layout is dictated by the staircase which was located in the central tower: it is likely that a master builder familiar with the beautiful masonry of the Caen plain was involved in the construction of this tower. The materials for the dormers certainly originate from this border region. A small side staircase leads to the upper chamber, in keeping with the medieval tradition of the oriel. A slim partition consisting of molded and matched panels divides the chambers on the upper floor. The interior of the *château* contains some exceptional decoration, in particular, three fireplaces whose design departs from the models in common use in the region. One of these, dating from 1584, can be found behind the gallery in the large hall on the ground floor: it has a flat overmantel, which probably once displayed a painting, framed by cable moldings with two superimposed cartouches bearing the coat of arms of the owner, Robert de Launay, "argent, an eagle displayed, sable" and of his wife, Marguerite Richard, bearing "six annulets,

arranged as 3, 2 and 1". This is topped by an imposing cornice centered on a grimacing horned face decorated with leaves and stylized gadroons, cable and wave moldings. However, the most original feature of this fireplace is the beautifully shaped piers which have, however, been significantly modified. The piers are decorated with caryatids surrounded by elaborate volutes; the figures – a man and a woman – bear an astounding degree of ornamentation and also figure on the corresponding fireplace on the upper floor.

There, one finds the same flat mantel, surrounded in this case by knotwork with palmettes and rosettes decorated with ribbons. The caryatids on this fireplace, which are surrounded by wide leaves decorated with volutes, are less curved in form and have a more hieratic attitude which further accentuates

The contrast between the outbuildings and the logis lies in the natural and informal character of the one, and the rigid, considered style of the other. The Italian-style gallery assumes the most unexpected forms using lovely traditional materials.

The unusual decoration of the upstairs fireplace is not the only example to be found in the Pays d'Auge of the exoticism which enhanced the repertoire of the artists of the province, but it is certainly one of the most accomplished.

the singularity of the representation. The sculptor has added more volutes: they surround the heads in the manner of an Ionic capital and form a support for the hands of the figures and the bases of the leaves. The figures are wearing strange belts and braces decorated with cartouches and their hair is arranged to look like feathers and beads. They are surrounded by bunches of fruit whilst the plinths and bases are decorated with masks surrounded by curtaining and knotwork. These motifs are related to those which began to appear in Normandy in the early years of the 16th century in the wake of the great discoveries, in which sailors from the province played a major role, sailing from the ports

of Honfleur, Rouen, and Dieppe. At that time, exoticism was a popular theme, particularly on the occasion of the solemn arrival of Henri II and Catherine de Médicis in Rouen in 1550, when the celebrations included "... fifty genuine savages recently arrived from overseas ... along with two hundred and fifty Rouen citizens ... dressed and equipped in the style of the savages of America...". Therefore, the caryatids at Cricqueville should probably be seen in the context of the subjects which inspired numerous representations connected with exoticism in Normandy at that time.

Judging by the surviving evidence on the elements of the wooden partition on the upper floor, the painted decoration was no doubt of the same style, scattered with cartouches and floral motifs. It featured alongside the glazed terra-cotta tiles, some of which are still incorporated in the old floors.

Les Demaines

The manor of Les Demaines occupies a prime location on the edge of the plateau. This belvedere, which stands amongst meadows and apple trees above the plowed fields of the plain, enjoys a view over the valley of the Dives. The timber *logis* is relatively long and incorporates some of the agricultural buildings. It forms a cluster of complex shapes, distinguished by two projecting structures and two large dormers. Several set-backs in the plan mark the projection containing the extension for the cider-press followed by the beginning of a two-story return wing with its high gable. A huge building with a gallery along the front supported by individual posts extended from this wing until it was destroyed in about 1950: this structure was either a secondary *logis* or may even have been the original *logis*.

The current *logis*, although disfigured – the staircase turret originally attached to the rear elevation was severed – is still of great interest due to the quality of both of its structure and decoration, which combines elements inspired by Gothic tradition and new Renaissance forms. The master builder deliberately avoided medieval practices: although he kept the central chimney block, he abandoned the traditional spatial organization and the usual arrangements for the window and door openings.

The windows on the main façade are still arranged in two vertical bays but are designed as simple rectangular openings without mullions or transoms, lintels softened by a slight curve, and with saltires on the upstairs window breasts. There is a single door in the right-hand end of the building and another opening in the gable, which is contrary to every tradition.

The complete lack of symmetry in the main façade is further highlighted by the two large dormers to the right of the chimney, which are not neatly aligned with the windows of the lower levels, are divided by a central mullion, and edged with end rafters in the shape of a pointed arch. A third identical dormer probably existed to the left of the chimney. This was mentioned in the brief description given by Arcisse de Caumont in 1867 and replaced at a later date by an opening of much smaller dimensions. The two projecting structures were later added to this homogeneous structure; the archaic decoration on the posts indicates that recycled timbers were used here.

The essential quality of this *logis* lies in its exceptionally refined decoration, which dates it in the second quarter of the 16th century. A twisted colonnette stands out from the main body of each post on the first floor of the façade. It merges at the top into the projections which appear as the posts gradually thicken as they approach the jetty.

The two projecting structures on the façade of the logis could be an example of a feature which was widely used in urban areas. Although some homogeneous examples found on rural logis have been traced to the 16th century, those at the manor of Les Demaines are an attractive addition built as part of a second construction phase involving the recycling of older materials.

The jetty and the frame posts have Gothic features and more modern decorative motifs placed side by side, like this frieze of light scalloped foliation on the bressumer.

This feature, still in the Gothic style, matches that of the moldings on the wall plates at this level, and especially the decoration on the lovely door with an ogee head, which is protected from the rain by the front overhang and framed by crocketed pinnacles curving up to culminate in a fleuron emerging from the feathery leaves. The jetty bressumer takes up the motif of the interlocked cable molding carved with egg patterns and imbrication, which is typical of the most elegant houses of this period. The cable-molding which covers the larger front overhang and joins up with that of the jetty seems to have been carved at a later date, at the time of the creation of this adventitious element.

Newer elements are identifiable within this decoration, in the form of light scalloped foliation below the inner edge of the ogee arch, on the last projection of the posts, on the window frames, and inlaid in the moldings on the sills or wall plate. The most innovative feature can be found on the gable door above the traditional ogee arch: the tapered crocketed pinnacles have made way for elegant balusters bearing bands and foliation which are undoubtedly a Renaissance feature, as are the large running foliage decorations, now almost entirely effaced, which follow the curves of the ogee arch and its row of pearls.

The interior decor is similarly meticulous and skillful. The more ornate fireplace on the ground floor has a rounded hood supported by two columns with polygonal bases and capitals.

A triple molding starts on the piers, intersects itself, and spreads out into a monumental ogee arch on the mantel. Two painted scenes representing the

There is no apparent reason for the total lack of symmetry in this logis, although it certainly does not detract from the harmony of the building. However, we can imagine how it looked with an identical third dormer on the left of the other two.

The astounding ash blond coloring of the carvings, which are protected by the central projecting structure, further adds to the quality of the ornamentation on the jetty, bay posts, and door frames.

The only direct concession to the sculpture of the Renaissance is found on the gable where the pinnacles and fleurons of the door with its ogee arch are presented as foliated banded balusters.

Annunciation and a hunt of St. Hubert can still be distinguished beneath the soot on both sides. As Charles Vasseur reminds us, there were "capricious running foliage decorations with little figures between the leaves" following the hollows between the moldings; these are still visible on a photograph from 1926. However, there is no longer any sign of the rich painted decoration which covered the whole room, whose "transverse beams and ceiling joists were painted with running foliage and cartouches", nor of the "traces of polychrome decoration" on the walls, the effect being completed by the flooring of glazed terra-cotta tiles. Charles Vasseur attributes the construction of this residence to Louis Thabarie, lord of Les Demaines in the 16th century.

181

Le Désert

Who would not dream of retiring to the "desert" were it in a place like this. In the Pays d'Auge, there are several toponyms involving the name "Désert", usually in combination with the name of a place, such as "Désert de Daubeuf" which is not far from here. A desert in this context is a clearing on the edge of a forest, many of which existed in the 15th century.

The estate of Le Désert was established soon after the Hundred Years' War by the Le Danois family, who invested some of their income from their main activity as prominent navigators in this clearing in the Touques forest. A letter from the royal officers in Cotentin dated Monday, 18 June 1492 mentions the "two ships belonging to Jehan Denis and Jehan le Danoys of Honnefleu, which recently arrived from Messina and Naples loaded with good-quality rich merchandise of great value, and took refuge in Barfleur, fearing the English". These Le Danois appeared on the list of brothers in the register of the Brotherhood of Charity of the parish of Notre-Dame in Honfleur: this mentions Guillaume Le Danois in 1457, Jehan Le Danois in 1461, Robinet Le Danois in 1492, and in 1513, another Jehan Le Danois who is identified as the "person in charge of provisions for the warships assembled in Honfleur under the orders of René de Clermont".

This contrast between distant maritime adventure and the peaceful country house is one of the charming aspects of the manor of Le Désert and is perceptible in both the location of the estate on the edge of the plateau overlooking the town and the Seine estuary and the appearance of the residence itself.

The manorial enclosure, about a hectare in area, is bounded by a flint wall of man's height. Now in ruins in several places, it contains several loop-holes near the gates on the north and south side, which were no doubt the original entrances. Inside this quadrilateral, the buildings stand in a regular parallel arrangement and close to the limits of the enclosure: the cowsheds to the south, a coach-house to the east, and the stables and press to the north. Only the *logis* is separate occupying a more central position facing the large pond and close to the oven and the well.

Apart from the contrast between the peaceful nature of this rural location and the defensive nature of this modest enclosure, there is also contradiction in the astounding architecture of this *logis*: a tall slim timber-framed upper floor is hardly what one would expect to find above this large ground floor with its solid masonry consisting of limestone and flint in fine irregular checkered patterns. The first level with its sober regularity and pure lines is firmly rooted in the land-owning tradition whilst the second reminds us of the daring work of the master carpenters of naval architecture, even to the extent of the provision of a look-out post at the top of the staircase turret, which seems to have been rocked sideways by the ocean wind. The plan of the residence is noticeably different from those generally in use in the second half of the 15th century: as usual the two main rooms form a regular rectangle, but the spatial organization does not follow traditional practice, in which the staircase turret and the upper gallery are located on the rear elevation. At Le Désert, the imposing polygonal tower stands in the middle of the main façade and dominates the entire *logis*. The entrance door is located at the foot of the tower beneath a lintel with an ogee arch with pinnacles at its corners, and gives direct access to the two rooms on each level. The staircase continues right up to the attic where a second spiral stair leads to the rectangular look-out chamber. The tower dominates the structure to such an extent that its roof

The manor of Le Désert is one of the most uniform and complete 15th century ensembles still in existence today. Even the enclosure walls, garden, and orchards have survived.

rises a good few inches above the main roof ridge and this largely accounts for the unusual silhouette.

Is it possible that this tiny upper room, which is reached directly from the outside, was the determining factor behind the most unusual position of the tower and of the entrance door?

It has been suggested that the tower was a later addition. However, this theory ignores the tradition of the oriel so widespread in Normandy. The aim of creating an ideal observation post overlooking the estuary must have been sufficient justification in itself if the personality of the owner is taken into account.

Let us again turn our attention to the ground floor. The perfection of the lines, the absence of movement in the masonry, everything indicates that it was designed and built with exceptional care. The main façade received most of the attention: its two mullioned and transomed windows, one on either side of the tower, have a complex structure with cyma reversa moldings, which are also found around the entrance door; this contrasts sharply with the simple chamfer found on the rear elevation. The same applies to the band at the base of the walls, which is reduced to a single cavetto on this side. The four sides of the rectangle are supported by the same number of angled buttresses, following a practice which was common at the end of the 15th century, although usually reserved for larger buildings.

Was the original plan to build the whole of the manor house in stone? The answer to this question can be found by examining these buttresses. They are all constructed in an identical manner, intersected halfway up by a drip molding and topped with weathering – all, that is, with the exception of one, the buttress on the north-west corner. The upper course of the weathering on this buttress reveals the start of the right corner of the upper courses which extended just a few inches and were never laid. This theory is also supported by examining the masonry parts located above the last course of the first floor: the impeccable pattern of dressed black flint alternating with hard limestone gives way to rougher masonry with the ashlar and flint cut in simple squares, particularly on the north and south gables. In the absence of any documentary evidence

The original design involved a two-story structure of checkered limestone and flint masonry. Financial constraints seem to have resulted in the upper floors being constructed in timber. The most original aspect of this logis lies in the dissociation of the staircase and the open gallery on the upper floor, which are usually both situated on the rear elevation. The symbolic and imposing presence of the tower on the main façade, in which the main door is located, was no doubt a major consideration in the design process.

on this matter, financial constraints seem to be the only possible explanation for this modification to the original design.

The master mason was therefore succeeded by the master carpenter. On the main façade, the timber-framed upper floor is slightly jettied and wind bracing is provided by diagonal braces fitted against the posts.

A molded sill which sits on the timber framework determines the height of the mullioned windows on this level which are vertically aligned with those on the ground floor; the window breasts are decorated with saltires.

The five bays of the gallery on the rear elevation, which oversail by almost a yard, are much lighter in appearance. The four posts spread out into double angle braces and support the sizable roof slope above the guard rail, which was clearly reworked in the 18th century, as indicated by the double diagonal braces on each bay.

Inside the *logis*, each of the rooms has its own character. The large room on the south side, reduced in size by the later addition of a partition, still contains its immense fireplace, whose richly molded mantel rests on piers with two colonnettes of different diameters. A fireplace of more modest appearance with a bare mantel and a mysterious sculpture on the capital of one of its piers stands on the north wall. I will leave it to some inquisitive zoologist to identify the strange animal, which is closer to a kangaroo than a rabbit, and the long cylinder which the animal is cautiously approaching. Could this be a memory from a distant expedition, or is it the fantasy of a mischievous sculptor? I am more tempted to go along with the first theory.

The floor of this room has kept its large stone tiles, polished by generations of hobnailed shoes. The walls faithfully copy the checkered pattern of the exterior facing, however, it would appear that a coating of lime plaster had been applied over the dark rough flintstones; this coating is still partially visible in the large hall and on the walls of the staircase. The ceiling with its neatly trimmed beams and joists ends in wide cross-bars on the façade walls and, strangely, shows no traces of smoke. The fireplace with the enigmatic capital also seems hardly to have been used.

The same division into two rooms of unequal size can be found on the upper floor; the two chambers overlook the staircase landing on one side and the gallery on the other. The larger room, on the south side, was renovated in the 18th century: its monumental fireplace has disappeared and been replaced by a simple fireplace with no piers or overmantel. Several red ocher lines on the walls emphasize the contour of the plasterwork of the partition separating the two rooms, a modest decoration, and the only one of its type which we are aware of.

The smaller chamber is perfectly intact. A magnificent fireplace occupies the center of the gable wall and contrasts starkly with the austerity of the simple whitewashed floor. Here one finds the same piers with colonnettes, polygonal bases, and capitals bearing a corbel with a molded end, all cut

from the same block of fine-grained limestone. The hearth and the fire-back are finished in tile fragments positioned horizontally or on their edges and are intersected by the relieving arch. The mixing of materials continues on the mantel which is made of tufa and supported by a molded timber lintel positioned at a slight slant.

The traces of the original windows revealed simple solid wood shutters which could slide up and down in vertical grooves in the window jambs. A particular harmony of half-shades and absence of bright colors reigns in Le Désert, this place where the maritime location and the influence of "neighboring" regions inspired an original expression in the art of construction.

As a symbol of the contrasts embodied by this residence, the country house of an ocean voyager, precious ship graffiti is drawn with an unsteady hand here and there on the lime nogging or the stones of a buttress, taking us back five centuries to the time when Binot Paulmier de Gonneville, who, as a neighbor, was no doubt received at Le Désert, left his manor of Le Buquet and set sail for the virgin territory of Brazil.

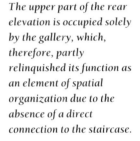

The upper part of the rear elevation is occupied solely by the gallery, which, therefore, partly relinquished its function as an element of spatial organization due to the absence of a direct connection to the staircase.

Les Évêques

Few of the manors of the Pays d'Auge have inspired lithographers and artists as much as this one. It was certainly on the route of the early sea bathers attracted by the growing popularity of the town of Trouville. It was the very symbol of the "picturesque" as expressed by artists and those who wanted to promote a new kind of regional architecture. The manor of "Les Évêques" ("the bishops") presented the ideal image of the timber-framed "Norman" manor. A legacy of the Middle Ages and enhanced by the prestige of its episcopal name, it had the seductive volumes, variety of materials, range of colors, and imaginative forms to appeal to the fertile imagination.

The various graphical representations of this manor constitute a perfect summary of the changing status of this class of cultural inheritance. In 1867, Arcisse de Caumont published a bird's eye view in his *Statistique monumentale du Calvados* showing the manorial organization in a careful and purely descriptive drawing. The lovely drawing produced a few years later by Charles Mozin is no longer an archeologist's observation. It represents the manor with extraordinary accuracy and precision, evoking at once the atmosphere of the farm which the manor had become, the worn

The manor known as "Les Évêques" has a very small enclosure, which meant that the various, usually well spaced, buildings had to be positioned close together. As well as the main logis, *there is a small secondary single-story* logis *with double doors and a dormer.*

The only bishop who actually took up residence in this manor was probably this clumsy effigy, carved at a later period on the central post of the small logis after it had been confused with the parish of the same name in the Orne region, where the bishops of Lisieux owned an estate.

lathing of the tiled roofs, and the robustness of the timber structures. All of these impressions are depicted in the minute detail, in which he also portrayed in the ribs of a ship lying high and dry in the Touques estuary, making it possible to imagine with accuracy the slightest repair to the framework, the entire situation being translated with the sensitivity that came naturally to this friend of the pre-Impressionist circle.

This manor was eventually popularized by photography at the beginning of this century in issue 136 of the periodical *La Vie à la campagne* (Country Life) where it featured in a series entitled "Old *logis* of Normandy – rustic manors". Here it was presented as the archetypal country house, "made interesting by its large gables and the effect of the overhangs" and intended to act as an inspiration to architects in the design of country houses.

Despite all of these interpretations, the manor of Les Évêques has retained its authenticity and today more or less tallies with its description in *Statistique monumentale*. Still partially surrounded by walls, its buildings stand in an irregular pattern in the courtyard, which today is only missing the porch for the carriage and pedestrian gates, the central dovecote, and the cowsheds and stables which used to stand along the east side.

The main body of the manor includes a two-story *logis* on the north side, which was rebuilt, extended several times, and partially reconverted for agricultural use. This contrasts with a connecting single story secondary *logis* adorned by a large central dormer.

The name "Les Évêques" is relatively recent: there was no fief of that name in the parish of Canapville. It seems to have acquired the name after being confused with another place of the same name situated in the *département* of Orne, near Vimoutiers, where the bishop of Lisieux owned a

The stone tower and the adjacent chimney stack are the oldest parts of the logis. *The timber structure which was added later on comprised, from its origin, a porch which protected the entrance to the storeroom.*

"*domus episcopi*" mentioned in the visits of Eudes Rigaud, Archbishop of Rouen, in 1258. This fact is no longer disputed since at that place, known as "the hamlet of the bishops", there is still a *motte* where the episcopal manor probably stood. The confusion persisted – or was possibly even encouraged – when a primitive carving of the head of a bishop wearing a miter was mounted on the middle post of the secondary *logis* of our manor of Canapville near Touques.

The construction of the oldest parts of this manor can possibly be attributed to Loys Despassam who lived "near the château of Touques" in 1416 and two years later was appointed vice-seneschal by the Duke of Clarence, brother of Henry V, and put in charge of the administration of the income of the bishopric of Lisieux. The new king of England, Henry VI, then granted him his noble sergeantry in the forest of Touques. Despite having served its occupants so well,

the manor and land belonging to Loys Despassam and inherited by his daughter after his death, were then sold by decree as soon as the English had departed and were acquired by Benest de Launoy, counsellor in the lay court, living in Clermont. A few months later, on 8 April 1448, he sold the estate, described in the bill of sale as "a free vavasory located in the parish of Canapville, comprising a *logis*, the land around the said *logis* and all the other workable land planted with crops or used as pasture and meadows below the residence", for 260 *livres* to Guillaume de Bertreville (or Betteville).

Two years later, on 19 April 1450, the manor was sold to the "venerable and discreet person Jehan du Fossey, master of arts and lay bachelor, for 300 *livres*", after which his family owned the estate for over two centuries.

Recognized as the "free vavasory of Canapville" granted by the king in his viscounty of Auge, the

All the dormers and ornamental gables over the doors are well built and varied. The gable above the doors on the small logis is the only one in which a section of the king post appears at the top, enabling the two principal rafters to be held in place more securely.

row of stone corbels, probably designed to hold the angle braces supporting a sharply oversailing timber-framed upper chamber, resting on what was formerly the last leveling course and positioned three courses above it. This element has disappeared having later been replaced with a simple extension of the tower built using slightly different stone. The fireplace on the first floor stands in a wide recess in the wall; it has no piers or mantel and is covered by a single segmental arch. None of these features survived in the Pays d'Auge after the occupation by the English. The piers of the fireplace on the second floor project vary slightly and support the stone mantel which curves towards the flue and rests on a timber lintel; this fireplace was restored at a later date.

The rest of the residence was without doubt damaged and gradually rebuilt by Jean and Étienne de Fossey: they were responsible for the addition of a wing to the west of the chimney block. This wing is still extant and comprises three long-post bays facing the courtyard and a jettied structure on the rear elevation and the gable; the profile of the overhang is still visible on the courtyard side, although now obscured by a subsequent extension. This first phase of reconstruction was executed with great care and included a painted decoration which is still discernible on the ceiling beams, comprising, in particular, a group of fleurs de lis, which could be interpreted as a symbol of loyalty to the king of France after the troubled period of the Hundred Years' War.

A second phase of construction was undertaken on the east side above a storeroom with stone walls and half below ground level which is probably a surviving part of the residence built by Loys Despassam. The new structure consisted of a three-bay timber floor. It had a much higher roof ridge, was supported by beams between two plates, and had no jetty.

It contains a continuous row of windows with a shared sill provided by a molded girding beam. A highly original polychrome pattern was used for the nogging on the window breast and in the gaps between the plates; this consists of rectangles of red brick alternating with rectangles of lime mortar, and was probably carried out at a later date. The

manor and its land passed from Jehan to Étienne de Fossey, a squire, mentioned in 1484. Then came Jehan, mentioned in 1490, 1510, and 1511; Pierre, mentioned in 1534; Jacques, in 1565, and Daniel. His son, captain Jean de Fossey, received from the king a "mandate to raise and lead one hundred soldiers" on 8 July 1635. The presence of the de Fosseys at Canapville ended in the next generation following the death of Henry, who had no direct descendants and left the estate to his four sisters. It was gradually restored by the Costart family who kept it until the end of the 18th century.

All that remains of the residence built by Loys Despassam are the masonry elements, in this case the polygonal staircase turret and the chimney block which is vertically aligned with the turret. Each element has unusual features. The turret has a

The small logis, which originally had hardly any windows overlooking the valley, has had many windows added with positive results.

central bay has a dormer whose end rafters form a pointed arch giving it a perfectly regular appearance.

We do not know the reasons which led to the addition of a beautiful porch to this façade. It may have been intended to protect the entrance to the half-buried storeroom with a porch similar to those which appeared in the region of Caux in the following century.

It is certainly true that, thanks to its jetty, its end rafters in the shape of a pointed arch, and its roof line, which is the same as that of the adjacent dormer, this structure blends elegantly with the body of the residence, subtly breaking the symmetry, an act which stands in sharp contrast to the design principles generally accepted at that time.

The *logis* at the manor of Les Évêques is not clearly separated from the buildings for the running of the estate, as would ordinarily be the case: the barn, cellars, and lofts extend the building as far as the east corner of the enclosure. It includes complex structures, with a clear contrast between, on the one hand, the new extension to the residence containing a straight-run staircase, which stood parallel to the façade and rested against a large gable with a jetty and end rafters, and, on the other hand, the shorter almost totally blind structure. The modifications to the façade on the courtyard side make it difficult to discover the exact chronology of the building, and make it impossible to find out why such importance was placed on the external staircase and the gable on which it was built. At most, one could hazard a comparison with one of the two *logis* at the manor of Saint-Loup-de-Fribois, which has a similar arrangement. We are, thus, inclined to attribute the completion of this residence to Pierre de Fossey in the second quarter of the 16th century.

The secondary *logis*, which stands on the west side of the courtyard, could also have been built in the 16th century. Its timber framework only covers a single floor, centered on two twin doors and surmounted by a large gable window consisting of a series of four windows along its entire width with the window breasts bearing saltires, the only place in the manor where this motif is used. This building was then extended on both sides so that it joined the main residence. Daniel de Fossey was probably responsible for the construction of the square stone and timber dovecote, in the final years of the 16th century, which unfortunately burnt down in 1920. It had a lovely hipped roof and a dormer on the same axis, which was supported at the base of its slope by pronounced sprocketed eaves, and featured a terra-cotta finial which merited a mention by Arcisse de Caumont.

Until the early part of the 17th century, the only means of access to the courtyard was through a porch containing a double gate in the east wall. A new entrance was then created in the south wall, in the form of a simple pedestrian main gate. This gate was covered with an open stone pediment, crowned with a quadrangular vase, and may have overlooked the gardens which have since disappeared.

The exquisite quality of this manor lies not only in what has been added to the house by its present owners, but also in the work of the modest craftsmen of the past, as exemplified by the attractive molding at the base of the screw of the cider-press.

Fribois

There used to be a priory called Notre-Dame in the former parish of Saint-Loup-de-Fribois. The priory, which was founded at the beginning of the 13th century, was a dependency of the abbey of Sainte-Barbe-en-Auge. The group of buildings near the parish church is often thought to be part of the remains of this establishment. This, however, is not the case: the archives relating to the sale of national assets contain a very precise description of the true site of the priory on the bank of the Vie, in the place called La Chapelle-Fribois, several hundred yards from this manor. Furthermore, it does not have the characteristics of a priory manor and is clearly recognizable as a lay manor with its buildings grouped together on the bank of the Algot, a tributary of the Vie, and still encircled by a network of water-filled moats.

Nevertheless, this manor has several unusual features which can still be observed today: apart from the farm buildings, the manor of Fribois comprises two very elegant timber-framed buildings which stand several dozen yards apart and both look like former manorial *logis*. In such cases, one of the buildings is usually a former *logis* which was abandoned and converted into an agricultural building

when a new house was built in the contemporary style. It is doubtful, however, that this is the case here as the two buildings were built no more than a few decades apart.

The building which tends to receive more attention is situated on the west side of the site. It is built on a very compact rectangular plan, has five bays on two floors, and is covered with a pitched roof which was later reshaped to produce a hipped end on the south gable. A block of three fireplaces occupies the center of the building, leaving sufficient space to accommodate the staircase within the body of the building. The interior spatial divisions provided a large room and a smaller room on each floor.

Although the plan of this residence is similar to the models often used in the late 15th and early 16th centuries, its structure is much more unusual. Whilst it looks like a jettied structure – its east façade has an overhang clearly marked by the presence of a highly molded timber – closer examination reveals it as a long-post structure, which the carpenter made to look like a jettied short-post structure. He simply reduced the thickness of the posts of this sturdy frame over the entire height of the first floor, created the transition using a decoration of single or double brackets, and added a very thick intermediate plate. This plate is elaborately molded with three tori which taper to a point as they approach each bay post, thereby simulating the decoration traditionally used on the bressumers of jetties. This is not an isolated example, as several *logis* from this period have this feature, and it dispels some of the theories surrounding the origin, function, economic and the technical advantages of the jetty, in that it plays a purely decorative role here.

The timber infill framing consists solely of vertical members, the braces being concealed on the inner

sides of the walls. A girding beam ran midway along the upright wall members of the upper floor and was held in place by the thickened portions of the bay posts and window posts.

The first floor of this façade had a mullioned and transomed window with a single chamfer, traces of which can be found on the third bay post in the north part, and probably also a small rectangular window opening in the south part. On the upper floor, two twin windows opened above the mullioned window on the first floor. The window which doubtless existed on the south part has not left any trace.

The small amount of decorative carving found in this *logis* is limited to the frame of the door on the north end: the lintel is decorated with an elegant blunt ogee arch surmounted by two vine branches. The figure on the corner post is more of a mystery; the weather has eroded his features making them less clear. One can make out the upper half of a man under an ogee, his long hair hanging down on each side. He is holding a stick diagonally, in a pose very

similar to that of the "savage" carved on one of the porch posts of the manor of Desmares in Lisieux, which is known to date from between 1482 and 1505 because of the presence of the coat of arms of Bishop Étienne Blosset de Carrouges on the ogee of the same structure.

The second "*logis*", which is sometimes portrayed as an exceptionally well built farm building, was clearly always intended to be lived in. The present gable has the traces of a door and empty mortises on the upper floor indicating that the building used to be about two bays longer with the last bay probably forming a porch on the first floor. It includes a rubble first floor on the south façade which is used as a storeroom. The living space was limited to the upstairs rooms which were accessed from a large covered staircase. A straight flight parallel with the east façade leads to a landing sheltered by an avant-corps which is presented like a real gable, decorated with a projecting truss with a tie beam and a collar, the principal rafters and the straining beam forming a blunt trefoil at the top.

Two substantial logis in a single manor which were built in close succession using radically different techniques and ornamental repertoires. It is possible that the older structure, on the right, was relocated to this site at a later time. Such practices were common and are confirmed by documentary evidence.

The second logis of the manor of Fribois is one of the most important examples of long-post structures with a simulated jetty, which is purely esthetic in function.

There are two doors on this landing, each leading first into an antechamber and then into a room with a fireplace.

This arrangement has been preserved in its entirety in the west part, with the exception of the partitioning, and must also have existed in the east part, where only the antechamber has been partially preserved, despite the disappearance of the floor, removed during the conversion of the storeroom into a cider-press and cellar. The ceiling beams, the joists, and the spaces between them of this antechamber show the substantial remains of the painted decoration produced at the end of the 16th century, consisting of a series of *trompe l'œil* coffers in yellow and red ocher separated by rosettes with interlacing.

The structure of the upper floor of the south façade consists of an interrupted row of small windows with wooden shutters which slid along in grooves in the window posts, above a continuous girding beam which formed the sill and a window breast displaying saltires. The same pattern continues on the frontispiece, originally designed as a front overhang supported on two posts. The north façade is not as refined in its detail. Its framework is composed of long posts and it has only two small

twin window openings. According to dendrochronological analysis, the oaks used in the construction were felled between 1470 and 1480.

The function of this building still needs to be explained. Despite the technical differences between them, there is not much of a gap between the construction dates of these two "*logis*". They cannot, therefore, be successive dwellings and must have been used simultaneously. It is obvious that the isolated building standing on the west side served as a *logis*, but the function of the "east residence" is less clear: what was the purpose of the chambers and ante-chambers on the upper floor above the storeroom which were so brightly lit and heated by at least one if not two lovely Gothic fireplaces and reached by this large external staircase? The matter becomes even more obscure when we consider the west end of this building. A timber-framed extension was added to the building containing the storeroom and living area. The extension has the same structure as the original building but the two are very badly joined. The extended building contains a hall on the first floor, with a fireplace dating from the end of the 15th century, and another room of the same type on the second floor; this part has evidently lost a bay following a fire, the traces of which are clearly visible. Uncertainty will remain until the history of this manor is finally revealed.

The covered external staircase is the most original feature of this logis and gives it its monumental character.

Mystery also surrounds this carving on the north corner of the first logis: the man's posture and the way he is holding the stick are reminiscent of the "savage", a decorative motif in common use at the start of the 16th century.

The presence of the bunches of grapes on the adjoining lintel is less of a mystery: vine growing and wine production were still common in the Pays d'Auge until the end of the last century.

Glatigny

Jean Faulcon built his manor in the second quarter of the 16th century not far from the port of Touques, from where his family originated. He kept the *logis* apart from the other buildings, which were scattered in the vicinity, and rejected the idea of a closed courtyard, the traditional arrangement which closely involved the lord in the daily life of his estate.

Although, no doubt, from a land-owning family, he distinguished himself from the other lords in the area. Had he traveled to distant countries, or participated in some armed campaign which took him out into the world? He had his *logis* built by a very skilled master carpenter who was highly trained in the best traditions and commissioned him to create some very elaborate ornamentation with a distinctly modern accent which definitely reveals something of his personality.

His descendants certainly appreciated the lovely timber dwelling. However, they too wanted to leave their own mark using the very latest techniques and add the refinements which had become part of the lifestyle of country nobility. Thus, they added two north-facing brick and stone wings to the south-facing medieval timber structure and closed off the small courtyard with a high blank wall containing a pedestrian gate crowned with a tiny square turret. A bridge here crossed the moat surrounding the residential block.

The water-filled moat has only survived on the north side. The blank wall and the small square turret were unfortunately demolished in about 1960. Fortunately however, the manor of Glatigny has preserved the essential elements of its 16th and 17th century structures and remains an excellent example of the architecture of this period.

The large timber *logis* built by Jean Faulcon is based on a structure which conforms to medieval principles: it comprises eight bays on two floors and is rectangular in plan. Due to his wealth, Faulcon could afford a residence which was larger than those of many of his neighbors and comprised three rooms per floor. The carpenter did not show a great deal of imagination in meeting these requirements. He was content to build the usual structure of six bays with two rooms per floor, centered on the chimney block with doors at both ends, and to add the two bays for the additional room on to the west end.

The hall occupied the central position, as indicated by the wider bays and the complex accolade on the lintel above the entrance door. This arrangement is totally devoid of originality and explains the presence of the two twin doors and their dissimilarity. However, this façade succeeds in retaining its uniformity thanks to the arrangement of the windows in three vertical lines which is emphasized by the three mullioned dormers with their trefoil end rafters. The carpenter wanted a robust structure: there was no question of concealing the diagonal braces which support the two corner posts on the upper floor, the south-west corner post, and one of the bay posts on the lower floor, and which could not be positioned symmetrically. The mullioned and transomed windows were located in the middle of the bays in the right-hand section of the building where the rooms occupy three bays, whereas in the last two west bays, the center post served as a mullion. A continuous girding beam ran along forming the sill for the three windows on the upper floor. The decoration made a few small concessions to tradition in the form of the ogee over the three doors and a few scalloped colonnettes with crocketed pinnacles on the window posts. The jetty is still used here but with new-style molding, incorporating cymas and ogees, which appear again on the window sills. The spirit of the Renaissance is already perceptible: the thickened post ends

A small traditional château was built in brick and stone at the back of the carefully preserved timber logis. *This meant that the old timber-framed staircase turret had to be given a new look. The courtyard was closed in by a blank wall, which was destroyed in about 1960. The wall had a slim turret on a square plan, with round-headed window openings on two levels, and was reserved for pedestrian access.*

arranged in elegant spirals. These could be the heads of his wife and his daughter and heir Suzanne who passed the Glatigny estate to her husband Gilles de Giverville, squire and lord of the manor between 1620 and 1640.

The Renaissance façade is therefore still in its original state and only one modification was carried out with great skill in the latter part of the 16th century. Windows were scarce, particularly in the large central hall and the original window was later replaced by a wider opening; the sill was lowered, and the lintel raised, interrupting the cross-bar and the girding beam which had served as the lintel. The window posts and the mullion were decorated with fluted Ionic pilasters surmounted by volutes decorated with foliage which also appear on the window breast. A frieze of ovolo patterns and knot-

work decorates the transom and the sill, which is supported by two ledges.

Despite the very personal nature of the decoration of this *logis*, it was so old-fashioned in its structure and layout that it failed to satisfy the person who occupied it from the early years of the 17th century. Suzanne Faulcon could not allow the beautiful building inherited from her father to be destroyed and when her husband Gilles de Giverville decided to give his residence a new north-facing façade with two new wings, he left the old timber *logis* fully intact. These two wings stand opposite each other and have completely separate roofs. Construction started with the east wing, which is aligned with the gable of the timber structure. The brick walls contain vertical bands of rusticated, toothed ashlar, and the two levels are

The structures overlooking the courtyard show how the builder gradually mastered the art of laying courses and vertical bands of toothed ashlar. In the central section of the building, the window openings occupy complete bays and do not show any of the imperfections still visible on the east wing.

separated by a single platband. It is possible to detect a slight lack of expertise in the way in which the masonry has been executed on the east face of this wing: the windows, also framed with rusticated stone, do not seem to have quite enough space between the vertical stone courses, their keyed lintels clumsily interrupt the band, and their sills have no connection with the other lines on the façade.

The central door is attractively positioned beneath a small wooden porch but the cornice seems to have been left roughly cut, awaiting a molding which was never added.

Such imperfections do not feature on the west wing. The window openings are arranged in very neat vertical bays; only ashlar is used here and the brick is reserved for the infill consisting of glazed brick ends laid in a lozenge pattern. The rustication is very elaborate. To accompany the highly elaborate styling of the cornice, a beautifully molded band was positioned below it. This west wing consists of two bays and is joined to the north-west corner of the timber dwelling rather than being aligned with the gable, as is the case with the east wing.

The intention is clear but the project was not completed. Indeed, the old timber-framed *logis* was extended by an additional bay built of brick and stone, respecting the gradient of the roof but remaining slightly set back in comparison with the new west wing. The simple brick wall on the south end of the building, which has no toothing quoins, is clearly an unfinished job. This extension of the timber *logis* was in fact to become the central section of a new façade, a plan which would involve the construction of a second west wing, symmetrical with the first. This ambitious project must have been halted in 1619, the date which appears on a cartouche on the dormer of this "central section": it is true that the living area of the residence had already almost tripled.

The desire to leave the timber *logis* entirely intact produced a rather unusual layout in the courtyard which had to serve both wings and give the ensemble an attractive architectural harmony. The north wall of the old residence was faced with a new wall of brick and stone and the old turret containing the staircase of the original *logis* was left in its original position but decorated with the same combination

of materials, leaving three oculi following the shape of the staircase. Only the upper part retained its timber frame and was harmonized with the other upper floors by means of hung slating. Thus, the turret now stands in the south-east corner of the courtyard and the remaining space between this structure and the west wing was filled in a perfectly symmetrical manner by a central bay containing a door and an oculus surmounted by a small pediment and a bay on either side with windows and dormers.

A large Renaissance window replaced the single window with its chamfered mullion on the first floor of the timber logis.

The rich decoration on the timber frame, some of which has been recently restored (for example, the siren on the south-east corner), indicates a subtle hierarchy in the functions and uses of the different parts of the residence.

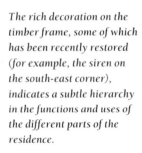

Grandchamp

Poised on a wide valley floor, the château of Grandchamp – former residence of the Marquises of Saint-Julien – does not really fall into the category of a manor. However, by studying it, we can fill in some of the gaps in our knowledge of manorial architecture. Indeed, it boasts the only surviving example of those innumerable timber towers, which served both as a *logis* and a keep and are mentioned many times in the documentation; it is a late example but unique in the region.

The château, a vast neatly composed ensemble surrounded by moats, has two quite distinct parts which differ in terms of both their volume and material. The first of these consists of an imposing timber-framed building which is built on a square plan and has two quadrangular turrets adjoining its rear façade. Its three stories are covered by a tall hipped roof containing two dormers with projecting hipped roofs. The four floors of the turrets with their narrow windows are linked by galleries of decreasing width and crowned by imperial roofs topped by lanterns.

The second part of the château consists of a long two-story brick and stone building which is aligned with the main façade of this timber structure. This structure has a slightly projecting avant-corps surmounted by a gable, which cannot really be described as a pediment due to its complete lack of styling. The slate roof, which is punctuated with tall brick chimneys, has a row of dormers with triangular pediments and brick window breasts which emphasize the pattern of the window openings in the façade with new slightly arched lintels. The north-facing rear elevation differs noticeably from the main façade: the first floor is presented as an open gallery looking onto the gardens through a series of centered openings and, although the windows on the upper floor are the same, the roof here

The original logis *at Grandchamp, the last remaining example of a large medieval timber keep, was slightly modified by various additions before being integrated into a new Classical structure.*

has dormers with pediments alternating with bull's eyes, and is not interrupted by an avant-corps.

History has only a few pointers to give in the analysis of this building and the piecing together of its chronology. We know that Jean Barate was lord of Grandchamp in the 14th century and Montfaut found the château occupied by Jean d'Anessy (Jean d'Anisy) in 1463. Having come into the possession of the Mallevoue family, Grandchamp then passed by marriage to the Le Prévost family, who kept it until 1760. Jacqueline de Mallevoue, lady of Grandchamp, married Nicolas I Le Prévost (grandson of Thomas Le Prévost, lord of Le Coin, ennobled in 1544); their eldest son, Nicolas II Le Prévost, lord of Grandchamp, alive in 1598, was a lawyer at the Normandy Court of Subsidies. The four Le Prévosts who owned Grandchamp after that were probably the direct descendants of Nicolas II: Richard-Tanneguy Le Prévost, knight, Marquis of Saint-Julien, captain of a company of the Household Cavalry, lieutenant for the king in Normandy in the bailiwick of Évreux in 1695 who lived at his château of Grandchamp (1719) and his château of Baclair (1724) and died before 1730; Raoul-Tanneguy Le Prévost, mentioned between 1730 and 1756, knight, Marquis of Saint-Julien, lieutenant for the king in the Normandy government, cavalry captain in the Vassé regiment, knight of Saint-Louis; François Le Prévost, mentioned in 1760, knight, Marquis of Saint-Julien, officer in the King's Regiment, lieutenant for the king in the government of Normandy; Marie-Henriette-Suzanne-Perinne Le Prévost, who married in 1760 in the chapel of the château Armand de Montault, cavalry captain in the Royal-Piémont regiment and who ended the line of the Le Prévosts at Grandchamp. The château then passed to the Lebourgeois family at the end of the last century before its present owner carried out the major consolidation and

A substantial hipped roof and dormers were added to the long-post structure during the Renaissance. The frontispiece and "pediment" were a later addition to the subsequent brick and stone wing.

restoration work necessitated by its acute state of disrepair following a long period of neglect.

Although Arcisse de Caumont wrote in his *Statistique monumentale* "At Grandchamp we find one of the great châteaux of the end of the 16th and of the 17th century, without any of the modifications which have made many châteaux of this period unrecognizable", we are by no means looking at a building which is completely free of inconsistencies and alterations, or which was built in just two stages. In fact, its construction was spread over several centuries, with numerous modifications and additions, and probably ended with the abandonment of the majestic masonry structure which would have reflected the status of the Le Prévost family.

Descriptions of and allusions to the architecture of Grandchamp are no less equivocal, illustrating the problems of interpretation posed by this building, particularly the timber-framed section.

Gabriel Ruprich-Robert expresses his perplexity in a letter dated January 1889 written just after he had finished his description of this part of the building: "... a section built in timber and brick, more or less typical of the methods of construction and decoration used in timber-framed manor houses in the Pays d'Auge and near Lisieux in the 15th, 16th and 17th centuries. The entire building must have been constructed at the start of the 17th century, including the square half-towers on the rear façade, although the style of these seems more recent ...". In short, having surveyed this section, our expert architect and talented watercolor artist was still hesitating between the end of the Middle Ages and the peak of the Enlightenment.

It is certainly difficult to distinguish the various structural and decorative elements which make up this part of the château, and if one were to follow Ruprich-Robert's theory that it was built in the 17th century, it is difficult to believe that it survived so long. It is, therefore, useful to establish which parts of this building belonged to the original structure, what possible alterations have been made to existing elements, and which parts have been rebuilt or completely restored.

Despite what Gabriel Ruprich-Robert says, the type of structure found at Grandchamp is not actually very common in the Pays d'Auge. It is the only extant château with such a sturdy and simple frame: its façade of five bays is composed of enormous long posts rising from the plinth to the wall plate, with each floor projecting slightly. The projection of each floor made it possible to leave some space free on the corresponding top plates for a very flat decoration of cable moldings and chamfers edged with blunt torus moldings. This frame is reinforced in a rudimentary but effective manner by means of single diagonal braces which were fitted with no particular concern for esthetics. These original elements give the impression of a structure which could not have been built any later than the end of the Middle Ages, in which the enormous timbers compensated for the weaknesses in the jointing technique consisting of simple shouldered tenon and mortise joints. The traces of the openings in the original façade are now too few to tell us anything about the original fenestration. Nevertheless, it would appear from the surviving mortises of the window posts and the vertical returns of the decoration on the top plates above the posts that there were window openings on each level in the second and fourth bays and a door in the first bay on the left on the first floor. A masonry bay on the east façade indicates the presence of three superposed fireplaces and the three-story structure which sharply overhangs the moat probably used to house the latrines.

This is the last surviving example of the medieval tower, *logis*, and keep surrounded by defensive structures and comprising three superposed square rooms fitted with all the necessary comforts, and probably served by a staircase in one of the corners. This very simple arrangement is found in numerous residences dating from the second half of the 15th century, for example the *logis* at the manors of Tordouet and Querville which have kept the original internal staircase but are only two stories high.

There are few elements which can help us pinpoint the date of construction. However, the fireplaces on the first two floors confirm the theories based on the analysis of the structure, plan, and decoration: the piers of the second floor fireplace with their colonnettes supporting the corbels, which are decorated with cavettos and ovolos, point to the 15th century. However, the painted decoration on the mantel was clearly not created before the mid-16th century.

The recently ennobled Le Prévosts would not have been at all satisfied with such an old-fashioned dwelling. They totally rebuilt the upper parts and renovated the interior decor and the carving on the façade in the late-Renaissance period: the wall plate was replaced with an elegant cornice carved with knotwork, cartouches, and palmettes, supporting the new hip roof containing two carved dormers which have the same set of decorative motifs. The upper floors projected only very slightly on the façades: the post on the south-east corner on the second floor nevertheless had a small fluted bracket cut into it with very shallow recesses and without the standard relief. The projecting elements on the upper floor were decorated with coats of arms on medallions produced under the same conditions; these are unfortunately illegible today. They no doubt included the coat of arms of the Le Prévost family.

This construction phase no doubt included the reconstruction of the fireplace on the third floor, which was given piers with brackets decorated with fluted volutes. The painted decoration of the walls was covered with ornamentation consisting of plant motifs encircled by cable moldings and stencil and line motifs on the transverse beams and ceiling joists. The medieval fireplace on the first floor was also decorated with a beautiful painting representing Faith, Hope and Charity surrounded by *trompe l'œil* leather motifs. On the right return, an inscription, which unfortunately has no date, gives us the name of the lord of Grandchamp, the person who was no doubt responsible for this huge renovation program: "Niollas (Nicolas) Le Prévos".

The presence of the leather-effect background, which is rarely found in the architecture of the manors of the Pays d'Auge dates this work after 1550, although we do not know whether it was commissioned by Nicolas II, the lawyer at Normandy's Court of Subsidies, or his father Nicolas I, son of the first Le Prévost at Grandchamp. However, the quality and novelty of these motifs could indicate that this is the work of a man of similar taste – as Nicolas II might be – to those in the circles of power, where the very latest decorative themes were preferred.

The internal layout of this *logis* had become completely outmoded and the staircase placed in the corner of each of the three vast halls was no longer considered adequate. An original solution was found here in the form of a staircase with four newels housed in the square turret built on to the north-west corner. In the interest of symmetry, a turret on the same plan was added to the north-east corner. This turret contained three small closets adjoining the existing large halls on each level and a small attic room. Although they are identical in shape, the two turrets display some perceptible differences: on the north-east turret, the timber frame, which is striated on each level by braces dissecting the timbers contains long narrow openings, whereas on the north-west turret, each floor is lit by two small windows at the extremities and there is a large cross brace on the top floor. They were, however, constructed at the same time, i.e. the late-16th century, as demonstrated by the bare pilaster decorations on the corner posts. The were also fitted with superposed awnings supported by the projection of the top plates, a feature which was also added to the south façade at that time, but which has since been removed. The joists on the top floor extended to form a sort of cornice with modillions and supported the beautiful imperial roofs which are topped with lanterns.

The new plan for the château of Grandchamp probably included a central section aligned with the main gate. The only part of this plan to be completed seems to be a wing which was joined to the old timber residence.

This type of roof necessitated the use of slates rather than tiles: the lords of Grandchamp could afford this and the exceptional lead openwork decoration which can still be found on the ridge of the main roof.

The Marquises of Saint-Julien and lords of Grandchamp would not have been content with a simple timber *logis* for long, whatever improvements had been made to its spatial organization and decoration. The date 1681, which appears on the timber-framed outbuilding adjoining a small round tower near the bridge leading into the courtyard seems to correspond to an ambitious and partially successful project modeled on the great residences of the Classical period.

This involved the extension of the timber-framed structure to the west with a large brick and stone structure whose squat first floor contrasted with the elongated windows of its second floor and which terminated in a rather untidy rubblework gable. A large regular garden extended to the north and was bordered by a moat formed by a diversion of the river; the end of the garden was marked by two small timber and brick pavilions. The position of these pavilions marks the point that the new brick

and stone building should have reached. Was the intention to create a wing to match the old medieval timber residence? If this were the case a more suitable internal layout would have been designed for the central part of this new building.

It is much more likely that the builder planned to construct the main body of the château in the axis of the bridge leading to the courtyard, and that he began with one of the two return wings intended to accompany it, i.e. the north wing which was attached to the old timber *logis* and overlooked the newly laid gardens. After this ambitious project was halted, a central frontispiece of no great character, an entrance hall, and a staircase were added to ill suited positions in this north wing.

It is no great shame that the Marquises of Saint-Julien were unable to fully realize their ambitions: this would inevitably have led to the disappearance of the feature which gives the château of Grandchamp its exceptional character, namely that last timber keep, a unique surviving example of an ancient tradition.

LEFT:
The two square turrets on the rear elevation represented a initial step in the improvement of the comfort and interior layout of the old logis.

RIGHT:
Detail of the ornamentation carved on the slight cantilevers of the long-post structure.

Houlbec

I t is rare in the Pays d'Auge for such a small building to be so well defended, or at least to give the impression of being an impenetrable stronghold with no less than a ring of deep moats and four stone towers protecting the small *logis*, which originally consisted of just two large superposed rooms.

In 1456, Jean Le Bouteiller, lord of Houlbec, pledged loyalty and homage to Guillaume, baron of Courcy, for the land he had just given him. In the early years of the 16th century, one of his heirs, who was, no doubt, impressed by the nearby powerful fortress of Courcy, probably had the idea of creating a small château of his own, adapted to an appropriate size for his modest fief. The small dimensions of the square dovecote, which stands not far from the residence and the 80 *livres* given as an estimate of the value of the estate in 1552 when the "nobleman Henri Le Bouteiller" was lord of "Houllebec", indicate that this was a fief of fairly low status.

The buildings connected with the running of the estate are grouped to the north and the *logis* stands alone on its platform surrounded by water. The central part of the building is rectangular in plan, and the first floor and whole of the south gable are constructed in stone, which obviously explains the presence of the chimney on this wall; the chimney culminates in a molded stack with weathering marking the thickness of the wall. The other three elevations are timber-framed and have been modified at various times since they were originally built.

The main façade is on the long east side of the rectangle and is marked by the two symmetrical towers at its extremities: they are circular in plan on the first floor but hexagonal on the second floor and crowned with a steep hexagonal roof. The first floor is built entirely in stone and supports a timber framed second floor which has been substantially

modified: the cornice and the middle post appear to be the only remaining parts of the original frame and the wide windows, the rather thin upright wall members, the window breast with saltires, and the large pediment are 18th century additions. The contrast between the materials of the main façade was less pronounced in the past as it was partly hidden by a coating of lime plaster which can be seen in the print published in *Statistique monumentale du Calvados* in 1867.

The towers on the rear elevation differ significantly from each other. The circular staircase tower on the south-west corner with its conical roof is constructed entirely in small rubble stones: a very slight difference between the two levels indicates that alterations have been made, or possibly that the original structure was similar to that of the two front towers with the upper floor constructed in timber. The large quadrangular tower on the north-west corner has a stone first floor which is perfectly merged with the rest of the masonry: in other words, it was not added at a later date. The upper floor is timber-framed and faced with clay tiles which are fixed with mortar and nailed in place on the two most exposed sides. This means of protection (and decoration), which was widely used throughout the 18th century in the south of the Pays d'Auge, was installed at the time of the major renovation work carried out on the residence. Apart from its diminutive proportions, this *logis* with its rectangular plan and four corner towers was unexceptional; however, Houlbec manor does incorporate some very unusual elements like the timber galleries running between the towers on the south and west sides. These are, in fact, part of the original structure, as shown on the south side by the presence of a small strip of stone protecting the edge of the tiled roof, and by the transverse beams on the west side which project quite far to support

A pleasant garden tones down the heavy defensive appearance of the manor of Houlbec, which, however, remains completely isolated on its platform surrounded by water-filled moats.

the floor of the gallery. Both galleries would have originally been open between the bay posts and had a window breast bearing saltires.

The timber framework on the upper floor of the square tower and the east façade bore very simple decoration which only featured on the structural elements: this consisted of a few moldings on the cornice and the horizontal timbers, which were covered when the clay tiles or the lime plaster was applied, and a few carved elements on the thickened post tops. These are now very worn and show an illegible coat of arms and a curious "monster" in a vertical position, which some believe to be part of a recycled timber member.

Nothing was left to chance or the imagination in this small *logis*: the defensive provisions were designed to be extremely effective and the interior layout was very neat. The only important modification made since its construction, apart from the creation of most of the large windows, is found between the two towers on the north façade, whose original timber-framed gable still exists. This takes the form of a new façade which was built in the 17th century and aligned with that of the quadrangular tower.

The dovecote, the barns, cow sheds, and coach-houses are situated in the outer bailey.

*The 15th century dovecote
still has its trefoil dormer.
The holes in the timber
frame for the long pegs
which anchored the clay
pigeonholes on the inside
are still visible.*

*Houlbec has retained all of
the original features of the
spatial organization in its
logis such as the timber
galleries linking the towers.
In many cases, only traces
of such elements survive on
masonry buildings.*

Langle

The manor of Langle, also known as "Vieux manoir" ("Old manor") or "the manor of Le Lieu Gervais" stands in the former parish of Brocottes amidst the apple orchards of the Doigt valley.

The *logis* stands on the axis of a long drive and looks out onto the manorial enclosure which is still identifiable on the current site; a pond and a few dips in the ground level appear to mark the position of the former moats. Two outbuildings stand parallel to the drive on each side of the *logis* and border a neat courtyard. Most of the agricultural functions are fulfilled by a large building which stands further away towards the west.

This was long believed to be the former priory, a dependency of the Premonstratensian abbey of Belle-Étoile built on the estate which they had been given in the 13th century by the lord of Beaufour. However, it is more likely to be the seigneurial manor constructed by the La Rivière family at the end of the 15th century: a member of this family, Michel de La Rivière, presented his proofs of nobility before the Elect of Lisieux in 1540. According to a statement of debts owed by the parishioners of Brocottes to their priest, Étienne Binet, dated 1656, the fief then passed into the hands of the de Courseulles family.

The timber-framed two-story *logis* is constructed on a rectangular plan. The original five-bay structure had a door at each end of the first floor, and was roughly symmetrical with a central chimney block and a stair turret with a conical roof joined to the rear elevation. The layout of the two rooms on the upper floor was dictated by a narrow overhanging gallery which was covered by the extension of the roof on that side. The living space was extremely limited and the *logis* was lengthened by two bays on the east end in the early 16th century.

The decoration on the frame is still entirely in the Gothic style: despite the effects of the weather, a lintel bearing an ogee with pinnacles to the side of it and enhanced with vine branches can still be identified on the casing of the left door. The thickened post tops, which are decorated with a rather roughly cut bracket, support a jettied structure on transverse beams whose decoration departs noticeably from that normally found on this kind of rural edifice: the top plate above the moldings on the girding beam is decorated with a series of monsters, an unusual motif for this part of the frame which normally features a simple drip molding.

The date 1545, which appears on a frame post of the central window on the upper floor, has been widely interpreted as the date of construction of the dwelling. This is not the case: this post, which intersected the Gothic cornice, was inserted into the original frame in order to replace the narrow mullioned window with a wide window opening decorated in the Renaissance style. The old continuous girding beam which formed the sill was removed and all the windows in the residence were altered in this way, before being modified again at a later date. Only one window has survived in its original state; it can be found concealed by a pentice on the rear elevation. The mullion and transom are decorated with cable moldings with a floweret or a shell at their intersections. The same type of cable molding was used on the upright posts of the window breasts on the upper floor, where it is still clearly visible.

The three rooms on each level and the open gallery on the upper floor were again judged inadequate. The gallery was closed in – probably in the 17th century – and small pentice rooms were built beneath the overhang, thus preserving the precious Renaissance window.

The manor of Langle avoided any further modifications to its façades, apart from the addition of a

A ditch, now barely visible, marks the borders of the manorial enclosure. The medieval logis has survived. The construction of the two aligned outbuildings in the 18th century made it possible to create a proper courtyard.

LEFT:

On the rear elevation of the logis, the wide overhang of the gallery has been concealed by the construction of pentices on each side of the staircase turret.

The Gothic residence has retained part of its refined decoration, in particular the door with an ogee arch on the left. The windows on the upper floor were enlarged substantially in 1545 and even encroach on the cornice above.

short return wing on the east end of the rear elevation, whose frame of purely vertical timbers dates it again in the 17th century.

In the following century, many manors saw the disappearance of their medieval *logis*, which were considered too outdated, although the outbuildings were often preserved. However, at Langle, the former manorial enclosure was instead reorganized and two symmetrical outbuildings were added, one on either side of the axis of the dwellings; these new structures housed the stables, the bread oven and the distillery. Each is built on a square plan and crowned with a gambrel roof with very pronounced sprocketed eaves, which was later extended slightly to cover a lower building. The timber frames of these buildings are very neatly arranged in a herringbone pattern, and finished with red tile nogging which matches the warm colors of the roof. The window openings with segmental arch lintels com-

plete the effect of the unusually high-quality finish for buildings of this category.

These carefully constructed additions were no doubt intended to precede the total reconstruction of the residence – it seems unlikely that the owner would have put so much effort into the reconstruction of the outbuildings without planning to update the dwelling to modern standards. Fortunately, the plan was never carried out, and the manor of Langle today still presents a homogeneous ensemble with its medieval *logis* integrated into a space which was expertly reorganized in the late decades of the 18th century.

Work then began on the organization of the space beyond the limits of the medieval enclosure. This involved the creation of the south avenue, centered between the two lines of the outbuildings, and a pond on the north side of the site, which has since been filled in.

Le Lieu-Binet

L e Lieu-Binet was certainly never a fief but one of those country houses owned by a wealthy middle-class man with the resources required to build a large residence in the middle of his small estate. Today it is no longer possible to locate the date 1646, said to have been carved on the building, which would have corresponded very closely to the building practices employed here.

Timber was no longer builders' preferred material with brick and stone masonry now enjoying greater prestige: Le Lieu-Binet is the perfect expression of this development, and embodies a particularly creative interpretation of the new materials. The residence stands at the foot of the east slope of the Touques valley and is largely open on its south façade, while on the opposite side a long section of roof overshadows the upper floors; the roof here is supported by a single wall with a timber framework almost devoid of windows.

The roofs form large harmonious volumes punctuated with unexpected details. Although the two large dormers with sprocketed eaves and hipped ends follow the traditional models, it is very rare to find a covered staircase presented like a genuine porch, as in the case of that leading up to the right-hand door in the main façade; this is preceded by a staircase sheltered by the extension of one side of the roof. A similar feature can be found in the *logis* of La Pipardière, which predates it by almost a century, and at Glatigny. The care taken with the arrangement of bricks between vertical courses of toothed stones, and the quality of the masonry details such as the flat band, the small molded cornice on the top leveling course, and the casing of the central door with its projecting keystone were accentuated by the highly elaborate composition of the plan and elevations.

The master builder very cleverly took advantage of the sloping site when positioning the different

levels: a half-sunken storeroom is surmounted by the hall with the central door leading into it followed by the independent secondary living rooms, accessed from the external staircase which encroaches on the timber floor. The fenestration is also unusual: only the hall has the advantage of a proper window, the other windows being limited to two rows of four small square or rectangular openings, placed very high up between the cornice and the band, or very low down between the two doors. The main staircase on the inside is in an unusual position in the south-west corner of the masonry section and designed as a spiral staircase serving both the storeroom and the other floors. Considering the relative comfort of this building, it difficult to understand the absence of impressive ornamentation.

The residence of Le Lieu-Binet cannot have been designed to be like this from the outset. It appears to be the product of an ambitious first phase, as demonstrated by the quality of the masonry work, which was subsequently reorganized to accommodate the constraints of a more modest plan involving the incorporation of some of the agricultural functions, such as the press and cellars, into the main body of the residence. This would also explain the extension of the building to the rear and the large roof.

The first phase of construction was probably limited to the parts built in brick and stone. A timber-framed story was probably planned from the start, as at the manor of Querville: it was constructed with timbers of medium quality at the same time that the residence was extended by several yards towards the west using the same materials, as demonstrated by the positioning and number of diagonal braces above the slate-clad window breast.

This *logis* needed a unifying element and this was provided by its imposing roof, which was in perfect

proportion to the whole and supported by the canted walls of its gables. The architect achieved this result by making the dormers exceptionally large, almost too large in relation to the length of the slope, and by making their breasts taller then those on the floors below. The effect was even more pronounced before the disappearance of the central dormer, whose position is now marked solely by a single break in the eaves.

Another hypothesis has been put forward by Michel Cottin, who suggested that the timber floor and the roofs were part of an older building, the lower part of which was reconstructed using more "noble" materials. Bearing in mind what we know

about the ingenuity of the carpenters of this province and their skill in "using up the leftovers", this theory cannot be ruled out until the matter is finally resolved by dendrochronology.

Le Lieu-Binet is one of the familiar images of the Pays d'Auge, whose whimsical character is bound to elicit surprise and admiration. Since it is not a manor in the true sense of the term, it is easier to understand the liberties taken by the builders who, having produced a quality building, then proceeded to adapt it to a form more suited to the demands of agricultural production for which it was the base.

The only element of spatial organization at Le Lieu-Binet is the very approximate alignment of the apple and cherry trees planted in the courtyard.

Waiting and chattering impatiently at the foot of the steps outside the house. Le Lieu-Binet still has some remarkable original features like this hinged door with its ogee ironwork and large square nails.

The logis has a wide variety of window openings: the enlarged basement lights of the storeroom, the large window of the hall, the small openings squeezed in between the vertical stone courses and the oculus lighting the spiral staircase.

Mardilly

When Martin de Rupierre decided to reconstruct his manor house in the early part of the 17th century, his intention was no doubt not just to replace his ancient timber *logis* with a more comfortable abode, but also to assert his standing as someone far removed from a mere vassal rendering homage for his fief at Mardilly.

The Rupierre family were already established in Mardilly in the 13th century and also occupied several fiefs in the Touques Valley. Invested with important military offices, the Rupierres took up opposing stances during the Hundred Years' War, some championing the French king's cause, others backing the English side. This led to a number of confiscations, more than compensated for by acts of leniency when peace returned. Their descendant, Martin de Rupierre, came out for the Catholic League with the same enthusiasm, in testimony of which the Duc de

The impact of slate accounts for much of the quality of the house. It was a costly material, yet perfectly adapted for use on the four bell-shaped turrets.

Stone is handled with extreme restraint at Mardilly. Forgoing all sculpture, the master builder makes use only of the interplay of elementary rustication, the pediment, and the lintel with rusticated voussoirs.

Longueville conferred on him a certificate confirming "that he had served the King, with arms and impedimenta". He had then gone on his travels and got to know the builders of several large estates; among the cousins that preceded him at Mardilly was an advisor to Catherine de' Medici. However, he did not have the resources to fund the construction of a large mansion and was unable to set the work in hand until after his marriage to Catherine de Hudebert on 26 September 1604. This alliance with a quite humble local family was, however, insufficient to finance the new house, and at the end of his life, even after selling off some of his lands, Martin de Rupierre found himself overwhelmed by judicial seizures.

Martin de Rupierre wanted a residence of quality, which had a regular layout, perfect symmetry, and would conform to the new rules for the art of building. A fighting warrior of the League could hardly set himself up in a mere country house: he wanted it to be strong, planted on the site of the ancient fortress, and capable of defending itself against sudden raids from bands of partisans. He made it restrained in its proportions, rich in its simplicity and balance, and austere and noble in the quality of its materials.

There is not the slightest crack in this splendid block of stone, this sandstone with its russet glow, perched on a slight glacis atop the mound of the ancient defensive formation. Four turrets cling to the corners, perched on corbeled projections and becoming detached at the arris of the great slate roof. Adjoining them on the slopes of the hipped roof are two tall chimney stacks.

The house was very small, bearing in mind the sumptuous and costly materials used; all the more subtle is the treatment by the architect in endowing it with real grandeur. This is achieved by the justness of the proportions between the main block and its minuscule turrets, and between the high roof

with its steep straight pitch and the bell-shaped roofing of the corner features.

The proportions are stressed by a discreet articulation of floors, separated by a platband, which also marks the base of the turrets, and above all with a fine modillion cornice supporting the eaves of the roof. Monumentality is also achieved by means of a bold distribution of openings, both false and real. The axial doorway is emphasized by a rusticated surround, a lintel cut into a segmental arch, and a broken pediment on top which breaches the platband. The central staircase accesses two principal rooms on each floor, which are compact enough to need barely more than a single window per façade.

The master builder gave the main façade an exceptional stateliness by endowing it alternately with blind openings and windows of the same size. They are all capped by straight lintels with projecting keystones aligned on the platband, stand on breasts with quadrant corner pieces, and are finished in a slightly reddish brick. There is no attempt to make the blind openings seem otherwise by recourse to *trompe l'œil* devices. Quite the opposite in fact; they are filled out with brick identical to that used in the window breasts and emphasized by the diagonal lines of three superimposed lozenges picked out with glazed headers.

Three pedimented dormers finally add rhythm to the façade by stressing the window bays. A more open solution could not have been adopted on this façade, which initially looked on to a courtyard; the openings on the moat are also reduced to strict necessity. Martin Rupierre valued the security of his home.

The master builder of Mardilly did his utmost to create a robust but perfectly balanced residence, to the extent of getting us to forget that more than half the windows are blind, just for the sake of harmony.

The relic of a water-filled moat which once surrounded the motte *of the first castle, perhaps? The water remains, though more idiosyncratically laid out on the rear elevation. The building still bears the trace of the apertures of the staircase and the slight prominence of the latrines.*

Behind its highly "civilian" look lie a number of features which ensure that the house could be properly defended: the modillions beneath the dormers are in fact really machicolations allowing the foot of the house to be raked, and an internal well enables the defenders to stay under cover even though a spring rises beyond the moat. He also gave the house an individual character by his original handling of color. Though ochre is predominant, the contrast with brick is lessened by a sparing use of terra-cotta in closely similar tones on the window breasts and chimney stacks, which stand out against the somber shades of the slate.

Le Mesnil-de-Roiville

For anyone fortunate enough, the discovery of Le Mesnil-de-Roiville remains an unforgettable experience. Nothing prepares you for it, and the extraordinary adventure of its rescue by Henri Pellerin, and its reconstruction by an inspired restorer in the 1960s, hits you at the first glance. As modest in its scale as it is perfect in its proportions, as sober in its façades as it is exuberant in the volume and decoration of its roofing, Le Mesnil-de-Roiville is a building possessing every subtlety and contrast.

Contrasts abound: between light widely-spaced timber-framing and massive masonry pierced with narrow loopholes; between the house and the water suspended above it and held back with great effort; and between a winding shady drive and the severity of building lines and volumes. Equally eye-catching are the subtleties of ornamental sculpture, the nogging formed with fragments of red tiling, and the paving made of glazed terra-cotta.

The history of Le Mesnil-de-Roiville is more difficult than many others to pin down with certainty, as a consequence of the original fief of Roiville being split into two estates and records referring to one or the other being kept under the same name. Christophe Gouhier (1452–1504) acquired the fief of Roiville from Pierre Rouxel de Médavy, a close relative of his wife Isabelle Rouxel. Their descendants Guillaume, Charles, François (mentioned in 1625), and then Jacques continued to own it until at least 1698. The dismemberment of the fief continued, leading to the establishment of a quarter fief of Mesnil-le-Roiville, probably in the mid-16th century. First we come across one Pierre Rioult, esquire, installed there, then Jacques Gouhier, who passed Le Mesnil to Olivier Le Sec. François Deshayes acquired it on 29 September 1654 and then swapped it with Philippe Deshayes, counsellor to the king at the administrative seat, bailiwick

and viscounty of Orbec, on 23 October 1668. The latter's oath of loyalty for the fief to the king on 16 March 1679 contains the first brief description of Le Mesnil-de-Roiville as comprising "a demesne in fee and not in fee, houses and buildings ..., a dovecote on legs, warrens and fisheries in the River Vie, rights and fees in the parish of Royville ..., woods, gardens, meadows, pastures, arable and non-arable fields..." The Gouhiers appear again in 1758, in the person of Adrien Gouhier, an esquire.

Today there is no trace of the "dovecote on legs" of 1679, and it is difficult to discern the "buildings" mentioned at that date among the present structures. All that remains is the main house, handed down to us in the condition much as its builders left it, spared by alterations, respected perhaps for its exceptional quality.

The house of Le Mesnil reveals a plan of almost perfect symmetry. It has a central rectangular timber-framed block of six bays, comprising two rooms on each of the two floors, flanked by chimney stacks set right at the ends, and covered with a tiled hip roof. At the ends, deeply recessed into the corners, are two small square timber-framed pavilion blocks with the same elevation, covered with pitched roofs of four slopes. A tower built of beautifully dressed stone, centered on the rear façade and pierced with loopholes, contains the staircase. Its massivity and the solidity of its material contrasts with the slenderness of the pavilions in the main façade, while its slate roof dominates the whole roofing system, forming the strongest accents in a symmetrical composition.

The evidence indicates a plan and elevation based on a few simple principles of harmony. The plan is perfectly inscribed in an isosceles triangle. Its base is aligned with the façade with the two pavilions, while its sides are formed by the corners of the façade behind these same pavilions, of the central block and of the staircase turret.

The plan of the house is inscribed in an imaginary but precise isosceles triangle incorporating the corners of pavilions, main house, and staircase turret. The logic of the elevation is maintained by the strict alignment of the sills and girding beams, and the ridges of the pavilion roofs and body of the house.

The alignment of the ridges forced the builder to reduce the slope of the roofs of the central block, to take account of the difference of depth compared with the pavilions. He then judiciously adopts the same slope for the hipped roofs of the dormers on both.

Sculpted decoration is confined to the dormers in the roof, and contrasts with the strictly geometric composition of the lower parts. Ovolos, fluted pilasters, and gadroons stand out against a lattice of tiles.

If we assume the builder measured in units of one foot (approximately 30 centimeters), we find that the central block consists of two rooms of 20 × 20 square foot, while the little pavilions are perfect 10 × 10 foot squares, and the staircase turret is an almost perfect square 15 × 15 feet.

Thus, there was no master mason or master carpenter dictating the architectural design but a master builder familiar with mathematical proportions and the innovations popularized by the first 16th-century treatises on architecture; a builder well-educated enough to break loose from the medieval layout that had prevailed hitherto. Volumes are carefully individualized and articulated, while respecting a strict symmetry allied with a wholly novel differentiation of the volumes and functions of each room.

The elevation bears witness to the same discipline. The long-post frame of the central block and the corner pavilions rests on a plinth made of massive blocks of stone. It is structured on two floors in a strict verticality unbroken by a single diagonal, the angle braces providing the cross-bracing being placed on the internal face of the wall. On the main façade, the builder has taken the refinement to the point of making each stud exactly the same in height on each level, by means of an expedient apparently not used by any other builder in the Pays d'Auge. Normally, the height of the studs on the ground floor is reduced, to compensate for the presence of the stone plinth. At Le Mesnil-de-Roiville, instead of making the girding beam that customarily separates the two floors in timber-framed houses correspond to the upper floor level, the master builder has placed it distinctly higher, at the actual level of the rail of the windows on the upper floor. This removes the window breast feature, and creates a deceptive reading of floor levels. The symmetry of this façade relative to the axis constituted by the molded top plate was even more perfect before the window rail on the upper floor was lowered to this axis. Indeed, the builder originally arranged his rails in complete symmetry with the lintels of the ground-floor openings.

The same harmonious relationships prevail in the window and door openings. The windows are arranged in two vertical bays in the central block and one bay in the façade of each pavilion, accentuated by perfectly aligned dormers. The window openings are four foot wide in the central block and two foot wide in the pavilions, while the pair of doors forming a center feature are eight foot wide. The same principles guided the design of the roofs. A flat projection shows the pitch of the hipped ends to be strictly identical, whether on the pavilions, the central block, or the staircase tower; and, on top of the pavilions, on the same axis as the window openings, we find diminutive ridges two feet long, which can have no other justification than to correspond to the breadth of the openings below. The ridges themselves are exactly aligned with those on the central block. The same recurs in the similar design of the staircase tower roof. Is this merely an accident?

The decoration of the elevations is thus confined to the harmony and rigor of its line, though a discreet frieze of small squares frames the windows of the pavilion blocks, matched by a double-square motif on the central block, to maintain the same harmonious logic.

On the dormers, in contrast, the decoration waxes profuse, turning the posts into fluted pilasters both on the window breasts and round the openings, with the addition of single brackets in the form of foliated volutes on the central members dividing the windows. The horizontal of the rails carry a relief of delicate ribboned gadroons.

Though the windows of the façades have retained no trace of their ancient joinery, the twin front doors still exist, now carefully restored. Their matched and molded vertical boards display the same rigor and simplicity as the façade, with not a single horizontal member visible at the foot. In the dormers, we find the same paneling as occurs on the interior doors.

The interior decoration shows the same attention to detail. Sober stone fireplaces – parts of which remain rough-hewn – contrast with alternating cartouches and squares on the soffits of the bressumers in front of them. Color undoubtedly played a very important part in an interior of this quality, but all trace of it has vanished except for the superb glazed terra-cotta tiling carefully restored on the ground floor. Outside, color remains above all in the exceptional tile nogging, which is handled with a degree of simplicity in the façades but reaches the level of virtuosity in the breasts of the dormers and around the windows, with the application of a lattice motif making use of tiny pieces of terra-cotta.

Such harmony leads us to presume the house of Le Mesnil-de-Roiville was built in a single phase. However, the diversity of materials – the stone tower and the timber main house – have led some people to distinguish two phases of construction. In this theory, the tower would be the oldest part of the building – a simple lookout tower linked with the nearby Fort-Fresnay – to which the timber-framed dwelling was added later. This is a feeble argument: the structure of the tower indicates it has never contained anything but a staircase. A lookout tower would have included several small rooms on top of each other, accessed via a small spiral staircase. Another theory is that the earliest house consisted only of the core block, to which the two corner pavilions were later added. Admittedly, their narrow hipped dormers cling to steeply pitched slopes while the dormers of the central block are much wider and project from a much flatter surface. Yet the structures and decoration are identical, and the stone bases below embody a perfect continuity.

It seems therefore that the whole building was conceived as a single scheme and that the concern for defense – evident in the presence of solid grilles on all the ground-floor windows – prompted the master builder to construct a stone tower, admittedly in a different stone, fortified towards the valley by several loopholes suitable for use with firearms, positioned to fit in with the rhythm of the stair treads. Close examination of the plinths of the whole rear part of the manor, which are closely linked with the central block, bears out that on this side, the building was constructed on a pronounced glacis, soon hidden by substantial earthworks, no doubt to prepare for gardens on both sides of the house, overlooking the valley.

Ancient mortises in the embrasures of the upper floor doors of the central block accessing the staircase have given rise to the theory that these were made in a second phase of works when the staircase tower was built. Nothing of the kind – their position corresponds to recycled pieces of timber. Other details allow a better insight into the life and defensive concerns of this house: the massive twin front doors and the grilles of the lower-floor windows already constituted a first line of security. At the least danger, the second line of defense was ready – it was enough to take to the stone staircase and slide across solid iron bolts integral with the strap hinges of the interior doors, real structural works strong enough to resist assaults from a posse of marauders. Thus, the staircase would be transformed into a small keep, furnished moreover with all possible conveniences to sit out a siege lasting several hours.

The decoration is still in the Renaissance style: the gadroons on the rails and the fluted pilasters of the dormers are very like those in the timber gallery at Le Mesnil-Guillaume dating from the 1560s, and the composition heralds the advent of Classicism of the end of the 16th century. This construction of the house of Le Mesnil-de-Roiville must, therefore, be attributed to this period.

We still have to identify and discover more about the character of the master of works or architect to whom we are indebted for such an innovative creation.

A paragon of balance, rigor and sophistication, it is difficult to credit that this major work was allowed to fall into a condition of utter distress, abandoned, almost roofless, open to wind and weather, and that in 1956 a tree was pressing against its precious floors, in the midst of rubble.

The floor of the reception room is decorated with glazed terra-cotta tiles from Le Pré-d'Auge, put together to form quatrefoils enclosing stylized leaves.

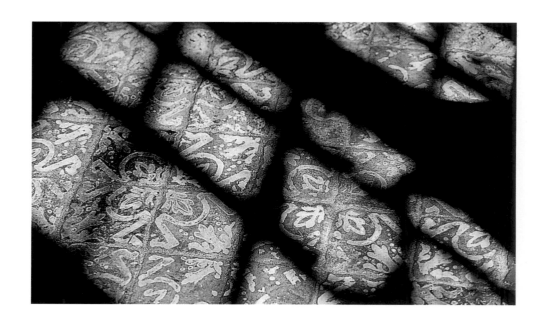

The alternation of backgrounds of green or yellow glazes is arranged generally in groups of four tiles, but was often randomly repositioned as wear began to show.

The reception room is austere in its handling. Though the bridging beam of the ceiling is decorated with alternate cartouches and squares, on the chimneypiece the decoration is incomplete, as is evident from the corbels of the fireplace and two of the three consoles of its cornice, which remain rough-hewn.

Ouilly-du-Houlley

The Pays d'Auge still includes several imposing medieval fortresses, and the château of Ouilly-du-Houlley should be included among their number. It is clearly in a different category from the manor houses, but a brief presentation may help us to identify some alternative ideas and discover some similarities of execution and decoration.

The layout took maximum advantage of the terrain. The formation occupies a free-standing spur in the plateau, at the confluence of the river Paquine, a tributary of the Touques, and a brook whose narrow valley winds round the stronghold. The spur is fortified on the eastern side by a wide dry moat which had a drawbridge thrown across it. The château has preserved its massive defensive walls in their entirety, punctuated by towers and a castellated gatehouse. The medieval arrangement of the courtyard is still perfectly preserved: the house occupies the south-west corner, formed of two wings at right angles, dominated by an imposing, semi-projecting stair tower crowned by a bell turret. The servants' wing, stables, and coach-houses are arranged along the north wing and as a return forming an east wing towards the gatehouse that occupies the central part of it. A chapel dedicated to SS. John and Philip formerly occupied a singular position tucked away

against the gatehouse, itself forming part of the defensive system. Its east end jutted out into the courtyard. As in many castle chapels, the lord could attend services from a raised loft. He reached it from the house via a private entrance while the guards and servants were kept on the ground floor of the sanctuary, which was accessible only from the courtyard.

The powerful barony of Ouilly was made up of four knight's-fee fiefs and was endowed with rights of high justice. It is recorded from the late 12th century. In 1180 it was in the hands of Martin d'Oullie, mentioned at this date in connection with the Exchequer of Normandy. Certain parts of the enclosure wall in the north-west corner could date from this period, as the stonework of the walls and their glacis abutments testify.

The archives are then silent until the first half of the 15th century, and we do not know under what circumstances the barony of Ouilly fell to the Leveneurs. In 1450, Philippe Leveneur married Marie Blosset de Carrouges, uniting two powerful Norman families, which would each provide a bishop for the diocese of Lisieux in the following decades. Following a partition concluded in 1464, Ouilly was awarded to Philippe de Manneville, whose family would retain it for nearly a century. It is interesting, as a demonstration of the force of feudal ties, to note the misadventure that befell Philippe's son Jehan de Manneville in 1469. Knight, lord and baron of Ouilly as he was, he did not deign to appear at the Musters of the nobility of the bailiwick of Evreux ordered by Louis XI. The penalty was equal to size of the insult. His fiefs were taken and "placed in the hands of the King ... by whom they would be controlled and governed until he had appeared as and from the place where he had presented himself". Everything would later return to normal, but it is clear that respect for one's pledged

The ancient fortress of Ouilly, which was endowed with a fine Gothic house, was totally remodeled in the 17th century. On the south front of the logis, the windows and doors were largely repositioned and the wall was given a cornice of projecting corbels, interrupted by pavilion blocks in the center and at the corners. The glacis was then revamped as a series of stepped terraces.

Who could this character be, if not the master of the household or one of the family? Richly dressed, with heavy features, he lurks at the corner of the cornice of the tower of the Gothic house.

The doorway of the Gothic logis at the foot of the tower. A masterpiece of medieval woodwork.

word and oath of loyalty to a feudal overlord could not be taken lightly.

No doubt Jehan took the construction of his new house much more to heart. He set up his corner tower and his bell turret, and decorated his exposed gables with a series of rosettes. The masterly moldings on the mullioned windows still stand out against the fine, perfectly regular stonework, as the surviving west wing bears out. But the greatest virtuosity of the builders was reserved for the delicate cornice on the tower: a frieze of carved and twisted foliage is succeeded by delicate tracery of curves and counter-curves developing horizontally, punctuated at each angle by beasts and human figures. Could it be the master of the house or some other member of the family perched elegantly on the corner above the door, despite the discomfort of the position his hands casually resting on his doublet? The elegance of the Gothic house is confirmed by evidence from the handling of the entrance doorway, which is undoubtedly one of the most remarkable examples of medieval domestic door work in the Pays d'Auge. The lower part has three linenfold panels; above, the upper panels are decorated with tracery of fleurons separated by applied colonettes adorned with a scale motif. The door knocker positioned halfway up is a masterpiece of the locksmith's art. It takes the form of a dove striking against an openwork plate supported by a capital and capped by a canopy accommodated on one of the colonettes.

At the examination of the Elect of Lisieux in 1540, it was René de Maintenon who presented his proofs of nobility as lord and baron of Ouilly, but we do not know under what circumstances his family entered into possession of the estate. It seems probable that neither he nor his son Gaston de Maintenon, who married Marguerite de Nollent in 1551, carried out any important alterations to the château save for some internal decorations. In contrast, when the Longchamp family took over in the early 17th century, radical changes were made. The medieval *logis* had to be adapted to the new demands of the Classical age. The top course of the walls was embellished with fine cornices on projecting corbels, a treatment which recurs generally on the buildings of the period. The south wing side of the house took on a monumental dimension, centered on a pavilion block, in which a number of brick features make an appearance. This duality of materials is most elaborate in a new chatelet, the square tower in the south-east corner, and above all in the rebuilt service quarters of the north wing and the return block forming an east wing. On the defensive structure containing the complex mechanism of the drawbridge, vertical and horizontal courses of stone elegantly divide the brick walls into little rectangles, in accordance with a highly symmetrical arrangement where the elevation of the central bay consists of a semi-circular arched doorway, with a window on the floor above it and a pedimented dormer above. The flanking side bays contain much smaller doors and oculi above them.

The east service wing comprises a first floor beneath an augmented roof. The materials in it are applied particularly skillfully, with polychrome effects featuring strongly. Slate was reserved for pavilion blocks, towers, and turrets, constituting the usual trinity with brick and stone. The dialog here only involves terra-cotta and stone. The brickwork, whose tones blend with those of the roofing tiles, alternates in long bands with the slightly ochered limestone, intersected by the vertical courses of the door and window openings. Finally, the roofing is punctuated by the rhythm of the dormers with their tall pediments, the bases of which are broken to accommodate a large stone keystone that reaches right down to the lintel of the opening. This splendid motif appears on all the structures built in the courtyard, right up to the roofs of the old house, tailoring it to the tastes of the day. No doubt we owe these alterations and works to Jean de Longchamp, who called himself "knight of the Order of the King, counsellor in his Council of State and Privy Council, governor of the town of Lisieux, baron and castellan of Ouilly, lord of Fumichon, Baudet, La Lande, Baratte and other titles and domains". They probably pre-date the death of his wife Jehanne Dumoulin around 1614. One of his two daughters brought the demesne of Ouilly to César d'Oraison, "knight and Marquis de Livarot", who was also governor of the town of Lisieux in 1637, 1672, and 1683. From the end of the century, Ouilly passed into the hands of the du Houlley family, who would finally give it the name by which we know it today.

Les Pavements

The buildings of the manor of Les Pavements rise alongside the ancient road leading from Lisieux to Dreux. Les Pavements is a toponym which probably preserves the memory of the paved stone road of antiquity. The buildings were once enclosed by a wall, of which only the south section parallel to the road survives, plus the return at right angles towards the north.

It was in this corner of the walls that the manor house was constructed, a carapace of reddish tiles, with restrained and yet subtle lines. The other structures were positioned randomly, in most cases backing on to the great south wall. The entrance was, as today, on the axis of the road, with a slight deviation; an enclosed garden stretched out opposite, bounded by the course of a stream.

The fief of Les Pavements has been recorded since 1426, its first lord known to have been Richard de La Reue, esquire, procurator, and controller for the town of Lisieux from 1439 to 1453. His successor in the latter post, from 1453–62, was Jean de La Reue. First Raymond Bordeaux, in 1851, then Charles Vasseur, identified the blazonry above the doors of the house – probably already very eroded – as being the allusive (punning) arms of the de La Reue family. Referring to an imprecise genealogy published by La Chesnaye-Desbois, Bordeaux and Vasseur attributed this house to Thomas de La Reue, esquire, lord of Lisores and Norolles, counsellor *en courte-laye* and lieutenant general of the bailiwick of Évreux, who married Guillemette Guédon in 1470 and is still mentioned in 1530. Jean de La Reue, lord of Les Pavements, is mentioned in 1544, then Olivier de La Reue, who died in 1595. The La Reue family died out with Françoise de La Reue, wife of François Lombart, esquire and courtier, who on 30 December 1660 sold to the Ursuline ladies of Lisieux "a farm situated in the parish of St. James, in the canton of Lisieux, village of Les Pavements, half of which is dependent on the prebend of Les Chesnes, the whole for the price and sum of 5,000 *livres*".

The Ursulines kept the estate of Les Pavements until the sale of national property in 1791. The valuation report was dated 11 December 1790, and describes all the buildings surviving today, which on 17 January 1791 were awarded by adjudication to a landowner, Jean-Baptiste Groult, for 43,000 *livres*.

The house faces west, and presents a timber upper floor shingled with fixed tiles, with a large dormer above. This structure is placed at the south-east corner of the enclosure, executed in masonry irregularly checkered with dressed stone and rubble and carried on a timber-framed first floor on the two other fronts facing the courtyard. The plan of the house, very compact and almost a square, breaks with the tradition of the extended rectangle. It provides interior spaces reduced by the thickness of the stone walls but slightly augmented on the upper floor by jettying, using the top course of the enclosure wall as a support.

It is worth noting that three sides are jettied in this way: the west side towards the courtyard, the south side, and the east side on the masonry wall – an exceptional feature which clearly indicates, in conjunction with the care given to the sculpted decoration, the importance that the builder intended to give the façades that were visible from the road, at the corner of the enclosure. It is probable that the fourth side would also have been jettied if the builder had not decided to append here the servants' wing, now disappeared. The arrangement of this jettying, carried at the corners on massive dragon beams visible from inside, corroborates the view that its chief purpose was decorative above all other technical or functional advantages.

The south-west corner of the jetty of the main house features an enigmatic figure carved into the end of a dragon beam, beneath a small female medallion figure. Above the lower bressumer with its fine bowtell molding, the upper bressumer has dentils in low relief.

The bulk of the two-story building is crowned by a generous roof with two slopes. This simplicity contrasts with the fashion of the day, whereby the roof was commonly peppered with dormers and punctuated by the projections of stair turrets. It seems that at Les Pavements the aim was to simplify the outline as much as possible. The chimney stack, perfectly centered, barely rises above the ridge tiles when viewed from the courtyard. The sole dormer, which occupies the entire breadth of the central bay, presents a gable scarcely lower than the ridge and a roof subtly linked to the main pitch by rounded valley tiling. Finally, the staircase accessing all three floors, which would normally form a projection on the rear elevation, is integrated within this vast dormer, attached to the chimney masonry behind the west façade and throwing out openings laterally on each floor. Its location is clearly marked in the joists of the ceilings, in the form of an octagonal opening made to contain a timber framework for the stair. Fragments of it survive, reused in a partition on the upper floor.

The manor house of Les Pavements is also notable at the same time for its modest dimensions and the unusual design of its timber frame, articulated in three bays. A structure of this sort is generally reserved for buildings comprising a single room per floor, pushing the chimney back against one of the gables and banishing the spiral staircase to a corner. Here, the two rooms on each floor only occupy one bay and a half, and the masonry of the chimneys shares the major part of the central bay with the stairwell. This ternary rhythm thus allowed the creation of the dormer, which extends the whole width of the central bay. It is of a type very like those found originally in the houses at Tordouet, Querville (in Prêtreville), or Prestreval, and Barneville-la-Bertran, all of them long gone.

We indicated earlier how the composition of the façade keeps to a very elaborate overall design. The recent restoration of the house has enabled the original arrangement of the lower story to be re-established, especially the mullions and transoms of the windows. It is noticeable, however, that the builder was not able to carry through this scheme to its logical conclusion. Hampered by the corner wall on which the buildings rests, he could

not achieve perfect symmetry. He had to push the door that one would expect to find in the south-west corner to the left of the ground-floor window; but this in no way impairs the harmony of the design. The composition of this façade corresponds to the traditional arrangement in use at the end of the Middle Ages, in which the two access doors to the two rooms on the upper floor are often placed at the ends of the building.

Surface treatment and sculpture have not been overlooked in this rigorous analysis: they remind us powerfully that, if in terms of volumes and some details (e.g. the door lintels of the west front, with their ogee arches braced with rosette motifs and crowned with fleurons), the building is still informed by the Gothic spirit, the ornamentation makes a beginning on renewing the repertoire, initiated

The composition of the west façade reveals a masterly design, which is analyzed on page 79. The absence of apertures in the central part, including the great dormer, is explained by the presence of the staircase in this position.

magnificently in Normandy's great construction sites of the Renaissance.

To begin with the jettying: the robust rounded moldings of the 15th century have made way for fine bowtells and talons separated by slender fillets, incised with dentils on the top layer. Beneath the ogee arches over the doors, the usual colonettes have given way to scarcely noticeable, very flat pilasters consisting of a slight recession bordered by an ogee and supporting Corinthian capitals where the volutes project from a corbel with stylized foliation. These shallow reliefs and terse moldings, somewhat eroded by time, contrast with the generally flowing curves of the sculptured bressumer of the jettying. What became of the "grotesques" of the previous century, whose open maws would gulp down the stop-ends of the beams? On the house at Les Pavements, they take the form of elegant dolphins, fish with twisting shapes, or sea monsters metamorphosing into foliage. Above the enigmatic human figure decorating the south-west corner, which seems to cut a profile derived from the far-off Americas, appears a diminutive medallion figure, in the spirit of the antique-style pseudo-cornice picked out in a frieze of dentils. There is another innovation on the windows: the moldings of the mullions differ from those of the transoms, thus adhering to the scheme adopted horizontally on the jettying (fine moldings) and vertically on the posts of doors and bays (recessions lined with bowtells).

The interior of the house has retained a number of sculptured features: the angle braces linking the girding beams of the upper floor to the bay posts are decorated with cascades of foliage, applied volutes, and small cartouches.

The timber-framed façades of the service quarters are totally devoid of decoration except at the end of the long building parallel to the road, where a little house on two floors was erected. The grotesques and fine moldings of the main house recur here, only this time handled with much less assurance. These are undoubtedly later work, made some decades later with the chisel of a deft but less sophisticated carpenter.

It is worth comparing the main house with several contemporary buildings. It was probably to Les Pavements that a master carpenter came looking for a model for the splendid Renaissance window that he inserted in the rear elevation of the medieval house of Querville at Prêtreville, unless it was the same hand at work, so similar is the detail.

More obvious is perhaps the affinity between the house at Les Pavements and two houses at numbers 48 and 52, place Victor-Hugo in Lisieux, unfortunately both destroyed in 1944. These, but especially number 52, had the large central dormer fringed by the same rafters with festooned edges interspersed with the same fleurons and small circular fluting. The shallow jettying adopts the same fine moldings, possesses the same type of grotesques-cum-foliage, and is adorned at number 48 with a frieze of dentils, the same decoration of sunken pilaster panels lined with bowtells and the same handling of the Corinthian capitals very similar to the model (capitals with volutes and a flower stem in the middle).

The simplified structure of the jettying of these two houses and the more advanced nature of their decoration suggests a date for these two houses some years after the manor house at Les Pavements and a connection with the circle of the de La Reue family, since their arms figure on the paneling of the neighboring house at number 45, also destroyed in 1944.

How credible is the very hypothetical date of 1561, now illegible, in the middle of the rich decoration of the façade of the main house at Les Pavements? If the two escutcheons referred to undoubtedly relate to the de La Reue family, they are not enough to discover with certainty the name of the builder(s). It is less likely to have been Thomas de La Reue and his wife Guillemette Guédon. Thomas was still living in 1530 and had shown an interest in architecture by involving himself in the construction of the church of St. James of Lisieux, where his arms and those of his wife are still visible on the bosses of the vaults of the south aisle of the nave. More likely is that it was Jean de La Reue, mentioned in 1544, at a date close to the middle of the 16th century. The identification of another escutcheon, discovered on one of the angle braces of the upper floor, as that of the Gasteblé family – azure with a gold chevron, accompanied by three ears of corn leafed of the same – will perhaps allow us to pin down the dating once we can establish the family's links with the de La Reues.

OPPOSITE:
The slightly later façade of the small house of the service quarters more or less follows that of the great house, but the decoration is limited to a few voluted consoles.

RIGHT:
The traditional grotesques of the jetty have become transformed into animated foliage and sea monsters, with human medallion figures here and there, today concealed beneath the tiled cladding.

Raising the lintel of the door unfortunately resulted in the mutilation of the great foliage fleuron, but at least the wheel (roue) of the arms of the de La Reue family was spared. It is still visible on the escutcheon in the middle of the ogee arch.

Le Pavillon

The *logis* at the manor of Le Pavillon figures among the 16th-century buildings to have benefited from the attention of a master builder who was devoted to the search for a scientific articulation of volumes, and the subtle interplay of materials and their polychromy.

Here, timber-framing stands aside for stone and brick, and the rectangular plan has made way for a scholarly design based on a hierarchical principle. It consists of a central block covered with tiles and two built-out pavilion blocks covered with carefully detached slate roofs. This symmetrical arrangement is only marred by the presence of a narrow clearly truncated turret on the rear elevation. The special character of this house is vested essentially in the design of the main façade, which is given a portico of four tall openings with semi-circular arches that function at once as Italian-style gallery and as an access staircase leading to the *piano nobile*. Though various details of the construction, such as the scholarly *bretèches* linking the pavilions to the central block, demonstrate complete technical mastery, it does seem that this happy result is due to the adaptation of an initial, much less elaborate design.

Despite appearances, the masonry bond presents a certain heterogeneity. The core of the building is executed in brick with stone dressings for the vertical bands of toothed ashlar, quoins, and string courses, and decorated with diamond latticing on the façades of the pavilions (which on the return walls is found only on the lower part). Oddly enough, between the stone piers supporting the arches of the gallery, the wall fronting the steps is partly implemented in an irregular brick/stone checkerwork that bears no relation to the arrangement of the piers, which is hardly consistent with the general rigorous linearity evident elsewhere. Though this checkerwork features on the other ele-

The two kinds of masonry used here could belong to two distinct periods: an initial phase of construction in an irregular checkerwork, broken off at the level of the plinth; and a second phase when the piers of the gallery were laid on top, on a background of brickwork divided by vertical bands of toothed ashlar.

vations of the central block as well, likewise restricted to the base, it is all the more noticeable for its absence on the masonry of the pavilions and rear turret.

The sole possible explanation would be that the original late-16th century scheme for this house must have been limited to a simple building on a rectangular ground plan. The fashion for Italian-style galleries, the examples of the châteaux of Cricqueville or St. Germain-de-Livet, the taste for designs that enhance the sense of volume, the arrival of a talented master builder – any or all of these factors probably induced the client to modify the original plan while retaining the elements already built. This would also explain the clumsy way the stone pillars are incorporated in this irregular checkerwork, as a survival of works interrupted at the level of the first string course marking off the base.

However original this formula of gallery plus steps as a central feature of the design, it can still be compared with other examples, like that of the timber-framed *logis* of Le Lieu-Cordier at Manneville-la-Pipard, which dates from 1618. This has just one flight of steps leading to the gallery, but like the *logis* at Le Pavillon presents twin doors, which appear here as an idiosyncrasy derived from practices more appropriate to timber architecture. The other elements of the arrangement of the façade are more classical: the openings, for example, are set into vertical bays on the axis of the pavilions, and emphasized by stone dormers with molded pediments.

The function of the four-cornered turret of the rear elevation is not obvious. Its masonry, which turns brutally to the south-west on a brick-built corner, indicates that it is a truncated feature, remains or commencement of a real tower intended perhaps to contain a monumental external staircase

The fashion for the Italianate gallery prompted builders to conjugate it through all its forms. In this case, the result was a monumental feature applied to a modest house.

The checkerwork of brick and stone is limited to the lower level of the main block, on to which are grafted the rear tower and the two pavilion blocks linked by slender bretèches.

Contrasting with the modernity of the gallery, the logis at Le Pavillon remains astonishingly loyal to the archaic feature of twin entrance doorways, inherited from timber architecture.

on the axis of the house, following the medieval practice. The installation of staircases in the two small symmetrical *bretèches*, at the junction with the pavilions, no doubt rendered the construction, or preservation, of a single central staircase unnecessary.

While maintaining discretion, the architectural decoration is no less subtle for all that, superposing a series of horizontal motifs – a platband, then a slender bead molding beneath a cornice of cube-shaped modillions ringing the entire building. It is worth noting the extreme deftness with which the platband is integrated with the rounded projections of the brackets supporting the *bretèches*.

Such architectural lines were evidently not to be contemplated without considering emphasizing them by means of a few glazed terra-cotta or lead features. There survives a sole ridge finial, today placed midway on the central block, allowing us to imagine those that once decorated every angle of the roof, lightening its outline.

La Pipardière

The manor of La Pipardière is one of the finest ensembles to have been preserved in the Pays d'Auge, and has been particularly admired since the second half of the 19th century. It was, however, abandoned to oblivion and neglect for many long years. Having been shorn of its role as a seigneurial residence, the construction of a railway station cut off its approach, compelling residents and visitors to cross the tracks to reach the manor house. It then became just a farm building, increasingly hemmed in by urban sprawl and soon surrounded by all the nuisances of our civilization, including a purification plant, an industrial zone, and overhead power cables.

The avenue formerly culminated in an outer bailey that contained a chapel, then, on a discontinuous alignment, a coach-house, the stables, and a square dovecote. This brought the visitor to the south-east corner of a four-cornered formation surrounded by moats, then across a drawbridge to the south-east corner and through a gatehouse enclosing the courtyard. The house was strung out along the whole length of the east side. A much lower building began a return on the north side, probably built up against the wall or palisade of the enclosure, while two other structures of indeterminate purpose occupied the south-west corner and a position contiguous with the south corner of the porch respectively. Gardens extended to the north-east, bounded by two long stretches of water integrated into the network of moats.

The fine Gothic chapel was alas in the way and was mercilessly buried under the ballast of the railway line. All we have is Arcisse de Caumont's enthusiastic description of the building and its rich fittings – already sold off in 1867 – and Bouet's drawing published in his *Statistique monumentale*. The dovecote suffered the same fate, as did the two buildings in the courtyard, leaving extant only the house itself, the gatehouse, and a disfigured coach-house. The moats and water channels were filled in, and a slow agony began, precipitated by a degree of damage suffered in 1944 and repaired without the least subtlety. The closure of the railway could have marked the start of renewal. Instead, a highway bypassing the town of Livarot was built on the line of the railway encroaching on the manor, which proved the final blow. A public use had been sought for the historic building for more than a decade, but all potential buyers had been deterred by the scale of restoration work required.

It was left to an art-lover with a passion for the building to undertake its rescue by rebuilding it, with the agreement of the Minister of Culture, on another site as close as possible to its original valley, about 25 kilometers away. He had no inkling, as he dismantled the manor house of La Pipardière, that he was in his turn following an ancestral practice, and that four centuries earlier, almost half the house had been constructed reusing an older building, transferred to the site at Livarot.

Though we may regret that moving this historic building was the only realistic way of saving it, it was undertaken with the greatest care, which also enabled successive decorative schemes and the structure itself to be revealed and subsequently analyzed. Dendrochronological techniques were used to date the construction work.

The fief of La Pipardière takes its name from the Pipart family, known since the 12th century and established particularly in the valley of the River Touques, near Pont-l'Évêque. The marriage of a member of this family to the daughter of a baron of Livarot is probably how they came to set up their house in these parts, erected in knight's fee. The archives give us the name of Guillaume Pipart, recorded at Livarot in 1313, then that of his son Jean Pipart in 1386. His grand-daughter Jeanne, the last of the name, married Jean de La Haye around 1415, whose family would retain the fief of La Pipardière until the 17th century. The positions which the first of the line occupied give us an idea of his social standing: having sworn fidelity and paid homage to the king of England and thus been confirmed in his rights to the fief of La Pipardière on 9 October 1420, he was subsequently seneschal of the barony of Livarot from 6 September 1426 to 25 August 1428, probably undertook the duties of deputy procurator to the king at Orbec from 1430 to 1448, and sat as a deputy to the States of Normandy in 1443. Once peace returned, Jean de La Haye's commitments to the English occupier does not seem to have had any unpleasant repercussions. We do not know much about the manor before the first years of the 16th century. Its position at the bottom of the valley involved a defensive arrangement in the form of an enclosure surrounded by water-filled moats at the confluence of the Vie valley and a small stream on the eastern slope. While maintaining the original site, the son or possibly the grandson of Jean de La Haye decided to build a new house. Its history is now sufficiently documented by dendrochronology to be told here.

During the winter of 1507–8, woodcutters felled the last oaks required for the construction of the new building. It would number six main bays and two floors beneath a plain roof. Each floor would comprise a large room of three bays and a more modest room of only two bays sharing on both sides the masonry of fireplaces backed up in pairs. Vertical access would be ensured by a staircase built in at the end of the house, leading to the main rooms on each floor. The carpenter then traced the *épure* of the façades: long-posted structures facing the moat, short timbers and jettying on the courtyard side, with a special refinement on the south gable where the jettying turns by means of a dragon-beam assembly. Stiffening would be provided by braces on each floor, and two latrines would be set up overhanging the moat. The decoration would be very restrained: thickened, molded posts decorated with small consoles assembled in trefoils would carry the jettying, made up of three molded pieces with three toruses on the cross-bars, taken up again on a smaller scale on the girding beam below the drip piece. The same decoration would be applied beneath the eaves of the roof, to form a fine cornice there. The windows would be made of chamfered mullions and transoms and the sills would have simple moldings.

Finally, the carpenter placed the squared timbers on the diagram, forgetting to clean off a number of scraps of bark on three components. It was this sloppy workmanship that allowed the dendrochronologist, four and a half centuries later, to date the cutting with absolute precision. Building no doubt followed very soon after, bearing in mind the number of pieces dated to winter 1507–8 and the absence of other more recent pieces in the original structure of the building concerned.

The new *logis* was plain and robust. On the lower story an intricate painted decoration was applied to the beams, joists and the spaces between them, using a white and bluish-gray linear patterning in the big room and simulated inlays of precious woods in the small adjacent room, matching the glazed terra-cotta tiles. Some years later, it was extended towards the south by one bay, the timber frame standing on a stone-built lower floor and endowed with a chimney in the hipped roof. The same phase of the works probably also accounted for the construction of the gatehouse, in the extension of this stone wall. Half a century later it seemed insufficiently spacious to Philippe de La Haye, lord of La Pipardière in 1542, and very inconveniently served by the single interior staircase at the southern end.

The logis *constructed around 1508–10 comprised six bays, built of long posts facing the moat and jettied on the courtyard side. The extension of the house, on the same alignment, was carried out using a long-posted framework and false jetty that were 25 years or so older. The covered steps masked the join in the two phases of construction, but they are not integral to the frame.*

When the building was moved, every piece of timber had to be put back in its original position, including the roof rafters. The system of laths and counter-laths made of split chestnut was re-established. A decoration of alternate circles and squares in strapwork adorns the soffit.

The *logis* could easily be extended by adding several bays at the north end. A thrifty man, Philippe de La Haye told the carpenter to reuse the four bays of an older building. Analysis of its timbers has allowed us to date their felling to 1464–70.

We do not know where this structure came from, but it has much in common with others of the same type in use in this part of the Pays d'Auge in the second half of the 15th century. It was a long-post structure on two floors, but with the upper floor presenting a slight overhang obtained by thickening the bay posts and using intermediate plates of very large cross-section, molded in the same way that a bressumer would have been in jettying. The original structure, which still bore traces of its earlier internal decoration alternating yellow ocher and red ocher, has undergone a number of minor changes, notably the modification of the floor level on the upper floor and extension by a few inches

obtained by lengthening the tie-beams and transverse beams. The openings were also re-arranged.

The problem of the staircase called for an original solution. Functionally, it had to be placed at the juncture of the two structures, to mask the contrasts between them. External stair turrets were no longer in fashion, but Italian-style galleries and loggias were still much favored. It was the solution of a covered staircase that was adopted, built of stone but decorated with brick panels, positioned against the last two bays of the first house and the southernmost bay of the extension. A lofty, generous landing is contrived at the top, roofed as a kind of large dormer.

A subtle decoration scheme was applied to the timber braces. The canopy and hipped roofing are supported by slender wooden colonnettes linked by angle braces with volutes, and the soffit of the plate of the canopy is decorated with strapwork circles and squares in alternation.

The structure of the "dormer" canopy covering the top landing of the steps. Curved ties ending in volutes ensure the rigidity of the frame.

Arcisse de Caumont claims to have seen the date 1525 on the small pedimented opening facing the stone staircase; others discerned 1595. Probably the truth lies somewhere between the two hypotheses.

Philippe de La Haye may have been parsimonious as far as carpentry was concerned, but he did not hesitate to call in the best painters to carry out the remarkable decoration of the interior. His family was related to the great houses of the province, notably the Tournebus, Courseulles, Hautemers, and Osmonts. He therefore had his monogram, consisting of harmoniously interlaced letters set in a laurel wreath, painted on the beams of the ceiling in the great hall upstairs in the extension, alternating with the arms of Osmont and other allied families. On the joists and the spaces between them, linear patterns in yellow ochre on a brownish-red background and stenciled motifs embrace circles and squares filled with *trompe l'œil* marble and precious-stone effects *en cabochon*. They

manifest a virtuosity quite out of the ordinary. Nothing was then wanting from this exceptional ensemble except a fine polychrome finish to the façade. It would get this in the late 16th/early 17th century in the form of a lavish nogging made of red tiling that contains possibly the finest repertoire of motifs to be preserved in the Pays d'Auge.

In 1639, the fief of La Pipardière passed by marriage into the hands of the Fresnel family, who would keep it until the Revolution. It was thus not sold once in nearly five centuries but just handed down from one generation to the next. The two following centuries would be ones of progressive decay which, it seemed, nothing would stop.

If Philippe de La Haye were to return to Livarot one day, he would look in vain for the *logis* of his manor of La Pipardière. He would find it today closer to one of the fiefs of the first Piparts, and in a condition approaching that in which he handed it on to his heir.

LEFT HAND PAGE:
Painstaking scraping revealed superb ceilings beneath the plaster. The beams are painted in a reddish ocher lined in yellow ocher and marked with the interlaced emblem of the de La Hayes. The timber joists and casebays are decorated with stencil patterns, yellow on the flat, white on the edges.

RIGHT HAND PAGE:
The richness of this decoration is expressed in the trompe l'œil *cabochons and prisms of precious stones – jet, rubies and lapis lazuli.*

La Planche

These days the manor is lost in the low-land meadows of the Vie valley, not far from its confluence with the river Dives. Its name of La Planche is probably derived from the fief to which the rights of crossing the river, on some fragile wooden contraption, were once attached.

This fief of the barony of Cambremer held by the Bishop and Count of Lisieux was a full knight's fee to which were attached "rights of court, custom, jurisdiction, dovecote and mill", as well as "seigneurial

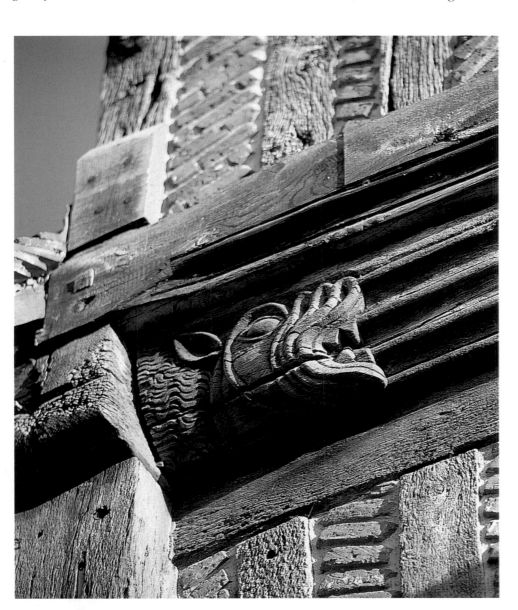

The huge mass of timber has bent at the points of maximum loading without damaging the framework. The base of the great dormer is supported by a jetty of six toruses evenly distributed on the girding beam and the wall plate with its grotesques.

rents, rents in corn, eggs, fowl, on men and vassals owing the same". A chapel dedicated to St. Thomas à Becket was attached to it, but in 1719 was transferred to the manor of La Pommeraye, in the parish of Berville.

The buildings of the manor were arranged round a courtyard ringed with water-filled moats. Of this arrangement, the alignment of two timber service buildings on each side of the main house survives. The impressive bulk of the dwelling stands out on a broad alluvial plain, without any other features except the trees bordering the streams, tracing a proud silhouette accentuated by the simplicity of line reinstated by careful restoration. Its two stories are covered by a tall tiled roof broached not by a few dormers of paltry dimensions but by the projection of the staircase turret on the rear (south) elevation and the large single dormer on the north front. These majestic timberwork gables were erected directly in line with the enormous masonry work of the central chimney stack. Their crests intersect, and not a single hip slope lessens this formidable verticality. In the same spirit, an open gallery provides access to the rooms of the upper floor, carried by the overhang of the transverse beams and supported on stout arch braces.

This enormous mass of timber erected in the last years of the 15th century demonstrates here its extraordinary ability to follow the movements of the structure. The two massive blocks of masonry of the chimneys press heavily on the water-logged substratum, dragging down the wooden structures that enclose them. The entire ensemble has shifted in sympathy with them, and the whole interior framework of the building has become bound together on its jetty in bending with the burden.

The north façade facing the courtyard adopts the traditional late-medieval design dictated by the presence of the chimney stacks, pushing back the

house in the Pays d'Auge. It is in fact nearly 20 meters long. The dynamism of this piece of work is accentuated by a remarkable handling of its surface treatment, made of simple toruses forming an ensemble of seven moldings adopted on both the jetty plate and the jetty bressumer. The windows of the upper floor are set in alignment with those of the lower floor, above a continuous molded sill plate forming a bearing, and attached to the angle ties at the ends to ensure rigidity of construction.

The biggest dormers usually occupy the whole width of a bay, their cheeks sitting on the principals of the trusses. In the presence of a structure of this size, a carpenter with no particular talent would have constructed three dormers on the alignment of the windows on the lower floors. Nothing of the kind at La Planche, where the master carpenter decided to take the dormer to a width of a bay and a half, to allow its crest to intersect with that of the great roof, and to position it very exactly between the bays of existing windows. This search for proportion is all the more sensitive in that the openings in this immense dormer are reduced to two small windows. At this dormer level, particular attention was paid to the decoration. The overhang of the dormer is supported by jettied bressumers decorated with snarling grotesques, the breasts below the two windows feature decorative saltires, and the gable is emphasized by a projecting truss, the king-post of which bears a sculpted salamander.

This abundance contrasts with the sobriety of the rest of the façade, where the posts make do with two little lampbase brackets where they begin to thicken in order to relieve the overhang of the bressumers, or to ease the transition of the sill bearing on the upper floor. The ogee arches over the secondary doors remain discreet, all the emphasis being placed on the door at the north-west corner. There we find everything that might lend a little pomp to this opening, which leads to the hall where, no doubt, vassals were received to pay their rents in cash or kind as already described: the door is flanked with buttresses crowned with tapering pinnacles cut in the body of the posts. They frame the ogee arch with its serrated leaves and crocketed finial, guarding the escutcheon once painted with the arms of the lord of La Planche.

doors to the corners of the two main ground-floor rooms.

The *logis* at La Planche has a third room on this floor at the west end, also served by an external door. Each room is lit by one mullioned and transomed window beside a bay post, or set in the middle of the bay. The jettying which separates the first two floors is handled with exceptional care and testifies to real virtuosity, both in terms of technical structure and decorative principles. It is carried on bressumers, in which the latter form a slight projection smoothed by quadrant beveling.

The cohesion of the timber frame is ensured by the principal feature constituted by the wall plate, cut as the longest piece of oak ever used in a manor

The timber work has been restored to its original very clear tonalities. The ceiling preserves the decoration of its joists in alternating tints of red, yellow, and green. Two griffins confront each other on the transverse beam.

The great hall contains a fine Renaissance decoration. The molded joists display alternate colors on the flat and cable moldings on the edge. The internal face of the bressumer is all that remains of the rich decoration that once covered all the walls.

Opposite the griffins, peaceful sirens with long hair and webbed arms frolic under one of the beams. A long tendril of stenciled roses winds along the edge.

On the beams, ornamental foliage painted in cameo style on a brown background. Between the foliage, cherubs surrounded by double volutes gambol in the midst of birds.

La Plesse

The name of La Plesse conjures up a time before the construction of the buildings we see today. A *plesse* or *plessis* designated a site that had been hastily fortified, enclosed by a hedge of thorn bushes, or by a simple palisade made of stakes driven into the ground, with a ditch in front.

The present manorial enclosure, which possibly perpetuates the outline of the original *plesse*, is laid out on a hillside as a courtyard, with farm buildings loosely arranged on each side of the *logis*. The former, likewise timber-framed, comprise the barns, dovecote, stables, cider-press, apple store, and cellars, bakehouse and brandy distillery, cheese loft, and other functions.

The fief of La Plesse, which depended on the powerful county of Montgommery, could have been held for part of the medieval period by a family called de La Plesse, which is better known in the Conches area. The presence there of a family called Le François is definitely recorded from 1520 until the second half of the 18th century.

The *logis* appears as a very balanced design on two floors, symmetrically pierced by three bays of windows beneath a hipped roof. This regularity is only broken on the main west front by the positioning of the doors and the enormous chimney stack that extends for virtually half the height of the roof on the right side. To the rear, however, all semblance of regularity vanishes in joyful abandon in (from left to right) a tangle consisting of a gallery whose initial overhang is buried beneath a later addition, a partially truncated staircase turret, then the continuation of the gallery, blanked off and altered, and finishing in a large length of walling hung with slate.

The oldest part is centered on the chimney stack and is limited to the first six bays to the south, which have preserved their openings in their original positions – a door at each end and two bays of symmetrical windows. It comprised two rooms on each floor, accessed by a staircase built into the unoccupied space between the chimneys and the east front.

The structure of the timber frame is not the same on both floors. On the ground floor, it is handled very vigorously, with a robust frame that is wholly preserved, with the exception of the center post and two angle ties probably intended to ensure the stability of this level. On the upper floor, slight differences can be observed in the alignment of four of the bay posts, cut in timbers having a very reduced section, and the presence of intermediate half studs thickened at the top, marking off half-bays, is also noticeable. On this floor, transverse beams still form a cornice: they are of modest scantling and are more carefully worked, with their quadrant-shaped

The logis *occupies the center of the courtyard on a steep slope. Its jetty forms a compact mass from which a weathered transverse beam emerges, beneath a bressumer with Gothic moldings.*

The original logis, notable for its diagonal braces, was centered on the chimney stack. This was then extended by three bays towards the north, with the timber frame displaying strictly vertical timbers. The extended building is unified by the nogging of red brick and tiling, contrasting with the bluish green tints of the windows.

stop-ends but bear no relation to their more massive counterparts in the floor below.

Profound changes have taken place in these first six bays, identifiable as much by the scantling of the timbers as by their decoration. The jetty is decorated with wide moldings on the bressumer. This molding is extended over the jetty plate, and is judiciously modified into a base directly above each transverse beam, or into a grotesque oddly positioned at the ends. The Virgin and Child sculpted in the body of the corner post at the north-east angle is conceived in the same spirit, and crowned with an elegant but blunted trefoil. The most significant figure is undoubtedly the little angel bearing a scroll and flitting beneath the half-stud that crosses the adjacent lintel. The two posts of the second bay have preserved their escutcheons on the ends of the transverse beams. On one of them, three charges can be made out placed 2 and 1, which could well be the arms of the de La Plesse family. This is only a hypothesis, bearing in mind the difficulties of reading due to the weathering of a façade constantly exposed to driving rain. However, it would allow us to date the construction of the *logis* not to around 1530, as the

general opinion has always been, but to well before 1520, the date after which the Le François family is known to have been at La Plesse. The profile of the moldings and the style of the sculpture belong in fact more to the last quarter of the 15th century than to a period when the Renaissance was in full bloom.

We are in Michel Cottin's debt for a detailed analysis of this house, which has established the profound transformations the structure underwent, particularly the creation of a staircase turret accompanied by an overhanging gallery, replacing the old, inconvenient internal staircase. This functional improvement, which may have been effected in the second half of the 16th century, was accompanied by a refurbishing of the main façade after the current taste, the decoration being out of fashion. However, renovation was limited to the replacement of the four bay posts indicated above and the insertion of window frames.

The new posts were more slender and carry escutcheons which are unfortunately indecipherable. Three of them are distinct from those of the ground floor in having a wide border.

The most readable one features a dolphin. Arcisse de Caumont notes an identical mammal, taking it

The stout timber frame of the ground floor carries a coat-of-arms which could be that of the Le François family. Upstairs, the original windows were enlarged at the end of the 16th century, cutting into the wall plate, following initial alterations to the main frame.

for a fish, at the manor of Tonnencourt, describing it as "un bar contourné" (a bass turned over on itself). It is also similar to one figuring on the façade of the manor house at La Valaiserie, in St. Germain-la-Campagne. It is probably a reference to one of the alliances of the Le François family. But the most interesting motifs remain the two portraits of bearded men with wavy hair, painted in a realistic style below the two central escutcheons.

The frames of the two upper-floor windows still attest the quality of these alterations. The jambs are decorated with pilasters carrying volutes with detached foliage, on a shaft adorned on the north side with a long sunken palm-leaf molding similar to those that would remain in fashion to the mid-17th century and executed on the south side in a series of small incised superposed squares, of a kind already noted at Le Mesnil-de-Roiville in the last years of the 16th century. These apertures, which are the successors of the

Gothic window, were probably built as twin openings, either side of a central mullion decorated in the same way as the jambs. Similar arrangements probably existed in the two ground floor windows, which still bear traces of their defensive grilles but have unfortunately been enlarged since.

It is difficult to date the extension of the *logis* by three bays towards the north. The total absence of all decoration, either sculpture or molding, deprives us of chronological reference points, but we may imagine that no 18th century carpenter would ever have accepted a commission for jettying three rooms. The strict verticality of the upright members, made possible by the concealment of the arch braces on the internal face of the wall, is entirely in the spirit of the 17th century, just like the steep slope of the hipped roof, rebuilt completely at the north end or cutting into the great medieval gable at the south end.

Pont-Mauvoisin

This building is better known as the manor of St. Hippolyte, named after the ancient parish of St. Hyppolyte-du-Bout-des-Prés, which was abolished in 1834 in a merger with the parish of St. Martin-de-la-Lieue. The latter name is in fact more evocative, because today the visitor has to look for the manor house at the bottom of the road leading to the end of the meadows, on the left bank of the river Touques.

The "pont", the "turreted bridgehead", thrown across the river and mentioned by Arcisse de Caumont, is long gone. It was probably not even the original entrance, but merely marked the axis of a carefully arranged group of buildings built on terraces rising from the river up the hillside which overlooks it.

The quadrangular enclosure was defended by the river and a system of walls and moats, the outlines of which can still be easily discerned. The distinction between the main courtyard and the outer bailey is accentuated here by a pronounced difference of level, marked by a retaining wall dividing the overall enclosure. The service buildings and the dovecote are ranged along the lateral walls of the outer bailey, focusing all attention on the *logis* placed centrally on the upper terrace. The same hierarchy was established in the use of building materials: timber framing for the outer bailey and fine stone and brick masonry for the house.

The fief of Pont-Mauvoisin is known from documents since the early 14th century, and had a somewhat troubled history until the early 16th century. It was in the hands of Richard Gain in 1311, and was in turn passed to the Basires, secured for the English, returned to Jean de Bonenfant between 1433 and 1437, and assigned to two knights called Nouvelet, who were established there from 1435 to 1504. In the course of the years that followed, the fief was restored to the Bonenfants (1504–11),

transferred to the Bernières (1511–26), and finally acquired by Jacques Le Pillois. The marriage of his daughter Geneviève to Jacques de Tournebu in 1533 gave Pont-Mauvoisin to the powerful Tournebu family, who had been established at the château of St. Germain-de-Livet since 1462. The last of the Tournebu line and inheritor of the two estates would die in 1810, but the first sale would take place only a century later.

Livet was always the major component in the Tournebus holdings in the Pays d'Auge, and Pont-Mauvoisin featured several times as the apanage of the cadet branch. Thus we find Robert de Tournebu senior, the son of the constructor of the château, assigning the work of his father to Anne, his first son and first president of the parliament of Normandy, reserving the fief of Pont-Mauvoisin to the younger son Antoine, gentleman of the Privy Chamber in 1619. The estates would be reunited in 1659 by lineal reversion into the possession of François de Tournebu.

The *logis* is an edifice of quite exceptional size, consisting of a two-floor masonry-built block on a rectangular plan, with two large timber-built dormers above. To the rear a square tower, clad in slate, contains the central staircase; this tower is lit by a timber oriel window and capped by a tall hipped roof. Two four-cornered turrets, used as latrines and completing the defense towards the hillside, graced the ends of the building. Only the southern turret with its small independent roof has been preserved.

The ground floor is built of limestone cut in large blocks brought from an ancient quarry on the opposite bank of the river. It is a very tough material that has preserved intact the fine lines of the plinth and the drip molding separating the floors, carried across the whole building. The upper floor is slightly recessed, and introduces a note of color in the form of bands

The access to the outer bailey, seen from the position of the "bridgehead" over the Touques, leading to the transition to the main courtyard on the upper terrace. Each courtyard has an independent side access.

of red brick intersected by the windows. This is an unusual arrangement in the Pays d'Auge, but appeared at the château of La Houblonnière from the end of the 15th century, and at Victot a century later. It is much more common in the Caux region in this period, for example at the château of Valmont.

The distribution of the apertures achieves perfect regularity on the upper floor, centering on a small window with twin openings. This is flanked by two much larger windows, and a smaller single window at each end completes the row. The later removal of mullions and transoms spared the fine moldings of the frame, whose rolls intersect in the corner and swell out at the imposts. The similarities with the château of La Houblonnière noted above do not stop at the use of brick in alternating band courses. We likewise find mullioned windows of the same type there, also framed with intersecting roll moldings, an indication that possibly the same master of works was in charge.

The design of the lower-floor windows is slightly simpler, sticking to a straightforward grid. Their distribution copies that of the upper floor windows, with the exception of the central section, where a door had to be fitted in without excessively darkening the comparatively poorly lit spaces within. Thus, the doorway could not be inserted directly under the central window on the upper floor. Its ogee-headed opening is framed by an ogee arch; the doorway shares the central section of wall with a large mullioned and transomed window. What might have looked an irritating dissymmetry is here turned to good account by the perfect alignment of the entrance with the lofty slate roof of the stair tower, which looks down on the tile roof from the background.

This arrangement also enables interesting things to be done on the interior, allowing access from the entrance to a first room that leads at the same time to the staircase and the principal room of the house, which itself benefits from generous lighting from two north windows. The first window to the left was opened out in the 18th century. This part of the house was probably used as a storeroom, accessible via a low door now blocked off.

The two pairs of large superposed windows, the upper lintels of which broach the cornice, were manifestly intended to support stone dormers of considerable size, like those still extant on the *logis* of the château of La Houblonnière. It was probably an economy measure that led to their realization in timber, seated on two short bressumers supported above the cornice. They are pierced with mullioned and transomed windows framed in a cable molding, set on a deeply molded sill above window breasts adorned with saltires. Posts and studs are decorated with motifs that have weathered badly. They consist of little pendant brackets, six now indecipherable coats-of-arms and small abutments as free-standing projections, cut in the thickness of the wood. The edge of the roof is treated like that of a real gable, as a crown-post roof with cusped principals. We must conclude, therefore, that the *logis* was built in two separate phases.

Its construction was long attributed to Jacques de Tournebu, i.e. after 1533, the date of his marriage to the Pillois heiress. This assumption was based on reading the arms of the Tournebus – "argent a bend azure" – off two of the escutcheons of the dormers, citing also the two "salamanders" that could still be made out on the crown posts of the dormers. The blazonry must be treated with caution: the salamanders for example are more like dragons, distant cousins of

The doorway of the logis, *centered on the tall roof of the staircase turret, leads to the main hall, which is suitably lit by the two mullioned windows to its left.*

jetty grotesques, than the royal emblem. Finally, can we really credit that an old captain of the Italian wars would continue to build in the style of the end of the previous century, without the least trace of Italianism appearing on the façades or in the interior decoration?

Stylistically, this *logis* belongs to the second half of the 15th century, and history bears out this hypothesis. This was the period from 1437 to 1504 when the fief of Pont-Mauvoisin resided in the hands of the Nouvelets, prior to an age of instability that lasted 30 years, in the course of which it was unthinkable to undertake a work of this size in a rather insignificant fief.

The construction of the dormers and the upper parts of the stair tower, i.e. the entire timber-built structure, is undoubtedly the work of a second phase which would be difficult to date from later than the 15th century. The octagonal dovecote in the south-east corner of the outer bailey, covered with a conical roof that originally terminated in a small lantern, also belongs to this period. It is built with great care, both structurally and decoratively. The three layers of close studding are separated by plates molded as drip moldings that are carried round the corner posts. The sculptor put all his effort into the top layer, cutting slender projecting pilaster buttresses out of the body of the posts and studs that rest on the drip molding and are crowned with tapering pinnacles.

Thus, when Pont-Mauvoisin became a Tournebu possession, the new owners undertook no major alterations. They made do with turning the gables of the *logis* into a hipped roof, and, perhaps, constructing the large retaining wall to emphasize the difference between the house and the outer bailey. The manor house was well built, and laid out in a fairly novel manner.

The row of outbuildings is interrupted by the secondary entrance to the outer bailey. The octagonal end building with the conical roof is the dovecote.

Le Pontif

The manor of Le Pontif is built on a huge quadrilateral on a slight slope surrounded by moats. Gardens occupy the major part of it, confining the *logis* and its courtyard to the eastern side, which is enclosed by walls. Water is present everywhere in moats laid out on successive planes. Channeled from the spring on the hillside, it bubbles into the fishpond integrated in the gardens and into the reserve ponds upstream. The working buildings were constructed outside the quadrilateral, in the surrounding grassy areas.

Le Pontif was a quarter fief of the seigneury of Asnières, at Pierrefitte-en-Auge, a dependency of the viscounty of Auge. It was a relatively modest estate, and the present buildings seem to go back no further than the early 17th century. It belonged, among other estates, to Jean de Mauduit, "counsellor to the king, steward in ordinary of his household and Chamber of the Counts of Normandy". Thanks to a most sympathetic restoration of the buildings and the re-establishment of its gardens, it has recovered the spirit of the cultured residence it used to be.

The materials are simple – greenish-tinged *pierre de marne* from the edge of the plateau combined with red brick and plastered rubble – and handled with great subtlety. The roofs are of tile, with a great flexibility of form.

The courtyard is closed to the north, possibly even defended, by two rectangular pavilion blocks flanked by two round staircase turrets which frame the semi-circular arch of the gateway. The roofs are fitted together very elegantly while the walls of rubble plastered with lime mortar seem to have preserved beneath their golden coloring an age-old patina, discreetly reinforced by chains of stone and a platband linking the curves of the towers high up. The sole touch of gaiety is lent by the cartouches of reddish-orange brick sprinkled on the lower part of the pavilion blocks and in the narrow spaces available above the platband. The reverse on the courtyard side shows a more generous application of brick confined between vertical bands of toothing ashlar.

The south front of the house presents a very orderly appearance, its rhythm set by the dormers crowning three bays of windows. However, the brick and stone masonry suggests several phases of construction. The entrance door, which could be expected to be in the axis of the building, is actually displaced to the left. The oldest parts seem to be to the right of this door, marked by a decoration of imbricated diamonds of glazed brick headers. They correspond to the design of the left side, where levels differ in relation to the rest of the building, as indicated by the dislocation in the platband course separating them.

To the north, the rubble masonry reveals the same chronology, the limit of the first building lying to the right of a small semicircular doorway. This first structure, which could date back to the beginning of the 17th century, must thus have had only one room above and below, with a habitable roof space on top, linked by a side staircase. In the second phase of construction, it must have been completed towards the east to make up suites of rooms, serviced by a new staircase at the same location.

It is to this period, probably towards the end of the 17th century, that we owe the fine orderliness of the courtyard, its pavilion blocks and the overall layout of the manor house, happily set in its valley surroundings and extended by a long outlook towards the upper hillside.

The manor house at Le Pontif offers a rare example of a manorial enclosure, still intact after three centuries, where concerns of defense, the amenities of the house, and the careful management of the estate have been reconciled in a most subtle equilibrium.

The manor logis and rear of the two pavilion blocks, seen from the fish pond.

The entrance porch to the courtyard is between two towers. The oldest part of the logis extends as far as the entrance, marked by the platband forming a break separating the lower and upper levels.

The garden, seen from the courtyard, articulated by trimmed yews, an avenue, and a cluster of limes.

The masonry of the pavilion blocks flanking the entrance is formed of vertical panels of brickwork on a background of stone and plaster on the exterior. This pattern, intentionally severe and cold on the outside, makes the inverse motif facing the courtyard that much more striking, with the warm tones of brick dominating.

283

Prétot

Imposing, indeed almost austere, the manor of Prétot stands proudly in the low-lying Touques valley, in the midst of the rich land holdings which constitute the estate patiently assembled by the Ballan family from the early 16th century. It was also named L'Osier manor after the osier willows whose shoots, which grow alongside the drainage canals, furnished their flexible stems for basketwork.

Men of the soil, but also men attached to the service of the province of Normandy, the Ballans crop up at various levels of the civil establishment, bearing witness to the evolution of landed property. The esquire Guillaume Ballan, who took over from his father the responsibility of receiver for the area of the Pays d'Auge, was also lieutenant for the bailiwick of Rouen. In 1634 he married the young sister of the dramatist Pierre Corneille and set up house at Prétot. It was there, in the quiet of this house in the fields, that the great writer enjoyed periods of peace several times between 1638 and 1668.

The *logis* at Prétot consciously diverges from medieval traditions. Sculpted decoration has totally disappeared, to the benefit of pure volume and strict line. It preserves the rectangular plan, the only small lapse from rigor being a little square turret on the rear façade. It contains two lofty floors beneath an imposing tiled roof, from the hipped slopes of which two detached chimney stacks rise at the extremities.

On the main façade, the two-light windows are arranged in three forceful vertical bays, accentuated by the double saltires and now-restored dormers, while an unemphasized bay with a single light introduces a subtle dissymmetry. The timbers have a very large cross-section, at the corners maintaining the tradition of long-posts. Not a single curve interrupts this uprightness, not even at sill level, where slightly curved timbers were normally used.

Everything at Prétot concurs with this sense of balance and stability. The structure asserts itself without resorting to tricks. In fact, the master builder introduced into his design a masterly line that lends force to the overall concept: refusing to conceal the oblique lines of the angle ties, he places them at the corners, and instead of having a series of superposed oblique braces on each floor linking the posts to the plate or sill, he has placed the obliques so as to form continuous lines, creating an illusion of a single piece of timber running through two stories and finishing off the composition in a perfect manner.

The fashion for polychromy would henceforth be limited to a simple alternation of brick and stone on the plinth and ashlar quoins on the brick chimney stacks, while the timber frame itself would merge into the silvered gray of the shingles, which still covered over the components of it several decades ago, showing up the lime nogging.

The preoccupation with defense was always present. The lower floor has now regained its grilles, and the stone masonry that constitutes the lower part of the rear wall still bears bullet holes in the

The rigor of the design and grandeur of conception is conveyed by the solid frame, which is pierced by broad sash windows.

To enhance the sense of monumentality, the builder positioned the diagonal ties in the extension so that they run from one to the other in a continuous line over two stories, suggesting a single block wedged between two chimney stacks.

The rear elevation – where the concern for defense is always evident – still includes an archaic tower shingles with chestnut tiles. But it contains only small closets, not the straight dog-leg staircase, which is included in the body of the house.

BELOW:
The same generous dimensions apply in the interiors, with high ceilings in the French style.

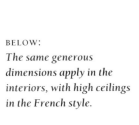

middle of tiny loopholes. The interior spaces derive from the same arrangement, with high ceilings in the French style and simplified lines in the fireplaces, which have no decoration beyond a simple console bracket on the jamb. The floors also contribute to the overall impression: magnificent paving of black flint cut into perfectly even pieces covers the vestibule floor while a similar but rarer stone adorns the ancient kitchen, where the black flint is striated with lines of gray flint.

It is difficult not to wonder about the presence of the small square tower on the rear elevation. Was it defensive worries that imposed this excrescence, and if it was necessary to create a closet-sized space, could it not have been integrated within the rectangular plan, at the cost of a small extension to the building? Should we not rather see in it a survival of the external tower that in residences a century earlier would have housed the staircase in the buildings? In this building, the staircase would in the future occupy a complete bay, totally integrated in the basic space of the house.

All trace of Renaissance art has disappeared at Prétot, and it is to the first quarter of the 17th century that we must date the construction of this innovative building, which has now been returned to its former glory.

Querville

Buried at the end of a valley, Querville is one of the most evocative manor houses in the Pays d'Auge. It is also one of the best preserved in terms of its original condition, its surrounding countryside, and its architectural history, which embodies three centuries of evolution in the art of living in one edifice. Snatched from the brink of ruin by courageous hands, it has rediscovered its vocation as a home, in the heart of an estate devoted to producing the best flavors the Pays d' Auge can grow.

The manor buildings are arranged round a polygonal courtyard originally ringed by water-filled moats. Entrance is via a gatehouse constructed in an irregular checkerwork masonry of limestone and brick. The outbuildings, byres, barns, cider-press, and outhouses still huddle up against the walls, framing a magnificent timber *logis* set on a ground floor of brick and stone. All that is missing is the dovecote once located in the forecourt, whose stone plinth vanished several decades ago.

Arcisse de Caumont supplies some detail about successive owners. In 1463, Montfaut found Henri de Querville there, one of a family owning various estates in the vicinity who would remain in possession until the end of the 17th century. Hector de Querville, who presented his proofs of nobility to the Elect of Lisieux in 1540, was governor of this town during the troubles which affected the region in the second half of the 16th century. "In 1616, Querville belonged to a nobleman, Jehan de Querville, squire of the place … . A tax roll dated 1683 mentions Damoiselle Anne de Querville among those exempt" (and she was no doubt the last of the name). The fief of Querville passed subsequently to "Messire Louis Marc-Antoine de Fauteveau – or Fautereau?, the family that owned the château of Mesnières, in the Bray region – and then in 1779 to Jean-Baptiste Davy de Boislaurens. After him, the Querville estate fell to one of his daughters, Madame de Vauvert."

The logis at Querville stands out at the end of the courtyard, seen here through the arch of the gatehouse.

It juxtaposes elements from several periods, like this post with a Green Man and the decoration of the rear elevation, still in a Gothic style but altered by the insertion of a large Renaissance window.

Erected in the 16th century, the gatehouse today powerfully conveys the defensive nature Querville manor house possessed right from the outset. Access through it is via a segmentally arched carriage gateway or the accompanying pedestrian doorway, which has a straight lintel. In the upper floor of the gatehouse is a small room, and above this an attic lit by a dormer with a hipped roof. A stone platband separates the first two floors, centered on two stones left rough-hewn, which perhaps once bore the painted arms of the lords of Querville. A staircase built of the same materials was subse-

quently built up against the gatehouse and is crowned with a timber latrine which very subtly imitates the proportions of the *logis*, even to the extent of adopting the same type of roof with four slopes and the same sprocketed eaves.

At first sight from the courtyard, the *logis* conveys a sense of unity, conferred on it by the sheer volume of the roof with its three dormers and the elaborate design of the first-floor masonry. The latter presents a sumptuous mosaic of brick patterned with lozenges picked out in glazed headers on each side of the central doorway, and vertical

The original logis was confined to the three right-hand bays. It has preserved the entire frame of the upper floor and used to feature a large dormer corresponding to the central bay. It was completed at the end of the 17th century by the addition of a frame of four bays on a brick and stone base.

The new axis of the building is solidly marked by a grand door with a pediment and double broken cornice, on which only the upper part is denticulated.

bands of toothed ashlar and jambs made of a golden limestone.

The differences of level between the two windows on the ground floor and the differences of texture in the timber frame on the first floor, where the pronounced window breasts on the left side vanish in the right third, suggest major alterations, which an investigation of the rear elevation confirms and clarifies.

This north façade reveals two phases of construction. On the three easternmost bays, a jetty separates the two timber-framed levels, the elements of which break off at right angles to a solid ashlar wall of stone and rubble with neat bonding stones and quoins. The first house was limited to the three timber-framed bays, and only consisted of two large superposed halls plus an attic floor lit by a large dormer facing the courtyard and occupying the whole width of the central bay. All that is left of this dormer are the mortises cut into the principals which were once occupied by the studs of the sides.

The original timber frame is wholly preserved on the north front. On the south side, only the upper floor is extant, lacking just the mullions and transoms of its single window. The decoration, which is perfectly preserved on the north façade, was effected with particular care. The jetty plate has a drip molding, then an ovolo flattened to an inverse point at right angles to each transverse beam, and on the bressumer a cable molding of scallops being "swallowed up" at each end by a grotesque with tapered ears and menacing claws. The same cable moldings on flagon bases recur on the first-floor posts, embossed with a floral motif which must mark the position of the transom of the original window.

The same decoration was found on one of the most famous houses in Lisieux, the manor house of La Salamandre destroyed in 1944, and still survives on any number of buildings from the first half of the 16th century. But other details also justify an attribution, if not to the same decorative hand, at least to a common inspiration in the authors of Querville and La Salamandre. The ogee arch and rosettes of the original door located at the northwest corner – now transformed into a window – with a fleuron above it, and even the floral motifs of the cable molding, the masks on the ogee, and above all the corner post at the north-west corner with its amazing foliage, lend this oak timber, already age-old when it was cut up for building, the aura of an enigmatic and condescending gaze on the centuries to come. An identical decorative system must have adorned the south façade: fragments of the bressumer bearing grotesques and cable molding have been found re-used in other parts of the building, sawn lengthwise for conversion into rafters, confirming the former existence of a similar jetty on the courtyard side.

The Renaissance left its stamp on the building in the form of the large window that replaces the Gothic aperture in the north front, inserted in the same position though with a greatly lowered sill. This features some fine ogee moldings and bowtells on the horizontals of the lintel, transom, and sill, and sunken panels on the mullion and jambs forming pilasters topped by delicate capitals with volutes and abacus flowers, similar to those that occur around 1550 at Les Pavements.

The service buildings extend on each side of the gatehouse facing the courtyard: storerooms, the cider-press, cellar, and granary, the timber frames of which rest on the back of the checkerwork wall.

The chronology of the phases of construction can be more easily discerned on the rear elevation where the medieval timber frame is preserved in its full height but is adapted to accommodate a large Renaissance window.

The *logis*, probably built by Hector de Querville, remained tiny, and access to the vast rooms on two floors via a simple staircase confined to one of the corners was no longer in fashion at the end of the 16th century.

It was probably Jehan de Querville who decided at the beginning of the next century to extend the *logis* towards the west, within the existing section, rather than completely rebuilt it. The extension more than doubled the size of the house. A first floor of brick with vertical bands of toothed masonry obliterated the overhanging jetty of the original house facing the courtyard, and a timber structure built in accordance with new principles was established on the extension. The studs are subdivided by an intermediate plate which acts as a sill, and the angle ties are henceforth confined to the upper tier. The composition is strongly centered

on a monumental doorway framed in plain pilasters, carrying an entablature broken at right angles to the keystone projecting from the lintel and surmounted by a curved, dentilled pediment with an oculus in the middle.

Brick nogging unifies the new façade, in which it is difficult to make out the shape of the original building. A large hipped roof, pegged down by an imposing chimney stack decorated with an applied pediment, covers the whole building. Thereafter no further alterations would impair the equilibrium of this sober design except for the addition in the 18th century of three dormers with segmental heads which were intended to accentuate the three window bays.

The considerable height of the ground floor of the original *logis* allowed some diversification of space in the extension. Making use of the strong slope of the terrain, a cellar was built without changing

The medieval logis only included a single large room per level, accessed by a spiral staircase set in a corner besides the large stone fireplace.

A staircase with fine octagonal balusters was constructed at the back of the main doorway. Above the door was a bressumer decorated with grotesques, which was reused in the alterations.

the harmonious height of the ceiling in the raised room built on top of it. The entrance door opens into a lobby, and the four levels are accessed via a sturdy dog-leg staircase which constitutes the high point of the decoration of the new *logis*.

Polychromatic effects are well represented in Querville, contrasting limestone, brick and timber. The occasional glazed brick, or the odd yellow or green-glazed tile on the roof, are there to remind us of the place that color holds in the attractions of Querville. It had some marvelous ridge finials, removed at the beginning of this century, and glazed ridge tiles decorated with foliated scrolls and stylized foliage, identical to those we find on the paving still carefully preserved. This blaze of color was probably arranged in large geometrical patterns like those recorded on the château of St. Germain-de-Livet.

La Rivière

Let us restore to the stud farm of Piencourt the name that this estate carried for more than eight centuries – after all, water is these days very much one of the charms of the place. The estate of La Rivière stretches to the bottom of the Calonne valley, the Calonne being a tributary of the Touques whose waters, by turn bustling or sluggish, carved out the plateau of Le Lieuvin. Numerous mills were at work, even quite close to the source, as records from the early 13th century bear out. One of these was leased out by the monks of the Abbey of Bec-Hellouin for the benefit of the third William of Bailleul, lord of a neighboring fief to La Rivière.

The place radiates serenity. The manor is set down among the greenery of the hillsides, and the waters reflect its image from the bottom of the valley. Time has slipped by since the day of Roger de La Rivière, who lived in this spot in 1198, and whose name history has been recorded just because of the forty sous bail he placed in the pocket of the royal receiver.

Unfortunately for the fief of La Rivière, the records are mute until 1469, the date when Louis XI summoned the General Muster, at which all vassals were bound to be present. Two vassals responded for the fief of La Rivière, which had been divided at an unknown date into two parts, held respectively by Julien Mallet, who presented himself with three horses, and Guillaume du Mesnil, who only brought two, in proportion to their respective obligations and the importance of their estates. Were horses already so important in this place? The Mallets were still recorded there some years later with Jean, son of Julien Mallet, and Tassine des Chenets, the Chenets being "lords of Cauverville and La Rivière-sur-Bailleul".

Sometime before 1562, the fief reverted entirely to the Le Mesnil family. It is not impossible to attribute to Jacques du Mesnil, whose wife was widowed in 1540, the construction of some parts of the present manor house, such as the huge service building which encloses the courtyard on the north-west, and it was probably his son Adrien who finished the works. The dovecote in the middle of the courtyard is perfectly preserved. Its octagonal frame is divided into three strictly vertical tiers and crowned with a fine conical roof. The escutcheon inscribed in the arch of the doorway probably bore the arms of the Le Mesnils, "gules a leopard or in a chief four barrulets argent".

The analysis of this *logis* is problematic, bearing in mind the numerous alterations undertaken in the course of the centuries. In terms of bulk, the most noticeable feature is an astonishing masonry tower, which stands out against the timber framework erected beside it on two floors. It is a round tower built of rubble plastered with red ocher checkerwork, simulating the elegant bond so popular with 16th century builders. It would not be inconceivable for this to be a remnant of an earlier building, because it is difficult to account for its present inclusion in a timber frame. Several manors in the area feature round stone-built towers at the corners of a timber frame, as for example at Le Vièvre, but in such cases the towers occupy a flanking position. The jetty on the façade is not very pronounced, and would suggest a construction date for the timber structure sometime in the last decades of the 16th century, though this hypothesis receives no confirmation from the arrangement of the windows and doors, which have been much altered. The centuries that followed would not bring any major changes in the existing components, though the interior decorations, the painted paneling of which has been partially preserved, will have been subject to refurbishing.

A dentilled cornice runs round the periphery of the most ornate room and highlights the lintels of

the doorways and the oval of a chimney mantel, while panels formed with applied moldings sport alternating cameo landscapes, foliation, and vases of flowers.

The 18th century on the other hand produced a remarkable transformation in the general arrangement. The courtyard was enclosed by a large brick and stone gateway on the axis of the house, two piers of which are still extant. The axis opens out into a wide view embracing the slopes of the right bank of the Calonne and a double avenue of lime trees ranged along the walls of the courtyard.

Today, the *logis* is a country house, and has happily adapted to this new existence. The site has been handled with sophistication and subtlety,

making the most of the freshness of its waters and its immaculate rich lawns. The ancient *logis* has taken on the charms of a country cottage. New apertures have been inserted into the timber frame, completing the large windows that replaced the medieval openings in the 18th century. The roofs have been embellished with dormers inspired by local traditions, but freely interpreted with the addition of a substantial hipped roof in the image of the first villas of the coast. Finally, without marring its dignity, the house has been discreetly extended towards the old service wing that clung to it. These days, La Rivière bears testimony to the new fashion that has enticed leading art lovers back to these manor houses after long decades of neglect.

The manor house of La Rivière in the rich man-made countryside of the Calonne valley.

A fine collection of painted
woodwork on a background
of applied panels is
preserved on the ground
floor of the logis.

La Roque-Baignard

The château of La Roque-Baignard is intimately associated with the memories of André Gide's childhood at this untroubled site set in a narrow valley. The brook that feeds its moats bubbles just a few minutes earlier out of the fishponds of the ancient Cistercian abbey of Le Val-Richer, the family seat of the 19th century statesman François Guizot.

Before it became so auspicious for meditation, this historic location was above all an ideal site for a fortress. The formation is established on an irregular polygonal plan, flanked by round towers which now stand in isolation alongside two residential buildings, and accessed by a gatehouse with a drawbridge in front of it. The large round tower of the dovecote is built on the north side, on a much smaller formation, and is likewise lapped by the running waters of the moat.

From the 12th century, the rolls of the Exchequer of Normandy mention here a family called de La Roque, notably Gervais and Jean de La Roque in 1180. In 1246, we find Robert de La Roque giving the living of the parish church to the Bishop of Lisieux. The fief of La Roque passed subsequently to the Baignard family, who would keep it long enough for their name to be added to the original toponym.

The present layout of the castle, which juxtaposes two substantial enceintes of very different kinds, is perhaps the result of switching the sites of the outer bailey and the castle proper. Today, the heavy tower containing the dovecote built on the smaller formation might well be a distant relic of the first keep. The old outer bailey, traditionally a much larger area, would then later have become the courtyard of the castle.

At the end of the 15th century, with the marriage of Catherine, the last descendant of the Baignards, to Jean Labbey, the castle and estate of La Roque passed into the hands of a distinguished family which would keep it for three-and-a-half centuries. Jean Labbey was the great-grandson of Colin Labbey, esquire to Bertrand du Guesclin, the famed Constable of France. Colin married Isabelle de Victot, and La Roque was handed down from generation to generation until the second half of the 17th century, when, taking advantage of a provision of the Customary Law of Normandy, Pierre Labbey de La Roque managed by means of lineal reversal to gain possession of the fief that had originally devolved to his brother, who had only a solitary daughter.

The family became extinct with Léopold Labbey de La Roque, who died in 1846 without issue. He was the son of Pierre-Élie-Marie Labbey de La Roque, born in 1752, who had to tackle the troubles of the Revolution, and saw his château take a drubbing during the looting of the charter-room in 1792. This great historian of Normandy, to whom we owe the publication of works such as Montfaut's "Enquiry" (1463) and the "Elect of Lisieux" (1540), completed the restoration of the château in 1803, finally fixing a black marble plaque to the back wall of the gatehouse that attributes its construction to François Labbey de La Roque in 1577.

François was the grandson of the first Labbey to be lord of La Roque, and everything about this building indeed indicates a work of the second half of the 16th century. It preserves the irregular layout of the ancient medieval castle, to the extent indeed of retaining its small angle towers built of plastered rubble and crowned with conical roofs. François also constructed a gatehouse on a square plan, flanked at the corner by a half-projecting diamond-shaped tower. The extensive alterations of the early 19th century left intact the fine masonry of red brick and long slots where the arms of the drawbridge used to go. However, the flattish pyramidal roof undoubtedly dates from the 19th century, as did the segmental arches of the windows and doorway.

The large *logis* facing the gatehouse has undergone major restoration work. Nonetheless, it preserves interesting polychromatic effects of brick and band courses of stone, echoing those on the gatehouse. We find once more, above each window bay, dormers with pediments and moulded jambs such as we encounter at the châteaux of Cricqueville and Victot. The builder's grandfather was lord of Héroussart, an estate on the western fringes of the Pays d'Auge, where this type of dormer was in fashion. No doubt François Labbey de La Roque called in a master of works originating from that area.

A second, more modest *logis* stands beside the moat on the west. It has clear echoes of the gatehouse, notably masonry of brick decorated with chains of toothing stones, but also the odd, lozenge-shaped, semi-projecting tower with a pavilion roof.

This structure was probably truncated, to judge by the tiny space left between the south gable and the first windowed bay. During the restoration completed in 1803, the small doorway with a semicircular arch was doubled by a much more monumental door intended to re-establish the balance of the house.

The gatehouse includes a similar lozenge-shaped tower. This building was heavily damaged during the Revolution, and restored by the penultimate Labbey de La Roque in the early 19th century. He was probably the one who set the stone tablet bearing the arms of his distant ancestor François, dating from 1577, into the wall above the entry porch.

Saint-Christophe

The proximity of the manor of Saint-Christophe and the chapel of the ancient priory of the Abbey of Cormeilles at Firfol has often given rise to conjecture as to whether they are, in fact, a single ensemble forming a small religious estate.

Nonetheless, the manor of Saint-Christophe presents all the characteristics of a secular manor, comprising a timber-framed *logis* of modest size, extended by service buildings returning at a right-angle at the end, and a covered well. The site lies within the confines of the Lieuvin plateau, where springs are rare. The round dovecote consists of a masonry first floor, partly in checkerwork, partly in dressed stone, beneath a timber frame with arch braces carrying the eaves of the roof. This tower no doubt once formed the corner of the manorial enclosure, and the pool alongside it could be the last remnant of the moats. Indeed, the summary published in Arcisse de Caumont's account mentions a linking feature – a wall or simple fence between the dovecote and the house – that is now missing.

There are still many gaps in the historical sources. We do not know for example whether François du Bosch, lord of Hermival and Firfol in 1540, or his successor Jean du Bosch, carrying the same titles, lived in this manor. As yet, we have no indication they did.

The *logis* and the outbuildings form a continuous building in which several phases of construction can be discerned. The most recent parts are on the north side, used as a barn, cow sheds, and cider-press. The middle component is probably the oldest. It is built on two floors, certainly much altered, but with an original structure of a very early long-post type with no intermediate plate and set on a high rubble plinth. An intermediate girder is pegged half way up in a rebate made in the bay posts, and the rigidity of the whole structure is ensured by a tall saltire. The presence of a small mullioned window and an aperture above the cross could indicate that we have here the location of the house prior to the end of the 15th century.

A much more elaborate *logis* was subsequently erected towards the south, on a much less common plan. It consists of one room above and below, in which there is nothing unusual, but access is via a spiral stair lodged in a square tower placed at the southern end of the façade. The entrance doorway is set into the foot of this tower, opening thence into the ground-floor room. The structure involved the use of the best timber-frame technology of the type current in Normandy in the second half of the 15th century. It is a short-timber structure with a jetty, on both the façade and the staircase, braced by two large saltires and an angle brace attached to the studs. This arrangement is as unusual as the plan. The structure of the staircase is integral with the building; in fact, the two transverse beams of the south side are extended to form the horizontal frame of the tower that contains it.

The moldings of the three pieces of the jetty and the cornice likewise display profiles rarely found in this region, like the "ribbed bowtell", which is much more common in Upper Normandy and recurs on the mullion and transom of the upper-floor window, flattened into "flagon" bases in the lower section.

This house has preserved its original layout in its entirety, including the two monumental chimneys, and two of its mullioned windows, still sporting their medieval frames, with internal shutters and vestiges of small openwork tracery in the Flamboyant style. To these features of the second phase of works, we must add a remarkable door with linenfold panels carved with a delicate border of slender trefoil foliage.

The two superposed rooms of the 15th century logis *form a sturdy building whose rear elevation is constructed in stonework laid in large blocks. The dovecote marked the south-east corner of the manorial enclosure. Its checkerwork wall linked up with the extension of the* logis *towards the south, whose overhanging gable was unfortunately destroyed.*

The extension of the logis towards the south in the first half of the 16th century was marked by the persistence of Gothic structural and decorative forms (e.g. grotesques) mixed with Renaissance motifs such as the fine statuette of St. Peter on the post and the gadrooned urns of the bressumer.

The sculpted decoration did not come to much. Today, all that is extant is a highly enigmatic leaf of oak on the middle post on the first floor, which is just as likely to have represented the signature of the carpenter as the punning arms of a client.

The two superposed rooms could not suffice for very long, and it was decided to extend the *logis* towards the south, on the alignment of the tower façade. The extension comprised three bays on two floors, the last being realized as an overhang carried on three posts. The master of the house thus had an additional room on each floor plus a south-facing, narrow, open gallery on the upper floor.

The whole decoration of the previous *logis* had been concentrated on the east front. The new building adopted a radically different scheme, applying lavish decoration to both east and south fronts. Unfortunately, the overhang has disappeared, and with it part of the sculpture described with such enthusiasm by Arcisse de Caumont. The parts still extant on the first two bays are enough to give us cause for lament, so successful is the handling of

Gothic motifs blended with Renaissance elements. The structure of short timbers, jetty and cornice was still de rigueur. Billet moldings and imbricated scallops still adorn the two mullioned and transomed windows. But grotesques would henceforth only gobble down interlaced rosettes or friezes of gadrooned urns, foliated scrolls, or scattered quatrefoil florets, the offerings of the new repertoire. The posts of the first floor are covered in Renaissance motifs in very low relief, alternating arabesques of gadrooned vases and delicate foliage. On top, cut in the body of the material, are the statuettes of St. Barbara and her tower, St. Peter and his keys, and St. John the Evangelist with his chalice, surmounted by a dragon. Although severely weathered by rain and west winds, the statues show the work of a skilled chisel, which handled the folds of the saints' clothing with great dexterity.

The statuettes on the upper floor, better preserved thanks to the eaves of the roof, were stupidly sawed off, and the features of the overhang so minutely described by Caumont were ruthlessly

The logis constructed with painstaking care in the second half of the 15th century was an extension of an older long-post structure. This may comprise only one room per floor, but affirms the depth of its builder's pocket with an imposing square upper-chamber tower containing the entrance gateway and the staircase. The extension towards the south implemented in the first half of the 16th century follows the alignment of the tower. It is built with timbers of very slender cross-section.

Very fashionable on timber-frame tie beams in religious buildings, grotesques adorn the extremities of the center beam upstairs in the main house here too, towards the south. The joists still bear traces of a now vanished painted decoration, preserved on the ground floor.

disposed of. Thus it came about that a bishop bene-dictens, a Trinity, a St. Michael slaying the dragon, a St. Margaret, and a St. Christopher which once adorned the center of the upper-floor gallery are now moldering away in some private collection of antique flotsam and jetsam.

The same refinement obtained in the interior decoration, still juxtaposing fireplaces and a beam with wholly Gothic grotesques and a painted first-floor ceiling – fortunately preserved – alternating joists and the spaces between them covered with interlaced rosettes and lozenges.

Despite the mutilation, the manor of Saint-Christophe still offers us one of the most fascinating survivals of the architecture and decoration in this region from the first decades of the 16th century.

The upstairs fireplace appears very archaic in comparison with the very elaborate decoration of the façades. The sole concession to modernity was the stylized foliage on the sides of the capitals.

Saint-Germain-de-Livet

Famous writers have wielded their pens to celebrate the delights of this dream residence and – to borrow an emotional phrase of Henri Pellerin's – its "immaterial beauty". We can scarcely avoid citing the enthusiastic eulogy by Jean de la Varende: "Livet! How will you concede that it is real, this façade, that it is in fact no more than a constructive flight of fancy; an ivory castle still, but one studded with emeralds! Indeed, a tiny jewel for a child princess, right at the heart of a narrow valley, set amid bubbling waters… ."

Livet is perhaps the monument that expresses the originality of the architecture of the Pays d'Auge with the greatest subtlety: the harmony and the contrast of stone, brick, and timber, a profusion of color, a perfect match in scale between the building and the man-made countryside, a continuity of history that, by means of alliances, has kept this piece of Normandy in the same hands for nearly 800 years.

The waters of the brook, a tributary of the Touques, were diverted to enclose the narrow polygonal formation where the Tyrels built – or rebuilt – their modest castle in the 12th century. Its irregular plan has survived to this day. Nicole Tyrel, the last of the name, married Ancel Louvet on 7 May 1352, a line that would stray from Livet just over a century later, to the advantage of the Tournebu family when in 1462 Jeanne Louvet married Pierre de Tournebu, who rebuilt the castle at the end of the Hundred Years' War. But it was above all Jean de Tournebu, their great-grandson, who created most of what we see at Livet today, which was probably reconstructed between 1561 – the date when his inheritance from his father-in-law brought him substantial means – and 1588, if we refer to the date and enigmatic inscription in the interior courtyard of the château. Preserved almost intact to the middle of the 19th century, Livet suffered its most serious destruction in 1865, on the order of the last of the Foucault-Tournebus, the ruthless Anne-Walburg-Crescence-Marguerite, countess of Bisson. Thereafter it was slowly reborn in the enlightened care of the Pillaut family, who in 1957 bequeathed it to the town of Lisieux.

The château proper is surrounded by broad moats crossed by means of a fixed bridge that replaced a drawbridge. Traces of the latter are still visible on the external wall of the gatehouse, which is flanked by two round towers. A huge forecourt lies in front of it to the north-east, enclosed by a wall once partly crenelated, that contained a carriage gateway and pedestrian gate. Still extant is the large timber-framed outbuilding built to the north-west at the end of the 15th century. But the octagonal dovecote built on three tiers of timber and brick with a lantern on top disappeared at the end of the 19th

The Tournebus constructed their new residence on a site once fortified by the Tyrel family, with one relaxed eye on the need for defense. While the south tower still has a number of loopholes hidden in the checkerwork of its walls, a tranquil gaze greets the visitor from the arch of the gatehouse, from the shelter of the fine entablature dated 1584.

The exact chronology of the phases of construction is difficult to determine. It is obvious, however, that the arcades of the gallery were inserted subsequently in a wall which was originally solid.

OPPOSITE AND RIGHT:
The gatehouse was, after the south tower, undoubtedly the first major phase of construction of the Renaissance period. Notable is the hesitant way the south-east curtain abuts it, giving nonetheless a dazzling response to the austere Gothic timber-built logis.

century, and with it the only display – at Livet – of the Tournebu arms "argent a bend azure".

Until the unfortunate demolition of the south-west and south-east wings in the second half of the 19th century, the château opened to view round an enclosed courtyard. The timber-framed *logis* to the north-west sits on very ancient masonry substructures, whose flat wall of the gable facing the moat could go back to the 12th-century castle. This *logis* occupies the entire north-west wing, and features a robust two-floor frame with a jettied upper floor beneath a roof with two large dormers arranged symmetrically in relation to the chimney stack. The frame is extended right to the west corner, the extension featuring a further, more modest dormer.

The house displays the normal design of *logis* built around 1500, a dating supported by the decoration with grotesques on the jetty bressumer.

The multi-colored checkerwork of the walls echoes the polychromy of the roof. On the latter, a number of glazed tiles still bear evidence of lozenge motifs and large finials of colored terra-cotta which glistened in the upper regions, above the carefully thought-out rhythm of the niches and semi-circular windows that alternate segmental and triangular pediments.

Though the apertures have retained approximately their original position, all the woodwork was refashioned subsequently.

A single major alteration took place after the mid-16th century, involving the entrance gateway and adjacent structures. Beneath the lintel of the entrance, there is now a fine Renaissance doorway with long vertical panels, sprinkled with iron nail-heads worked into rosettes.

On the first floor is the great hall of the *logis*, incorrectly called the Guard Room. The quality of decoration in it indicates its importance. A huge fireplace occupies the larger part of the cross wall, its lintel supported on thick piers with molded consoles and carrying a deeply molded relieving arch. The narrow staircase is oddly placed in a small tower, located between the fireplace and the wall facing the moat, which imitates a machicolated tower. The painted decoration achieves a richness

rarely equaled, covering the ceiling beams and preserved on the upper half of the walls and the mantel. The floral strapwork of the transverse beams is echoed by the geometric motifs of the fireplace. Ovoli underline the moldings, and an oval ribbon cartouche occupies the tympanum of the relieving arch. Two pilasters stand out at the corners from a landscape background where a pair of scrolls are positioned: in the foreground stand two mysterious figures in long garments, one of whom is tipping out jewels from vases. Are these related in some way with the scenes from the Old and New Testaments that frame them to the left and right of the fireplace? These feature Judith presenting the head of Holofernes at the tip of a sword, and Salome being given the head of John the Baptist on the salver brought by the executioner.

Another – less violent – scene completes this iconographical program illustrating the Holy Scriptures as, to the left of the window, David watches Bathsheba at her toilet. This contrasts with the battle scene developing on the rest of the wall.

The style of these paintings originates from a single hand. The design is unfussy, in firm, dark lines that flow easily round the folds of the clothing, particularly well preserved in the figure of Judith. Hands and faces are delicately realized, stamped with gravity of mien. Eyes and nose are finished in detail, with a wavy mouth. The coloring of the garments has remained bright and lustrous, with brownish red tones dominating. With the glazed terra-cotta floors of the upper floor, we have a precise notion of the importance of color in interiors of this quality.

In the western extension, which closely followed on this first *logis* and where a broad staircase was installed in the 19th century, we find a ceiling painted in black and white geometric motifs applied in broad rapid brushstrokes. It is the only example of its type in the Pays d'Auge, and was probably carried out before the end of the 16th century.

Undoubtedly Pierre de Tournebu must be considered the most likely builder of this house, in the second half of the 15th century, and his son Jacques, the man who commissioned the decoration, in the early 16th century.

Jacques de Tournebu knew about Italy. He served there as a captain of a company of Norman legionaries under François I. He does not seem to have embarked on major works at Livet, but the huge projects undertaken by his son Jean would not be strange to him. For that, substantial means were required.

The marriage of Jean de Tournebu with Marie de Croixmare in 1555 did, of course, make him better off, but most of all it linked him with a wife whose family had close links with Italy. In fact, among her near relatives was Marco Antonio di Segghizzo of Modena, the queen's major-domo and governor of Vernon. Connections with an environment so imbued with Italian influences were no doubt forged after the marriage of Jean de Tournebu and Marie de Croixmare. Links were close-knit enough for their son Robert to marry Madeleine di Segghizzo, daughter of Marco Antonio, in 1586. The boldness of the scheme chosen for the reconstruction of the château was thus justifiable. There was already a fashion for brick and stone checkerwork. The design adopted endowed it with a systematic character, contrasting plain terra-cotta on the courtyard side and green glazed brick facing the moat. The heavy tower had probably already been built, with its irregular checkerwork of brick and stone and narrow loopholes, as a counterpoint to the mass of the timber gable of the residence.

An elegant gatehouse on two floors, surmounted by a large slate roof and flanked by two towers on three levels, lent a monumental character to the entrance.

All the apertures have semi-circular arches or pediments, and a wide double band course carries the cornice of the central block round the two towers. The same irregular green-glazed checkerwork and double band course encloses alternating squares, and the same narrow niches recur on the great wall that abuts the east tower. Though the oculi of the gatehouse towers remain relatively plain, the five apertures of this type on the first floor of the east wall opt for strapwork decoration while, on the upper floor apertures with semi-circular arches, curved and triangular pediments alternate, each separated by a narrow niche. At the ends, the rhythm peters out in a much smaller unit.

The major feature facing the courtyard is the gallery, which extends from the gatehouse to the east tower, taking us aback with its reduced scale and the quality of its ornamental sculpture. It also disconcerts in that, though the building work reveals several design changes, the overall impression is of perfect harmony in a freely interpreted overall scheme.

Galleries are a feature much elaborated by the Renaissance, and their origin must be sought in Italy. They are found in most royal châteaux, and soon spread into all parts of the French kingdom, even to urban buildings. Here the four arcades of the first floor support a checkerwork upper floor, initially crowned by an exceptionally elaborate cornice. It is articulated by alternating windows and niches that are barely recessed into the stonework, rough-hewn and such that we can nowadays only discern the scallop of the upper part.

The design of an arcaded gallery normally follows simple principles, where the rhythm of the piers

Saint-Germain-de-Livet

determines the interaction of all other elements. The upper-floor apertures are usually inserted in the middle of the bays and not, as here, directly above the piers. This is to avoid affecting the stability of the structure. We should note that the windows are not of their original dimensions, as the dentilled bearings below them indicate, running on irregularly to the sides. The lintels also indicate clear reworking, cutting into the double-volute frieze running above. Finally, the fine cornice which still appears in prints from the beginning of this century – though unfortunately masked and partly obliterated as a result of an alteration to the eaves – was decorated with a series of stylized flowers, but apparently without the rigorous spacing that would have made the rhythms of the gallery scan. In the end, the main rhythm of the design is provided by the four niches, which have not undergone any alteration and which correspond exactly to the keystones of the arches on the first floor.

The master mason did not encounter too many difficulties in building a semi-circular arch in the gatehouse. On the other hand, the four three-centered arches of the gallery reveal a serious insecurity of stone-cutting, as the outline of the voussoirs particularly shows. Their joints converge at the center of the semi-ellipse instead of being apportioned among the three centers corresponding to the three arcs normally found in the outline of a three-centered arch. A final worrying observation: all these arches cut through more or less completely, though with some considerable indecisiveness, the platband separating the two stories, which suggests a later reworking or alteration.

A study of the relationship between the gatehouse and the gallery dispels our last doubts. The two floors of the gatehouse are separated by a frieze of limestone and brick squares, framed on every front by a platband and a pitch-faced rustication of interlaced lozenges and honeycombs. The motif is carried round into the wall facing the moat, but was obviously cut on the south front of the gatehouse when the interior wall of the gallery courtyard was attended to.

We can make out the first few inches of the frieze as commenced on this wall, almost immediately and very clumsily recut at the first arch.

The chronology of these two structures is thus

clarified: reconstruction began with the gatehouse and the wall facing the moat. Not long after, a lavish building with the same type of masonry and decoration and relatively few apertures was built in the space left free between the south tower and the gatehouse. A slight change of layout is evident in the transition from plain brick to glazed brick halfway up the upper story. Some years later, an inexperienced mason was commissioned to open an arcade of four arches on the first floor and alter the windows on the floor above, just as the fashion for galleries was developing. We should consider the indecisiveness as that of a builder faced with an exceptional project, which he translated into reality within the limits of his fellow masons' skills, who were more used to backing up the carpenters' work than creating the Italian dream of the Renaissance in the Pays d'Auge.

Jean de Tournebu's decorative artist was a man of great talent, as witness the facility of the strapwork decoration of the oculi on the façade facing the moats, the friezes of ovoli and *cyma reversa* volutes, and the decoration of the small windows with alternating pediments.

He probably left to the mason the decoration of the rustic work on the gallery arcade, rusticating and chamfering in turn from one voussoir to the

The great hall of the château occupies the major part of the ground floor of the timbered house, and has some of the most remarkable painted decoration of the 16th century extending over the whole area of wall and ceiling.

However, the checkerwork of glazed brick was only one of the elements of this color scheme. The occasional tile glazed yellow, brown or green still scattered here and there on the roof must be the last vestiges of a sumptuous decoration. This was indicated by the discovery of two primitive paintings from the late 17th or early 18th centuries, of whose objective accuracy there is no doubt. All the roofs in them bristle with immense glazed finials, and the glazed tiles are arranged in geometric motifs, a decorative scheme which is also attested in the engraving of the *Monasticon Gallicanum*, illustrating the abbey church of Préaux, in the diocese of Lisieux, at the end of the 17th century.

Various features allow us to date the chronology fairly precisely. We may suppose that this building work did not begin before 1555, the date of the marriage of Jean de Tournebu and Marie de Croixmare, and that full-scale construction came after 1561, when Marie came into a splendid inheritance from her father, the lord of Limésy. In 1578, according to the date carved there, we know that the same building team completed for Jean de Tournebu the construction of the seigneurial chapel adjoining the parish church, where there are close similarities with the decoration of the gatehouse and arches of the gallery.

The first date carved on the château is placed on the gatehouse, but in a location that indicates with certainty a major alteration. It is in fact on the admirable entablature applied to the front of the semi-circular doorway, carried on two Corinthian columns in a cartouche decorating the soffit, in the middle of a cable molding with four strands. The whole of the gatehouse must thus have been completed before this date of 1584, and we have to confirm that the quality of the new ornamentation on it achieves that of chasing.

The final clue is an odd inscription on the upper floor of the gallery, carved in three words and a date, …"FINIS CORONAT OPUS 1588". Jean de Tournebu thus completed the reconstruction of the château two years after the marriage of his son Robert to Madeleine di Segghizzo, thereby confirming the Italian contribution to the most complete work of the Renaissance in the Pays d'Auge.

Access is provided via an elegant Renaissance doorway with narrow panels framed by moldings and studded with wrought nailheads. This door is distinctly more recent than its Gothic frame of pinnacles and an ogee arch.

next. Its implementation on the arch of the gatehouse is particularly noticeable, where the rustication is alternately on façade and soffit. The result is one of an indefinible grace, arising out of the perfect harmony between the intimate character of the house and the richness of inspiration, where the splendor of color remains the dominant feature.

Saint-Léger

Lying between the Pays d'Auge and Lieuvin, and between Upper and Lower Normandy, the manor house of Saint-Léger seems to have been built with the intention of combining in one building the most beguiling expressions of architectural art in both territories. In terms of strict architectural line, the builder of the residence introduced an unusual variety of expression, contrasting the forms of façades with one another. In respect of harmony of color, he expanded the use of a very wide range of materials, displaying a virtuosity rarely equaled.

The *logis* of Saint-Léger long lay forgotten and mutilated in deep countryside. Fortunately, careful attention has now been lavished on it, though exercised with great discretion despite the extent of the works required, demonstrating the greatest respect for the spirit of its builder.

Saint-Léger was a knight's half-fief dependent on the barony of Bonneville-La-Louvet. In the 16th century, the Costard family became established here, and built up a position of some importance. In 1537, Pierre Costard was governor of the county of Harcourt, in the service of the most powerful family in Normandy. One of his descendants, Philippe Costard, would make an alliance with the Nollents, who were established at the château of St. André-d'Hébertot by marrying Marthe de Nollent in 1663.

Philippe Costard decided to have his residence rebuilt around 1625. He adopted a symmetrical scheme which he invested with an uncommon grandeur. It consists of a central rectangular block, on the west front of which he grafted two bastioned pavilion blocks. They are set forward, half outside the rectangle, the lines of their slanted façades converging towards the central door. At the ends of the east façade, two *bretèches* at the corners carried on *cul-de-lampe* brackets matched the two pavilions, while the square staircase turret in the middle forms

a pronounced projection. The bastioned pavilion arrangement of the ground plan does not seem to meet any defensive requirement, even if certain walls do show a noticeable batter. We might have concluded from the presence of a projecting staircase turret that there was once an earlier spiral staircase turret. Nothing of the kind – the turret contains the ends of long, straight flights supported by a string wall, as was the fashion in that period. Every effort seems to have been made in this *logis* to both integrate new features and preserve any old ones that, despite being archaic, could enrich the architectural expression.

The whole ground-floor level is built mostly of stone, but contrasts east and west again. Brick rules on the west front. Confined between stone quoins, its warm tones are sprinkled with decorative lozenge patterns made of glazed headers. The east front is dominated by a succession of toothed ashlar elements contrasting with a background of small paving blocks of gray and black flint laid in dry joints. Occasional apertures scarcely interrupt the rhythm, which continues to form returns round the end walls and the side walls of the pavilion blocks. Relief is limited to a few fine moldings on the top course and three fine, successively recessed ogee moldings forming the *cul-de-lampe*.

The builder erected a timber-framed upper floor on this masonry plinth where the removal of slate shingling has revealed a two-tiered structure consisting of a window level and a window breast level. On the latter, cross braces beneath the windows alternate with pairs of oblique braces in between. The rhythm is regular on the west front and freer on the east front. The decoration therefore amounts to an assembly of pieces of timber and volute consoles marking the tops of bay posts and jambs.

The arrangement of apertures for the most part follows the symmetrical scheme, with some

Such contrasts of form and color between the two façades of a single residence are rare. Saint-Leger plays the cards of surprise and the unexpected, cold shades and warm reflections, taut line and supple curve.

variation of rhythm. On the upper floor, single and double windows alternate; on the lower floor, the rhythm is a little freer.

The roofing accentuates the lines of this very elaborate plan. On the long roof of the central block with its two slopes and end hips, plain tiles are mixed with scalloped tiles, a motif repeated on the pyramid roofs of the pavilions grafted on to the west front. On the same front, three dormers emphasize the strong accents provided by the double windows on the lower floors. On the east front, only the northern *bretèche* is preserved. The main feature here is the staircase and above all the edicule that clings to its southern flank, a fragile timber-framed chapel supported on a sheaf of arch braces. Its three-sided apse overlaps the vertical of the staircase, a gay touch complementing the double curvature of its roof emphasized by scalloped slates. Such a diversity of forms and materials could have ended in an accumulation of disparate elements. In fact, the result is quite the contrary. Limestone, brick glazed or unglazed, black and gray flint, oak timber, lime plaster, plain tiles and scallop tiles, straight slates and scalloped slates blend harmoniously in one of the most elegant ensembles of manorial architecture in the Pays d'Auge.

The bastioned ground plan adopted for the main façade introduces a new dynamic in this elevation, accentuating the sharp corners of the pavilion blocks, which are echoed by the angles of the pyramidal roof.

OPPOSITE AND RIGHT:
Stone with its sharp edges carries timber and its rhythm of struts on the bretèche; a contrasting sheaf of curved timber braces carries the apse of the chapel, turning back into its southern flank.

No transition between the brickwork and its lozenge patterns of glazed headers on the front and the miniature two-tone checkerwork of gray and black flint on the side. It is the continuous pattern of struts between the rail and the plate that unifies the building.

325

Tordouet

The confluence of two watercourses was an ideal site on which to establish a fortification, and since the terrain was somewhat prominent, excavating a moat enabled the site to be turned into a "barred spur", making its defense that much more effective. At Tordouet, the two meandering *douets*, or brooks, mingle at the foot of the small castle, not far from where they run into the Orbiquet.

The homage rendered by the lord of the place for his fief of Tordouet, a full knight's fief held directly from the king, mentions a "manor constructed on a *motte*", a dovecote, and a mill. The site of the mill still exists downstream of the manor, while the dovecote stood away from the motte in the bailey, several of whose buildings still exist, along with fragments of their defensive walls.

The *motte* is not an artificial mound here but a natural feature of the spur adapted by means of a deep moat, now partly filled in. The irregular formation was small and surrounded with walls built of flint rubble, a fragment of which survives on the north side. It left little space for the construction of the house, enclosing the east side, and several buildings of prime importance in this reduced enclosure, such as the bakehouse.

It was a perfect illustration of feudal ties that the lord of Tordouet had fishing rights along the river, the right to take timber for his building and wood for his fire from the forest of Pabées, which belonged to the king, and to keep any number of pigs there. He also owned the livings of the churches of Tordouet and St. Cyr-du-Ronceray, and the small sixth-part fief of Monnay in this parish was a dependency of his. In return, he had to provide 40 days' vigil a year at the castle of Orbec and be in a position to equip himself in the service of his suzerain, to present him before him "in the clothing of a man of arms, accompanied by an archer and a page, mounted and adequately armed", as he did at the General Muster of the nobility of the bailiwick of Évreux on 17–18 March 1469.

The first lord of Tordouet whose name has come down to us is Henry du Buisson, at the end of the 14th century, whose son swore fealty for the fief to the king on 8 October 1413. Jeanne du Buisson, the last of the name, married Odon de Saint-Ouen, who could furnish evidence of his noble line back to 1265. He was then the one to swear fealty to the king for the fief of Tordouet on 8 June 1452. He presented himself 27 years later at the Muster of the Nobility of the bailiwick of Évreux, and died before 1484. The St-Ouen family retained the manor of Tordouet until the early 17th century, when alliances formed by Odon's descendants would induce them to set up in the Bessin region. They sold the estate of Tordouet to the Chaumont-Guitrys, who kept it until the Revolution.

The present *logis* is probably that of Odon de St-Ouen, and has survived almost intact. This makes it particularly interesting. It has never undergone any major alterations except for additions extending the southern end.

The original building stands on the east flank of the *motte* and its defenses. It was thus a matter of course that its first floor should be built of masonry. The builder made full use of his rights in this royal lord's forests, choosing the best oaks for the construction of the upper floor. This is an extraordinary structure dressed in timber that has no knots, to which its remarkable state of preservation can be attributed.

The masonry of the first floor is built with great care of small squared flints with bluish-gray tints, separated by two long-band courses in limestone. The same feature recurs in the frame of a semi-circular door and a window that today lacks its mullions and transoms.

This bond made up of alternating bands enjoyed some favor in the Pays d'Auge, though brick was preferred to flint. It did not, however, reach the level of exceptional virtuosity found in the masonry of this type in the region of Caux, particularly in the 16th and 17th centuries.

The north gable could be the oldest part of the roof. In fact it comprises numerous blocks of *roussier*, a kind of ferruginous sandstone quarried in the valley. It is also used for the construction of a thick pilaster buttress shoring up the mass of the chimneys.

The timber-framed floor comprises four bays resting on a double course of sill plates and creating a slight overhang on three fronts. (The north gable wall is the exception.) The jetty is returned at the corners by means of dragon-beams, allowing unmarred continuity in the austere molded decoration of the jetty bressumer and the jetty plate. The under-ceiling height reaches nearly 4 meters, and this leaves room for a very elaborate design of façade. A row of bays with transoms extends unbroken, matched by a corresponding number of window breast walls featuring saltires. However, the height is such that the builder was forced to leave solid space above the transoms, usually reserved just for the top plate. The crosses in the window breasts are jointed into the lower wall plate, then laterally into the vertical posts, enabling the continuous plate forming the window bearing to be positioned by pegging it on as a wall piece. The windows preserve lateral grooves, witnessing to the presence of sliding shutters that allowed the low openings to be hidden. The absence of grooves on the transoms seems to indicate that originally the shutters were simply oiled parchment, allowing a certain amount of light in but checking draughts, before glazed panes made their appearance.

The decoration of the timber frame is plain, and limited to moldings on the jetty, sill, and lintels of the apertures and transoms. Only the bay posts are adorned with large flat lamp-base motifs, at the point where they widen to carry the edge of the tie-beams. In the interior, the space comprised between the top course of the stone walls and the joists is occupied by a cornice whose moldings resume the motif on the external jetty bressumer.

The roof retains some very interesting features. A huge hipped dormer occupied the whole width of the third bay and presented an elevation very similar to that of the floor below. But most of all, this splendid, almost cubic, building was crowned with an asymmetrical roof, responding to the sole chimney stack at the north end. The south gable was protected by a steeply sloping open roof supported by the ends of the plates of the façades and relieved by angle braces still clearly visible.

The house built in the second half of the 15th century did not, therefore, contain more than a single huge room each on ground and upper floors, beneath a huge roofspace lit by the large dormer. The ground floor room was quite dark, bearing in mind the thickness of the walls. The only natural lighting was provided by two splayed window embrasures. An imposing stone fireplace, the canopy of which was supported by a relieving arch, occupies most of the north wall. The elegance of the great Gothic fireplace on the upper floor, on supports much more elaborate than those of the lower room, and the substantial lighting at this level, prompt us to wonder whether the great hall of the manor was not in fact at the upper level.

As in all manor houses with a single room per level built in this period, for example Querville, the

The original logis, *which only had one room on each floor and an attic space lit by a large dormer, was extended towards the south in two separate phases of building.*

square – timber-framed – staircase turret is set in a corner. In this case it faces the entrance door, which allows very direct access to the great hall upstairs. Other details militate in favor of the importance of this room, including a timber ogee arch later pegged on the lintel of the door leading to the staircase, as if to solemnize access. Finally, let us not forget it was only at this level that the outlook extended beyond the walls over the whole of the demesne.

From the end of the 16th century, this rather inconvenient residence was extended by one bay towards the south, while holding to the alignment of the original façade. Here the masonry is much more skillful, adorned this time with a pattern of limestone bands interspersed with alternating rectangles of limestone and squared flints. The timbering on the other hand is much more simple. It respects the position of the jetty, which it extends but without any moldings. Could the forests of the Pabées have been worked out? The builder was happy with reusing recovered posts and studs that still bore Gothic *cul-de-lampe* motifs. The fashion for straight gables was out, and the extension is

covered with a hipped roof aligned on the point of the old south gable.

In the years that followed, the *logis* was extended once again by a small building of much more modest dimensions, restricted to a single floor in the same masonry bond. It is also covered in a tiled roof hipped at one end, its ridge coinciding with the eaves of the main block.

No further alterations would be undertaken and the Chaumont-Guitrys, established mainly at Orbec, would consider the fief of Tordouet as simply an associated property occupied henceforth by a farmer. The useless walls gradually vanished bit by bit, while the great dormer was removed and replaced by a more modest opening.

In the 18th century, a rendering of lime with panels of red ground-brick mortar covered the breast walls of the west façade and the south gable, to protect them from driving rain. This very dilapidated decoration was removed at the time of the most recent restoration, returning the building to its medieval arrangement.

Le Verger

The site chosen for the construction of Le Verger lies at the bottom of a small valley facing west, watered by a tributary of the Touques. Clever management of the water in the form of two earthen dikes enabled two successive ponds to be created. The upper reach of these ponds encloses a small *motte*, on which there was only room for a *logis* and a single outbuilding including the bakehouse. The other outbuildings, cow sheds, and press are scattered around the ponds.

The ancient fief of Le Verger, an eighth fief of Fervaques, itself dependent on the barony of Auquainville, was owned in 1454 by Raoul Anfrey, who was ennobled in that year by Charles VII for his unwavering loyalty to the kingdom of France during the English occupation. A century later, the fief of Le Verger appears to have passed into the hands of the Louvières through the marriage of the Anfrey heiress with Claude de Louvières, who embarked on the reconstruction of the manor house in the second half of the 16th century. His father – another Claude – had died in 1562, and the son also disappeared by 1604.

Henri Pellerin justly rated the *logis* at Le Verger as something of an aberration in relation to the usual standards of architecture in the Pays d'Auge. Admittedly, the large cube-shaped mass of this strange timber-framed structure mixed with stone hewn in large blocks was, until its recent restoration, a distant stranger to the rules established during the Renaissance. Despite the red-brick nogging and the quality of its sculpture, the unfortunate dimensions of the building could not be ignored, crowned as it was by an intolerable flattened pyramidal roof, from which rose a heavy, squat chimney stack. At first, Pellerin aired the idea of a house devastated by a roof fire and rebuilt cheaply and in haste. "The manor house at Le Verger is no more than a façade", he wrote in 1955. He went back on the theory twenty years later, arguing instead for a probable southern, indeed even Italian, influence to justify the reconstruction on a square plan and with a shallow pyramidal roof.

Space was short on this confined formation. The problem was how to fit a conveniently oriented residence of good size on it. The only way was to compact it into a solid bulk on the north-west, sparingly endowed with apertures facing the moat and solidly built of stone on this side. The south and east fronts, with broad apertures facing the courtyard, could then be erected of finely worked timber, lavishly decorated in a Renaissance style and tricked out in a masterly nogging of red tiling. A study of the square plan reveals two substantial stacks of chimney masonry, linked by a spiral staircase dressed in the same material. This accesses four rooms on each floor, three with a fireplace downstairs, four upstairs. Floor levels vary widely.

The upper pond surrounds a narrow motte with its waters. Space is short on the motte.

This lack of space prompted the almost square plan, relieved by the generous slate roof. This was recently restored, complete with its glazed terra-cotta finials.

The arrangement betrays a number of second thoughts, and apparently indicates the commencement of a stone structure on the north-east side, completed soon after by fine Renaissance timber-framed façades to the east and south.

Their structure is very simple, sometimes breaking with the perfection of the stout timber frames which were still the rule at the beginning of the 16th century, with a clear differentiation between stories, separated by a jetty. At Le Verger, the five bays of the east elevation and four of the south elevation are marked vertically by long posts common to both floors. Horizontally, a window breast wall of saltires provides a strong feature of the façades between the two ranks of studs that correspond to the two levels of openings.

With some exceptions, all the openings have preserved their original distribution. For the most part, they consist of simple doors and twin windows, arranged with regularity.

The sculpted decoration is in low relief and superposes friezes of foliage volutes and curved gadroons on the plates, reserving ovoli and festoons of stylized foliation for the lintels.

The north and south façades display two exceptions upstairs: on the north front, a blocked-off doorway corresponded with the latrines directly above, which were reestablished during the recent restoration. On the south front, the fine sculpted door has been converted into a window, to avoid opening into a void. No doubt it once led to some defensive work such as a palisade that completed the protection of the *motte*.

It is worth pausing on the unusual arrangement of the sculpted decoration. Usually reserved for the single members of the frame, here it covers the verticals of the bay posts, the jambs and alternate studs. On the posts, we find garlands of foliage and fruit interspersed with coats of arms (unfortunately inde-cipherable) and vegetable volute motifs. The studs are trimmed with consoles of long carved foliage. Horizontally, the sculpted decoration adorns two sections of the cornice, the continuous sill beneath the two windows upstairs, and the rail marking off the window breast wall. The cornices superpose a cable-molded mid-rail and a bressumer covered with ovoli enclosed in a fine cable ribbon. The carvings have been very well preserved under the eaves of the roof. Whereas the rail is gadrooned, symmetrically incurvated per half-bay, the plate separating the floors is decorated with a frieze of foliated volutes.

The final component of this wealth of decoration is the treatment of the lintels and jambs, to which the same degree of care is applied on each floor.

The use of jetties disappeared in the second half of the 16th century, as long posts returned in force. They are decorated with long carved leaves, fluting, or opposed pairs of volutes.

The windows have cable-molded lintels or festoons of stylized foliation, supported by long leaf motifs turned back into volutes. On the ground floor, the two doors present an astonishing amalgam of intermingled ogee arches and foliage volutes, illustrating again the tendency to decorative excess.

The relationship of this ornamentation with that of the Old Manor at Orbec or the *logis* in the Rue du Perré in Vimoutiers is obvious. If we take as our reference point the date of 1568 carved on the Old Manor, the construction of the *logis* at Le Verger must have been around 1580. In fact, the simplified structure of the frame highlights the decline in the carpenter's art at the end of the 16th century. On the other hand, though the sculptor handles the geometric motifs – cable moldings, foliage, ovuli and gadroons – already used at Orbec and Vimoutiers with the same deftness here, he is much less at ease when he attempts original motifs such as the foliage volutes on the posts of the east front.

One major question remained unanswered, namely the shallow roof of the house. Traces of fire were discovered during restoration work. The carpentry and roof were reworked in 1841, according to a date carved on a sheet of lead. A close look at the base of the fine green-glazed Pré-d'Auge terra-cotta finial perched on the unlovely pyramid revealed its initial position, not at the top of an almost flat roof but at the end of a ridge. All that was needed was to find the second finial. A stroke of good fortune came during the cleaning out of the pond, when the vital fragment was found deep in the mud – a pretty female face, of the same glazed terra-cotta, in the same style as the masculine character that had fortunately remained on its roof for four hundred years. No doubt it also came off during the fire of 1841.

Thereafter, the silhouette the manor of Le Verger was to resemble that of the Old Convent of Vimoutiers, with the same compacted mass, though on a more modest scale, covered with a tall roof with four slopes and the same ridge with two finials. The remaining task was to establish the position for a possible dormer. The enormous open chimney stack on the east slope to the right left available the necessary space directly above the best window on this story. It was just where one bay of the cornice had

been changed, eaten away perhaps by the ravages of weather when it carried the base of the dormer at this location. The end result was to reestablish – more or less – a silhouette similar to that of the house in the rue du Perré at Vimoutiers, with which the manor house at Le Verger has certainly very many affinities.

The ridge finials posed an acute problem: the old intact finial was finally taken off. A faithful copy of the male character – a huntsman in baggy culottes carrying a gun – now perches on the ridge alongside the female character reconstituted on the lines of the finial couple in the same spirit preserved at the Seine-Maritime Museum of Antiquities at Rouen.

Today, the lord of Le Verger and his wife once again supervise the renaissance of their manor under the green glaze of their finials.

The latrine is directly above the pond. It was restored using the original mortises.

*Space was reduced, and the
fireplace in the room, which
is integral with the
staircase, seems to be
gathering strength in the
corner.*

Victot

In 1720, the Small Royal Stable numbered among its many young pages Jean Jacques René de Sainte-Marie, who became lord of Victot; and we might say that Victot has been the finest estate for horses in the Pays d'Auge ever since.

Set in the rich plain that marks the low-lying valley of the river Dives, the château is bound up with the image of these luscious pastures where the best horses have been bred and nurtured by the Aumont family for nearly two centuries. The successor to the page from the Small Royal Stable and the Le Normands of Victot in 1798 was, it so happened, Pierre Aumont, who became the "general purveyor" of horses to Napoleon's Grande Armée, securing for his brother the post of "general purveyor of forage".

Since the 1840s, it has been the stables constructed by Alexandre Aumont and not a broad avenue or an entrance gate flanked by lodges that have greeted the visitor to Victot. We are in the heart of the kingdom of the horse, and the whinnying of a stallion or the tranquil step of a brood mare are more welcome accompaniments of the visitor than the yapping of an ill-tempered dog.

We have also entered a remarkably preserved manorial ensemble, which juxtaposes its different features in such a way as to suggest what the original arrangement of this great domain might have been. The network of drainage streams feeds a huge rectangle of moats surrounding a square courtyard of outbuildings in the west and extensive gardens and orchards to the east. These moats are continued by a large stretch of water orientated towards the north-east.

The stables are timber-framed on a high plinth of limestone rather like the thin slabs of the Caen plains stone. Roofed with tiles covered with orange lichen, they are ranged to form a huge outer bailey. The first structure in the row is a small building on a square plan right by the entrance which was once no doubt the dovecote, still legibly recorded as such on the first cadastral survey in the early 19th century. The church of Victot, on the outside of the enclosure and very close to the entrance, preserves the memory of the ancient castle chapel, with a slender belfry and timber porch.

The château proper is included within the huge rectangular enceinte, midway along its south flank, but isolated on a formation which is itself surrounded by wide moats. There does not appear to be any logical planning behind this collection of buildings, which occupy two sides of a courtyard wide open to the south. They form a happy mixture of brick and stone checkerwork and half-timbering clad in slate, the brickwork being confined within quoins of toothed masonry and decorated with glazed patterns. These structures are flanked by a square tower on one side and a round tower on the other.

It is the art of color that gives this iridescent ensemble its real coherence, partly the multiple coloring of its walls, but even more the colors of its extraordinary roofs. A major proportion of the latter are made of tiles glazed in yellows, greens, and browns, while the ridges still sport several large

The great west house is surrounded by moats. A roadway runs between it and its mirror image in the water, allowing access to the outer bailey in front of the gatehouse.

glazed earthenware finials. Victot is a rare example of the use of scalloped tiles in Normandy. They are applied likewise on arris hips, formed of two glazed angle scallops, and are even placed transposed on the scallops of the slate cladding facing the moat.

Much has been made of the "two-house château" of Victot, by which is meant the way the two masonry-built blocks are linked at the end by a connecting timber-framed feature. To be more precise, the layout consists, on the one hand, of a great gatehouse with a drawbridge, a real mini-castle, focusing the basic defenses of the château, the *logis* itself, and on the other, set as a return at right angles, distinct from the first building and noticeably more developed. How the courtyard was originally laid out is no longer known, but it was

certainly once entirely enclosed by walls, against which sundry other buildings were erected in accordance with medieval custom. In the south-east corner, a large, square, set-back section seems to indicate the former presence of a substantial flanking structure that has now vanished or was once planned.

A summary glance at the sole remaining timber façade indicates from the profile of its high cornice that all or part of the medieval *logis* of Victot remained timber-built until the end of the Middle Ages. Apart from this modest relic, the rest of the buildings were reconstructed in the second half of the 16th century and early 17th century, and altered in minor ways in the following centuries.

The history of Victot is reasonably well-known. The fief was owned by Hugh of Victot in 1160, and

Horses stroll in the outer bailey, which is flanked along its entire length by service buildings, barns, and coach houses.

The gatehouse at Victot assumes a particular importance, constituting a mini-castle in itself, defended by a drawbridge and endowed with two generous dormers.

The date of 1574 written on the dormer above the drawbridge marks the completion of the gatehouse. It is accompanied by the Boutin family motto: "Death is good that brings back to life", above their arms of "argent a fess azure accompanied by three roses of gules, beneath a helmet plumed and supported by two unicorns". No doubt this goes to explain the parallels between the two châteaux and particularly the important role assigned to multi-color effects.

The gatehouse is built in a checkerwork of brick and stone erected in regular courses on two levels separated by a platband. The semi-circular arch and the accompanying window on the same level are decorated with rustication and quincunxes of nail-heads above the entrance. On the upper floor, the slots for the arms of the drawbridge have now been blocked off, but they nonetheless remind us of the problems of defense, always present in those troubled times.

The great west house, although built of the same materials, bears witness to an evolution introduced into this architecture some years after the construction of the gatehouse. The checkerwork has given way to alternating beds, and though a platband of stone still separated the two levels, the façades are mostly brick. Beds of stone henceforth marked the plinth, the sill, and the lintels of the windows of the first floor, but upstairs only the window sill level (prior to later alterations) with strong horizontals.

The façade facing the moats is centered on a slender square tower with a pavilion roof, and at the south-west corner abuts an imposing round tower built in a masonry bond which is perfectly tailored to that of the *logis*, the only difference on the two features being a fine cornice of volutes – not a simple molding any more – and a top layer of zig-zags made of small blocks of plain stone. Originally, only the façade facing the courtyard sported large dormers much more elaborate than those on the gatehouse. They had a semi-circular aperture flanked by narrow volutes and consoles, the spandrels and jambs being emphasized by flat flutes, the arch by a rusticated keystone and a deep pediment.

In the final years of the 16th century, a number of major alterations were carried out on the gatehouse, to make the château more comfortable. A first

remained in his family until the early 15th century, when Jeanne Gosse, apparently the last of the line, married Guillaume Boutin, bringing with her the fief that her descendants would retain until 1704.

"Guillaume Boutin and his aforementioned wife were most strongly suspected by the aforesaid English of being good and loyal French people", according to letters patent granted by Louis XI in 1463. It is thus very likely that the old castle took such a battering during the troubles of the Hundred Years' War as to justify its complete reconstruction. In 1570, Philippe Boutin married Geneviève de Croixmare, niece of the president of the Court of Aids (i.e. Customs & Excise) of Normandy. She was also sister of Marie de Croixmare, wife of Jean de Tournebu, who was at that date directing the reconstruction of the château of Saint-Germain-de-Livet.

turret, also on a square plan, was placed to the west, to the right of the drawbridge. It initially had a pavilion roof, but was later extended for the whole depth of the gatehouse towards the courtyard as a shingled, timber-framed structure of the same section. The turret was then replied to on the left by a large, heavy, and square tower with very similar architectural characteristics. The play of colors is reduced in this case to corner quoins of toothed masonry and window surrounds on a background of brick, accompanied by the final element of the trilogy that would typify the whole 17th century, i.e. slate. However, these two towers retain a close connection with the previous structures, notably in the continued use of voluted cornices and the same model of large dormer on the square tower, breaching the eaves of the roof in order to follow the horizontal alignment of the other dormers.

In the 18th century, changes were made simply to keep up with current fashions, e.g. increasing window sizes by raising lintels and lowering sills, removing the window above the gatehouse arch facing the court, and adding clumsy pediments to the first-floor windows on the great *logis* facing the moat.

The courtyard of the château was no doubt once enclosed by walls or structures on the south and east sides. The part of the building that extends the heavy tower in the south could be a relic of them, but the mediocre quality of its brick masonry and lozenge ornament suggest too late a date.

At the château of Victot we thus find a summary of the whole evolution of the art of polychrome architecture that the Pays d'Auge indulged in so happily between the end of the Middle Ages and the Classical period.

The richness and diversity of seigneurial architecture

It is possible to trace a succession of construction phases on the rear elevation of Anfernel manor house, which overlooks the valley. Above the section of flint and sandstone rubble masonry, which is underlined by a limestone string course, we see the fine brick checkerwork masonry laid in various geometric patterns and particularly carefully executed on the bartizan on the north-east corner.

Anfernel

The contrasting tones of checkered brick under the tiled roof turned silver with lichen and the scarcity of its window and door openings give the *logis* of Anfernel the appearance of a fortress. Its huddled mass contrasts with the gentle character of the timber-framed outbuildings which surround it scattered among the apple trees. The fief of Anfernel ran along the southern side of the Courtonne valley and along the plateau above it. At the end of the 16th century, the plateau lands were covered with woodland and ploughed fields of rye, barley, peas, beans, and oats, and livestock grazed on the slopes of the valley. The lord of Anfernel could keep a close eye on the running of his estate from his home. He soon

found the *logis* rather cramped, however, and, deeming it too small to meet his needs, he extended it by renting some neighboring land from the bishop of Lisieux.

The origins of the fief remain unclear. It may have belonged to the Anfernel family known in the region of Vire at the beginning of the 15th century, who may have carried out one of the many clearances undertaken after the Hundred Years' War, when prosperity was slowly being regained. Castelleyre, the name of one piece of Anfernel land during the 16th century, suggests an earlier settlement, but there is no further evidence of this.

Gabriel du Houlley, youngest son of Jacob du Houlley, is the first lord of Anfernel known to us. The elder branch of this family went up rapidly in society – in the following generation Adrien du Houlley, lord of Courtonne, Gouvix, la Roque, Argouges, les Essarts, Firfol, la Grandière and other places, was granted the titles of royal councilor and civil and criminal lieutenant general of the bailiff of Évreux in the county of Orbec.

However, the younger branch, which concerns us here, had to await the Paris Charter of May 1646, registered on 8 May 1648, when the King ennobled the son of Gabriel du Houlley, lord of Anfernel, who was also named Jacob.

The house itself forms a long rectangle running from east to west and is extended to the west by two short symmetrical wings, which only project slightly from the main body of the building. Window openings are found at various levels, testifying to various repairs and changes of fortune, and a large tiled roof lends coherence to the structure. The most original feature is an extraordinary *bretèche* on the north-east corner which has a cut-off corner and is supported by three inverted pyramids.

While the plan has been left unchanged, the elevation shows a superposition of masonry bonds which represent three phases of construction. The first of these is found in the ground floor and consists of small stones of brown and gray flint mixed with *roussier*, a ferruginous sandstone commonly found in the area. Dressed stone is used only to form the lintels and in the rather uneven toothing of the window and door jambs. The only decoration consists of a flat string course which rises to the level of the lintel of the main door on the north side, sinks as it passes the old window openings, and is realigned again on the west elevation. The same bond is used for half a floor above the lintel, but it is laid more regularly here with uniformly interspersed vertical bands of toothed limestone blocks.

Could it be that the *logis* of Anfernel was originally only two stories high? This is unlikely. It would appear that the builder wanted to level off his stonework neatly before constructing the much more carefully finished upper story, during the final building phase. In this last floor we find attractive regular stone checkerwork with alternating courses of limestone and brick, and courses of limestone and light brown flint. Particular attention was paid to the north wall where bricks are laid in a lozenge pattern on the four squares of the checkerwork in the middle of the panel; saltires, zigzag, and herringbone patterns feature on the bartizan on the north east corner. It is most likely that Gabriel du Houlley, who died before July 1591, built this house, which bears certain similarities to a neighboring house, the manor of Haulière in the Orbiquet valley on the banks of the Courtonne; here we find the same compact plan, the same silhouette of a fortified house, but less elaborate masonry than at Anfernel.

The manor chapel stands about fifty yards away from the *logis*. It is very simple, built on a rectangular plan and covered by a hipped roof with sprocketed eaves. The west-facing door and the lateral round-headed windows are equally sober, and this impression is reinforced by the very subdued polychrome highlight added by brick toothing capping the corners of the walls. The remains of a *trompe l'œil* altarpiece enable us to date this chapel to the mid-17th century. It is probably the work of Jacob du Houlley, carried out sometime between his ennoblement – recorded in 1648 and confirmed in 1666 – and his death towards the end of the century, before 1696, the year in which his son, the honorable Louis, lord of Anfernel, registered his coat of arms in the armorial of France.

The manor and lands of Anfernel remained in the possession of the Houlley family until 1754 when they were acquired by a Courtonne farmer named Guerrier, who immediately made various changes. He engraved this date on the lintel of a door on the north façade and changed many of the windows. Up until this time, the only light in the house was provided by narrow rectangular single casement windows. The leveling of the roof which counteracted the protrusion of the western wing, damage to the roof of the large *bretèche* on the north-east corner, and the removal of a much smaller *bretèche* which appears to have been attached to the south east corner, are undoubtedly his work. The younger son of the Houlley family did not have sufficient resources at his disposal to build a large elaborate home. He did, however, endow it with the hallmarks of the rank finally bestowed upon his branch of the family after a fifty year wait, and consecrated it by building a chapel.

L'Aumône

The logis at Aumône has every appearance of a seigneurial manor, but in fact it was the former leper-house of Cornica probably founded in the 11th century near the town of Pont-L'Èvêque. This was a charitable foundation which took in lepers at a time when this dreadful disease ravaged the province. Today, its origin is only recalled by local place names. The leper-house is situated close to 'chemin des ladres' (leper lane), which leads to the 'fontaine aux malades' (fountain for the sick). This was also the site of the chapel of St. Mark and St. Giles, of which no trace remains. The manor of L'Aumône has been a simple agricultural estate since its integration into the hospital of Pont-L'Èvêque in 1696.

Its unfortunate inhabitants found the comfort of a house sheltered by the plateau and protected from the west winds, its aspect enjoying the morning light over the Yvie valley and the warmth of the midday sun.

The outcrop of soft limestone in the area provided the light gold colored stone for the house, the timber framework being used only sparingly in the construction of the gable and the three roof dormers. Its robust quadrangular mass is centered around a staircase turret at the back, which also has timber framing resting on a stone ground floor and is covered with a hipped roof, the tall ridge of which is linked to the slope of the main façade. This apparent homogeneity is the result of several construction phases and the date 1584, which is engraved in the keystone of the round arch of the main door, refers to the main phase of alterations.

There are, however, also deviations from the symmetry which one would expect to find in a building constructed in a single phase. The twin window openings on the right-hand side of the first floor are slightly lower and the surrounding molding is the only projection in the otherwise flat wall at this level. Most noticeably, there is a break in alignment of the dripstone separating the two stories and in the stone courses.

The structure of the chimneys also differs significantly on each of the gables. On the west gable, the chimney stack projects considerably on both stories and the flue gradually tapers to the dimensions of

the stack. Inside, the mantels are supported by robust corbels or simple studs. On the east side, the only fireplace on the first floor is hidden behind the timber-framed gable and has a pair of small pretty studs with molded capitals which clearly originate from a more recent period.

The protruding chimney breast is part of an old tradition dating back to the time when the fireplaces of stone buildings, hitherto situated on the eave walls, were moved to the cross walls or gables: the hearth was included in the thickness of the wall or as an extra layer, thus eliminating the need for studs to support the mantel. This was no longer the practice in the Pays d'Auge after the 15th century.

The discreet ogee arches marking the twin windows of the first floor on the west side confirm this

The interruption in the projecting stone course on the main façade of the manor house of L'Aumône marks the junction of the two construction phases. The year 1584, which is engraved on the arch of the entrance door, probably indicates the year in which the building was completed.

medieval barn, built with a huge nave supported by two rows of posts flanked by aisles, some farm buildings, and the imposing mass of the manor house itself which consists of a main rectangular structure with a slightly taller side wing built at a right angle to it.

The name of the Barville family was associated with this land since 1198. The family lived there for more than three centuries until the death of Constantin de Barville in 1523. His nephew, Richard de Livet, inherited the estate and it remained in the family until the death in 1891 of Léon Marc de Livet, Marquis of Barville, Inspecteur des Eaux et Forêts, who planted the conifers which still adorn the lands around the manor, as well as the long avenue which separates it from the church. The estate does not seem to have been sold for seven centuries, but was simply passed from one generation to the next, always maintaining its association with the Barville name.

The oldest part of the main body of the *logis* faces south and has timber framing on the two stories, which are separated by a heavily molded jetty. The manor of Barville is situated in the most eastern part of the Pays d'Auge and the *logis* bears evidence of traditions from neighboring Lieuvin, such as the two oblique braces on the upper floor which do not, as is normally the case, link a bay post and a wall plate, but the rail and wall plate.

Although the frame has retained most of its original features, the window openings have been radically altered, to the point that it would be difficult to restore them to their original state. Most of the decoration on the frame has disappeared and only some bases and ogee arches which adorned the gables can still be discerned. Fortunately, the decoration on the jetty has remained largely intact. Although the drip molding on the jetty plate has been ruthlessly severed, the extensive moldings on the bressumer have been saved. It features alternate torus and cavetto moldings, finely absorbed and blunted where they meet the beams, in keeping with a design common in the late 15th and early 16th centuries. This *logis* was probably built by the last generation of the Barville family.

No doubt wanting to celebrate their ownership of the estate of the Barville, the Livet family added on a

dating, which relates to the left-hand side of the *logis* as far as the round-headed door to the right of the raised dripstone.

The original structure merely comprised two extremely large rectangular rooms with a fireplace, built one on top of the other and linked by a staircase fitted in a corner, probably facing the entrance door.

During the 16th century, the manor house was extended on its east side, to create a storeroom and, above it, a room with a fireplace (the proportions of the molding on the twin windows and the structure of the chimney confirm this date) and a new more convenient staircase was added in an external tower.

The three dormers were probably added during this final phase, especially the central dormer which is oddly formed as a kind of *bretèche*; its axial window is centered over the arch of the entrance door, on which the year 1584 is inscribed and dates this work precisely.

Barville

The main buildings of this estate stand on the manorial enclosure of Barville, not far from the parish church of the same name. These comprise a

much more imposing perpendicular wing during the second half of the 16th century. The new wing was higher than the original *logis* and designed along very different lines.

Jetties were no longer fashionable and high timber-framed gables had also fallen out of favor with the master builders. This extension was therefore built without a jetty and priority was instead given to the arrangement of the façade panels. It was also given a high hipped roof, the converging lines of which were emphasized with enormous finials.

An attractive frieze of saltires along the window breast contrasts with the severe vertical rhythm of the façade of the old house, and the tile nogging of the old structure is replaced with alternating layers of limestone blocks and pink bricks on the new structure.

The two structures were unified by the design of the roofs: the roof of the old west gable was refashioned into a long hipped roof, similar to that of the perpendicular wing, and fitted with small hipped-roof dormers with round-headed windows.

The three finials which crown the building are recent, however, those which adorned the extremities of the roof of the wing built during the second half of the 16th century are still extant: they are kept in a private collection made public by Étienne Deville in 1927. Completely identical, they testify to the exceptional workmanship of the potters of Manerbe and the Pré-d'Auge, whose work remains unequaled. The base, which forms the last roofing tile, is adorned with scrolls following the lines of the long roof panels and with bulbous and perforated leaves on the arris, as well as a delicate female head with a ruff on the cut-off corner. The latter is topped by a cylindrical feature with volutes, complete with bearded satyr heads on one and female heads on another, alternating with finely ribbed shells. The main piece above this comprises a large ovoid vase, the body of which is strewn with little jagged indentations around the outline, and the top part is decorated with two cherubs with short wings holding a flowing cloth and with two volute arches. The bird of prey with the threatening beak which crowns each finial is supported by a motif of four female busts, separated by scrolls of leaves and fruit.

Bellemare

Situated on the plateau approaching Lieuvin, the old fief of Bellemare features one of the strangest timber buildings in the Pays d'Auge. The *logis* stands in the middle of some farm buildings and is bordered by two ponds which appear to be the remains of moats. All we know of the history of this manor is limited at present to the name of one of its owners during the second half of the 15th century, Philippe de Bellemare, identified by Montfaut in his survey of 1463.

The *logis* comprises two separate structures which stand at right angles to each other under the same roof. The square stone house on the north side is flanked on the south by a large timber structure whose upper story is for the most part clad in slate. The stone work on the north wing is very varied: the first floor on the west side features robust masonry work of flint with large blocks of rough-hewn sandstone. This is topped by a second floor of rubble stone with deep courses of bonding ashlar, which is used on the entire north wall. Among various other changes, three windows, which feature molded frames and mullions dating from the late 15th century or early 16th century, have been added to the original structure. This is confirmed by the trace of the two-part rail which is still visible on the vertical elements.

The archaic character of the sandstone block stonework would imply that this is the oldest part of the building. However, neither the timber wall which forms the east side nor the stone wall extend to the south side, but instead abut the large timber structure which extends for over two bays towards the east.

This would seem to be the oldest part of the house, forming an exceptionally tall homogeneous rectangular two-story building. The east gable originally had a protruding truss matched on the west by the same straight gable, which was later aligned with the roof of the perpendicular wing. Traces of a large dormer window, which opened across the full width of the second bay, can be found in the attic. A very prominent jetty interrupts the timber frame on the south and west façades; the structure of this jetty reflects the archaic character of the *logis*.

The unusual profile of the logis of the manor of Bellemare where the wooden logis pre-dates the stone extension. This must undoubtedly be one of the most ancient timber structures to have survived in the Pay d'Auge, and the technique of its timber framing may derive from English practice.

In the south it is supported alternately by the overhang of the transverse beams interlocking with the bay posts, relieved by thick consoles and by separate brackets grafted on the intermediary posts. It is continued on the east elevation with the help of the enormous corner post consisting of a single member which thickens at the top to support an overhanging top plate, supported by two joists. This arrangement is unique in the Pays d'Auge, although it is somewhat similar to the jettied structure of the *logis* at the manor of Coupesarte where the jetty plates of the ground floor are similarly aligned on the bressumer of the upper floor, and there is a molded girding beam between the transverse beams. A horizontal intermediary piece, which was grafted onto the oblique braces on either side of the corner post, supports the series of small rectangular windows arranged in groups of two and three. The slate cladding on the upper floor conceals a much

reworked timber frame, which does not seem to have retained any trace of the original fenestration.

The plan shows one large room on each level and a narrow space in the last bay on the eastern side. There is no trace of the original staircase or of the chimneys: the chimney at the junction of the two buildings was obviously not added until the end of the 15th century, and that built on the east gable during the 17th century resulted in the blocking up of the three original small rectangular windows which can still be made out.

The final evidence of the archaic origins of this building can be found in the arrangement of the sole plates which are supported by a practically non-existent plinth. On the south east corner, the corner posts are joined to these intersecting sole plates which then continue along the entire length of the façades, including under the door sill. What we have here is a very old structure, a relic of distant times when all the vertical elements rested on a horizontal wooden frame which was barely raised off the ground.

Pending dendrochronological examination, it is difficult to date this unusual house. It is certainly earlier than the 16th century and one would be inclined to link it with some 14th-century English houses on the basis of its use of braces and the jetty on the joists, so common on the other side of the English Channel. If this is the case, then this could well be a house built during a period of English occupation during the Hundred Years' War.

Les Boves

The manor of Mesnil-Violaine is today known by its original title of Les Boves. It is beautifully situated above the narrow valley of Monceaux, at the edge of a plateau from where the alluvial plain of the Dives can be glimpsed to the west.

The timber-framed outbuildings of the manor are scattered liberally around the main axis which culminates in the stone and brick *logis*. There is greater emphasis on the warm tones of the materials used in the construction of the *logis* than on severe architectural lines.

Our knowledge of this half-fief with its own coat of arms goes back to the 14th century, when Jean Collet, son of Richard and comrade-in-arms of Bertrand Du Guesclin, married Agnès des Boves, heiress to the estate. In the 15th century we find Guillaume and Thomas and then, in 1540, Geoffroi Collet known as "squire, lord of Boves".

None of the buildings that remain standing today seem to date back to these times – at best, we can pinpoint an archaic technique which features in the timber framework of one of the buildings. This consists of a rail halfway up the wall, which is pegged onto the studs and rests on the thickening of the bay posts, in accordance with the technique commonly used until the end of the 15th century.

The chimney stack on the *logis* bears the base of a sundial, dated 1635, which fully corresponds with the dating hitherto suggested for this building. Jean Collet, lord of Boves, had married Hélaine Le Sevray the previous year and he immediately started on the

reconstruction of the *logis*. The quality and cost of this work may well have some bearing on the difficult financial situation in which he left his wife and sons. His heirs continue to disclaim the succession.

This *logis* combines clearly archaic features with a very interesting interpretation of new forms. It gives the impression of being the work of a master mason who trained on other prestigious sites and was here working to his own taste with a total lack of restraint in the matter of lines and proportions. The result is very tasteful, and the significant restoration work carried out has done it justice.

The *logis* has two stories on a rectangular plan; it is crowned with a hipped roof which features a more or less axial chimney stack framed by two dormers. The beautiful brick masonry work is reinforced by piers of toothing stones at irregular

A pond was added at the center of the courtyard at Les Boves, completing the simple layout aspired to by its builder. The master builder initially adhered to the regular grid of the standard timber logis *with doors at the extremities of the building but added two irregular side bays to meet the client's requirements.*

both of which opened to the exterior, before the far door was converted into a window.

The polychrome tones of the brick and stone were deemed sufficient decoration for this *logis*. The builder merely added a thin flat string course above each window lintel to mark the articulation of the stories and a second string course on the upper story at what was probably the level of the original timber top rail.

All of the secondary openings – providing ventilation for the cellar and lighting the old stairwell – take the form of small circular limestone openings.

The skillful restorer of this *logis* has discreetly added the two new windows on the east side of the façade and has restored the two dormers using the attractive design with a large keystone breaching the pediment copied from the château of Ouilly-du-Houlley, just as his distant predecessor would have done.

In order to guarantee the structural cohesion of his logis, the builder of La Brairie erected two separate buildings, one being a continuation of the other. They are almost identical and can only be distinguished by some subtle differences in their decoration.

intervals, for the most part aligned with the frames of the apertures. The distribution of the window and door openings and the position of the chimney are among the archaic features of this building: i.e. the central part resembles the façade of a medieval timber *logis*, with a door at each extremity and two bays with windows topped by dormers on either side of a chimney stack with four flues.

In order to adhere to the requirements set down in Jean Collet's plan, the master mason added a half bay on the west side and a complete bay on the east, an arrangement which the Classical period would have translated into a rigorously centered and perfectly symmetrical composition with a central door and two chimneys moved out to the gable walls.

Documents relating to the succession of Jean Collet enable us to examine the contents of the plan he drew up for his residence. The living quarters on the ground floor included "a hall and a kitchen" which probably corresponded to the two central rooms. Adjoining the kitchen was "a cellar with three tuns"; this was visible from the low narrow openings to the east which could still be discerned until the recent addition of the large window in line with that on the upper floor. Finally, there was "a dairy and laundry room" and "a stable" on the west side,

La Brairie

The toponymy of the location of the manor of La Brairie is a little confusing. Within little distance from each other, we find three houses named *le manoir de Bray* (the manor of Bray), *le manoir de la Brairie* (the manor of La Brairie), and *le fief de Bray* (the fief of Bray). The existence of three manors in such close proximity is inconceivable in all respects and suggests that these are the successive *logis* of one and the same manor of Bray, seat of the fief of the same name, which would have been divided up when the Bray family line ended in the late 17th century.

Massot de Bray lived here in 1406, Guiot de Bray in 1444, Jehan de Bray in 1454, followed by his son, also called Jehan, then Étienne and Jacques de Bray, and finally Claude de Bray, mentioned in 1612.

The oldest of the *logis*, today known as La Brairie, is a two-story timber-framed structure and stands on a steep slope, wedged by a large cellar of *roussier*, the ferruginous sandstone which is so plentiful in the Orbiquet valley. The rectangular plan is exceptionally well organized and culminates in the north with a large gable (see page 62), which is as ornate as the main east-facing façade. The first impression is of two twin buildings, almost identical in structure, one a few centimeters lower than the other with a clear split at roof level.

The 'first' building comprises four bays with a very powerful frame enclosed by two braces; the ground floor of this section has twin windows on either side of the second and fourth posts and a door resting on the third. The upper floor has an uninterrupted string of ten small identical windows, each bearing a breast with a saltire and a heavily molded rail marking a lower casement and transom. The windows also have a shared sill which runs across the entire width of the façade. A single dormer, which is supported by a jetty similar to that on the ground floor and decorated with a scalloped edge rafter, fills the width of the third bay.

The strength of this frame and the harmony of its proportions mean that the horizontal timbers need no decoration other than the discreet and effective drip moldings on the jetty plate, window sill, and bressumers. The rail is the only member with a more complex profile consisting of three unadorned tori between two cavetti. A hierarchy in the decor of the bay posts and the door and window architraves marks the amortizement of thickened parts to accommodate a beam or to allow the passage of a sill. The superimposed horizontal moldings end in small trefoiled brackets. There is a single bracket on each of the architraves and two on the bay posts, creating a subtle rhythm which accentuates the strong points of the façade.

The fireplaces on both floors are positioned on the south gable and heat only one room per floor; they are duplicated by a narrow passageway within the thickness of the wall of the rear elevation.

Curiously, there is no trace of a staircase in this 'first' building, or even the slightest trace of a stairwell in the floors which remain intact and in their original state. We must deduce from this that, although it has its own completely separate structure, the 'second' building was built immediately after the first with almost no interruption between the two projects. Several factors would support this theory: the frame of the gable of the first building was never fitted with its studs, and the dividing walls are on the joined gable of the second building; the stone cellar, which is half underground, extends beyond the second building half way across the area of the first, yet there are no signs of it having been altered.

The reason for this 'simultaneous' juxtaposition of two buildings seems to relate to a strong concern for perfect solidity which was very prevalent among the master joiners of the Middle Ages.

Generally speaking, until the beginning of the 16th century, the length of a timber structure of this type depended on the length of the main piece of wood required to stabilize it, namely the top or jetty plate, which was largely responsible for the cohesion of the jetty. Thus, in response to the client's requirements and the impossibility of finding timbers more than 18 meters in length, the master builder had to build the house in two separate parts, each with its own structural system. However, this did not prevent the two buildings from subsiding in different ways, which has caused the slight division mentioned above.

The stairwell was of course in the first bay of the second building, giving access to the corridor on each floor. There are several original features here. The second chimney breast (see page 74) is unusually placed on the west eave wall; this layout, inherited from a practice which had become obsolete over a century before, gives this structure, which is widely lit in the gable and directly accessible from the exterior, an exceptional presence which would not have been achieved with a chimney centered on the gable wall.

Similarly, the ceiling separating the two levels of this part of the building was constructed not with joists supported by beams but with a series of close thick planks. The frame is, of course, of the same design in both buildings, as is the decor, except for a slight simplification of the molding on the jetty rail, which has only two tori instead of three.

The main difference in this second building lies in the gable. The row of ten small windows on the façade is complemented by six windows on the upper floor of the gable above the four windows on the lower floor, which are limited in width by the two large oblique braces.

The jetty of the façade continues around to the gable (see page 57) and the great virtuosity of the

In the courtyard of the manor of Les Buttes, the beautiful, perfectly symmetrical façade of the house is aligned with the lovely small square dovecote, which is the only remaining trace of its noble origins.

carpenter is most clearly demonstrated here in the way in which he rested the diagonal dragon beam on an enormous post, which is thickened on top, and accentuated the effect by putting in a small frieze of three trefoiled brackets, rather than the two seen on the other bay posts. Finally the height of this gable is emphasized by the large protruding roof truss, elegantly shaped in a pointed arch under a tie beam at the top.

This kind of gable is exceptional in a rural setting, but much less so in an urban setting: prior to 1944, the nearby town of Lisieux still had several buildings very similar to this, so much so as to suggest the work of the same master builder. The most important of these had its eaves wall facing onto the Rue de la Paix and its gable on the Grand-Rue and was also built during the second half of the 15th century.

Les Buttes

The manor of Les Buttes could pass as a simple country house nestling on a hillside. The humble timber residence and its few outbuildings dotted around a gently sloping courtyard suggest little more than a small farm.

However, the presence of a tiny dovecote reminds us that this manor was part of a fief endowed with certain rights and prerogatives, including the right to build a dovecote – a sign of nobility.

The dovecote was always built to scale with the size of an estate, thus the fief of Les Buttes was not very extensive. The dovecote of Les Buttes is built very economically on a square plan with long corner posts. Its two-tier timber frame uses numerous recycled timbers and numerous diagonal members arranged as double or triple braces, or in a fern pattern.

The carpenter's work involved a very reduced simple design consisting of four vertical panels crowned by a pyramid roof with small dormers. It is far removed from the sheer virtuosity of the master carpenters of the Pays d'Auge who designed many such magnificent octagonal buildings with sculpted studs and posts and strived to ensure the perfect line of the polygon from the body of the building to the perfect cone of the roof, or constructed sloped roofs with radiating horizontal framing and further complicated the exercise by adding a lantern in the form of a pinnacle. The only refinement on the dovecote at Les Buttes is on the junction of the hip tiles which was originally crowned with a glazed terra-cotta finial, of which only the base and the iron rod, on which the various elements would have stood, remains. It is not surprising that these dovecotes were subject to such frequent repairs and reworking, considering the care with which they were maintained in order to preserve the rights that went with them. It was particularly important that their appearance of antiquity be maintained and the dovecote at Les Buttes seems to have some features which are much older than the actual *logis*, which was rebuilt at the end of the 18th century.

The manor of Les Buttes exudes an impression of grace and harmony conveyed by the balance of its volumes and the fine sobriety of the *logis*, which was designed by a sure hand along perfectly symmetrical lines. Its two timber-framed stories are built with long posts, linked by an interrupted mid-rail marking the division between the two stories. On either side of the central bay (which is slightly wider than the others) there are three even bays, alternately blank or with aligned windows. There are no moldings or carved details added to the fine outline of the timber framework, the quality of which lies in the arrangement of its elements, which are cut in handsome grained oak and adhere to the rule of "equally full and empty", sometimes mentioned in carpenters' estimates whereby the space between the studs is equal to their width. The members responsible for the rigidity of the frame in this instance are not mere technical elements whose sole purpose is to ensure stability; they also contribute to its decoration. Thus, braces in rows of four punctuate every second bay and alternately frame

the central bay and the two outer bays, while the window breasts on the upper floor are each adorned by two saltires with a half stud in between.

On the hipped roof, which has sprockets forming slightly projecting eaves, the three dormers with pediments and curved lintels emphasize the severe alignment of the straight linteled windows.

The only note lacking in this perfect balance of lines, supported by the discreet mass of the chimney stacks, is a subtle interplay of color. This is found in the grid of pink tiles used in the nogging, which is enhanced by a wide variety of motifs including rape and calyx plants, crosses, and grotesques.

Cauvigny

Somewhat off the beaten track, the manor of Cauvigny is hidden in the fold of a small valley in the hamlet of Mesnil-Imbert. It is carefully composed with a fine timber-framed *logis* at the top of a courtyard which is bordered with long outbuildings rising towards the hill. Here we find the laborers' quarters, stables, barns, byres, sheds, and the bread oven. The two-story *logis* is crowned with a large hipped roof which has regularly spaced dormers on every second bay. The sober design has no oblique lines in the timber framework of the eaves walls, and consists of strong bay posts and narrow studs, intersected at the top of each floor by an intermediary beam. The builder has allowed some diagonal members on the side walls: the upper section is crossed by two large oblique braces and the small sections which frame it have symmetrically sloping studs and two cross braces under the eave.

The bay posts are strictly vertical, from the sole plate to the wall plate but are made up of two pieces of timber separated by a large intermediary girding beam. Each story, thus comprises an independent structure, constructed using only short pieces of timber. The construction of the manor of Cauvigny goes back to the early years of the 17th century when it was becoming difficult to obtain very long wide timbers for a project of this scale, and when the technique using short timbers based on the jetty was largely out of fashion.

The logis *of Cauvigny is one of the rare buildings of this type. Built during the first half of the 17th century, it makes a clean break with medieval and renaissance tradition in favor of a new sobriety and simplicity of line.*

The decoration is extremely discreet and restricted to the bay posts. The carpenter made simple rounded consoles to suit the drip molding of the middle rail and the wall plate and emphasized the large horizontal divisions on each story with discreet pilasters.

This building is part of the same movement which saw the erection of other important buildings, such as the château of Le Breuil, which, it must be said, is not quite so plain: however, it shares the same principles of construction using short timbers applied to much bigger buildings.

The carpenter did not limit his efforts to this sober decoration of the walls, but also drew on his considerable talents to construct an attic which was made habitable by installing a fireplace at the north end. The king posts of the trusses are cut off at the level of a tie beam and culminate in molded quadrangular bases under a longitudinal beam, which supports the joists of a ceiling and links the rafters of each elevation. A similarly sophisticated attic structure can still be found in the roof of the château of Carrouges.

The *logis* did not originally have as many windows as it does now: there was originally a window in every second bay, aligned with the dormers. There were large windows on the second and the eighth bays with timber mullions formed by a continuous vertical stud which was intersected by the intermediary timber member which formed the cross-rail. The mortises and pegging reveal traces of the original level of the window sills which were considerably higher than they are today. The fourth and sixth bays, which are narrower than the others, had windows with a single transom, and there appears to have been a door in the center of the building on the ground floor.

Thus, in its original form, the house had an

attractive façade with alternating blank and windowed bays and a large ridged roof wedged between two chimney stacks, creating large rooms at the center of each story and small rooms in the outer bays outside the chimney breasts, with discreet windows on the gable walls.

No doubt the building seemed austere to Jacques Adrien de Corday de Cauvigny, born in 1703, grandfather of Charlotte Corday, who lived here until his death in 1795. The original windows allowed very little light to filter through and the interior layout was probably limited to a series of connected rooms.

Thus, he decided to remove the mullions and transoms from the existing windows, lower the sills, add segmental arched lintels, provide narrow windows for the chambers of the outer bays and a large window in the middle of the façade, and transform the central door into a French window, also decorated with timber finishings.

The interior was also completely reworked and the only surviving features are the 17th century fireplace in the kitchen on the ground floor at the northern end of the building, the attic fireplace, and the painted decoration of cartouches in a floral motif on the beams in an upstairs bedroom. A beautiful staircase with fine balusters was added at this time to provide access to the wide corridor on the upper floor which leads to the bedrooms with their paneled-timber finish, fireplaces, and wallpapers, which can still be seen today.

The brick and tile nogging which was added to all the façades and partially coated with lime mortar during the last century also originates from this phase of modifications.

Le Champ-Versan

The *logis* of the manor of Champ-Versan belongs to a category of modest but meticulous buildings, commonly found in the Pays d'Auge in the late Renaissance and early Classical periods. Having turned their backs on the inflexibility of medieval architectural logic, the architects devoted their efforts to the skillful articulation of lines and spaces, and seeking their models in the early architectural tracts drew up very detailed plans which

contrasted greatly with the reduced scale of the actual buildings.

Efforts were underway at the time to move away from the traditional strictly rectangular *logis* with a massive central chimney stack which dictated a plan consisting of largely undifferentiated spaces. The *logis* at Le Champ-Versan deliberately moves away from this model and is clearly inspired by other models consisting of a central structure flanked by small side wings. However, it shows little regard for symmetry and an extremely tasteful and unfettered approach to interpretation of the new models.

The *logis* comprises a central two-story structure on a rectangular plan with a hipped roof. Two small, almost free-standing, hipped-roofed wings with the same elevation extend from the corners of the rear elevation; they are joined by the narrow gallery on the ground floor which is covered by the extension of the roof of the main building. All of the roof slopes follow the same lines, which are also echoed in the two small dormers on the main façade. The chimney stacks give strong emphasis to the structure, the extremities of which are marked by various panels and breaks, in strong contrast to the sober lines of the central section. By shifting the chimneys to the

An oblique view reveals the unusual plan of this house and the two substantially projecting wings which were built on the main body of the building at the corners of the rear elevation, contrary to the practices in vogue since the Renaissance, which favored the erection of symmetrical wings on the main façade.

edges of the building, the master builders had free rein to change the layout of the *logis*, and the central main door now opened onto an entrance hall, and small rooms were added to the main rooms, halls, and bedrooms.

This desire to simplify the central section of the house to benefit the side parts is particularly noticeable in the reduction of the staircase area which, although it remained in the center of the building where it would have had to project into the roof, does not interrupt the long incline of the roof, which descends fully intact as far as the eave at the rear.

This inspired approach to the spatial organization is equally matched by an imaginative use of materials. The main façade is dominated by a timber framework whilst the two turret wings and the entire side walls – not just the width of the chimneys – are built in an attractive stone and brick checkerwork which is continued right up the chimney stacks. In the 18th century, much of the timber infill of the west turret was replaced with dressed stone, however the corner posts of the original frame were left intact. This timber framework was given rather cursory treatment. No longer the master builder's main concern, it was left up to the carpenter to create a structure which would interpret the lines of the plan without becoming the main feature of the building. Long posts are only used for the corners of the main body of the *logis* and the wings; the jetty no longer enjoys pride of place, and the only concession to tradition is the drip molding which runs along the girding beam separating the two stories. The diagonal braces are fitted with absolutely no concern for symmetry.

The original fenestration on the main façade was approached with the same freedom. The windows are aligned along the two main axes created by the dormer windows in the second and seventh bays. These were probably made up of two casements separated by a timber mullion, as indicated by the system which still exists in the two small dormer windows. The other windows in the fifth and eighth bays seem to have been added later during a construction phase which probably coincided with the disappearance of the mullions and the timber infill of the west wing, which had been eroded by bad weather.

Very curiously, the central door opens at the junction of two bays beneath the second floor post, which seems to go against all logic (see p. 78). The ogee decoration is also astonishing, as such ornamental molding seems very out of place on such an innovative building. It contrasts rather starkly with the refined decoration of the two hall doors leading into the two rooms on either side. These have finely molded lintels resting on door jambs with sculpted cable moldings, Ionic pilasters, and foliated consoles with scrolls and palmettes. All this exterior door and the two interior doors have in common is the presence of the same much finer cable moldings emphasizing the curves of the ogee arch and the pinnacles which frame it. However, the blank surfaces of the attached leaves and the surface of the three escutcheons were surely meant to be painted.

The manor of Le Champ-Versan has shared the destiny of that of the nearby manor of Le Camp-Bénard since at least the 16th century: at that time Regnault de Hesbert, squire, was "lord of Cambénard and of Champ-Versan", as were his successors until the end of the Ancien Régime: "Jacques-Pierre Bazin, advisor to the king, in the election of Caen" is mentioned in 1733, or "Jean-Baptiste Bazin de Sainte-Honorine, lord of Camp-Bénard, of Champ-Versan and other places, former Keeper of the Seals at the Rouen Parliament" who died on 21 July 1786.

Le Coin

The buildings of the manor of Le Coin today stand in a compact group on three sides of a quadrangular courtyard which is partially surrounded by water. Situated in the lower valley of the Vie, in the vast and rich meadows at the mouth of the alluvial plain which extends until the Vie meets the Dives, this was an ideal site for a manor, in terms of both defense and maintenance.

Whilst the spatial organization around the yard seems simple, the purpose of the individual buildings (free-standing to the south and west and adjoining on the east) is not evident. In functional terms they seem to embody a combination of living quarters and outbuildings and structurally also include various stone, timber, and mixed edifices.

A sketch of the manor, drawn by G. Bouet in 1852, reinforces this idea in that it contains buildings which have disappeared. In view of the reliability of the artist in question and his frequent collaboration with A. de Caumont, this is probably a very accurate image and is indeed confirmed by the first Napoleonic land survey.

An isolated two-story timber *logis* occupied the north side of the site. A stone dovecote with a conical roof pierced with three dormer windows marked the north west corner. The buildings making up the south and west sides of the courtyard were linked, but the most remarkable building – a small square two-story pavilion with a high roof marked by the elegant silhouette of two finials – stood on the south east corner. A tiled awning ran along the middle of the timber framework and extended to the adjacent buildings. On the upper floor, narrow passageways linked the pavilion to a jettied gallery on the gable wall of the south building and to the building on the east side.

The oldest part seems to be the stone building which forms the central part of the east wing and has beautiful masonry of small limestone slabs with dressed stone reserved to frame the window openings, all of which remain intact. To judge by the width of the door opening onto the courtyard, the two small windows which frame the door, and the two windows on the upper floor, this was probably originally a *logis*. The profile of the cornice and the discreet contours of the edge of the door lintel may suggest that it originated in the 16th century, but it is difficult to set a precise date because all of the interior features, in particular the fireplaces, have disappeared. It is very difficult to determine the order of the other elements around the courtyard at that time.

A new residence was built (probably just after the Hundred Years' War) adjoining the south gable wall of its predecessor. Built on a narrower, more elaborate plan, it has a staircase turret at the back which provided access to the two floors of the *logis*. The staircase turret is in stone with carefully finished quoins of dressed masonry. The body of the actual *logis* consists of a sturdy timber framework with very thick long posts. On the court-yard side, traces of all the windows can still be made out on the five

bays which are reinforced with four braces. The entrance door on the north end gave access to the main room which extended across three bays and was lit by a wide mullioned window, which is almost completely sealed off today. The kitchen occupied the two remaining bays and was mainly lit by a large mullioned and transomed window on the south gable. This kitchen also originally had its own door opening directly on to the yard. On the second floor, the stair landing provided access to two different sized rooms which were situated on either side of the chimney breast and lit on the courtyard side and on the south gable by windows identical to those on the first floor. The window sills were formed by a continuous rail which was fitted onto the thickened ends of the posts.

Did the roof originally have dormer windows? It was easily accessible from the wide stone staircase, but no trace of dormers remains. However, the light provided by the two small double windows in the gable would have made the area habitable. The square tower has a timber-framed upper chamber which projects slightly in the direction of the moat and to which a decorative jetty has been added. At a much later stage, lean-tos were built on either side of the stair turret, extending the roof slopes on the rear elevation.

A timber structure extending the north gable of the 14th-century stone building was built on exactly the same lines. This was probably an out-building, which may have had more basic living quarters on the upper floor. It does, in fact, have small rectangular windows, the jambs of which still bear the side grooves for the sliding shutters which were used around this time in many quality *logis*.

If Bouet's drawing is accurate, and we have no reason to believe otherwise, another timber structure stood on the north side of the courtyard. The drawing reveals its features: a long plan, two stories separated by a jetty, an end door next to a bay with mullioned and transomed windows. The plan seems to have been perfectly symmetrical on either side of the chimney breast and the only dormer which is still visible must have had a counterpart above the windows. Thus, this residence bears all the characteristics of those built in

High quality stone was found in abundance in the valley of the river Vie. It was used to build the earliest house preserved in the courtyard of the manor of Le Coin. A new house was built as an extension to the original logis at the end of the Hundred Years' War using the long-posted technique. Stone was not, however, completely excluded from this new structure; it was used in the construction of the staircase turret, which has a timber-framed upper chamber.

sort of *logis-porche* (porch lodge) of a type well known in other regions, particularly in Brittany, but very rare in the Pays d'Auge, except in the case of castle gatehouses. Did a sharecropper live there? Was the demesne, which he could tend for his own profit, very extensive?

So many questions remain open, to which history may one day provide the answers. We know only that in the middle of the 16th century this fief belonged to Thomas Le Prévost, who sought and was granted letters of nobility in 1544. The investigation revealed that "he had lived in good legitimate marriage, ate and lived well, was of sound virtue, reputation, conversation, morals, and conditions". His request was granted "in return for a payment of 787 *livres* and 10 *sols* to Master Jean Laguette (the king's general collector) and payment to the inhabitants of Mesnil-Mauger of a loan redeemable on the tenth *denier* representing the tallage posed upon him." He must therefore have had considerable means at his disposal to enable him to rise to the nobility. His son Thomas retained the manor of Le Coin and passed it on to Jean Le Prévost, while one of his nephews set up home at the manor of Coupesarte, another, Robert Le Prévost, squire of a small farm in 1616, then an ordinary gentleman of the king's chamber later became a knight of the order of St. Michel, and a third became lord of Grandchamp through his marriage to Jacqueline de Mallevoue. The fortune of Thomas Le Prévost therefore gave rise to a distinguished line of descendants, with whom some of the most interesting manors of the Pays d'Auge are associated.

It was no doubt as a sign of loyalty to the king that Thomas decorated the large dormer window above the entrance to the manor with an escutcheon bearing three fleurs-de-lis. The dormer itself may have been added on top of an older *logis-porche* in 1544. It has a long-post timber framework, very similar to that used in the 15th century house, but with slightly thinner studs which enables us to estimate its construction at a slightly later date. This *logis* had only one room on the first floor adjoining the porch which housed a staircase giving access to the two rooms on the upper floor, one of which was built above the entrance passage. The east gable wall still bears traces of the joints

such great numbers during the first half of the 16th century. But why is there a third house?

It may well be that the first 16th-century *logis* was deemed too dark, so during the following century it was complemented, or rather replaced, by another with more windows and a better layout.

Its main drawback was probably its west-facing aspect, leaving it exposed to the heavy westerly rains. The construction of the new *logis* finally provided a good south-facing elevation, which was mostly open onto the courtyard, and stood opposite the entrance porch, beyond which the south moat was crossed.

Did the owner of Le Coin house several families at his residence? Did he enjoy the presence of his 'people' within his manor? Whatever the case, he decided to make the entrance to his manor into a

supporting the overhanging gallery featured in the Bouet drawing.

Finally, the purpose of the surprising little square pavilion on the south-east corner, which is linked to the upper floors of the porch-lodge quarters and the 15th century *logis* by passageways, remains to be clarified.

Because it served a common function for the two buildings, we can only suppose that this structure housed the latrines, which we know to have been one of the particularly appreciated elements of comfort, and which Thomas Le Prévost would have needed to support his application for nobility and to prove his ability to lead a life compatible with his new social rank. This "privy tower" could easily have been accommodated by adding a door to the timber framework of the gable wall of the 15th-century house (still visible) and by building a bridge to the gallery of the porch-lodge.

In addition to the modifications mentioned above, the manor of Le Coin has suffered many changes in fortune since the late 19th century, and, as a result, the *logis-porche* today enjoys a position of prominence it did not originally have. Over the course of time, we can trace the downgrading of successive houses, transformed at each stage into outhouses, making the history of this remarkable group of buildings particularly complex.

Conty

Facing the estuary of the Seine and looking up to its ever-changing skies, the manor of Conty looks out over the sound, which, far from being the border between the two Normandies, – the result of an absurd administrative division, – is in fact their ancient link, the favored route from which the Normans set sail to discover the world, and, in turn, a path of invasion and commercial artery leading from the heart of Europe.

The *logis* overlooks the road from Honfleur to Trouville, from both its staircase turret with its cladding of heavy slate facing a modest quadrangular frame and its strongly projecting gallery supported by protruding transverse beams on arch braces. A tiled roof crowns the main body of the building

and slopes gently over the gallery overhang, follows the canted walls of the turret, and has a massive chimney stack on its southern slope. The sloping ground is offset by a stone faced cellar which significantly increases the height of this elevation and the well-organized layout would suggest that this is the main entrance. However, the latter is actually situated on the opposite side of the building, facing the hillside, on an elevation now distinctly lacking in character. A fine stone staircase leads to the door built into the east side of the staircase turret below the gallery. This is indeed an exceptional feature and is part of the original structure.

Everything in this *logis* reminds us that it is located in an area which was very open to exchange

The logis *of the manor of Conty is one of the only ones to have kept its open gallery on the upper floor, supported on great arch braces: the only one, also, to have retained its cladding of thick slates. The access door in the wall of the staircase turret is a later addition of the 16th century.*

and influences. The timber framework has the usual form found in the Pays d'Auge, but it also has the motif of the double brace fitted into two horizontal members on the two levels of the east gable wall which was so common on the other side of the Channel. Moreover, the wide variety of materials used include tiles with tones of light and dark ochre, (which differ strongly from the pink and red-brown tiles more usual in the Pays d'Auge and probably originate from the banks of the Caux), simple mortar pointing on the sharp-edged roof, and a thick cladding of slate on the staircase turret. Slate was actually quite rare in the Pays d'Auge but spread widely from Brittany and is found on modest buildings close to places accessible to open sea vessels along the coast of the Pays d'Auge, such as Honfleur and the Touques estuary. Its use was normally restricted to more elaborate *logis* in the interior of the region. Finally, the stone plinth bears the traits of techniques frequently used in the area around the Caux, such as layers of knapped flint, black ores from the cliffs alternating with gray ones from the nearby plateaux.

The carved decoration, which is very simple, consists of a single cable molding on the sill of the mullioned window situated under the gallery and was typical of the motifs used in the mid-16th century.

There is still some doubt as to the original size of this *logis*. Could it be that its two rooms, one on top of the other joined by an external staircase, are all that remains of a larger residence originally extended over two bays to the west? An examination of the west gable wall, which with its random rubble masonry could not be more different from the meticulously laid adjacent foundations, would lead us to believe this. The staircase turret would thus have been in the center of the building, which is where it is normally found. However, this theory is eliminated by the fact that the quoins of the west gable are in their perfect, original state.

Historical facts confirm the dating suggested by the architecture and decoration of this house: on 25 August 1566, Jehan de Conty, known as du Mont, burgher of Honfleur in 1588, heir to his father, Jean de Conty, paid homage to Étienne de Vatemare. On 7 June 1618, we find here "nobleman Jehan de Conty, advisor to the presidential seat of Caux at

Caudebec" in 1596, 1603, and 1614. His son, Pierre de Conty, occupied the same posts, and on 7 October 1648 paid homage to Gilles de Giverville, lord of Vasouy. The estate passed into the hands of the Bourgeot family through the marriage of Suzanne de Conty to Pierre Bourgeot, corn-chandler at the salt warehouse in Honfleur. Their son, a lawyer also named Pierre, paid homage to Charles de Giverville on 14 July 1701.

Le Coudray

The strong wall, of which only the south part remains, is a relic of the fortifications which formed a quadrilateral surrounded by moats, and gives us an indication of the importance of the former fief of Coudray. It was a full fief with its own coat of mail, endowed with the privilege of high justice granted by the king at an unknown date. Although the house was destroyed at the end of the 18th century, the manor still has its very large dovecote, an enormous building used as a barn, and outbuildings supported on the enclosure wall, which were recently partly converted into living quarters.

The Coudray family owned this fief until the mid-15th century when it passed into the possession of the Lyée de Belleau family for almost two centuries through the marriage of Jeanne du Coudray to Guillaume de Lyée, lord of Lyée, Tonnencourt, Belleau, and la Fosse.

Reading the old descriptions of this manor, we can only regret the disappearance of a building which is mentioned by Arcisse de Caumont as being situated between the house, which occupies the east side of the courtyard, and the barn on the north of the site: "the prison of high justice, a strong remarkable building, made of horizontal pieces of timber, laid one on top of the other and joined at the ends". According to some, it seems to have been a unique example of a stacked timber construction in medieval western France. However, let us reexamine the short extract, which fails to describe how the pieces of timber were linked at the ends. The cohesion and stability of stacked buildings is assured by the assembly of the horizontal pieces, without recourse to any vertical pieces.

I have compared this observation with an old photograph, on which it is still possible to see the remains of a timber structure supported on the west gable of the barn. It was constructed with strong wooden posts joined to a low sole plate, with the space between the posts filled with thick pieces of timber, probably – to judge from the absence of warping – connected to the posts by tongue-and-groove joints. This was, therefore, a timber paneled structure with no upright studs, in which a method of infilling was used comparable to that found in several buildings of the late Middle Ages in Denmark.

This construction technique is similar to that found in some buildings in Normandy, in which thick timber panels were used as infill, such as can be seen on the façade of the former residence of the Abbess of Saint-Amand in Rouen, making it look more like an assembled prefabricated unit than a work of carpentry. This building at the manor of Coudray, which according to Caumont had disappeared, was not, therefore, demolished until much later.

It is unusual to find a manorial barn (see page 35) built with the meticulous attention to detail found in the barn at Coudray: boxed heart timber with no knots, a perfectly upright and proportioned structure which has not fallen into disrepair. The structure is supported by continuous plates – cut through at a later date for the addition of new doors – which intersect and project to accommodate the posts. This frame rests on a plinth punctuated at each bay by large blocks of sandstone.

One would be justified in questioning the purpose of this building, which deviates from the usual plan of the large seigneurial barn. This normally comprised three central aisles with a sort of 'nave' separated by two rows of free-standing posts from the two side aisles, and all covered by the long slope of a single roof. Such barns normally had one or two doors in the side aisles, or a gable door allowing the entry and exit of carts. At Coudray, the vehicle entrance is in the second bay on the west, the first being occupied by a coach house. The building has never had an intermediary floor and indeed, if it had, this would have caused confusion as to its purpose. It does, however, have twin doors between the

second and third bays on the west side, the purpose of which is uncertain, but which are related to the original division of the building into two distinct areas, both of which are unobstructed from the ground to the roof. Another puzzling fact is the elaborate decor, which comprises posts sculpted with the figure of Saint Barbara, recognizable by her tower, a bishop or mitered abbot, and the Lyée de Belleau coat of arms on the south-east corner post, bearing an escutcheon "argent a lion sable a tongue gules", a fine drip molding on a mid-rail which extends to the bay posts, and a flattened console on the center post. The Lyée de Belleau coat of arms enables us to date this building with certainty to the second half of the 15th century. It is most likely that the roof was reshaped into a hipped roof when the vast outbuildings backing onto the south wall were built in the 17th century.

As indicated by its decoration of small consoles with scrolls, the large octagonal dovecote with a lantern was rebuilt at the center of the east side of the courtyard during the second half of the 16th century.

The outbuildings supported on the rear of the south enclosure wall stood opposite the monumental barn of Le Coudray. These were converted into living quarters following the destruction of the main logis and have a strictly vertical timber frame.

*The manor of La Coudrairie
was designed with great
freedom of expression and a
tasteful combination of
elements from Classical
architecture, such as the
mansard roof.*

La Coudrairie

Whatever the scale of the job commissioned, the master builders of the manors in the Pays d'Auge showed great spirit of innovation and the ability to interpret a wide variety of architectural forms. At La Coudrairie, we find one of the best examples of their work applied, however, to one of the most modest *logis*.

The structure of the timber framework is completely in keeping with the practices in vogue at the end of the 17th century, with three distinct horizontal bands: the first band extends up to the top of the windows on the ground floor, the second to the window breasts, and the third to the top of the windows on the first floor.

The attic has been designed as an habitable floor of the house whose surprising proportions arise from the unusual treatment of the mansard roof. This form, which breaks up the line of the slope in two different pitches – the upper and lower slopes –

was very rare in rural areas. In fact, it is only found in the *logis* at the manor of Le Bois-Simon in Auvillars, the manor of Malivoye in Reux, and at the vicarages of Saint-Jean-de-Livet and Auvillars. More often seen in urban settings, this shape is usually associated with the raising of the eaves walls above the floor of the attic.

The use of a mansard roof without this raising of the eave wall gives the manor house of La Coudrairie its unusual proportions and the exceptional emphasis on the lower slope of the roof, which has sprocketed eaves and is supported on wooden corbels onto timber brackets on the posts.

Each of the three dormers, which are aligned with the windows of the lower floors, has a small hipped roof which ends at the junction of the two roof slopes. The pitch of the dormer roofs matches the upper slope of the mansard roof precisely. The verticality of the design was originally even more marked before the cross-braced window breasts which separate the windows of the two floors were partially covered by small tiled awnings.

The second interesting feature at La Coudrairie is the tasteful interaction of the timberwork and the masonry. The dialogue between wood and tile is always harmonious in the Pays d'Auge. Here, however, the forms used fail to produce a clear differentiation between the walls and the roof, and the materials used tend to accentuate this impression. The almost vertical tiled lower slope of the mansard roof could almost be interpreted as an extension of the timber wall. And the tile cladding, which covers almost half of the timber framework, seems to emphasize the illusion of the roof up to the point where it even echoes some of the other forms, such as the awnings on the lower section.

The dialogue between the materials does not stop there. What simpler way to give a monumental character to a small timber *logis* than by giving it a stone doorway with a brick and tile pediment? This is not unique, for we also find it used equally tastefully at the manor of Le Vigan in Saint-Martin-de-Fresnay, which is undoubtedly copied from the first example found at the manor house of Bellou. However, at La Coudrairie, the two gnarled pear espaliers which frame the doorway play down any such claims of monumentality.

Will we ever know why Pierre Thomas undertook the successive construction of two almost identical houses not even one hundred meters apart? The south house has conserved its remarkable group of aligned farm buildings which surround the access porch to the courtyard.

Apart from these observations, this *logis* represents an interesting milestone in the development of the layout of this type of building. The tiny central hall leads directly onto the main staircase with balusters and three flights per floor, which on the ground floor provides access to the salon on one side and the kitchen on the other, and then the bedrooms on the first floor.

Finally, thanks to its authentic state, we find some extremely interesting and unusually well preserved finishings in this *logis*, such as its series of interior doors, or the casements of the central window on the first floor, the two parts of which (originally decorated with stained glass panels) were later fitted with glazing bars.

La Cour Thomas

At La Cour Thomas in Heurtevent, there are two oddly similar houses which stand parallel to each other and about 40 meters apart. Should they be considered as two houses commissioned by the same person who was "anxious to bequeath to his children an inheritance that would avoid any jealousy", as suggested by Henri Pellerin? Each house appears to be an autonomous entity, complete with its own outbuildings, one facing south, the other north. Only historical facts, which have not yet been fully investigated, could uncover the reasons behind this very unusual situation.

This land was owned by Jean Thomas, a merchant, in 1709. It was probably his son Pierre, "advisor to the king, owner of the salt warehouse in Livarot", who undertook the successive construction of the two houses for each of his sons: Michel, who occupied the same post as his father in 1745, and Charles-Gilles, who married Jacqueline-Françoise Remond of Saint- Évroult in 1749.

The layout of the two timber-framed *logis* follows the practices common throughout the 18th century: a long rectangular plan with two stories covered by a hipped roof with perfectly symmetrical windows.

The north house seems to be the older of the two. It stands between two service buildings to form a quadrangular courtyard. It is centered on the double entrance door and has a large central dormer with a molded pediment, which is framed by two smaller dormers. The timber framework is constructed in three levels, with blank bays decorated with braces and studs alternating with bays with windows extending the full height of the first and third levels. The central level serves as the window breast of the second floor windows and is decorated with a row of cross braces. It is possible to observe a skillful progression in the distribution of the window openings: at the extremities of the building there are small single casement windows, then windows which occupy almost the whole width of a bay and finally, in the central bay, there is the entrance door and the second floor window

framed by panels fitted in a fern pattern. The same progress can be seen in the layout of the braces which are doubled on the breast of the central bay and are singly above the door and on the other window breasts. The only difference between the rear and main elevations is that on the rear elevation there is a single dormer with a pediment instead of the three dormers of the main façade. A model of balance and distinction, the decoration of this house is limited to these sober lines, the design of the timber framework, the molding on the dormers on the north elevation, and the ovolo cornices.

This house also features superb tile nogging with very intricate patterns, perhaps the most varied found from the 18th century, when simple triangular motifs were generally the norm. Concealed under the eaves, we find almost a veritable alphabet laid by a meticulous mason. The letters T, H, O, M, A, S are legible in the nogging of the first bay on the north and there are subtle geometric variations below each of the letters. The construction date of 1737 is discreetly marked in terra-cotta figures on a base of light ocher mortar on the west wall, followed by what may be the initials of the carpenter and the mason.

The south *logis*, which is probably a little more recent, has less elaborate dormers and less variation in the tile nogging. The layout of the courtyard is also more free: it deviates from the strict axial layout by introducing lateral access via a covered porch built in the middle of one of the farm buildings and indicated by the extension of the external slope of the roof.

La Croix blanche

The *logis* at the manor of La Croix blanche is a model of simplicity which makes it an outstanding example of 15th century architecture in the Pays d'Auge. On the west side, the two-story timber building abuts an imposing stone mass. Could this be the remains of an older building? This seems very likely if we look at the beam embedded in the stone and faced with the stop ends which support the jetty on the first bay of the timber framework. The execution of the large stone gable confirms this

At the manor of La Croix Blanche, at the end of the 15th century, a timber logis *was built against the large chimney-stack, which was probably the only remaining trace of the earlier building.*

assessment: in keeping with the principles applied during the two previous centuries, it consists of a slightly projecting central part in line with the hearth and the chimney flue, which is emphasized by two drip moldings. Similarly, the gap between the two materials is toothed less carefully here than at the corner of the building. This suggests that an extension was added, leaving only the western block of the original structure which housed the two chimneys (see page 300).

Nevertheless, examination of the profile of the corbels on the first-floor fireplace and the piers of that on the second floor confirms that this first structure cannot be dated earlier than the beginning of the 15th century.

The sobriety of the entire volume, i.e. both the western block and its timber extension, reflects an archaic interior layout with an interior staircase, of which no trace remains. The location of an external staircase, which was added at a later date and disappeared at some unknown time, is still visible on the north elevation.

The timber framework is curiously laid out in irregular bays, which clearly reflect the original layout of the building. However, this is difficult to make out because of the numerous changes it has undergone. The original position of the door and

window openings is no longer evident because of the many new openings which have been inserted into the timber frame. However, it is possible to make out the original position of the door on the first floor, which occupied the traditional position in the last bay of the south face between two posts decorated with escutcheons and marked by the lintel pegging, which is still perfectly visible. On the upper floor, light was provided by two small double windows on either side of the second bay post, which are still in place, and by two single windows to the east, which have been doubled in more recent times.

Apart from a bare jetty on the north elevation, decoration is only found on the south elevation. The molding on the continuous rail which forms the window sills on the first floor and the jetty rail, which consists of two tori around a cavetto, enables us to date this timber structure in the second half of the 15th century. However the decoration is still very plain: the usual drip molding on the wall plate is here replaced by a simple chamfer and the thickening of the posts to the right of the original windows is only marked by some horizontal grooves.

However, the presence of escutcheons with plain fields on two of the posts on the south elevation could indicate that these façades actually featured some color which accentuated and set off the simple shaped features, representing in *trompe l'oeil* what would normally have been produced by the sculptor's chisel.

La Hogue

La Hogue is a hamlet in the municipality of Beuvron. Dating back to 1234, the manor is concealed behind hedges and bushes of hawthorn and holly. The manor house occupies the focal point of the site and stands on the west side of a large courtyard surrounded by the farm buildings. Due to the absence of a spring or stream, a covered well was built in the center of the yard.

This modest structure is rather interesting. It would appear that it was built at the same time as the *logis* and shows the same attention to detail,

The main façade of the logis *at La Hogue is dominated by the tall volume of the roof wedged between the two large chimney stacks on the side slopes.*

especially in the proportions of the four-sided roof, each side of which rises above sprocketed eaves at the end of the slope.

The master carpenter who built the *logis* and the well seems to have had very personal preferences when it came to spatial organization; he arranged these spaces carefully and was not afraid to use some archaic principles for aesthetic gain.

In the mid-17th century, the fashion was for houses on a rectangular plan, from which all projecting features were consciously banished: galleries disappeared, as did the staircase turrets which previously jutted out from the rear elevations. The lord of Hogue wanted a quality *logis*. His master builder designed an east-facing two-story house with fine slender lines, crowned with a steep tiled hip roof, which was accentuated by green-glazed terracotta finials.

Two tall chimney stacks constructed in rectangular rubble stone with stone toothing rise from the side slopes of the roof.

Nothing particularly archaic so far. until we look at the pavilion at the center of the west elevation: the four sided roof of this structure is at right angles to the line of the roof of the main body of the *logis*. Thus, instead of hiding it inside the house, the

The main decorative feature of the façade of the manor house of Le Lieu Hocquart is the continuous frieze of saltires along the window breasts of the first floor. The central bay is emphasized by a dormer window with discreetly carved cheeks.

master carpenter dared to revive the staircase turret – probably for the last time – and to make a monumental structure of it. The volumes are large and simple and emphasized by the curve of the sprockets in the eaves. The inclines of the roofs are exactly the same on every slope, whether they form part of the main building, the staircase pavilion, or even the two dormers on the east façade, which, however, have a slightly more extended sprocket.

The timber structure is designed with long thick posts which form a five bayed timber framework consisting of three horizontal sections. The arrangement of the timbers provides the only decoration on the façades, the most striking feature of which is the large window breasts which are decorated with a continuous series of very narrow saltires separated by half studs which are aligned with the studs of the other sections. This same pattern accentuates the pier panels of the two geminated doors on the east elevation.

The layout conforms to the principles favored at the time but shows a certain resistance to perfect symmetry: a central door could have been inserted into the axis of the center bay, but the master builder preferred to preserve the old tradition of double doors on either side of a bay stud, thus retaining different spaces for the two main rooms of the first floor, and distinguishing the living room from the kitchen. Access to the two rooms on the upper floor is provided by the positively monumental staircase echoing the scale of the structure which houses it.

We must climb this staircase to find the most sophisticated room in the house, which has a remarkable fireplace: unusually, its hood is painted and it has a cornice with dentils, combining the science of *trompe l'œil*, seen in the ovolo frieze of the frame, garlands, and tumbling fruit and flowers, with landscape art in the central scene which depicts the flight into Egypt (see p. 74). There are some other painted fireplaces from this period in the Pays d'Auge, but none of such high quality, particularly with regard to the treatment of the two angels supporting the central oval, whose bodies end in stylized scrolls of vegetation.

Now all that remains is to discover the name of the enlightened commissioner of such a work. Was it Jean Levesque, 'lord of Hogue', known to us only for standing as godfather to the son of one of his neighbors, Philippe Collet, on 18 September 1648 in the church at Beaufour? It would be especially useful to know the circles in which he moved and the circumstances which led him to require the services of the artist responsible for the painting on the fireplace.

Le Lieu-Hocquart

A country house, rather than a manor in the medieval sense of the term, the *logis* at Le Lieu Hocquart is directly inspired by the stone architecture found on the opposite bank of the Dives, beyond this rich valley floor in the nearby plain of Caen. It was probably built – as suggested by Jean-Paul Corbasson – by the Poupart family who were linked to the Hocquart de Turretot family, who gave the place its name.

If we substitute the timber framework of the façades of this *logis* with the fine courses of stone masonry framing panels of rubble filling, so common in the houses in the plain of Caen, we can easily recognize the long outline of the houses built there in such vast numbers during the 18th century with their two stories covered by a gently sloping tiled hipped roof, punctuated with dormers. The traditions of the Pays d'Auge are not forgotten and the extremities of the roof are still highlighted by the tiny glazed terracotta finials reduced to simple upturned green-glazed vases. The door and window openings, aligned in vertical bays, have segmental arched lintels.

The interior layout respects the classical plan of the houses of this period with interconnecting rooms on the first floor, and the bedrooms off a side corridor on the upper floor centered around the hall and the staircase. The influence from the neighboring region is even more evident in the fireplaces with their fine Rococo decoration (see p. 75).

However the architecture of this house most certainly belongs to the Pays d'Auge and the master builder brilliantly demonstrates how this model, originally conceived for the use of stone, could be subtly interpreted in timber.

The entire timber frame uses long posts, whose arrangement is scrupulously in line with what could have been achieved with vertical stone piers framing the openings of the central section. The timber framework is made up of three horizontal sections comprising a window breast of cross braces sandwiched between two levels of vertical studs intersected by diagonal braces. The horizontal members define the façade in the same way as bands of dressed stone enclosing the rubble infill. This association is perfectly evident in the central bay: taking into account the reduced width of the window on the upper floor compared with the double leaf entrance door, the jambs of each opening are linked by curved timber features in a pattern closely based on the design of stone façades.

The elevations are rigorously symmetrical with a skillful gradation on either side of the central axis, which is marked by the entrance door below a double casement window and a dormer with console-like decorations. The next bays have identical windows crowned with simpler dormers with arched lintels. The outer bays have single casement windows and narrow doors. The two top and bottom sections of the timber frame are of identical height on either side of the window breast which remains the strong point of the composition. The cross brace motif in the axial bay is the most intricate, giving way to increasingly simpler motifs towards the ends (see p. 46).

The master builders of the mid-18th century seem to have banished all sculpted decoration from their façades. Exceptionally, the master builders of Le Lieu-Hocquart seemed to want to convey something of the sumptuousness of the interior decor on the exterior and added some Rococo decoration to the consoles on the central dormer (in the form of bases decorated with guilloches on the lower cheeks) and an inverted floral heart to the pediment over the lintel. Throughout, he demonstrated his ability to transpose the layout and decoration of stone architecture to this timber structure, and even went so far as to create a remarkable carved timber stair banister as an imitation of the wrought iron patterns in use at that time.

Le Lieu-Rocher

The manor of Le Lieu-Rocher offers the surprising contrast of an imposing residence built on regular lines coupled with a relatively free layout. The

This modest 17th century logis was turned into an imposing residence when two large side pavilions were added a century later. The two long rows of outbuildings formed a fitting courtyard.

arranged in groups of four at the corners of the ground floor and groups of three on the upper floor; they are limited in number because the upper level of the timber frame is shorter to allow for the intermediary level of the window of vertical half studs. The windows are aligned in two vertical bays on either side of the axis defined by the center post, to which the lintels of the two twin doors are joined. The lintel of the door on the right-hand side has been raised to come into line with the adjacent window; the door on the left has been inappropriately blocked up and a French window created in the adjacent bay. The architect had subtly accentuated the two central bays, by bringing the breast of the upper floor down to the level of the first-floor lintels and by setting it off with a grid of three parallel diagonal braces resting on the posts. Unfortunately, this harmony has been lost because of the changes made to the doors. This composition adheres to that used in many houses of this period, which like Le Lieu-Rocher were originally covered by a hipped roof. It was, therefore, quite natural to have a simple farmyard in front of the *logis*, the buildings of which were timber-framed and designed along the same principles. The only differences were to be seen in the modest cob nogging on the outbuildings as opposed to the tiles used for the nogging on the house, and the rather crooked timbers contrasting with the straightness of those used in the main *logis*.

house is at the center of the composition, with the detached outbuildings aligned on either side in two long low groups which are more or less parallel.

Such an opulent building would normally feature a truly grand courtyard, and in this case we would expect to find it on a carefully chosen ostentatious site overlooking the beautiful landscape of the valley of the Oudon, with the farmyard and lower courtyard pushed back to the sides.

To understand the reasons behind this layout, we must look at the original structure of the house. It is made up of a central timber-framed body with six bays on two stories and flanked by two large perpendicular wings. The central body seems small compared to the wings, which have ceilings almost one and a half times the height of those in the main part of the house.

These observations, coupled with the uneven heights of the stories and the significant difference in the construction techniques, clearly indicate two very distinct construction phases.

The central building was probably built in the middle of the 17th century on a very simple plan. It is a very robust structure with long perfectly symmetrical posts with structural elements providing the only decoration. The diagonal braces are

In the mid-18th century, the owner was in a position to expand considerably and two large wings were added at right angles to the modest house. Built on an ambitious scale, they were based on a design which was very common in the châteaux of the 17th century, for example at Pin-en-Lieuvin where the roofs of the slightly protruding wings tower above that of the main body. The side elevations are windowless, the only decoration being two immense chimney breasts extending from the long-posted timber framework. The parallel braces are here grouped in fours or fives and there is a narrow window breast with cross braces at mid-height. The exceptional character of this house originates in the enormous windows which are grouped in threes on each floor of the main façade and fitted with fanlights.

The addition of brickwork to the wing façades

during the 19th century, could have cast doubt on the authenticity of this design had the right-hand wing not retained a part of its timber frame still intact, and, in particular, the arched timbers which frame the windows of the upper floor. The *logis* of Le Lieu-Rocher is the only surviving example of such systematic use of this window shape, which was very common in Normandy from the Regency period on.

Timber architecture is based on the principle of the line while stone architecture developed the principle of the arch, and it is very unusual that the latter be used with such outstanding results in a timber structure. Thus, having exhausted the creative possibilities of their medium for a time, the master carpenters turned to copying the forms dictated by stone and were far from unsuccessful in their endeavors.

Lortier

A stone entrance porch and an avenue lined with hundred-year-old lime trees lead to a beautiful timber-framed house with a tiled roof. Built parallel with the valley below, the manor of Lortier is situated on the left bank of the river Touques, half way up the hill, above the church and the remains of the ancient fortress of Auquainville.

We also find this place name written as *L'Ortier*, which is most likely linked in some way to the fortress. *L'Ortier* was probably the "garden" of the ruined castle and the cultivated land immediately around it may have then been established as an independent fief. Its history is quite well known to us, as is that of its successive owners up until the 19th century. Bought by Laurent Amiot in 1361, it was owned by Jehan Amiot in 1444, whose family were resolute supporters of the French. His property was therefore confiscated by the occupying forces and given to an English knight by the name of Griffith Don. Jehan Cuillier – a relative of Jehan Amiot – astutely continued to farm the Lortier fief, thus allowing the family to discreetly stay in the area. An elderly Jehan Cuillier, who was not ennobled until 1471, was represented by his son Geoffroy at the parade of nobility of the bailiwick of

Évreux at Beaumont-le-Roger in 1469, "armed with brigands and spears and two horses", an indication of his considerable rank and fortune. Jehan Cuillier was actually lord of Cheffreville and Parc, and he was only the joint owner of Lortier with Jehan Amiot. On the death of Jehan Cuillier, the seigneury of Cheffreville passed to the elder son, Jean, and the fief of Lortier to his younger son François. During the early years of the reign of Louis XIII, the last in the line passed Lortier on to Pierre Le Bas, lord of Coudray, who undertook the reconstruction of the manor. Cut-off from the farm buildings, the *logis* was built on a rectangular plan with two stories crowned by a hipped roof with regularly spaced dormer windows, three of which are placed along

An avenue lined with hundred-year-old lime trees leads diagonally to the center of the main façade with its discreetly arched door and window frames.

The manor house at Malicorne now stands in the middle of the strong wall which once enclosed the fortified site. The staircase turret, unfortunately truncated, has recently recovered its hipped roof.

the main façade. On this side the frame is built with long posts and the timber infill framing is strictly vertical with no visible diagonal braces; it is only interrupted by a mid-rail which separates the two floors. However, the façade is not completely regular: the window openings, accentuated by the hipped dormers, are arranged in three vertical bays of double casement windows and, in addition, there are several single-framed windows distributed less uniformly at each level. Furthermore, there are notable differences in the scantling of the timbers used: the timber framework of the middle section, which is centered on the biggest chimney stack and the two dormers to the right, is more regular and uses thicker timbers than those in the other parts of the building. Similarly, the dormer on the left, of less precise proportions than the first two, confirms the presence of significant extensions, even though the house appears very uniform at first sight.

The original structure consisted of only the right-hand side centered on the biggest chimney stack and the two elegant dormers, the roofs of which have the same pitch as the main roof. A wide entrance door, now filled in, but whose lintel remains intact, marked the left extremity. A new door was later inserted, replacing an adjacent window. The regularity of the window openings is rigorous here, broken only by the presence of a post which divides the windows below the right dormer.

These harmonious proportions have very discreet timber decoration which is limited to the molded sills of the dormer windows. However, in some places the masonry infill shows traces of rose tiling and geometric shapes on the breast of the left dormer and the north gable, the color of which matches that of the chimney stack which is made of bricks and stone laid in a sawtooth pattern.

The *logis* as it stands today represents the product of two successive construction phases. Two new rooms were added in an extension to the left gable, topped by a simpler and starker dormer. A subsequent extension built at the rear at the end of the 18th century gave the manor house its finest access with a plan double the depth of the house which breaks the symmetry of the side elevations.

It was at this time that the fine wood paneling and interior fireplaces were added, the simplicity of which is in keeping with the scale of the house. This decoration was completed by the reworking of the finishing on the doors and windows with glazing bars, the rounded heads of which give the entire building its most distinctive feature.

Malicorne

The manorial enclosure at Malicorne sits at the junction of two streams which initially filled the moats around the *logis*. As a result of major earthworks this is not so easy to detect today, but it is still possible to sense how powerful this fortified site once was.

A coat of arms, decorated with two bird wings, bearing "faces with ermine wings", on one of the fireplaces in the house, indicates that it was built by the Osmont family, established in Normandy since the 10th century and well known since 1267.

The first mention of the Malicorne fief is when Louis Osmont, squire, described in an act of 17 February 1450 as an *atorné*, i.e. proxy for his mother, took over this estate. He submitted his proof of nobility to the 'Elect of Lisieux' in 1463, and presented himself to the monitors of nobility of the bailiwick of Évreux six years later. His son, who married a "noble lady", Robine Fortin, on 24 February 1497, succeeded him and passed Malicorne on to

Jean Osmont. The latter is known for having been at the worst disturbances during the Wars of Religion on 22 July 1562, and was commissioned by the Duke of Aumale, governor of the province of Normandy, to "raise and assemble either on horseback or on foot the number he deemed sufficient of peasants and residents of the bourgs of Saint-Julien de Foulcon (le Faucon), to take command in preventing the pillage and vandalism being committed by the rebels in the province." René, son of Jean Osmont, served as man-at-arms in the company led by the lord of Montmorency and there followed an impressive line of descendents in armed service until the early 19th century.

We are not therefore surprised to find traces of strong walls at Malicorne, inside which the timber *logis* was erected, perched on an enormous plinth.

All that remains of the side facing the yard is a beautiful cornice – above the more recent unattractive stonework – whose fine molding makes us regret the disappearance of the timber framework. However, the rear elevation on the moat allows us to imagine the original layout.

The framework here is of a very rare size and quality, exceptionally fitted with a jetty and a cornice, identical to that of the side facing the yard, and flanked by diagonal braces on each floor.

The façade is centered on a projecting hexagonal staircase turret, which is now truncated but must have originally been quite tall to reach the living quarters in the attic. The roof trusses still retain traces of the enormous dormers which took up the entire width of the second and fifth bays on the yard side.

The positioning of the chimneys on the two gables deviated from the practices of the time. The timber house was fitted into the enclosure wall so it was natural to have at least one chimney breast backing on to it.

In keeping with the *logis* itself, the decoration is sober and powerful. The moldings of the jetty and the window sills are accompanied by discreet patterns on the heads of the thickened posts, in the form of an ogee above a double base.

The most refined decoration is seen on the four windows inserted in the middle of the second and fifth bays, only one of which remains intact. It con-

sists of two double windows, the lintels of which flourish in floral ogees scattered with serrated falling leaves.

We must examine the whole of this window and its breast to grasp the quality of design; the decoration simply accentuated the structural logic. The main lines are provided by the three jambs, from which project three fine pilaster buttresses with molded bases. They appear on the corner, above the springing of the ogee, and end in sharp pinnacles punctuated with tiny gables and crockets. The decoration is very obviously copied from stone architecture, but it has been transferred to timber with perfect ease, conveying the constructive principles very clearly, i.e. the continuity of the jambs, with hardly any visual interruption by the sill. The latter appears as an almost independent feature, with the small bracket buttress behind it.

The size of the timbers used also add to the harmony of the ensemble, a harmony achieved as a result of a skillful plan which guided the work of the carpenter.

The lord of Malou wanted to ensure the defense of his manor by building a gatehouse equipped with effective devices. Traces of the grooves into which the draw-bridge fitted can be found under the lovely molded timber dormer.

Malou

The confluence of two streams into a little tributary of the Touques, an isolated dale with grassy slopes under the shade of apple trees provided a perfect site for the manor of Malou.

The outbuildings still form a circular arch upstream from the polygonal platform, on which the *logis* stands. Defense was obviously a priority: the uneven ground was encircled by wide moats, still very noticeable today and accentuated by the downthrow of earth inside the surrounding walls. This archaic shape, which was almost a *motte,* was doubtless the site of a small timber fortress accessed from a bridge across the deepest part of the moat on the upstream side.

In the 16th century it was decided to provide better defenses for the original site by surrounding it with a stone wall. Work was started at the most vulnerable point – the drawbridge, the gatehouse, and the two adjacent sides. The thrust of the land of the platform was contained on either side by slightly sloping stone walls, supported by a thick rounded cordon.

This gatehouse is not free-standing: it backs onto the main body of the house and was inspired by the forms used at the château of Saint-Germain-de-Livet or in the old manor of Beuvillers – from where a gatehouse was recovered from the ruins and transferred to the château of Crèvecœur. Two tiny cylindrical turrets with cone-shaped roofs frame a round-headed door, forming a relatively effective fortification, in which we can still see the grooves into which the two arms of the drawbridge fitted. The masonry consists of high-quality stone, and a simple cornice in the upper part and brick and stone checkerwork in the lower part of the turret elevation constitute the only decoration.

"The ploughman should build according to his income and possessions, because it frequently occurs that a construction that is too big costs more to maintain than to build. It is therefore necessary to plan the size of the latter so that, should some misfortune come to pass, it can be repaired with the income of one or two years from the non-tied land on which it stands". This sound advice, which appeared in the translation of Palladio published in 1554 by H-J d'Arces in his *Treize Livres des choses rustiques* ("Thirteen books of rural matters"), and echoed in most of the other anthologies and treatises of the time, was wisely heeded here – albeit belatedly. His desire to build an expensive stone building was, it seems, beyond the means of Jean Gouvis, lord of Malou, mentioned in 1540, and the work was stopped, limited to this gatehouse, which was sufficient to affirm the seigneurial prerogative, if not to actually ensure the defense of the house. Work did not begin again until a century later as can be seen in the use of large panels of brick with stone dressings on the elevation of the sides adjacent to the gatehouse. But yet another century was to pass before the north part of the *logis* was fully completed, this time using a simple timber framework to finish the upper floor. The reconstruction of the three other sides of the surrounding wall was never undertaken.

Today, the contrast between the two sides of the manor is very striking. Viewed from an upstream perspective, the *logis* of Malou gives the impression of a small fortress defended by its high walls and its gatehouse with two turrets. The two arches of the fixed bridge are still in place, but closed on each side. Approached from downstream, the courtyard is now a terrace planted with a peaceful garden and the hedge around the kitchen garden is the only allusion to the palisades which probably defended it.

Le Marescot

The manor of Le Marescot nestles in a dale at the foot of Montpinçon hill, not far from the source of a tributary of the Oudon which, after some steep meandering, joins the Dives valley. It has stood there for centuries and has seen many changes, subject to the fortunes and misfortunes of time.

However, this modest ensemble has an extraordinary air of authenticity which comes from the splendidly conserved wooded landscape, the courtyard with its very loose arrangement of buildings surrounding the house, the scent of apples floating in the air at certain times of the year, and the small population of farm animals coming and going, as they have always done.

The timber-framed cowsheds, cider-press, and barns made of thin oak or elm planks, and the sheds

The logis *of Le Marescot presents a series of harmonious volumes, dominated by its quadrangular staircase turret, its two tall chimney stacks, and the roof finials.*

with fine arched braces have been positioned as required, the product of the carpenter's talent or the fortune of the owner of the time. They have been situated in such a way as to allow access to the meadows, stream, and wash-house, which are closed off by an embankment.

The *logis* is not exceptional. It is easy to imagine the fine lines that the master builder would have given it during the latter years of the 16th century: a high tiled roof from which two chimneys emerge on the steep sides and a staircase turret in the center of the rear elevation, which has gradually been enclosed by side extensions; however the upper part remains intact. The finest details have been retained, such as the handsome green-glazed roof finial with is pigeon or kestrel still perched on an

upturned baluster, the vase, the bressumer with small modillions which is all that remains of a fine jetty, and the unusual brick and stone checkerwork in which one of the chimney stacks is built.

The house has retained its original silhouette and fenestration, but most of the timber frame has been replaced over the years. It includes some very varied patterns, from the clumsily defined single diagonal braces to the rather strange large saltire which can be seen all along the upper floor but serves no apparent purpose.

The carpenter who carried out the last renovations faced the formidable problem of strengthening the jetty at each end of the building. In theory, it would have been necessary to remove the different pieces carefully, repair the most damaged ones, and reinstall them on the basis of the original composition. However, he chose not burden himself with such constraints and merely replaced the two superposed posts at each corner of the building, with a single post cut in curved wood following the profile of the old jetty.

At no stage was any thought given to leveling the yard, nor to setting the house on a flat surface: the natural gradient has prevailed and as a result the ground floor is rather low. This made the timber framework of the first floor more prominent and its two horizontal sections thus acquired unusual dimensions, the monumentality of which is confirmed by the astonishing liberty of the flight of ten steps leading up to it.

Timber architecture lends itself to extremely close analysis. This should not be taken too far in the case of Marescot. We should simply allow ourselves to be seduced by the harmony of the beautiful setting.

Les Mathurins

The open gallery was a very popular architectural feature at the end of the Middle Ages and throughout the 16th century. Built to provide access to the different areas of the house and space for circulation,

The "manor" of Les Mathurins is one of the most curious buildings in the Pays d'Auge. Its precise purpose and its builders remain uncertain, but everything indicates that it was indeed a "place of health" set up by the Mathurin monks who ministered on behalf of a charitable establishment in Lisieux.

service, and social activities, it appears in a particularly unusual and attractive form in Les Mathurins.

Extending along eleven bays across the west elevation, comprising a long passageway supported by a frame of elegant timber columns, and linking two hip-roofed pavilions on an almost square plan, the gallery is the dominant feature of this building: together with the square pavilions, it may once have constituted one side of a manor courtyard. There is a timber-framed farm building on the southern side of the site, but there is no trace of a house on the west or north sides, nor is there any indication that a building was removed from either pavilion. Finally, there is no record of a fief of Mathurins in this district. This unusual building must, therefore, have served some other purpose.

The Mathurin monks were asked by Bishop Jourdain du Hommet to provide the services of a charitable institute founded in Lisieux in 1165. On 14 June 1584, after a number of serious epidemics, a ruling of the Council of State authorized the town to collect "the *deniers* of the octroi (duty on goods brought into the town), up to the sum of four hundred *écus* (crowns), to help build an appropriate place for the isolation of infected patients, and one hundred *écus* for the maintenance of barber-apothecaries". It is tempting to think that "the manor of Les Mathurins" could have been this "appropriate place for the isolation of infected patients", particularly because the main features of the building can be dated to the end of the 16th century and the Mathurins owned various property in the parish.

It is easy to imagine our monks sending the sick, who could no longer tolerate the unhealthy conditions in the town, out to their estate less than three miles away in the Touques valley. Did they enjoy the sun and the fresh air on the two floors of the gallery which was protected from the east winds by the slope of the hill and the blank wall behind it? And once evening came, did they retire to the side pavilions, each of which had a room with a fireplace? If this is the case, this is an exceptional and early example of an architectural structure predating the sanitorium or clinic.

Although a building like this would appear to have been constructed in a single phase, a closer examination reveals at least two construction phases: the first involved the erection of the north pavilion and the gallery, followed some decades later by the addition of the south pavilion. Both comprise a timber-framed upper floor resting on a stone first floor, but have some subtle differences.

On the north pavilion, we find a regular pattern of stone and brick checkerwork topped by a vertical timber framework, on which there is a slightly protruding rail which forms the window ledge and extends to the projecting latrine on the north wall. The other walls have a large angle brace.

In the south pavilion, the ground floor is built in brick masonry alternating with vertical bands of toothed ashlar. The first floor, which is supported by a course of slightly molded stone, is timber-framed and subdivided into two horizontal bands with cross braces along the window breasts. There is a rare example of a perfectly intact 17th century window on the east wall, which still has its casements ready to be fitted with bordered stained glass and its small-framed interior shutters.

Decoration is limited to some discreet slightly molded scrolls on the top of the corner posts. This pavilion seems to have been built half a century later than its symmetrical counterpart. The ground level, built in brick with stone dressings, probably origi-

nates from the renovations carried out in the 18th century when a timber staircase with carved wood balusters was fitted in the last bay of the gallery.

The gallery, with its timber studs bearing Ionic capitals and crowned by elegant scrolls with a row of vertical beads, remains the most sophisticated feature of this house. However, due to its western aspect, the studs have been badly eroded by the effects of weathering. The bay studs on the second floor are slightly fluted and crowned with scrolled consoles, indicating a lingering Renaissance influence on this structure.

Even more decorative features were recorded in the 19th century, such as glazed terra-cotta finials on one of the roof dormers, which have since disappeared: one of them featured a vase of fruit topped by a stud and another had garlands and bouquets of flowers and fruit intertwined with crescents, all typical motifs from the latter years of the 16th century.

Le Mont-de-la-Vigne

Vines were cultivated in abundance in Normandy until the beginning of this century, especially here in the valleys of the Vie, Dives, and Laizon. Many names of places, parishes, and families reflect this,

The powerful fortress of Le Mont-de-la-Vigne, seat of the seigniory of Montfort, was built on a particularly suitable site – a natural knoll, very rare in the valley floors of the Pays d'Auge, where vines were cultivated until the last century.

and the site of the château of Montfort is much better known as "Mont-de-la-Vigne".

This natural isolated knoll on the valley floor, an exceptional feature in the Pays d'Auge, provided a particularly suitable site for a fortified building and its best exposed slopes were clearly ideal for viticulture.

The slopes alone could not provide adequate defense and the castle was built on a large platform surrounded by walls and moats on an irregular plan. They are still well preserved and their layout has been gradually systematized in the course of successive alterations.

The wall, eroded in places yet still featuring buttresses on its south side, has five round towers. These defenses do not seem to date back further than the 15th century: it has the type of loopholes used at that time and windows with drip lintels. This extensive use of brick is unique to Le Mont-de-la-Vigne; it is sometimes found in interior facing, such as in the staircase tower at the manor of Sainte-Marie-aux-Anglais. Its use here can be explained by the availability of facilities for brick production in this wide clay-floored valley. Two large farm buildings with 17th-century timber frameworks lean against the north and south walls on either side of the entrance bridge, which reveals the large *logis* at the end of the yard and conceals the little chapel, situated close to the tower of the north-west corner, which in turn shelters the charter house.

This fortress was the seat of the powerful seigneury of Montfort, owned by the Aché family, who claimed to be of royal descent. The last Marquis of Aché, François Placide, leased most of his land to Gilles de La Roque in 1702, keeping, however, "the manor and the stable". Le Mont-de-la-Vigne passed briefly into the hands of Guy du Val, lord of Bonneval, before being returned to Gilles de La Roque, who was already beneficiary of a farming tenancy which had been given to him almost twenty years previously. In the opinion of the lord of Bonneval, these common hands were not worthy of enjoying the honorary rights and the seigneurial income attached to this estate so quickly and Gilles de La Roque had to wait until 4 August 1726 to receive them when he finally became lord of Montfort in full. Although he described himself as "counselor-secretary to the King, house and crown of France" and "squire" from 1714 onwards, and thus tried to avoid paying tallage, his prerogatives were not fully recognized until twelve years later. In the meantime, the tax-paying parishioners took him before the king's grand council, protesting against the "so called title of secretary to the King" with which he had decorated himself, although "he is a trader and merchant, at the present time he and his two unmarried sons who live with him, work several farms". This clearly demonstrates the social changes that took place between the Middle Ages and the beginning of the 18th century.

The *logis* was badly damaged by bombing in 1944 and has been extensively restored, yet its original layout is still clearly discernible. Built at the end of the 15th century, it is situated between the charter house and the south-west tower, marking a break in the lines of the surrounding walls. Today the house is bricked into the west wall, which supports the first floor of the building with its prominent jetty. The other elevations are dominated by timber-framing which is exceptionally well-built and still quite well-preserved on the south side overlooking the moat.

The defensive nature of this house is reaffirmed by the lack of windows; there is only a series of small square windows in the upper part of the first timber-framed story. However, there were many more windows on the upper story.

The *logis* is not completely devoid of decoration but it is limited to the molding of the sills, lintels, and the jetty bressumer which bears a triple torus, which terminates on either side of the ends of the transverse beams in a perfect quarter circle. The imposing volume of this main house was cleverly achieved by the courtyard gable with its overhanging truss and the large arched braces, which extend its outline.

A smaller perpendicular return wing was added to the house during the early years of the 16th century. This was supported by the surrounding walls at the rear and decorated on the courtyard side by a beautiful jetty decorated with grotesques.

Mont-Fleury

The manor of Mont-Fleury, which stands on the hillside of an isolated valley, offers the surprising contrast of a modest house with numerous architectural features borrowed from a range of larger-scale edifices. This contrast is all the more striking because it applies to a simple isolated house completely devoid of any reference to scale due to the disappearance of the outbuildings which originally stood nearby.

The main section of the *logis* was built during the early years of the 17th century with a timber framework on the two stories. It was designed on a very symmetrical scheme over seven alternately blank and windowed bays centered on a door in the middle, above which there is a single casement window. The two other windows on the upper floor are two casements wide, crowned by simple dormers with hipped roofs which reflect the lines of the main roof. This layout must have originally been used over the whole height of the building before changes were made to the second floor.

The house was simple and the carpenter interpreted the generally symmetrical scheme with a certain freedom, particularly with regard to the positioning of the braces, preferring to ensure maximum stability for his work rather than respect a perfect balance of lines on either side of the central bay. He used medium quality timber, neither perfectly straight nor particularly thick, but the single cross braces of the center bay and dormers, and the double cross braces of the side windows are very carefully constructed.

The person who commissioned this building, who remains unknown, undoubtedly believed that he had a quality residence in the fashion of the time, well balanced by its two chimney stacks at either end. His successor, it seems, came from a different background, attracted by more complex layouts, nobler materials and forms as yet unknown in the timber-frame architecture of the Pays d'Auge.

He wanted a stone *logis* with alternating panels of small orange-colored brick with courses and bands of stone, and started by truncating the bay posts just below the girding beam and reconstructing the upper floor.

He wanted to modernize the interior layout as quickly as possible and to this end added two square semi-protruding pavilions at the corners of the rear elevation. Was he perhaps inspired by Champ-Versan or Criquebœuf? His stonemason did not seem to have completely mastered the art of building large stone structures, and would have been more accustomed to adding a small sill or nogging to a timber framework than to erecting an entire two-story building. He thus came up against the problem of unstable foundations, but beautifully mastered the cornice molding and the string course linking the window bays.

The most elegant feature of the *logis* is the outline of the roof of the southern pavilion, which seems to unique of its kind among the manors of the Pays d'Auge. There are many four-paneled roofs, with

The great monuments of Normandy have sometimes been interpreted with extreme elegance, such as the axe-head roof with which the seigneur of Mont-Fleury crowned his logis at the end of the 16th century.

Most of the timber framing on the rear elevation of the manor of La Motte is concealed behind slate cladding and tiled pentices. The beautiful cider-press which stood nearby unfortunately disappeared when the manor was abandoned. It has, however, been restored since.

parish, to which it would then have given its name, but the research has so far been fruitless. The house forms an imposing mass with large and refined volumes which have not been changed by the various additions to the rear elevation.

The pure volume of the roof is achieved by the way in which the lines of the ridge on the roof of the only dormer on the main façade and those of the gable roof of the staircase structure join the ridge of main roof. The simple lines of long posts in the rear façade contrast with the short posts of the jettied main façade. In keeping with the same principles, the carpenter did not want to expose any diagonal members in the timber framework of this two-story house, and he has carefully hidden all the braces on the internal side of the walls.

Given such refinement, one would have expected a strict distribution of windows. Although the doors were originally in their traditional place at the extremities of the main façade, the windows – the mullions and transoms of which are still visible on the jambs – were distributed randomly, and did not feature as usual in the center of a bay or on either side of a post. It would appear that the carpenter concentrated on perfecting one element of the work – he was concerned above all with erecting a perfectly stable structure. This concern is particularly evident in the attention paid to the very thick wall plate. It is cut from a single piece of timber and its length determined the length of the *logis*.

Decoration is reduced to some high quality details, such as the series of bases in a line beneath the row of windows on the large dormer marking the passage of the sill, or underlining the thickening of the bay posts where they support the jetty. In addition, there are the common rafters with shaped edges in the dormer and the moldings which are very neatly detached on the jetty bressumer. These features all date this house to the late 15th or early 16th century.

The outbuildings were completely modified on several different occasions: there was a remarkable cider-press dating from the 17th century, but it has since disappeared. The quality of the materials, combining stone and brick, further enriched the volume formed by the narrow wing at right-angles which housed the cider-press. The roof ridge of the

narrow ridges, the gradient of which is softened at the end of the slope by gently sprocketed eaves. However, none seem to have this "axe-head" outline with the progressively inflected curve, which gives such lightness to the structure.

This design was most likely based on the Renaissance wing of the Mondrainville mansion in Caen, which was inspired by an Italian style casino, or the entrance pavilion of the Château of Gaillon, or the bell tower of one of many churches in the Caux region which also feature this magnificent silhouette.

La Motte

The parish of La Motte has today disappeared and only the manor of the same name still stands some distance from the ruined church. This place name has led us to look at the corresponding hillock, which may have been the seat of the main fief of a

wing intersected that of the main body of the building, and the hipped side slopes harmoniously take up the same symmetrical lines.

The distribution of rooms in this *logis* conforms to the layout common at the end of the Middle Ages in the Pays d'Auge. The staircase turret adjoins at the center of the rear elevation and shows no concern for composition or decoration; it is built on a rectangular plan, covered by a gable roof, and is clad with tiles. It is the only weak point of the design, no doubt the product of a momentary lapse.

The staircase turret opens onto a gallery on the first floor. The gallery is completely integrated into the volume of the building but can be made out by the asymmetry of the roof. It was probably never very open to the exterior and just perforated by some small windows.

Ouilly

This building is sometimes incorrectly referred to as "la ferme d'Ouilly" [the farm of Ouilly], although its well known history and its architecture place it unmistakably in the manor category. The apparent modesty of the *logis* and remote location are no doubt behind this confusion, which close examination clearly dispels.

The fief of Ouilly was first known as Val-Herbout and was owned by a family of that name known in the area in the 13th century.

It passed into the hands of the lords of Ouilly-le-Tesson near Falaise and it has since borne their name; the fief belonged to Richard d'Ouilly in the 14th century. The situation is more complex from the end of that century, when the fief was divided: "the manor, the Ouilly forest and most of the arable lands" then belonged to a Rioult family, while the seigneurial rights became "the property of a younger branch of the house of Courcy", who were probably linked to the Ouilly family. It was not until 1611 that the fief and its land were reunited when Gabriel Quesnel de Coupigny, descendant of the house of Courcy, finally ceded the seigneurial rights to Jacques Rioult, whose family had already been established on the land for more than two centuries, and had submitted proof of nobility to the 'Elect of Lisieux' in 1463.

The *logis* of Ouilly extends over a long rectangular and apparently regular plan following the incline of the valley; its two stories are covered by a roof with two hipped slopes on the south, and a single one on the north side, which have two identical dormer windows and two chimney stacks of different size.

The slight overhang between the two floors cannot be classed as a jetty. It is only a few inches deep and it is not supported by a 'corbel' or other supports, joists, transverse beams, or brackets. Actually, each bay is marked by long posts, slightly thickened to accommodate this overhang, which is supported by intermediary plates of the same section as the posts. The first three bays on the north side stand out as having a slightly stronger structure and perfect straight lines, diagonal braces on the upper floor, very elaborate joints between the posts, and discreetly molded plates. It was probably a small house built at the end of the 15th century by Pierre Rioult, son of Jacques Rioult, who presented his proof of nobility in 1463. It was a *logis* with only one room on each story, but nonetheless stamped by the coat of arms on one of the posts which can no longer be made out today.

The prosperous period which followed coincides

The oldest logis, *at the right-hand extremity of the current structure, only consisted of three bays built with long posts with a slightly oversailing upper floor and just one room on each level. It was later extended by several bays using slightly less complex techniques.*

Providing access to the interior rooms was probably not the only function of the staircase turret at Piencourt manor: it was also a symbol of seigneurial prerogatives.

The sophistication of the house is also demonstrated in the interior finish. Traces of paint decoration remain on several ceilings, with small landscapes framed by cartouches with coffers of precious wood in *trompe l'œil*. They are finished rather clumsily, it must be said, but they do indicate a residence of quality. To these fragile traces we can add the final remains of the once elaborate roof decoration comprising the base of a glazed terra-cotta finial dating from the Renaissance, whose little cherubs on a deep blue base mark the southern point of the roof.

Piencourt

Piencourt is without doubt the only manor which still has a house perched on an original feudal *motte*. Although partially filled in, traces of the moats are still visible. They originally encircled a perfectly round hillock, which was so small that there was no room for even the smallest courtyard. A second enclosure, which can barely be made out today, surrounded the *motte* and protected the bailey, including what may have been the parish church, preceding the later chapel (see p. 33).

An examination of the basement of this building reveals the presence of a wall on the west side, the stonework of which was about three meters thick – the last remains of a strong stone keep, which is related to the history of this fief.

The name "Willermo de Péencourt" appears in a charter of 1126, and written as "Guillelmo" in a deed dated 18 June 1139, and on two documents originating from the chartulary of the priory of Saint-Lambert de Malassis. The family tree of these Piencourts can be followed very accurately in a series of other records until 1214, testifying to their importance.

It was logical to find the Piencourts strongly fortified in their "motted" stone keep, but it is rare to find a castle site so well-preserved, despite its continued occupation to this day. The Baudry family succeeded the Piencourts at some unknown date: in 1428 Cosme Baudry was the viscount of Évreux and of Orbec and his direct descendants remained on the land for almost three centuries. René-Jacques de

with the large extension built on to the south side of the *logis*. The four bays were built respecting the principles used during the previous century, but without the same mastery in the art of carpentry: the bays are wider and this created the need to support the upper floor with intermediary posts, the wood is not so regular or thick and the windows are distributed at random in the middle of a bay or on a post.

The carpenter concentrated his efforts on the window sills and the cornice, which bear a fine dentil decoration with a frieze of tiny consoles, in which we can clearly see the mark of the Renaissance. It was continued to the old house, where the sill of the upstairs window was probably recut when in place and the cornice matched with that which had just been added on the extension. The two dormers with hipped roofs and window breasts with saltires must also have been added at this time. The year 1518, which features on the panel of the sun dial on the chimney stack, clearly dates this new building and the slight changes made to the original structure.

The only changes introduced since 1518 include the construction of a staircase tower on the south gable and the addition of the fine tile nogging, both carried out before the end of the 15th century.

Baudry, lord of Piencourt in 1668, bore "sable, with three right hands in silver".

According to a late inscription made on a fireplace in 1821, the current house was built by the Baudry family in 1502. However, it is more likely that it was built during the second half of the 15th century on part of the foundations of the keep at the top of the *motte*. The defensive function was perpetuated in this great *logis* and the ground floor is built completely of stone. It has a few generously lined windows fitted with window seats. The year 1502 refers only to the construction of the timber-framed polygonal staircase turret with a conical roof.

The timber first floor is built on a jetty which runs along the four sides of the house, supported at the corners by dragon braces. The bracing was left undecorated except for the discreet moldings on the east elevation. The house was severe, with windows being equally scarce on the lower and upper floors. The south gable still bears an almost intact example of the small twin windows at the center of bays alternating with blank bays. The only decoration on the façades was the scant molding at the top of the bay posts.

The only trace of color on this somber house was on the first level of the timber framework of the turret, with its alternate infill of tile, squared flint, and stone triangles completed during the 16th century.

It may have been continued in the upper levels, but this is concealed from view by the slate cladding. Was it continued on all the elevations? There remain what may have been two panels of infill in the center of the east elevation, decorated by a curious vertical checkered pattern of small black flint and limestone, perhaps recycled.

The building was modernized at the beginning of the 19th century by the owner of the manor, a *Monsieur* de Bonnechose. He recovered the first floor with wood and the ground floor with a coat of lime on a lathing of rived oak, decorated with false toothing stones on the frames of the windows on the east elevation, completed in the center with a small pediment with roundels.

After this transformation, dated 1821, the manor house of Piencourt was subjected to a drastic restoration around 1950, during which the building

regained its exposed timber, but the window openings were damaged.

La Quaize

We are already familiar with the taste for lurid color that reigned among the builders of the Pays d'Auge during the 16th century. The manor house of La Quaize is a fine example of this. It was brutally altered by extremely careless renovation around 1960, but painstaking restoration has since returned the authentic features to their former glory.

Overlooking a beautiful landscape at the junction of two secluded valleys, the house is very small, and must have seemed even more so when its two stories were covered by a high tiled roof, which was

The tranquil approach to the manor house of La Quaize gives no hint of the elaborate detail of its carved decorations and stunning polychromy (see p. 65).

reduced in size around the middle of the 19th century. A scattering of glazed tiles can be seen on the slopes of the lowered roof, the last vestiges of the "clever designs of this great roof", mentioned by Arcisse de Caumont; these were accompanied by a "double finial" on top of the roofing tiles. The irregular checkerwork masonry plays on the polychromy of the white stone and pink brick on the first level of the north gable and on the west elevation. But the outstanding originality of this house lies in the nogging on the main east-facing façade overlooking the manor courtyard. We have become accustomed to both the prodigious variety of geometric tile patterns developed by the stonemasons from the middle of the 17th century and the combinations of materials in fashion during the previous century involving squared flint in various colors, tiles, and small blocks of dressed stone. Some rare examples show the use of glazed brick, as in a 17th century house in the Rue du Bouteiller in Lisieux which was spared in the bombing of the last war, but this was only used for monochrome features. At La Quaize, the nogging of glazed brown, red, green, and yellow bricks combined in various patterns is a fine example of the importance and the boldness of colored details in the Pays d'Auge (see page 65).

With regard to authenticity, it must be said that the nogging we see today had to be recreated using materials found in the area complemented by new elements. Fortunately, a photograph from 1927 shows us the original design with the nogging featuring on the two levels of the right-hand side of the façade, but only on the first floor of the left-hand side. It has now inappropriately been extended to include the whole façade and removed from the window breasts on both levels.

The timber frame of this house has undergone few changes, but shows some significant differences on the main façade and the jetty. The first three bays on the south side are very regular with their posts aligned from one level to the next, in contrast to the three bays on the north side which have obviously been remodeled. The timber infill framing of the whole of the façade has also been altered significantly, making it difficult to identify the original window openings.

The wall space below the windows of the first floor in these first three south bays was inappropriately given a continuous series of saltires, although originally there was only one per bay, and there was only a single window on the central bay. On the ground floor, the main door, which was blocked up for a long time, once again opens under an ogee arch, close to the north east corner.

Although the chimney stack stands in its normal central position, the narrowness of the plan did not allow for the staircase to fit between the chimney and one of the elevations. With no tower to house it, the staircase was therefore placed in an unusual position – in the south-east corner. This explains the slight protrusion of the entrance door.

The decoration of this part of the *logis* is exceptionally rich, combining features of Gothic ornament with new Renaissance ideas. The jetty and the cornice are very traditional in structure but include a host of fine moldings, separated by wide flat pieces, carefully detached to the right of each post. Grotesque figures feature at the ends of each jetty bressumer, becoming sea monsters or foliage (see page 43). The door still has an ogee lintel but it is supported by two jambs decorated with concave panels, intersected by lozenges, and crowned by scrolls; finally, on either side of the fleuron, two half studs support the tumbling fruit which definitively breaks with the Gothic decoration. This sculpted mass, which is badly eroded, is a direct copy of that at the *logis* of Les Pavements, though it is probably slightly later and clearly carved by a less confident hand. The traces of polychromy found in the relief of these façades have allowed for a faithful restoration, imposed by the colored scheme which features on this *logis*.

The east elevation also has an group of coats of arms on jig-saw shaped escutcheons, which are attached to the door and window jambs, and a single escutcheon on the top of the third post.

The west elevation, which has timber framing divided into two horizontal sections scattered with saltires, has only one visible escutcheon in the center, embossed with a simple heraldic cross, topped with a bishop's miter.

This is the coat of arms of Jacques d'Annebault, Bishop of Lisieux from 1543 to 1560, which dates the construction of this *logis* precisely.

The fief of La Quaize came under the barony of

Glos and, therefore, the bishops of Lisieux. The man who built the house, Silvain de Fatouville, would have wanted to render homage to his overlord with this escutcheon, with a view perhaps to appeasing the 'Elect of Lisieux' who demanded tallage payments from him in 1540, deeming his proof of nobility to be insufficient. It is true that at this time the Fatouville family was only recently established at La Quaize.

There are mentions of several members of a "de la Quèze" or "de la Quièze" family in the parish of Glos between 1320 and the middle of the 15th century; the last descendant married Jehan Quesnel, squire, who passed this fief to the Fatouville family in unknown circumstances. The coat of arms of Silvain de Fatouville "with gules, on a silver band, crabs in sable at the top, and at the point two tips of the same" features once again on the entrance door. The *logis* must have been exceptionally elegant for such a small building in the late 16th century.

It remains, however, to explain the reasons for the disparity between the left-hand side of the east elevation and the group comprising the right-hand side and the gable wall adjoining it at right angles.

There are indeed structural differences, already suggested by the absence of harmony between the bays on each level, the strong diagonal braces on the second floor, and, especially, the window breasts with interwoven cross braces, which feature along the full width of the gable and all along the upper floor.

This kind of layout, especially that of the sills, is more typical of the late 17th century. It is, therefore, very likely that all these elements, including the paint decoration on the joists of the upper room on the south side, were altered at this later stage, without significantly modifying the general aspect of the *logis*.

The logis *of Les Quatre Nations represents one of the great successes of 18th century timber architecture. Thanks to the abundance of windows, the architect succeeded in banishing all vertical timbers from the infill framing of the façade.*

Les Quatre Nations

What were the "four nations" that gave this place its name? There is no trace of a fief with this place name, nor of any family with such a name and no mention of the authorization of seigneuries. There is, however, a cemetery in Caen named "Les Quatre Nations" which is shared by four parishes. The estate in question here is situated on the borders of four parishes with many enclaves. Thus, the name could, perhaps, reflect the geographical location.

The old road from Caen to Rouen was nearby, as was the famous fair known as "the Dozulé market", which features on a map drawn by Cassini: this was a big market held on the Monday before Easter Sunday, and big fairs were held on the day after Saint John's Day, and on Saint Samson's Day.

All of the details adhere to this principle, including the fanlight and panels of the entrance door.

This suggests that the *logis* regularly accommodated travelers from far away, indeed from four nations. However, this hypothesis is completely contradicted by the architectural layout of the old hostels in this region, which can still be seen at the "Auberge de l'Aigle d'Or", an inn in Pont-l'Évêque. These had a series of bedrooms above the great hall and the kitchens, with huge sheds and stables built around a closed courtyard.

The layout of Les Quatre Nations is completely different and does not differ significantly from neighboring estates. Most of the outbuildings are grouped in a small outer bailey. The oldest date from the 16th or 17th century and have been greatly altered. Only the cider-press was built – or rebuilt – a little distance away from and at the same time as the manor house, although both buildings were no doubt originally linked to the rest of the outer bailey.

As with all 18th-century timber-framed buildings, all the specifications of the material are abandoned in this house in favor of a return to the architectural forms and decoration of stone building, and it is modeled on buildings in the nearby plain of Caen, on the opposite bank of the Dives. There is a lot of space and there are many windows. The *logis* was built with two stories on a rectangular plan, crowned by a four-sided roof, with a wide overhang at the bottom of the slope where the eaves are steeply sprocketed.

The layout is rigorously symmetrical and there is a skillful gradation between the central axis of the middle bay, where there is a wide double-leaf entrance door, and the end bays which are substantially wider than the two intermediary bays. The frame is perfectly orthogonal, made up of long posts connected at the height of the second-floor window breasts by a plate which is intersected at each bay, and sits on a low sole plate supported by a rubble plinth.

Remarkably, apart from the door and window jambs and the intermediary posts, the infill framing does not have any vertical pieces: all of the panels are constructed using diagonal pieces of timber, giving large fern patterns on the blank gables and the piers between the windowed bays of the north and south elevations.

Multiple diagonal braces intertwine in the spaces

between the openings on each floor. Apart from the frame and the window ledges, there are no other horizontal members in this timber framework. The segmental arched window lintels, the lower sides of which are normally simply trimmed as in the manor house of Le Lieu-Hocquart, are here shaped in a complete curve which gives the whole elevation a particular distinction, further accentuated by the double line of the fanlight with its curved glazing bars.

This clever decorative scheme also gives a remarkable stability to the building due to the numerous diagonal members. The master builder achieved maximum effect by placing long opposing diagonals on the end bays, perfectly wedging the composition, and contented himself with shorter fern sprigs on either side of the central bay and a tiny pier panel between the two large windows of the two main rooms of the second floor.

This is not decadent carpentry, as the timber framing of the 18th century has been rather hastily labeled, but the result of intelligent collaboration between a skilled designer and a master carpenter who had not forgotten the lessons of the past. Indeed, he revived the well-proven technique of the diagonal beam in the ceilings of the upper floor at the corners of the building – a practice that had been abandoned for over two centuries.

The interior decoration is equally elaborate. The carpenter played his part, of course, providing molded ceiling beams and a skillfully curved stair string. The stone mason was responsible for the series of six chimneys constructed in brick and stone toothing and topped by a fine ovolo and cavetto molding. The sculptor then added curves to each hood and molded mantels which are the same as those with which he decorated the leaves of the entrance door.

It may seem surprising that the joiner who showed such skill in the carving of the panels of the interior and exterior doors was not commissioned to give the house some elaborate wood paneling. Perhaps the commissioner of the building had come to the end of his budget having contracted the services of a highly skilled blacksmith who gave this house its collection of crafted locks and a remarkable stair rail, which is worked in large creeping scrolls, curving over and back and arranged around a simple heart design at the center of each section.

Les Roches

We do not know how this *logis* acquired the name of "Les Roches" [the rocks]. Does it refer to the slight knoll in the middle of the low meadows of the Vie valley, or perhaps the great stone tower of the *logis*?

This building actually lies in the former manor of Querville which bore the same name as the parish joined to that of Biéville-en-Auge. The painted coat of arms on the chimney hood in the hall of the house testifies to this with its two escutcheons "in silver with a string of gules", which are the arms of Jacques de La Lande, lord of Querville, who is mentioned in the D'Hozier armorial.

The manor buildings are situated on a small terrace bordered by the stream and a network of watered ditches, and include a barn, a cider-press, and sheds, all of which are timber-framed.

Only the house breaks with the homogeneity of material. It is a simple two-story timber-framed structure built with long posts and has an imposing stone staircase tower at the rear, bearing a timber-framed upper chamber with slate cladding. The chimney block is impressive and groups the four flues in an enormous stone stack decorated with a small sundial.

The logis of Les Roches has an imposing quadrangular staircase turret which could be interpreted as the remains of an older building. However, this is not the case, and the size of the work mainly corresponds to the symbolic affirmation of seigneurial prerogatives.

The strictly vertical timber framing of rather narrow members could indicate a structure of the late 16th century: the hipped roofs on the main body of the building and the upper chamber in the staircase turret would seem to support this hypothesis. However, the great fireplace on the first floor with its cavetto and ovolo piers is still rather Gothic in style. The rail added to the upright members of the upper floor and the small double windows in the center of the panel are more indicative of a building of the previous century. In addition, the long posts show the characteristic thickening where the rail passes, with the exception of those of the last bay on the west side.

The stone staircase turret is often said to be the oldest part of the building and has even be suggested as originating from the 12th century. However, there is nothing in its simple masonry to indicate that it is such an old structure. On the contrary, the rustication decorating the frame of one of the interior doors, and the posts of the upper room, which are thickened with scrolls, seem to indicate work originating from the late 16th or early 17th century.

Thus, in its original form, the *logis* at the old manor of Querville would only have been made up of a simple long-post block on a rectangular plan with five bays and either an interior or exterior staircase housed in a timber turret. It must have been subsequently extended by one bay on the west side and given its stone staircase turret with the upper chamber providing a view over the entire estate at the bottom of the valley and, if required, some basic defense.

La Roque

Nothing seems to have changed at the manor of La Roque in the last two centuries, and today's owner has wisely retained its perfect simplicity. There is no elaborate portal, but a simple gate opening onto the road, no ostentatious flower beds or winding avenues, but a simple lawn scattered with umbels, no gleaming timber façades, but façades covered with the lovely gray tint which oak acquires with time and the acquisition of a light coating of lichen.

The *logis* and its outbuildings form one of the most captivating ensembles of timber architecture, consisting of a loose arrangement around a courtyard which is almost completely enclosed by buildings. Barns, cow-sheds, cider-press and cellars, stables, sheds, and the bakehouse are all lined up in two rows of timber-framed buildings, interrupted on one side by the pond and its washing place and covered by mossy tiles which have been added on as the need arose. They present an interesting range of simple roof shapes resembling a 'forage dormer' and a splayed awning, and a wonderful variety in the timber infill, which is either strictly vertical or with multiple oblique braces. The two stories of the house, framed by the two tall chimney stacks emerging out of the hipped ends of the roof, terminate and dominate the back of the courtyard.

The manor of La Roque stands at the edge of an imposing fortified site, still easily discernible, within a vast enclosure bordered by moats. It was probably the castle of Radulphe de Montpinçon mentioned in a charter of 1074. When the fortress was abandoned, the seat of the deposed estate was most likely reduced to the site of the former outer bailey, the location of the buildings of the present day manor of La Roque; none of these buildings date further back than the 16th century.

A discreet view of the rear of the manor house of La Roque from the neighboring knoll. It is probably the remains of an important fortified site mentioned as early as 1074. Its timber framing is concealed by slate cladding on the elevation facing the yard where the outbuildings stand.

With its very symmetrical composition, centered around an entrance door topped by a large fanlight with glazing bars and balanced by the two groups of double windows on either side of the bay posts, the façade of the *logis* is now very Classical in its appearance. However, some of the decorative features are much older and there are some curious joints in the frame.

The upper floor projects slightly due to the overhang of the girding beam separating the two stories. It is not a jetty but a simple device to which the carpenter has united on a single piece of timber the decoration, which was normally divided between the two upper parts of the jetty, i.e. a drip molding which tops and protects a beautiful ovolo cable molding, where a hollowed out ribbon borders triangles of stylized foliage. On examining the timber frame at each end of this façade, we find traces of two large Gothic-style doors, which are now blocked up. Close scrutiny reveals traces of ogee decorations with foliate motifs topped with high florets. These are very similar to the decoration at La Quaize, Les Pavements, and the church at Auquainville, which have been precisely dated to the second quarter of the 16th century, a date confirmed here by the scrolled consoles worked into the heads of the posts and some upright studs decorated with long hollowed panels.

This Renaissance *logis* already had a very symmetrical composition, emphasized by a large chimney breast – the traces of which can still be seen in the form of a header in the middle of the building. It had, however, already moved away from the use of a jetty, retaining only its decorative elements to conceal the joints of the transverse beams behind the posts.

The small structure, which extends over two bays on the left-hand side, seems to be older than the larger structure. Indeed, its jetty enables us to date it to the beginning of the 16th century. However, its various alterations may be explained by the later remodeling of an older building.

The large building must have been in rather bad condition in the middle of the following century, especially its central section – the decorated plate is now actually missing. Restoration work was carried out incorporating more recent trends, and a main door was added giving direct access to the central staircase which was built in the former place of the chimney breast, which was shifted to the extremities of the building. The Gothic doors were blocked up and ruthlessly chopped up and only the elegant decoration of the wall plate was saved by the carpenter, who was content to replace the missing central part with a simple, roughly squared beam. The windows have more or less retained their original positions and are simply decorated with cross braces on the window breasts of the upper floor. In fact the commissioner of this work was more concerned with the renovation of the decoration and the interior layout. This has been carried out with great elegance and includes the fine stair balusters and the exquisite array of fireplaces in stone and stucco fitted with large, delicately molded hoods.

Les Samsons

The manor of Les Samsons is built on a particularly suitable site close to the confluence of one of the many tributaries on the left bank of the Orbiquet. There is an abundance of water and the manor overlooks the rich meadows of the estate on the wide valley floor. The free-standing buildings are arranged around a single courtyard, with the manor house occupying the best site, nestled on the hillside facing due south.

This *logis* has only recently been called 'Les Samsons', which was probably the name of one of its owners at the beginning of the 19th century. It is in fact, the old manor of the Masselinaie fief, a "complete fief" originally owned by Colin de Mailloc and later by his daughter Marie de Tournebu, who sold it to the Bishop of Lisieux, Pierre Cauchon.

The latter gave it to the cathedral chapter on 17 January 1441 "during the time when Jehan de Mailloc resided with the king, his land being occupied by the English", according to a statement made on 4 January 1538 by another Jehan de Mailloc for his full fief at Mailloc.

The long silhouette of the house, the importance given to the east gable facing the valley, and its setting following the slight slope in the land, have

The manor house of Masselinaie, better known as "Les Samsons", is made up of several parts, the oldest of which stands in the center. The square pavilion was added after the 15th century and another narrower extension was built on the other side at a later date.

bressumer, which in turn supported the hearth of the upstairs fireplace. The master builder of Les Samsons moved away from the model of the central chimney stack found at the time in all buildings of this size. The other bressumers show no trace of having been interrupted. We must, therefore, conclude that this house had only a single large room on this floor stretching over five bays, a layout which remains exceptional in this type of building.

The upper story has maintained its original layout on the façade, with the exception of the first bay which was significantly changed after a fire. The three central bays had three windows with mullions and transoms and saltire braces on the breasts. The rhythm of the timber structure on this floor is also rather peculiar, because the bay posts and the door and window jambs are constructed in the same rigorous style, forming a series of vertical elements significantly thickened at the top, supporting two twinned wall plates which serve as a cornice.

We find structures of this type in several buildings dating from the 14th century, such as the house situated at 28 Grande-Rue in Caudebec-en-Caux (destroyed). A similar layout was used on the first floor of a more recent house situated at the Rue de la Paix, near the church of Saint-Jacques de Lisieux (also destroyed). In the absence of dendrochronological dating, it is difficult to put such an early date on this part of the *logis* of Les Samsons. The decoration of the jetty is also too limited to offer a precise date. The simple chamfer of the brace does not, however, seem to be earlier than the mid-15th century.

As in almost all buildings of this era, the rear elevation consists of a long-post frame which, however, retains the system of thickened posts on the upper floor as used in the main façade.

The main body of the *logis* has been extended on the east side since the late 15th century through the addition of a stone storeroom at ground level bearing a timber upper floor. This storeroom originally only had a door with a segmental arch in the gable wall and narrow window openings on each of the other walls, which have since been inappropriately reshaped. A very talented master carpenter was commissioned to complete the timber-framed upper floor and he built it as an actual square pavilion with

resulted in its frequent comparison with the *logis* of La Brairie. However, although chronologically close, these two buildings are based on quite different construction principles.

The two very large roof dormers lend the structure an apparent coherence, which does not, however, stand up to an examination of its timber structures. It is in fact made up of three distinct parts: from east to west there is a wing with a stone first story topped by a three-bay timber frame, next to which stands a two-story five-bay timber structure, and finally a small, much narrower, timber structure set back on the south façade but aligned on the north elevation.

The central part seems to be the oldest, because of both its very simple structure and its modest decoration. The entrance door, which has now been closed up, occupied the first bay on the west. Its straight lintel was integrated into the posts by a small curved shoulder in sharp relief. The next three bays, which have undergone significant change, probably each had a window in line with those on the upper floor. The fifth and last bay is unusually narrow: in fact, it is the width of the only fireplace on the ground floor. The hood of this fireplace, which no longer exists, was supported on a

three bays, supported on the stone walls of the store-room by means of a jetty running along the three sides, the overhang of which is only a few centimeters deep. This feature is constructed with great technical virtuosity, using a dragon beam to form the two exterior corners thus, harmoniously lengthening the skilled molding of the jetty plate and bressumer.

The structure of the south façade is very symmetrical, centered on the window in the middle bay, the mullions and transom of which can still be easily made out today. Bracing is provided by two straight braces linking the horizontal members and cross-hawed over the studs. The carpenter did not want to interrupt the vertical harmony which he had carefully accentuated using an elegant Gothic decoration of thin tapering pilasters cut into the body of the posts and relieved on every second stud, thus respecting the binary rhythm already used in the construction of the upper floor of the first house. This decoration with pilasters crowned with crocket pinnacles is very similar to that used on the dovecote of the manor of Pont-Mauvoisin, so much so as to suggest the work of the same craftsman, or the same workshop. The big central dormer window, supported by a cornice which meticulously follows the pattern of the jetty, stretches along the whole width of the central bay and has been built along the same lines. However, its axial window has only two double openings above a single sill.

The second dormer was probably added to the second last bay on the western side during this phase of construction in order to maintain the symmetry of the whole building. The two are of similar proportions and have the same projecting truss; they were decorated again half a century later with the same roof finials, which have since disappeared. The east gable faces the entrance to the manorial enclosure, thus it could not be left blank. It still has a window with its mullion and transom intact and is curiously protected by an awning which provides maximum light and is once again decorated with Gothic pilaster buttresses.

In contrast, the rear elevation is extremely plain with a completely unadorned jetty and the cornice. The windows are simple rectangular openings. A small latrine, overhanging the ditch, was added on this side, facing the hillside.

The addition of a storeroom and a large room with a fireplace (since removed) was not deemed sufficient. The same master builder built another extension on the west side, in the form of a small, much narrower structure of unknown purpose aligned with the rear elevation. It has two bays, but of much smaller proportions, the same jetty as the east wing, and the same windows as the central section with saltires on the window breasts.

Les Tourelles

The manor of Les Tourelles clings to a hillside at the bottom of a narrow valley. The manorial enclosure is still almost completely intact, with a continuous line of outbuildings on two of the four sides, the positioning of which is dictated by the slope of the land (see p. 32).

Windows and doors are dotted along the one and two-story timber façades of the sheds, stables, and barns which all bear traces of various renovations. It is possible to trace the evolution of the different types of joints – from keyed tenons to pegged rails – which were used in the traditional joinery techniques from the 16th to 18th centuries.

The large octagonal timber dovecote occupies the dominant position and is embellished with discreetly molded tile nogging. Its beautiful conical roof is echoed in the tapering forms of the two stone turrets which frame the entrance to the *logis*.

These turrets have, in fact, given the *logis* its name and they are certainly its most original feature, although their modest size would cast doubt on their efficacy as defensive structures.

However, although they were built to add an element of sophistication, as suggested by their fine molded cornices and the quality of the masonry and ashlar facing, they could have frightened henchmen who would not have known what was hiding behind their loop-hole openings. They are above all symbolic and, in this respect, as important as the dovecote.

Visitors passed through the towers – linked by a wall with a porch which has since disappeared – and walked past the dovecote to reach the house, the façade of which opened mainly onto the valley.

La Touzerie

In most manors, the *logis* occupies the dominant position: it is often the only multistory building and its very size imposes the functional hierarchy. The manor of La Touzerie does not follow this principle. The impression conveyed is one of a group, in which the layout of the farm buildings – built at different times – is exceptionally strong. Despite standing in the middle of the ensemble, the *logis* originally occupied a position of almost secondary importance.

The farm buildings actually stand in two parallel lines running north to south around 100 yards in length and following the pronounced slope of the site. The house stands at a perpendicular angle between these two lines of buildings, but without actually enclosing the courtyard in the upper part; a little further up the hillside, there is a large, well exposed garden, still partially enclosed by walls. The view from the house towards the north extends unobstructed to the steep-sided valley of the Vie.

This was in fact a farm, with a carefully arranged, highly functional layout designed to keep it under the close watch of the master, who was able to survey operations from his well-positioned *logis*. The most distinctive feature of this manor is the way the different tasks are neatly divided into as many buildings, as opposed to the normal practice whereby the various jobs were combined in the same long simple buildings; the functions were only indicated on the outside by the door and window openings.

Timber framing has advantages and disadvantages. There is a natural tendency to isolate buildings as a precaution against fire. Furthermore, timber walls visually convey the interior structure of the volumes, which are subject to specific constraints and the limit on the load that the floors could support. The result here is an exceptional variety based on the different functions and chronology of the buildings, which encompass almost a century and a half.

The variety is toned down, however, by the similarity of the materials used (timber framing with cob and lime nogging, limestone plinths, and tiled roofs) and the consistent use of uniform shapes, such as the hipped roofs.

The logis has conserved all of its elements, including the small symbolic defenses providing access to the courtyard, which is centered around the logis and the dovecote and surrounded by outbuildings.

It has undergone significant changes, which, however, have not altered the quality of the volume. The timber elevations have been completely altered, and it has become almost impossible to make out the original position of the window openings. On the oldest part, which dates back to the early years of the 16th century, they were probably much as they are today – aligned with the two fine dormers with trefoiled edge rafters flanking the large stone chimney stack. It seems that this house never had a jetty but with a mid-rail drip moulding, a feature repeated in the extension which appears to have been completed some decades later.

Color is introduced at Les Tourelles with an original touch which deviates from the usual practices of builders in the Pays d'Auge. Although brick and tile nogging was used on the dovecote, the locally extracted stone and bronze-toned sand gave the plaster a strong color which matches that of the materials used in the chimney.

The east side is mostly taken up with buildings related to the crops – barns, apple loft, cider-press, cellar, the distillery and its still – alternating with the laborers' quarters. Opposite this are the cow sheds, stables and other buildings concerned with animal husbandry. The latter were built to a simpler plan and are smaller in size: this balances the mass of the two lines as one is slightly higher on the slope than the other.

The farming requirements were thus satisfied and these structures could have been completed by a truly monumental arrangement based around these two rows of buildings. Instead, rather than creating a central avenue which would have disrupted the agricultural functions of the large yard, it was decided to provide access to the *logis* by means of a simple covered porch built into one of the buildings on the west side, with a larger opening on the north side reserved for agricultural purposes.

The manor house itself was probably not built before the early years of the 17th century and it was extended considerably during the 18th century by the addition of a second perpendicular structure on the west side. Originally, this *logis* was only a small building, built on a long plan with long-post framing on its two stories. The three central bays are built with vertical studs, completed at each end by two bays with four rows of braces; their addition lends a certain strength to the whole, an impression reinforced on the yard side by the window breasts with cross braces.

This very long plan originally made it possible to fit wardrobes and cabinets in the upper-floor bedrooms between the chimney breasts and the gable walls. However, this element of comfort would not satisfy the requirements of the master of an estate of this size for very long. There was a large empty space between the house and the farm buildings, sufficient to add one – or even two – perpendicular symmetrical wings, as at Le Lieu-Rocher.

Only the west wing, whose features date it to the second half of the 18th century, was actually built. It consists of a first floor with a timber framework of exceptional quality resting on a brick ground floor whose corners are marked by a pier of bonded stones. The technique of the *surcroît* is used where, which makes it possible to increase the size and

living space of the top story substantially by separating the roof tie beam and the attic floor. This technique has existed since the end of the Middle Ages and was used a good deal in urban structures at the time in Upper Normandy. It spread widely throughout the towns in the Pays d'Auge – particularly in Lisieux – from the end of the 16th century. It was not until the 18th century, however, that the *surcroît* roof spread to country houses, its purpose here being not so much to increase their living areas, but to give height to the elevation. This was achieved at La Touzerie by accentuating the contrast between this increased height and the hipped roof whose eaves have a wide sprocketed section at the bottom. It is supported by the thickened posts of the extended roof, a contrast emphasized all the more by the narrow frieze of saltires which runs along the bottom of the timber framing. In an attempt to unify the building, the architect continued the pattern of the braces used in the older structure in the new perpendicular wing, but only in rows of three.

La Valette

The *logis* of La Valette belongs to the category of buildings with very simple plans and decoration which were built in large numbers in the Pays

The outbuildings of a manor have rarely given it such a monumental character. The house stands crossways between two long parallel rows; its modest size was altered by the addition of a large perpendicular wing in the 18th century.

d'Auge just after the Hundred Years' War. Its principal merit lies in the fact that despite almost continuous occupation, it has conserved its original layout almost intact – in almost all other places this was deemed too modest and too sober and was thus updated in the style of the day. The balance and attractiveness of the building seem to have helped it to escape any radical transformations.

The master carpenter created a long-post structure along a series of four bays with a vertical rhythm which is uninterrupted by diagonal members; the braces were fitted on the internal face of the timber frame. A rail cuts across the upper floor at mid-height and was joined using a rather unusual process which uses a lot of timber. Actually, this member, which originally consisted of a single piece of timber and mainly served to prevent the splitting of the long posts, is joined from above on vertical tenons on jowls. This design involved a substantial waste of materials because a much thicker piece of timber was required than if the rail had simply been pegged horizontally onto the studs and the posts.

The central position of the chimney stack meant that the two doors were moved out to the ends of the façade, a symmetrical layout echoed in the window openings which are superposed and supported on the bay posts. The decoration on the windows is very simple, taking the form of a chamfer on the mullions and transoms, the main purpose of which was to increase light filtering through to the interior. The staircase is housed in a large square turret on the rear elevation, which is aligned with the center of the chimney stack, and like the main body of the house is crowned with a simple gable roof. Partially protected by a sheath of embedded tiles, the volume has been made somewhat wider by the later addition of two timber-framed lean-tos, the roofs of which consist in the extension of the main pitch.

Only one substantial change has been made since the 16th century when the owner of the estate needed more space. The existing staircase tower provided comfortable access to the attic, so it was decided to add a large dormer along the whole width of the third bay on the main façade. The dormer broke the symmetry that had been perfectly maintained until then, but did not upset the elegant balance of the structure. The harmony was respected by giving the dormer a large gable built as high as the main roof.

The same owner then commissioned some very clever decorative features. The dormer is set on a jetty with a molded rail, framed between the two protruding beams and a wall plate with a stopped chamfer. It was initially perforated by four small rectangular windows above a window breast with saltires, however, only the two central windows remain intact today. The system used to join the sill, which is supported on the vertical tenons, was preserved and a fine decoration of bases was added to the thickened top of the posts; this decoration is repeated in the upper part to house the slight overhang of the gable. All that remained to complete the job was to add a trefoiled edge rafter accompanied by two wide festoons to give this dormer window a lightness it may otherwise have lacked.

La Vallée

Irrigated by the waters of the Reux stream, the lands of this estate, which is frequently confused with "Lieu Day" in the same parish, stretch along the

The logis of La Valette is a handsome long-post structure built during the second half of the 15th century which has remained almost intact. The only significant modification involved the addition of a wide gabled dormer one century later.

lower valley of the Touques, with moats bordered by willows, pollarded poplars, rushes and reeds. The manor house stands in a central position in the middle of the farm buildings which are arranged in two groups: the cider-press and the dairy stand on either side of the entrance to the main courtyard, while the cow-sheds and stables are in an outer bailey behind the house.

Despite its two stories, the most attractive part of this house is the roofing, which shrouds, protects, and conceals the timberwork. The orange colored tiles undulate on the riven oak lathing of the roofs and the slopes of the hipped roof shade the gables and the pediment of the dormer windows and cover the staircase tower on the rear elevation. A wide awning separates the two floors on the main façade, continues around to the gable walls, and extends to cover the widening of the second floor on either side of the staircase turret.

Rarely has a timber-framed house been so carefully protected from the rain: the roofer clearly had an obsessive fear of water damaging the timber frame and not only hung tiles on the cheeks of the dormers but also embedded tiles in mortar on the north-east and south-west sides of the staircase tower. Thus, despite the absence of a jetty, each of the vertical panels could let even the slightest drop of rain run off and in this way made it possible for the house to survive for over three centuries. This technique of fitting peripheral awnings was quite common around Pont-l'Évêque, but not implemented as elaborately as here at La Vallée.

The layout of the *logis* is based on the traditional medieval model, with some loose interpretations tending to increase the diversity of function of each volume. The chimney stacks are at the core of the house standing back to back in two groups of two, thus determining the position of the four rooms with fireplaces. The staircase turret has been built in the same line, but it is fitted into the widening of the rear elevation, with small secondary rooms built on either side. On the first floor we find the Classical layout, with a gallery which is narrower than the width of the rooms below it. The house extends to the southwest over three bays to give a large room on each floor, which originally had no fireplaces.

All the door and window openings have maintained their original position and some of their casements, such as the doors of the main elevation with their iron nailing. The asymmetry of the composition is balanced by the offset of the dormer window on the left hand side, which breaks with the usual layout of windows in vertical bays.

The exterior decoration is limited to the polychromy of the chimney stack built with bricks with ashlar quoins and to the molded lintels of the doors and windows on the upper floor. Inside it is continued with two fireplaces decorated with fluted pilasters and medallions.

Vilembert

The manor of Vilembert stands in an isolated spot at the edge of the forest of Touques at the start of a small steep sloped valley. A mound of earth terminates the pond, over which an imposing wall projects. This wall supports the narrow platform, on which the manor is established.

This was the residence of the warden of the ducal forest, whose job it was to manage the plantations and copses, to collect the dues for the

No other master builder ever took such precautions to protect a timber-framed house from the weather: the dormers, the staircase turret, and all of the elevation are hooded with awnings and hipped roofs.

The carver has decorated the cornice below the overhang of the roof of the extension built during the last quarter of the 16th century with gadroons. The fearsome fangs of one of the Le Touques forestkeeper's dogs feature on the end of this transverse beam.

various functions, and to police the area in his charge.

A small square dovecote with a timber-framed first floor resting on a stone ground floor faces the house and its outhouses, which are built at perpendicular angles.

As a result of the many modifications made to the east wing, we can barely make out the original layout of this structure, which probably houses the oldest part of the *logis* and the outhouses. It has only one floor and some of the decorative features would suggest that it originates from the mid-16th century: the heads of the posts are decorated with scrolled consoles, sometimes sheltering a plump little cherub, a decoration very similar to that seen at the south porch of the church of Sainte-Catherine de Honfleur, and on a house behind its free-standing steeple, attributed to the same carpenter. It also features the same curved lintels marking the two geminated windows which today are blocked up.

A single-story return wing resting on the large supporting wall was added to this very simple house in the last quarter of the 16th century. As it had only one floor, the first house was rather cramped and did not have a great hall.

This extension was able to provide one, with a quality of decoration rarely achieved prior to this in such a small house. It is centered around a very wide window, the mullion and transom of which have disappeared; its sill is decorated with vertical ovals. The doors at each end have projecting lintels which are simply molded or have stylized foliation and contrast with the elaborateness of the section above. The posts bear scrolled consoles, bordered with foliage, sometimes on top of the bust of a man or a woman and sometimes a bird with a threatening beak and talons. The cornice spreads out into a series of rails with fine gadroons bordered by ribbons, similar to those found on the Renaissance gallery at the château of Mesnil-Guillaume. The overhang of the roof tie-beams between these features is carved with a frightening animal head with short ears, piercing eyes, and terrifying fangs, and with another human face with bulging eyes, an open mouth, and heavy cheekbones.

Could this have been the keeper depicted on the façade of his house together with his wife and one of his fearsome dogs, who probably accompanied him in the forest on the trail of some terrified brigand, under the eye of one of the birds of prey who frequented these plantations?

This part of the *logis* is topped by a single dormer in the roof, built in line with the large window of the ground floor. The three sides of its roof follow the slopes of the main roof with the pronounced sprockets at the end of the slope. It has the same decoration of gadroons as seen on the sill and, most remarkably, it has one of the only Renaissance window frames still in place in the Pays d'Auge today.

Each of the two casements is divided into two horizontal compartments. The upper compartment was probably fitted with stained glass and lined with an interior shutter. Below this was a compartment with three panels: the two side panels are decorated with four projecting ridges (the last remaining trace of linenfold panels from the Gothic period) and frame a delicate panel of indented wood, from which a leather cartouche stands out, hanging on a bow of ribbons above tumbling fruits. A tiny interior shutter may once have hidden this indented panel, an exceptional testimony to the art of joinery at that time.

References

Anfernel (*Glos*)
PELLERIN H.: "Le manoir d'Anfernel", in *Le Pays d'Auge*, March 1977, p. 3 to 12.

Argentelles (*Villebadin*)
MESNIL DU BUISSON Comte R. DU: *Le Pays d'Argentan*, December 1968.

Aubichon (*Lisieux*)
PELLERIN H.: "Le manoir d'Aubichon", in *Le Pays d'Auge*, May 1964, p. 3 to 7.

L'Aumône (*Saint-Hymer*)
BUREAU J.: "Le manoir de l'Aumône", in *Le Pays d'Auge*, December 1963, p. 6.

Le Bais (*Cambremer*)
BUREAU J.: "Le manoir du Bais", in *Le Pays d'Auge*, January 1961, p. 4 to 8.

Barville (*Barville*)
DEVILLE E.: *La Céramique du pays d'Auge*, Paris, 1954, Pl. IX.
REYBAUD Cdt: "Manoir de Barville", in *Le Pays d'Auge*, February 1954, p. 15-16.

Bellemare (*Firfol*)
CAUMONT A. de: *Statistique monumentale du Calvados*, tome V, Caen 1867, p. 105.
DETERVILLE P.: *Charme discret des manoirs du pays d'Auge*, Condé-sur-Noireau, 1985, p. 99.

Bellou (*Bellou*)
COTTIN M.: "Le manoir de Bellou", in *Le Pays d'Auge*, April 1993, p. 2 to 15.

Boisjos (*Coudehard*)
ROUSSEAU X.: "Boisjos", in *Le Pays d'Auge*, January 1983, p. 7 and 8.

Boutemont (*Ouilly-le-Vicomte*)
PELLERIN H.: "Le château de Boutemont", in *Le Pays d'Auge*, September 1970, p. 3 to 10, and October 1970, p. 5 to 10.

Les Boves (*Les Monceaux*)
PELLERIN H.: "Le manoir des Boves", in *Le Pays d'Auge*, September 1976, p. 13 to 17.
NÉDÉLEC Y.: "Généalogie très provisoire de la famille Collet des Boves", March 1984.

La Brairie (*Glos*)
LECOURT Abbé: "Histoire de Glos-sous-Lisieux", in *Le Pays d'Auge*, July 1968, p. 19.

Le Breuil (*Le Breuil-en-Auge*)
BUREAU J.: "Le château du Breuil et le souvenir de Tancrède de Rohan", in *Le Pays d'Auge*, July 1953, p. 9 to 13.
NÉDÉLEC Y. "Le château du Breuil-en-Auge, note provisoire", in *Société d'archéologie de la Manche*, Mélanges, eleventh series (1982), p. 1 to 10.

La Bruyère (*Auvillars*)
BUREAU J.: "Le manoir de la Bruyère", in *Le Pays d'Auge*, January 1965, p. 11 to 14.
IMPEY E.: "Seigneurial Domestic Architecture in Normandy, 1050-1350", in *Manorial Domestic Buildings in England and Northern France*, edited by Gwyn Merion-Jones and Michael Jones, Volme 15 of occasionnal papers from the Society of Antiquaries of London, London, 1993, p. 108-111.

Les Buttes (*Saint-Georges-en-Auge*)
DETERVILLE P.: *Charme discret des manoirs du pays d'Auge*, Condé-sur-Noireau, 1985, p. 181-183.

Caudemone (*Auquainville*)
MENEGOZ M.: "Découverte de décorations picturales du XVIᵉ siècle à Caudemone et à Grandchamp", in *Bulletin de la société des antiquaires de Normandie*, tome XXXVII, 1926-1927, p. 414 to 418.
PELLERIN H.: "Le manoir de Caudemone à Auquainville", in *Le Pays d'Auge*, July 1978, p. 1 to 10; August 1978, p. 1 to 8; October 1978, p. 1 to 8.

Cauvigny (*Le Renouard*)
DETERVILLE P.: *Charme discret des manoirs du pays d'Auge*, Condé-sur-Noireau, 1985, p. 169-170.

Le Champ-Versan (*Bonnebosq*)
HENRY J.: "A Bonnebosq: le XVIIᵉ siècle nous a légué le manoir du Champ-Versan", in *Le Pays d'Auge*, May 1983, p. 3 to 6.

La Chénevotte (*Orbec*)
PELLERIN H.: "Le manoir de la Chénevotte", in *Le Pays d'Auge*, August 1971, p. 5 to 11.

Chiffretot (*Les Moutiers-Hubert*)
CAUMONT A. de: *Statistique monumentale du Calvados*, tome. V, Caen, 1867, p. 746.

Le Coin (*Le Mesnil-Mauger*)
NÉDÉLEC Y.: "Le manoir de Coupesarte, note historique provisoire", in *Société d'archéologie de la Manche*, Mélanges, tenth series (1981) p. 212.

Conty (*Vasouy*)
RAUDIERE P. de La: "Le manoir et la terre de Conty à Vasouy", in *Le Pays d'Auge*, April 1957, p. 11 to 15.

La Coudrairie (*Ouilly-le-Vicomte*)

Le Coudray (*Tortisambert*)
CAUMONT A. de: *Statistique monumentale du Calvados*, tome V, Caen, 1867, p. 633-634.

Coupesarte (*Coupesarte*)
LESCROART Y. "Le manoir de Coupesarte", in *Congrès archéologique de France, Bessin et pays d'Auge 1974*, Paris 1978, p. 180 to 187.
NÉDÉLEC Y. "Le manoir de Coupesarte, note historique provisoire", in *Société d'archéologie de la Manche*, Mélanges, tenth series (1981) p. 211 to 214.

La Cour Thomas (*Heurtevent*)
PIEL Abbé: *Inventaire historique des actes transcrits aux insinuations ecclésiastiques de l'ancien diocèse de Lisieux (1692-1780)*, Lisieux, 1892-1895.

Courson (*Notre-Dame de Courson*)
PELLERIN H.: "Le manoir de Courson", in *Le Pays d'Auge*, November 1962, p.5 to 12.
LESCROART Y.: *Le manoir de Courson, contribution à l'étude de la construction à pans de bois aux XVᵉ et XVIᵉ siècle*, M.A. thesis, Paris IV-Sorbonne, 1973.

Crèvecœur (*Crèvecœur-en-Auge*)
CAUMONT A. de: *Statistique monumentale du Calvados*, tome V, Caen 1867, p. 422-423.
PENAULT P.-J.: "Le trésor de Crèvecœur", in *Le Pays d'Auge*, April 1995, p. 2 to 15.

Criquebeuf (*Bonnebosq*)

Cricqueville (*Cricqueville*)
PELLERIN H.: "Le château de Cricqueville", in *Le Pays d'Auge*, August 1964, p. 3 to 9, and September 1964, p. 9 to 14.
COUZY H.: "Les châteaux de Cricqueville et de Victot et l'architecture polychrome en Normandie", in *Congrès archéologique de France, Bessin et pays d'Auge, 1974*, Paris 1978, p. 126 to 130.
BOTTINEAU-FUCHS Y.: "L'exotisme en Haute-Normandie au début du XVIᵉ siècle", in *Études normandes*, 1978, n° 3-4, p. 63 to 83.

La Croix blanche (*Grandmesnil*)
DETERVILLE P.: *Charme discret des manoirs du pays d'Auge*, Condé-sur-Noireau, 1985, p. 171-172.

Les Demaines (*Lécaude*)
CAUMONT A. de: *Statistique monumentale du Calvados*, tome V, Caen 1867, p. 403-404.

Le Désert (*Honfleur*)
BREARD C.: *Le Vieux Honfleur et ses marins*, Rouen, 1897, p. 80 – 81.
BUREAU J.: "Le manoir du Désert", in *Le Pays d'Auge*, August 1962, p. 3 to 5.
LESCROART Y.: "Le manoir du Désert", in *Le Pays d'Auge*, May 1982, p. 3 to 10.

Les Évêques (*Canapville*)
BUREAU J.: "Les manoirs de Canapville", in *Le Pays d'Auge*, July 1954, p. 7 to 9.
GUIDECOCQ P.: "Le manoir de Canapville, dit manoir des Évêques", in *Le Pays d'Auge*, October 1992, p. 2 to 11.

Fribois (*Saint-Loup-de-Fribois*)

Glatigny (*Tourgeville*)
BUREAU J.: "Le manoir de Glatigny", in *Le Pays d'Auge*, November 1964, p. 15 to 20.

Grandchamp (*Grandchamp*)
LESCROART Y. "Le château de Grandchamp", in *Congrès archéologique de France, Bessin et pays d'Auge 1974*, Paris 1978, p. 173 to 179.
NÉDÉLEC Y. "Le château de Grandchamp, notule complémentaire: les Le Prévost de Grandchamp et Saint-Julien-le-Faucon", in *Société d'archéologie de la Manche*, Mélanges, tenth series (1981) p. 218-219.

La Hogue (*Beuvron-en-Auge*)
LESCROART Y.: "La construction à pans de bois à Beuvron", in *Art de Basse-Normandie*, n° 58, 1ᵉʳ trimestre 1972, p.34.
CORBASSON J.P.: *Notes inédites*, 1992.

Houlbec (*Écots*)
NÉDÉLEC Y.: "Le manoir de Houlbec", in *Société d'archéologie de la Manche*, Mélanges, tenth series, 1981.

Langle (*Brocottes*)
BUREAU J.: "Le Vieux manoir à Brocottes", in *Le Pays d'Auge*, February 1965, p.15 to 18.
LESCROART Y. et PELVILLAIN H.: *Dossier de recensement*, Conservation des Monuments historiques de Basse-Normandie, 1985

Le Lieu-Binet (*Lisieux*)
CAUMONT A. de: *Statistique monumentale du Calvados*, tome V, Caen, 1867, p. 304-305.
COTTIN M.: *Vie rurale et construction en pans de bois en pays d'Auge aux XVIIᵉ et XVIIIᵉ siècles*, L'Oudon-Montpinçon, 1987, p. 32.
DETERVILLE P.: "Le manoir du Lieu-Binet", in *Le Pays d'Auge*, January 1987, p. 10 to 16.

References

Le Lieu-Hocquart (*Beuvron-en-Auge*)
LESCROART Y.: "La construction à pans de bois à Beuvron", in *Art de Basse-Normandie*, n° 58, 1er trimestre 1972, p. 34.

Le Lieu-Rocher (*Vieux-Pont-en-Auge*)
DETERVILLE Ph.: *Grands et petits manoirs du pays d'Auge*, Condé-sur-Noireau, 1982, p. 176-177.

Lortier (*Auquainville*)
CAUMONT A. de: *Statistique monumentale du Calvados*, tome V, Caen 1867, p. 707.
PELLERIN H.: *Notes inédites*, 1974.

Malicorne (*Saint-Désir-de-Lisieux*)
MAGNY E. de: *Nobiliaire de Normandie*, Paris 1862, p. 255-273.
CAUMONT A. de: *Statistique monumentale du Calvados*, tome V, Caen 1867, p. 302-303.

Malou (*Norolles*)
CAUMONT A. de: *Statistique monumentale du Calvados*, tome IV, Caen 1859, p. 422.

Mardilly (*Mardilly*)
PELLERIN H.: "Le château de Mardilly", *Le Pays d'Auge*, February 1963, p. 9 to 15.

Le Marescot (*Montpinçon*)
DETERVILLE Ph.: *Grands et petits manoirs du pays d'Auge*, Condé-sur-Noireau, 1982, p. 165.

Les Mathurins (*Ouilly-le-Vicomte*)
CAUMONT A. de: *Statistique monumentale du Calvados*, tome V, 1867, p. 8 to 10.
PELLERIN H.: "Les Mathurins", in *Le Pays d'Auge*, December 1954, p. 1 to 4.
DETERVILLE P.: *Grands et petits manoirs du pays d'Auge*, Condé-sur-Noireau, 1982, p.132-133.

Le Mesnil-de-Roiville (*Roiville*)
PELLERIN H.: "Le manoir de Roiville", in *Le Pays d'Auge*. November 1956, p. 1 to 5.
COTTIN M.: "Le Mesnil-de-Roiville", in *Le Pays d'Auge*. December 1993.
ROUSSEAU X.: *Notes inédites*, manoir du Mesnil-de-Roiville.

Le Mont-de-la-Vigne (*Monteille*)
PELLERIN H.: "Le château du Mont-de-la-Vigne", *Le Pays d'Auge*, April 1970, p.15 to 21; May 1970, p. 7 to 13.

Mont-Fleury (*Saint-Pierre-des-Ifs*)
DETERVILLE P.: *Charme discret des manoirs du pays d'Auge*, Condé-sur-Noireau, 1985, p. 83-84.

La Motte (*Saint-Pierre-des-Ifs*)

Ouilly (*Livarot*)
CAUMONT A. de: *Statistique monumentale du Calvados*, tome V, Caen 1867, p. 684-685
DETERVILLE P.: *Charme discret des manoirs du pays d'Auge*, Condé-sur-Noireau, 1985, p. 191 to 193.

Ouilly-du-Houlley (*Ouilly-du-Houlley*)
CAUMONT A. de: *Statistique monumentale du Calvados*, tome V, Caen 1867, p. 78-90.

Les Pavements (*Lisieux*)
DUFLOT D. et LESCROART Y.: "Le manoir des Pavements", *Le Pays d'Auge*, February 1989, p. 2 to 13.

Le Pavillon (*Fauguernon*)
DETERVILLE P.: "Le manoir du Pavillon", *Le Pays d'Auge*, April 1985, p. 3 to 7.

Piencourt (*Piencourt*)
CHARLES J.: *Notes inédites*. Conservation des Monuments historiques de Haute-Normandie, 1987.

La Pipardière (*Livarot*)
CAUMONT A. de: *Statistique monumentale du Calvados*, tome V, Caen 1867, p. 678 to 680.
PELLERIN H.: "Le manoir de la Pipardière", in *Le Pays d'Auge*, December 1967, p. 5 to 10; January 1968, p. 13 to 19.

La Planche (*Notre-Dame d'Estrées*)
RAULT F.: "Une famille de notables, les Manchon", in *Le Pays d'Auge*, May 1972, p. 17.

La Plesse (*Saint-Germain-au-Montgommery*)
CAUMONT A. de: *Statistique monumentale du Calvados*, tome. V, Caen 1867, p. 652-653.
COTTIN M.: *Notes inédites*, Conservation des Monuments historiques de Basse-Normandie, 1987.

Pont-Mauvoisin (*Saint-Martin-de-la-Lieue*)
CAUMONT A. de: *Statistique monumentale du Calvados*, tome V, Caen 1867, p. 313 to 317.
NEDELEC Y. "Le manoir dit de Saint-Hyppolite" in *Société d'archéologie de la Manche*, Mélanges, eleventh series (1982) p. 21 to 27.

Le Pontif (*Coquainvilliers*)
CAUMONT A. de: *Statistique monumentale du Calvados*, tome V, Caen 1867, p. 454-455.
COTTIN M.: *Vie rurale et construction en pans de bois en pays d'Auge aux XVIIe et XVIIIe siècles*, L'Oudon-Montpinçon, 1987, p. 27.

Prétot (*Canapville*)
BUREAU J.: "Le manoir de Prétot", in *Le Pays d'Auge*, April 1961, p. 1 to 6.

La Quaize (*Glos*)
PELLERIN H.: "Le manoir de la Quaize", in *Le Pays d'Auge*, October 1968, p. 5 to 9 ; December 1968, p. 11 to 16.

Les Quatre Nations (*Dozulé*)
PELLERIN H.: "Le manoir des Quatre Nations et les foires de Dozulé", in *Le Pays d'Auge*, May 1972, p. 20 to 25.

Querville (*Prêtreville*)
PELLERIN H. "Le manoir de Querville", in *Le Pays d'Auge*, July 1955, p. 8 to 10.

La Rivière (*Bailleul-la-Vallée*)
Charpillon M. et Abbé Caresme: *Dictionnaire historique du département de l'Eure*, 1868, p. 196.

Les Roches (*Biéville-en-Auge*)
CAUMONT A. de: *Statistique monumentale du Calvados*, tome V, Caen 1867, p. 426.

La Roque (*Montpinçon*)
DETERVILLE P.: *Charme discret des manoirs du pays d'Auge*, Condé-sur-Noireau 1985, p. 175-176.
COTTIN M.: *Vie rurale et construction en pans de bois en pays d'Auge aux XVIIe et XVIIIe siècles*, L'Oudon-Montpinçon, 1987, p. 37.

La Roque-Baignard (*La Roque-Baignard*)
CAUMONT A. de: *Statistique monumentale du Calvados*, tome IV, Caen, 1859, p. 168 to 171.
PELLERIN H.: "Le château de la Roque-Baignard", *Le Pays d'Auge*, January 1963, p. 7 to 11.

Saint-Christophe (*Firfol*)
CAUMONT A. de: *Statistique monumentale du Calvados*, tome V, Caen 1867, p. 97 to 105.

Saint-Germain-de-Livet (*Saint-Germain-de-Livet*)
PELLERIN H.: "Le château de Saint-Germain-de-Livet aux XVIIe et XVIIIe siècles", in *Le Pays d'Auge*, November 1971, p. 5 to 12, and December 1971, p. 5 to 10.
PELLERIN H., BERGERET J.: "Le château de Saint-Germain-de-Livet", in *Le Pays d'Auge*, supplement to no. 6, June 1982.

Saint-Léger (*La Lande-Saint-Léger*))
BUREAU J.: "Le manoir de Saint-Léger-sur-Bonneville", in *Le Pays d'Auge*, July 1957, p. 6 to 9.

Les Samsons (*Saint-Martin-de-Mailloc*)

Tordouet (*Tordouet*)
PELLERIN H.: "Le manoir de Tordouet", in *Le Pays d'Auge*, January 1967, p. 11 to 15; February 1967, p. 19 to 23; March 1967, p. 3 to 10.

Les Tourelles (*Saint-Germain-de-Montgommery*)

La Touzerie (*Castillon-en-Auge*)
DETERVILLE P.: *Charme discret des manoirs du pays d'Auge*, Condé-sur-Noireau, 1985, p. 197 to 199.

La Valette (*Le Mesnil-Simon*)

La Vallée (*Reux*)
BRIER M. A. et BRUNET P.: *L'Architecture rurale française*, Normandie, Paris, 1984, p. 242 to 249.
BUREAU J.: "Le manoir de la Vallée de Reux", in *Le Pays d'Auge*, November 1972, p. 19 to 21.

Le Verger (*Fervaques*)
PELLERIN H.: "Le manoir du Verger", in *Le Pays d'Auge*, June 1955, p. 3 and 4; December 1975, p. 3 to 7; February 1976, p.3 to 9; March 1976, p. 3 to 9.
LESCROART Y.: "La Renaissance au manoir du Verger", in *Le Pays d'Auge*, October 1984, p. 3 to 9.

Victot (*Victot*)
SIMON G.A.: *Les Boutin, seigneurs de Victot, et le château de Victot*, Caen, 1926, 12 p.
PELLERIN H.: "Le château de Victot", in *Le Pays d'Auge*, September 1957, p. 1 to 9.
COUZY H.: "Les châteaux de Cricqueville et de Victot et l'architecture polychrome en Normandie", in *Congrès archéologique de France, Bessin et pays d'Auge*, 1974, Paris 1978.

Vilembert (*Saint-Gatien-des-Bois*)
DETERVILLE P.: *Charme discret des manoirs du pays d'Auge*, Condé-sur-Noireau, 1985, p. 147-148.

Picture credits

p. 4: V. Azzaretti
pp. 19 top/bottom, 29, 39 bottom, 56, 69: R. Quenedey, *Recueil des documents d'architecture civile, la Normandie*, Paris 1929
p. 26: Th. du Moncel, *Album pittoresque de Trouville-sur-mer et de ses environs*, 1856.
p. 28: Archives of the Higher Committee for Historic Monuments, Paris
pp. 31, top, 44 top, 53, 55 bottom, 57 left, 61 top, 66 bottom, 71 top, 72, 76, 79: Y. Lescroart
p. 49 bottom: engraving by Ch. Mozin, 1845

Acknowledgments

We should like to express our thanks to:
the Regional Council of Lower Normandy,
the owners of manor houses who have willingly opened their doors to us,
and the photographic equipment manufacturers Pentax, Fuji and Panodia.

Régis Faucon used the following equipment to take the photographs in this book:
Pentax 67 body (medium format)
Pentax 55 mm/ 75 mm offcentering lenses, 105 mm/165 mm/200 mm and 300 mm lenses
Fujichrome, Velvia 50 films, 120 format
Binders, filing pockets, and slide mounts by Panodia